THE EARLIER AND LATER UPANIṢADS
A Comparative Study

THE EARLIER AND LATER UPANIṢADS

A Comparative Study

Smt. Mrinalini Vivek Manohar

BHARATIYA KALA PRAKASHAN

DELHI (INDIA)

First Edition : 2011

ISBN : 978-81-8090-275-8

Published by : **C.P. GAUTAM**
for BHARATIYA KALA PRAKASHAN
3421-A, IInd Floor, Narang Colony,
Tri Nagar, Delhi-110035.
Phone : (O) 27393083, 32967505
E-mail : bkp3421@yahoo.co.in

Laser Typesetting by : Twinkle Graphics, Delhi-110088.

Printed at : G.S. Offset Printers

CONTENTS

FOREWORD

Upaniṣads represent the highest peak of Indian culture. Schopenhauer called them "the production of the highest human wisdom". For him, the reading of the Upaniṣads (even in second-hand Latin translation!) "has been the solace of my life and will be the solace of my death". Upaniṣads are universally accorded such high regard and praise for their profound philosophico-spiritual revelations. They are also considered as source of all later Indian philosophical doctrinal developments.

But this is true only of some ten or thirteen or seventeen earlier Upaniṣads. The hundred odd other Upaniṣads, generally considered later, are neglected as being sectarian and mostly derivative as to their philosophical content. It needed to be seen whether these later Upaniṣads served any worthwhile purpose, whether they possess any spiritual value, or whether and how do they fit into the vast pan-Indian panoramic thought-pattern.

The present doctorate study of Dr. Mrinalini Manohar "The Earlier and Later Upaniṣads : A Comparative Study" (carried out under the insightful guidance of Prof. Alka Bakre) is an important treatise, particularly significant from the point of view of these later Upaniṣads. It is a serious and systematic inquiry into this particular problem.

The design adopted in this study is deceptively simple. The subject is initiated with some general observations on place, age and necessity of composing these – earlier as well as later – Upaniṣads and meaning and implications of the term '*upaniṣad*'. Then, a very brief review of the principal teachings of the Upaniṣ ads serving for the development of later theistic-sectarian principles as well as philosophical systems is attempted. This serves as a proper background for a broad yet unified view of the main philosophical tenets of the Upaniṣads – Brahman, the One Ultimate Reality, appearing also as Ātman 'Individual Self' through *māyā,* through cosmological as well as transmigrational stages and shows how some of the later Upaniṣads try at consolidating, theosising and mystifying these tenets. Chapter–III is titled as "The *Ālambana*-s of the Upaniṣads". *Ālambana* is a symbol, a tangible support to make the Abstract perceptible to the senses and mind. In the earlier Upaniṣads, the symbols of Brahman were imperceptible but endowed with qualities while the deities were in subordinate position; in later Upaniṣads, these deities acquired new meanings and, in sectarian contexts, were individually raised to the status of Brahman. The next two chapters, taken together, show the ways and paths to reach the Ultimate (leading to Salvation) – be it *nirguṇa* Brahman or *saguṇa* Īśvara. Earlier Upaniṣads expounded *Upāsanā* in its various aspects – its teacher, its prerequisites, its elements, levels, methods of approach, kinds etc.; later ones indicated *bhakti, yoga, saṁnyāsa, tāntrika* worship, and *mantras* etc. The miscellaneous topics like social conditions, doctrine of *Karman* and sectarian injunctions, literary aspects of the earlier and later texts, the changing concept of *mokṣa* etc. also have been appropriately discussed in a separate chapter. The final chapter of 'Conclusion' makes a brief but pertinent overview of the foregoing discussions and makes some important observations. The chronological overview of all the Upaniṣads indicates a polytheistic tendency culminating into a monistic one in the earlier Upaniṣads and then again this monistic tendency leading to a polytheistic one in the later Upaniṣads. However, in the ultimate analysis, the Upaniṣads – whether earlier or later – expected the aspirants to have the knowledge of the Highest Reality and achieve salvation. Also, the later Upaniṣads identified individual divinities with Brahman, simplified the act of focusing attention, left ample scope for aspirants in their choice of deities in accordance with their individual set-up, widened the scope of the pursuit of *dharma,* and transformed the philosophy of a few into a religion for the masses, retaining, at the same time, the importance of philosophy.

The concluding observations are well-supported by the well-informed and studied foregoing discussions. They are significant in that they point to the fundamental unity of Indian thought which has yet constantly kept developing in diverse directions through millennia. They substantiate and underline the most fundamental characteristic of Indian culture: Unity in Diversity.

I would aver that this is a well-written book; it covers a wide range of material in the form of earlier and later Upaniṣadic texts, patiently analyses its contents, detects and shows the threads of continuity of thoughts and ideas and draws careful conclusions leading to an overview of the entire thought-structure which can be called its 'thesis'.

The approach to the problem is broad and general aiming at covering a wide spectrum of later Upaniṣads in their essence which are otherwise too varied and numerous in their multi-sectarian variety to be covered in a single study. Again, in their essential content and approaches, these are so similar, so analogous and concordant that their individual or even sectarian group-wise studies would apparently be repetitive and even perhaps mutually redundant. Dr. Mrinalini's approach is, therefore, wise and sensible. She has done well in attempting a comprehensive view of all of them and in showing the continuity of the concept of the Supreme in its essential characteristics from the *nirguṇa* Brahman in earlier Upaniṣads to the *saguṇa* Īśvara (in His *avatāras* or varied forms) through later Upaniṣads down to their modes of worship. We realize that these would percolate into their beliefs and attitudes and activities in daily life, thus, constituting the essential unity of Indian culture in its apparently diverse forms. Call it Brahman or Viṣṇu or Rāma or Kṛṣṇa or Śiva or Śakti or Mother Goddess, they all -- in their ultimate essential characteristics – point to one and the same Supreme, the diversities shedding themselves as only too apparent to be adhered to, and then also only by the short-sighted dogmatics. The Vibgyor colours of rainbow ultimately spin themselves into Pure White. And what is true of Indian culture is also true of universal culture.

I congratulate Dr. Mrinalini Manohar and her guide Prof. Alka Bakre for this really contributing doctorate study and welcome it in its published form.

Vadodara,
22 June 2010

Dr. Rajendra Nanavati

PREFACE

The earlier Upaniṣads indeed occupy a unique position in the development of Indian philosophical thought. They exhibit a wealth of profound thoughts and are explored fully by various eminent scholars of the east as well as the west. However, the contents of the later Upaniṣads seem to be different from those of the earlier ones. For the same reason, I was induced to undertake an attempt at studying them with a comparative angle.

In this endeavour many have helped me. At the outset, I wish to express my deep sense of gratitude towards my guide, Dr. (Smt.) A.B. Bakre, ex - R.G. Bhandarkar Professor and Head, Department of Sanskrit, University of Mumbai who has been my support throughout. I am extremely grateful to her for going through the manuscript of this work painstakingly and making a number of valuable suggestions.

My sincere thanks are due to all the professors of the Department of Sanskrit and those of the visiting faculty because of whom I developed keen interest in the study of Sanskrit texts. I extend my thanks to the non-teaching staff members of the Department for their timely assistance. I am greatly indebted to both the units of Mumbai University library, *i.e.* Jawaharlal Nehru library, Vidyanagari, Mumbai and Fort library, Fort, Mumbai, as also to the Library of Asiatic society of Bombay, Town Hall, Mumbai and the library staff of all these libraries for their courteous and kind behaviour.

My special thanks to Dr. W.R. Antarkar who willingly allowed me to borrow books from his personal collection.

I acknowledge with thanks the University of Mumbai for awarding me the Ph.D. degree scholarship during the year 2000-2001.

I owe a considerable gratitude to all my family members who have been patiently helping and encouraging me all along.

Smt. Mrinalini V. Manohar

LIST OF ABBRIVIATIONS

Agni Purāṇa	*Agni. P.*
Aitareyopaniṣad	*Ait. Up.*
Aitareya Āraṇyaka	*Ait. Āra.*
Amṛtanādopaniṣad	*A. Nāda. Up.*
Atharvaveda	*Av.*
Atri Saṁhitā	*Atri. S.*
Bhagavadgītā	*Bh. G.*
Bhāgavatapurāṇa	*Bhāgavata. P.*
Bṛhadāraṇyakopaniṣad	*Br. Up.*
Bṛhajjābālopaniṣad	*Bṛ. Jābāla. Up.*
Brahmasūtra Śāṅkarabhāṣya	*Br. Sā. Śā. Bh.*
Brahmāṇḍa Purāṇa	*Brahmāṇḍ. P.*
Chāndogyopaniṣad	*Chānd. Up.*
Gaṇeśottaratāpinyupaniṣad	*Gaṇeśa. U. Tā. Up.*
Gaṇeśapūrvatāpinyupaniṣad	*Gaṇeśa. P. Tā. Up.*
Īśāvāsyopaniṣad	*Īś.Up.*
Jābāladarśanopaniṣad	*Jābāla. D. Up.*
Kalisanataraṇopaniṣad	*Kalisana. Up.*
Kaṭhopaniṣad	*Kaṭh. Up.*
Kauṣītakibrāhmaṇopaniṣad	*Kau. Up.*
Kenopaniṣad	*Ken. Up.*
Kṣurikopaniṣad	*Kṣuri. up.*

Mahopaniṣad	*M. Up.*
Mahābhārata	*Mbh.*
Mahānārāyaṇopaniṣad	*M.N. Up.*
Maitrāyanyupaniṣad	*Mai. Up.*
Maṇḍalabrāhmaṇopaniṣad	*Maṇḍala. Brā. Up.*
Manusmṛti	*Manu. S.*
Matsya Purāṇa	*Mat. P.*
Muṇḍakopaniṣad	*Muṇḍ. Up.*
Māṇḍūkyopaniṣad	*Māṇḍ. Up.*
Nṛsiṁhapūrvatāpinyupaniṣad	*Nṛsiṁha. P. Tā. Up.*
Nṛsiṁhottartāpinyupaniṣad	*Nṛsiṁha. U. Tā. Up.*
Nāradaparivrājakopaniṣad	*N.P. Up.*
Nārāyaṇapūrvatāpinyupaniṣad	*Nārāyaṇa. P. Tā. Up.*
Nārāyaṇottartāpinyupaniṣad	*Nārāyaṇa. U. Tā. Up.*
Paramahaṁsaparivrājakopaniṣad	*P. Haṁsa. P. Up.*
Praśnopaniṣad	*Praśna. Up.*
Pūrvamīmāṁsāsūtra by Jaimini	*Jaimini. Sū.*
Ṛgveda	*Ṛv.*
Rāmapūrvatāpinyupaniṣad	*Rāma. P. Tā. Up.*
Rāmottaratāpinyupaniṣad	*Rāma. U. Tā. Up.*
Rudrākṣajābālopaniṣad	*R. Jābāla. Up.*
Śāṇḍilyopaniṣad	*Śāṇḍ. Up.*
Sarasvatīrahasyopaniṣad	*Sarasvatī. R. Up.*
Śatapatha Brāhmaṇa	*Śat.Brā*
Saubhāgyalakṣmyupaniṣad	*S.L. Up.*
Saṅkarṣaṇopaniṣad	*Saṅk. Up.*

Siddhāntasāropaniṣad	*S. Sāra. Up.*
Śukarahasyopaniṣad	*Śuka. R. Up.*
Sūryatāpinyupaniṣad	*Sūrya. Tā. Up.*
Śvetāśvataropaniṣad	*Śvet. Up.*
Taittirīya Āraṇyaka	*Tait. Āra.*
Taittirīyopaniṣad	*Tait. Up.*
Tripādvibhūtimahānārāyaṇopaniṣad	*Tvmn. Up.*
Triśikhibrāhmaṇopaniṣad	*Triśikhi. Brā. Up.*
Upaniṣadsaṁgrahaḥ	*Up. S.*
Uśanaḥ Saṁhitā	*Uśanas. S.*
Yajurveda	*Yv.*
Yogakuṇḍalyupaniṣad	*Y.K. Up.*
Yogatattvopaniṣad	*Y.T. Up.*
Yogarājopaniṣad	*Y.R. Up.*
Yājñavalkyasmṛti	*Yāj. S.*
Yājñavalkyopaniṣad	*Yājñ. Up.*

CHAPTER I

INTRODUCTION

The earlier Upaniṣads, the compositions dealing with the spiritualism, the fragments that are extracted from the Āraṇyaka portion of the Veda-s hold a unique place in the spiritual and philosophical thought of India. These metaphysical treatises represent the earnest efforts of the erudite thinkers of ancient India, to solve the mystery of the origin, the nature, the destiny of a man and the universe, *i.e.*, more scientifically, the value of 'knowing' and 'being'. According to Max Müller, it is "a system in which human speculations seem to have reached its very acme."[1] The Upaniṣads which are replete with sublime conceptions, and with the intuitions of the universal truth, are the vital part of Indian spiritualism from time immemorial. They have survived through many changes-religious and secular-and have shown an unequalled variety of appeal all along. Though remote in time from us, the Upaniṣads are not remote in thought.[2] Indian thought has constantly turned to these treatises for fresh illumination and guidance. They have inspired generations with vision and strength, for they are the mine of inexhaustible wealth of thought, significance and spiritual power.

The later Upaniṣads are also treatises dealing with the spiritual aspect. A vast literary, religious and philosophical activity is found in these compositions. Majority of these Upaniṣads belong to the *Av*, a fact which shows how the seers concerned had taken a lead in propagating the post-Vedic, Purāṇic Hindu religion.

These works have grown out of the glorious tradition of this country. They have widened the path of knowledge so as to enable the common man to freely tread upon, not taking into consideration the rigidity of religion which consisted of *varṇāśramadharma.* Granting all the changes such as mode of dress, mannerisms, relation of an individual with other members of society throughout the ages; the dominant theme that has permeated the thought process of the Hindu mind has been the same. That is, the Reality or God is one. He is conceived in different ways and forms – the thread of unity running through and through all kinds of diversities.

The Place of the Origin of the Earlier Upaniṣads

It would be interesting to recapitulate briefly the place of the origin of the Upaniṣads. As the direct tradition fails us, we are compelled to infer from the texts themselves. Scholars unanimously agree that the Brahmanical sacrificial cult flourished in the region of the confluence of the Gaṅgā and the Jamunā.[3] It is the region between present Delhi and Agra, and to the east thereof, the place where the tribes of the Kurus and the Pāñcāla-s lived. From there, the Āryan Indians and with them, their Vedic culture started spreading, towards the north of the Ganagā and towards the east, upto where Bihar of today is placed. This whole area is considered as a holy land of the Veda-s. This same area is regarded as the land of the origin of the Upaniṣads.

In the earliest Upaniṣads, the land of the Kurus and the Pāñcāla-s is mentioned.[4] In the progressively later texts, the king of Videha, Janaka is referred to.[5] Videha is the area where Bihar of today is situated. This shifting and movement of the Āryans towards the east is important from the chronological point of view, because in the latest portions of the older Upaniṣads, the striking contacts of the Buddhism, in the sprouting form are seen.[6]

A Brief History of the Later Upaniṣads

The Upaniṣads of the three older Veda-s continued to live in the tradition of the *śākhā-s* of the Veda-s and were transmitted from generation to generation. But this was not the case with the *Av.* Since it was not employed at the sacrifice, there was no firm tradition of the school. As a consequence, many new compositions were added freely into the Saṁhitā-s of the *Av.* This explains a large number of the newly composed Upaniṣads, as the Upani-ṣ ads of the *Av.* It is true that many of them trace back their doctrines to the Śaunaka or Pippalāda. By the time the *Av.* obtained the designation as the fourth Veda, many new Upani-ṣads had been added to the *Av.* A great number of the Upaniṣads went on increasing till the time they were assembled into a collection. Deussen says that "everything which appeared in the shape of the Upaniṣad, that is, mystical text, whether it were the expression merely of the religious philosophical consciousness of the limited circle or even of an individual thinker was credited to the *Av.*"[7] These assembled collections fall into two classes according to Deussen. (1) They either contain the Upaniṣads in their entirety or (2) they limit themselves to the Upaniṣads of the *Av.*[8] The first category consists of the collection of *Muktikā* and Oupenk'hat (Persian); the second category includes the collection of Colebrooke and Nārāyaṇa. The collection of Colebrooke includes fifty two Upaniṣads, and the collection of Nārāyaṇa is in agreement with that of Colebrooke, excluding a few variations in the order of the compositions. The collection of 108 Upani-ṣads of *Muktikā* includes all the treatises of Colebrooke and Nārāyaṇa. Apart from these, there is also a collection of fifty Upaniṣads under the name Oupnek'hat, which was translated from Sanskrit to Persian in the year 1656 A.D. at the instance of Sultan Mohmed Dārā Śakoha, which was later translated into Latin by Anquetil Duperron in 1801-2 A.D.

The Period of the Earlier Upaniṣads

All the principal Upaniṣads are seen to be having earlier and later parts,[9] but when all the Upaniṣads as a whole are taken into consideration, one can roughly estimate the period to which in general the Upaniṣads belong. Though it is very difficult to fix an exact date of any of these Upaniṣads, the upper and the lower limits of the whole Upaniṣadic period may be fixed without much difficulty as being between 1200 and 600 B.C.[10]; just prior to the rise of Buddhism. Modern critics generally agree upon the point that the Upaniṣads which represent the Vedānta in its pure original form, and which are the earliest philosophical treatises of the world belong to the 7th and 8th century B.C. The ten Upaniṣads commented upon by Śaṅkara, the *Śvet. Up.* and *Kau. Up.* mentioned in his commentary on the *Vedānta-sūtras* and the *Mai. Up.* are generally accepted as the older Upaniṣads[11]. Deussen and other European scholars also look upon these thirteen as the older Upaniṣads. Even Belvalkar and Ranade treated these thirteen Upaniṣads as the older ones and have discussed in detail, how from the philosophy of the Brahman developed in these thirteen, they can be arranged chronologically.[12]

The Period of the Later Upaniṣads

Considering a very large number of the later Upaniṣads, the unavailability of the dates of the compositions make it considerably difficult to fix an exact date of each of the Upaniṣads. But according to the elements such as Sāṁkhya, Yoga, *Saṁnyāsa* present in them; and the mention of some of these Upaniṣads by the *ācārya*-s in their works, roughly the period–when these Upaniṣads flourished can be estimated. The sectarian Upaniṣads which interprete Śiva, Viṣṇu etc. as the personifications of the Brahman, are of later date because they proclaim the worship of qualitiful Brahman. (*saguṇopāsanā*). Probably, they were composed when these sects were prevalent. The Upaniṣads proclaiming Yoga, *Saṁnyāsa* may be of earlier date and the Upaniṣads containing the element of Rādhā etc. are of later dates. Later Upaniṣads cover a very long range of time and might have been composed between 200 A.D. and 1400 A.D.[13] An attempt will be undertaken to throw more light on chronological details in the appendix section presented at the end.

Why Were the Earlier Upaniṣads Composed

Dharma, artha, kāma, and *mokṣa* are the four human values (*puruṣārtha*-s). Of these, *artha* and *kāma* are the secular values, while *dharma* and *mokṣa* are the spiritual ones. During the sacrificial period, *dharma* was of prime importance, as it was considered as the means to the goal, the Supreme ideal, that is *mokṣa* or release. The term *'dharma'* connotes many shades of meanings. During Brāhmanic period, it was interpreted as the performance of sacrifices. Rituals were performed for the material benefits such as health, wealth and progeny. Also, it was believed that through the performance of sacrifices, merits (*apūrva*) could be collected. And through the collection of the merits, one could enjoy life in the heaven after the fall of this material body. The aim in view was to reach the heaven. But the fruit in the form of the heaven was temporary. The departed one has to return to this earth, when all his merits are exhausted and again start with a fresh account. After having realised the shortcomings of this idea of *mokṣa* and *dharma*, an intellectual movement started. With a view to take the seekers to the Eternal Truth, from where there is no return, and which is the Ultimate goal of human life, the Upaniṣads were composed.

The seers of ancient times, perceived with their intuitive knowledge (*prajñā*) and reasoning that behind the flux and variety of phenomenal life; the sum and the substratum of all is One Reality, imperishable because it is not conditioned by time, indivisible because it is not conditioned by space, immutable because it is not conditioned by causality; in a word Absolute and transcendent,[14] and, therefore, eternal, unalterable, undecaying. 'It' alone 'is'. To acquire the knowledge of that One, without a second, the Upaniṣads were composed.

Upaniṣads as Significant Part of the Vedic Religion

The philosohical reflections of the sages scattered in the Veda-s, Brāhmaṇa-s, Āraṇyaka-s, (*i.e.* the Upaniṣads) were incorporated in the official systems of the Vedic religion and this was done by means of the fourfold scheme of life prescribed for the members of the priestly caste. According to this scheme, a man after living first the life of a student, then that of a householder fulfilling his ritual obligations, becomes at the approach of old age, a hermit, meditating on the inner meaning of the ritual, and finally an ascetic devoting himself purely to the quest of mystical knowledge. The Upaniṣads which were the ending portion of the Veda-s, are also termed as the Vedānta.

The Brāhmanical idea of sacrifices was modulated in the days of the Upaniṣads. With the exception of the *Muṇḍ. Up.*[15], their general tone is not to condemn the acts of formal sacrifice, but the form is entirely transformed into a new concept altogether–that is, a mental sacrifice which is helpful in the process of acquiring spiritual knowledge. We find many examples of such a 'transformed' sacrifice in the Upaniṣads. For *e.g.* the *Br. Up.* gives a cosmic interpretation of the *aśvamedha* sacrifice.[16] With due respect, ignoring its common form, this sacrifice is interpreted allegorically. It is used as a vehicle of religious truth. The *Chānd. Up.* instructs us about the inner sacrifice, which is described as the real sacrifice where oblations are offered to the life-breath (*Prāṇa*) within us. Further, it is stated that, he who knows this inner sacrifice is relieved of his sins and even if a man were to do the acts of charity for a *cāṇḍāla,* he may verily be regarded as having sacrificed to the Universal Soul.[17] The *Kau. Up.* again teaches us to perform the act of mental sacrifice and says that the ancient sages did not go for formal sacrifice knowing that an endless sacrifice was going on continually within themselves.[18] The religion of the Upaniṣads is pre-eminently inward and spiritual. Therefore, there is a strikingly different tendency from (the preoccupation with) the technicalities of sacrificial rites which was the characteristic of Brāhmanic religion. As stated earlier, in the *Muṇḍ. Up.,* the sacrifices are condemned. They are declared as unsafe boats and those who rely upon them are deluded like blind men led by one who is blind; which means that the actual act of the performance of sacrifices will lead one to the transitory goal, hence one will not be able to reach the ultimate goal. Thus, these Upaniṣads formed a significant philosophical part of the Vedic religion.

The Need for the Genesis of the Later Upaniṣads

'Dhāraṇāt dharmaḥ' is one of the definitions of *dharma*. (*Mbh. Śānti. P.* 109.11) *Dharma* was the sheer necessity of everyone. *Dharma* was given utmost importance. Without *dharma*, it was like groping in the darkness. The Vedic religion, which comprised of ritualistic part (*karmakāṇḍātmaka*) and philosophical part (*jñānakaṇḍātmaka*) was extremely difficult to follow. The ritualistic acts (*karmakāṇḍa*) which comprised of sacrifices, included many tedious technicalities formidable to a common man. They were to be performed under the guidance of Brāhmins. The philosophical thoughts in the Upaniṣads (*jñānakāṇḍa*) were deep, impervious; therefore unintelligible for a man of ordinary intellect. In these circumstances, it was imperative that a commoner should be protected by some religion. These circumstances consequently gave rise to a new Hindu religion. The philosophical thoughts became accessible to massess through the *Purāṇa-s Bhāgvatadharma* etc. During this period, the new Upaniṣads were composed for the same reason. To put forth in a simple compact sentence, it may be said that it was the need of the changing times.

The tendency of human mind is such that it clings to the objects of its interest. Evolution in science brings in comforts for the body and the mind; but the typical characteristic of human mind is that it is never satisfied. It craves and searches for more. This outward tendency of mind was known to the seers of these Upaniṣads. They contemplated and searched for the remedy. To turn the restless mind inwards, and to keep it engaged in activity, they recommended various methods such as worship, *japa* etc. By resorting to such methods, the mind slowly becomes steady, quiet and turns inwards. When victory over the mind is achieved, dissolution of the mind is possible. The dissolution of mind leads to the unity with the Highest Reality. Keeping in view these tendencies of mind, they were described in these Upaniṣads. The *Kaṭh. Up.* declares, "sharp as the edge of a razor and hard to cross, difficult to tread is that path[19] (of knowledge)." It requires worship (*sādhanā*) on the level of intellect and mind. For a man of common intellect; this *sādhanā* to meditate on the unmanifest is very difficult. And it is the right of every man to seek the God. To lead a man slowly on the path of knowledge, to help him develop pointed intellect, (*ekāgrabuddhi*) various *sādhanā-s* are propounded by these Upaniṣads. Only a chosen few tread the path of knowledge, while keeping in view the masses; these Upaniṣads were composed.

The term Upaniṣad

The word Upaniṣad is derived from *upa, ni,* and the root *ṣad,* that is sitting down near somebody. Max Müller understands it as a "session or assembly consisting of pupils assembled at a respectful distance round their teacher to listen to his instructions.[20]" Śaṅkara derives the word Upaniṣad from the root *ṣad,* which means, 'to loosen, to reach or to destroy' with *upa* and *ni* as prefixes and *kvip* as termination.

According to Śaṅkara, the Upaniṣads were so named because they loosen or destroy the inborn ignorance or because they 'conduct' to the Brahman.[21] In other words, the treatises that deal with the knowledge of the Brahman are called the Upaniṣads. This knowledge was secured by a student at the end of his studentship. The Upaniṣads form the ending portion of the Vedic study and the essence of the Veda-s and therefore, are known as Vedānta. Sāyaṇa opines that the word Upaniṣad denotes theosophy or Brahmavidyā. He explains that the prefix *upa* means near, and nothing can be nearer to one than one's own inner soul. The three meanings of the root *ṣad,* namely to destroy, to decay, to know are applicable to theosophy (Brahmavidyā). Thus, theosophy is called an Upaniṣad because,

(*a*) It leads to the Ātman, the inner Self, Brahman, which itself is devoid of duality and thereby brings about destruction of ignorance. (*avidyā*)

(*b*) It destroys that ignorance (*avidyā*), which is the root cause of all the evil, and leads one to the knowledge that the

Supreme Being devoid of duality is none other than one's own Self.

(*c*) It destroys altogether all germs of outward activity by way of cutting their root (that is *avidyā*).[22]

This meaning of the word Upaniṣad is in derivative sense. The word Upaniṣad, in the conventional sense means a 'mystery' and a 'secret'. The Upaniṣads contain the explanations of the mystic words like *'tajjalān'*[23] and the mystic significance of the syllable Oṁ, which are intelligible only to the initiated. The term Upaniṣad then became an alternative name for mystery. The word Upaniṣad also means a 'secret' (*rahasyam*).[24] The evidence can be found in the texts itself. Instead of *iti Upaniṣad,* at the close of the passage, the expressions such as *guhyādeśaḥ*[25], *paramaṁ guhyam*[26], *guhyatamaṁ*[27] are used.

This secret was imparted only to the tested or the chosen few. According to the *Chānd. Up.,* the knowledge of Brahman should be imparted by a teacher, only to the eldest son or to a worthy pupil and no one else[28]; this secret was to be communicated only to the son or an ardent pupil[29] who had attained tranquility.

In the case of the later Upaniṣads, the term Upaniṣad is used in a broader, liberal sense. In addition to the derivative and conventional meanings of the term, the word is explained in a special way by the scholars. Oldenberg suggests that the word Upaniṣad means an adoration-*upāsanā*, that is, reverential meditation on the Brahman or Ātman.[30] This explanation befits the later Upaniṣads for they propound various worships (*upāsanā-s*), which are the means to reach the goal of human life.

Dange's Exposition of the term Upaniṣad

While explaining different shades of meaning of the term Upaniṣad, Dange, S.A. has suggested one more meaning.[31]

In the *Ṛv.* (II. 6. 1), in the verse, *imaṁ me agne samidhaṁ imaṁ upanisadaṁ,* the word *upasad* (fem.) means a praise. Hence, the import of the word is, that 'praise' which is residing (*sad*) near (*upa*) the god.

Also, in the *Ṛv.* (II. 21. 5), the words *'abhisvarāniṣadā'* suggest 'a praise in high pitch'.

In the *Ṛv.* (X.53.2), in the verse, *arādhi hotā nisadā, 'niṣ adā'* is the means (*sādhana*) of *upāsanā* of the divine priest *Agni.* The words *upasad* (*upa+sad*) and *niṣada* (*ni+sad*) clearly indicate the meaning 'praise'. Hence, it is possible that the basic idea behind the word Upaniṣad is formed through the combination of the meanings of the words *upasad* and *nisad.* Therefore, in the word Upaniṣad, the meanings, 'subtle praise' and 'eternal truth' are comprised.

The word not only indicates the act of sitting near the preceptor for the acquisition of eternal knowledge; but it also suggests that *karmakāṇḍa* is not the goal of human life; contemplation of the eternal principle is one's own goal. The proof of this is found in the word itself. For instance, the *Kaṭh. Up.* means, the contemplation of the contemplator of the *Kaṭha- śākhā.* So also, in the later Upaniṣads, for *e.g. Sūryopaniṣad* means, the contemplation on the eternal essential principle in the Sun.

Regarding the use of the term 'Upaniṣad' for this new, later literature, Vaidya, C.V, objects and states that, "their authors have abused the high name of Upaniṣad and have wrongly used the sacred authority of that Vedic word to preach their worthless doctrines. We would call them Purāṇic or Tāntric. Winternitz calls them non-Vedic proper."[32]

Philosophy of the Upaniṣads

The Greek word 'philo' mean 'love' and 'sophia' is ordinarily translated in English as 'wisdom' and the compound 'philosophia' from which the word philosophy is derived is translated as the "love for wisdom." Philosophy etymologically connotes, the love exercising one's curiosity and intelligence rather than the 'love of wisdom.'[33]

According to The Concise Oxford Dictionary, Philosophy is "the use of reason and argument in seeking truth and knowledge of reality, especially of the causes and nature of things and of the principles governing existence, the material universe, perception of physical phenomena and human behaviour." It is also "a particular set or system of beliefs reached by this."[34] Durant Will states that philosophy is the study of experiences as a whole or of a portion of experience in relation to the whole.[35]

Each of these definitions of philosophy is adequate in itself. As contrasted with the western philosophy, with its analytical approach to the Reality and experience; Indian philosophy is fundamentally synthetic. Religion and philosophy, knowledge and conduct, intuition and reason, man and nature are all brought into harmony. Metaphysics, ethics, psychology, epistemology, facts, values, all are treated as aspects of single comprehensive reality. Indian philosophy believes in the intimate relationship of philosophy and life, theory (doctrine) and practice that is, "it is for life and it is to be lived." as is aptly described by Radhakrishnan, S.[36]

The chief mark of Indian Philosophy in general is spiritual. It makes unquestioned use of reason but intuition is accepted as the only method through which the Ultimate may be known. However, one can go a step further and say that it is not enough to just know the truth, and become one with it, and live it for oneself; but to transmit its knowledge to other aspirants.

All the thoughts of the Upaniṣads revolve around Brahman-the Eternal, Infinite, Divine power, which manifests itself in all existing things; which creates, sustains and withdraws the universe into itself again. The word Brahman is used in the Upaniṣads to indicate the Supreme Reality. It is derived from the root *bṛh*, which means, to grow, to expand, to exceed, to burst forth. The derivation suggests thriving forth, ceaseless growth (*bṛhattvaṁ*). Radhakrishnan states that, 'Śaṅkara derives the word from the root *bṛh*. meaning to exceed, and means by it eternity and purity.'[37]

The Upaniṣads use the word Ātman as a synonym of the word Brahman. The word is derived from the root *an* - to breathe. It is the breath of life.[38] Gradually, its meaning is extended to cover life, Soul, Self or essential being of an individual. Ātman is the principle of man's life, the Soul that pervades his being, his breath (*Prāṇa*), intellect (*prajñā*) and transcends them all.

Ātman is that, which remains when everything that is not 'Self' is eliminated; which is equated with the Brahman.

'Brahman' is the older and less inteligible expression while 'Ātman' is the later and more significant expression. 'Brahman' is the unknown cosmic principle that needs to be explained. Through the knowledge of the Ātman, the Brahman finds its explanation.

The Brahman is the first principle so far as, it is conceived in the universe. The Ātman is known as the inner Self of a man. One of the examples is furnished by the story of Gārgya, in the *Br. Up.* Gārgya ventures in vain to define Brahman. Finally, he is referred by the king, to the Ātman for its explanation.[39] The meaning of the words Ātman and Brahman is brought out clearly when they are placed side by side in the sentence in the *Br. Up.*– verily this Ātman is the Brahman.[40] This identity of the Brahman with the Ātman, of God with the soul is the fundamental thought of the entire doctrine of the Upaniṣads. It is briefly expressed in the famous four *mahāvākya-s.*[41]

The Concept of the Brahman in the Later Upaniṣad

The deities Śiva, Viṣṇu, Devī, Sūrya, Gaṇapati etc. gained importance during the period of the later Upaniṣadic days. Different sects arose in honour of these deities. The later Upaniṣ ads which are mostly sectarian in character, equate their favourite deity with the Supereme-Self or the Brahman; and consider the personal aspect of the deity as a stepping stone to reach the impersonal one. The realization of the Brahman is the goal of a man according to the teachings of the Upaniṣads. These later Upaniṣads describe the physical aspects of the deity, so also the metaphoric aspect. The abilities of the Brahman which is the Supreme Reality-of creating, maintaining and dissolving the world are attributed to the deity of worship. Through the meditation of these aspects, that is through meditating upon the manifest form, one can reach the unmanifest God.

To achieve the aim of human life, that is to perceive the imperceptible Brahman, the earlier Upaniṣads propound different ways. They are technically called *vidyā-s. vidyā* means the path-in the form of worship–to reach the Īśvara. Many *vidyā-s* such as Bhūmāvidyā, Prāṇavidyā, Śāṇḍilyavidyā are described in the Upaniṣads. They are designed to suit the capacity, intellectual and mental temperament of the disciple.

Many *upāsanā*-s are advocated by the later Upaniṣads such as *pūjā, japa, mānasapūjā,* recitation of *mantra*-s, worship of *yantra-s* etc. These Upaniṣads proclaim that the *upāsanā*-s propounded by them lead one to the path of knowledge and ultimately the Brahman.

Earlier Upaniṣads as the Source of Later Indian Philosophy

From the Upaniṣads spring various streams of thought which gradually become systematised into systems of later Indian Philosophy. The thoughts in them are the basic blocks with which the later *ācārya-s* built their theories. In the Upaniṣads, we see the roots of later Indian philosophies such as Sāṁkhya, Yoga, Buddhism, Śaivism etc.

Roots of Buddhism in the Upaniṣads

The end of the Upaniṣadic period and the rise of the Buddhism are contemporary; one being anterior to the other. The *Chānd. Up.* says, "in the beginning verily Not-Being (*asat*) alone existed."[42] From this sentence, one understands that a reference was made here to a doctrine which later became fulfledged in the denial of the existence and presence of void in Buddhist literature. "When a man is dead, people think differently about the spirit that inspired him, some say it still lives and some say it ceased to exist." says the *Kaṭh. Up.*[43] Here, we have the seed of *anattavāda,* another thought of the Buddhists. Again in the *Kaṭh. Up.*, the thoughts that the objects of sensual enjoyment wither away the vigour of the senses,[44] and the life is as short as a dream run parallel to the thoughts of Buddhism, that everything in the world is full of sorrow, and everything is transitory. (*sarvaṁ duḥkhaṁ, sarvaṁ kṣaṇikaṁ*). The *Br. Up.* mentions the life of a mendicant who casts away the world and rises above the desires of the world to attain God.[45] This thought fits well with the order of the *bhikkhu*-s in Buddhism. Again, in the same Upaniṣad, it is stated that, when a person departs, different parts of that person return to different parts of nature, from where they had come, the soul goes in space and only his *karman* remains.[46] This is the Buddhist doctrine. Hume, R.E. opines that the later Śaiva sects that were founded on the *Av,* were closely connected with the Buddhist sects. Perhaps in this way the influence of the Buddhist thought was transmitted to the *Praśna. Up.* and *Muṇḍ. Up.* of the *Av.*[47] Ranade, R.D. opines that though the philosophy of the Buddhism is fundamentally different from that of the Upaniṣads, they have found sufficient inspiration from them to be traceable to them as a parent.[48]

Upaniṣads – The Foundation of Sāṁkhya Philosophy

There is an ample evidence in the *Chānd. Up., Kaṭh. Up., Praśna. Up.* and *Śvet. Up.* to infer that the thoughts; on the basis of which the Sāṁkhya-s developed their philosophy; later on became a complete system in itself. The *Chānd. Up.* mentions three colours red, white and black.[49] The origin of the three *guṇa*-s in the Sāṁkhya philosophy can be traced here. Later, the same concept was used in the *Śvet. Up.*[50] The mind and intellect, the *mahat* and *avyakta* and the Puruṣa play a very important part in the Sāṁkhya philosophy. We find their roots in the *Kaṭh. Up.*[51] The idea of the *liṅgaśarīra* in the Sāṁkhya philosophy is already embodied in the *Praśna. Up.* which reiterates the nature of Puruṣ a with sixteen *kalā*-s.[52] The *Śvet. Up.* was written at a time when the Vedānta, Sāṁkhya, and Yoga were not separated as different systems. As Ranade, R.D. has pointed out, "the *Śvet. Up.* wavers between the theistic and deistic view of the Godhead."[53] The *Śvet. Up.* describes God as the one who brings maturity to the Nature (*svabhāva*). He presides over the development and utilizes the *guṇa*-s.[54] God is also described as the Lord of Pradhāna, Prakṛti, individual souls as well as *guṇa*-s.[55] Here, in this Upaniṣad, God is described as a magician and Prakṛti as his power.[56] Also, God creates this world with his power, and the individual soul is described as bound by the fetters of *māyā.*[57] In this manner, we get the theistic description of the Godhead. Some passages describe God as living apart from Prakṛti in a transcendental sphere, and the individual soul bound by its ignorance, lies by Prakṛti, caught in the meshes of her love.[58] Also, God is described as merely a spectator (*sākṣin*) and a witness who is devoid of *guṇa*-s.[59]

The Roots of Yoga as Found in the Upaniṣads

A detailed description of the philosophy and practice of Yoga is found in the second chapter of the *Śvet. Up.*[60] The verses describe the posture during the time of meditation. One is advised to control the senses by means of mind, which is known as *pratyāhāra* in the system of Yoga. Thirdly, one is directed to control breath, which is known as *prāṇāyāma* in the later system. Also, the environment where one should meditate, is advised (*sthāna*) and so on. Lastly, one has to achieve the state of *samādhi,* where the individual soul unites with the universal soul. The *Kaṭ ḥ. Up.* mentions *dhāraṇa.*[61] *Dhyāna* is mentioned in the *Śvet. Up.*[62] Except *yama* and *niyama* of later Yogic philosophy, that is the eightfold system of Yoga (*astāṅgayoga*), these various elements of Yoga are described in the earlier Upaniṣads.

Yoga and Physiology

Physiological structure is an important aspect of the later Yoga Philosophy. The circulation of the *Prāṇa-s* and cleansing of the blood-vessel (*nāḍīśuddhi*) are also of prime importance in this philosophy. The *Chānd. Up.* describes the blood vessels as tawny, blue, white and red.[63] In the *Kau. Up.*, we are told that the blood vessels go from the heart to the body and they are described as a hair divided thousand times.[64] They are tawny, white, blue, red and yellow. The *Bṛ. Up.* describes the colour of the vessels as white, blue, tawny, green and red.[65] The *Mai. Up.* ponders over the seven elements (*dhātū*-s), four *mala*-s and three *doṣa*-s.[66] This physiological aspect of the Yoga later gave rise to physiological science and further led to the sciences of medicine.

The Upaniṣads and the Nyāya System

We do not find many traces of the Nyāya and Vaiśeṣika systems; in the Upaniṣads. Some words of the Upaniṣads are used in the Nyāya and Vaiśeṣika systems; but it is doubtful whether the words are used in the same sense in the system as in the Upaniṣads. The word *tarka* occurs in the *Kaṭh. Up.*[67] The word again is found in the *Mai. Up.* twice. The terms *dṛṣṭānta* (instance), *hetū* etc. of the Upaniṣads, subsequently became the peculiar terminology of the Nyāya school of philosophy.

The Upaniṣads and the Vaiśeṣika System

The views of Kaṇāda are supported by the Upaniṣads. The word *aṇu* is used in the *Mai. Up.*, as an adjective of the wind–the smallest particle of the wind. So also we come across the words such as monād, diād, triād.[68] It is doubtful that these words were used in the Upaniṣads in the same sense, which Kaṇāda attached to them. The words *pramāṇa, prameya* used in the Upaniṣads, later had a fixed meaning in the schools of philosophy. The doctrine of the *purītat* found in the Upaniṣads is chosen by the Nyāya and Vaiśeṣika systems of philosophy; and a change is also introduced in the doctrine of those systems. For instance, in the *Bṛ. Up.*, it is said that at the time of sleep, the soul moves through the *nāḍī*-s to the *purītat* and causes the physiological action of sleep.[69] Picking up this idea, the Nyāya and Vaiśeṣika systems substitute the 'mind' for the 'soul'. The reason for this change may be, one can easily think of sleep about mind and never about the soul, which is always regarded as unsleeping.

The Upaniṣads and the Mīmāṁsā

The philosophical thoughts of the Upaniṣads are the essence, nectar of the Vedic and Brāhmanic philosophy. There is not much in common between the Upaniṣadic philosophy and Pūrvamīmāṁsā. Basically Pūrvamīmāṁsā deals with the acts and rituals to be performed for the gain of the merits and thereby entry into the heaven. The Upaniṣads probe into the nature of the Ultimate Reality. The *Īśa. Up.* declares that one who follows the path of works go to the pitchy darkness and one who treads the path of mere knowledge goes to greater darkness still.[70] On the one hand, mere works which *Pūrvamīmāṁsā* advocates are not sufficient and on the other hand, mere knowledge is insufficient. The gist is that, both works and knowledge are to be synthesized, and by going beyond both works and knowledge, one is released.

The Root of Śaivism in the Upaniṣads

Though the concept of Rudra, Śiva was being developed since the days of the *Rv,* we get a fuller doctrine of Śiva in the *Śvet. up.*

The idea of *paśu, pati* and *pāśa* of Śaivism can be seen here in the seed form. The Upaniṣad says, "Rudra is the only Lord God, there is no other God."[71] The Upaniṣad maintains that having known Śiva, who is hidden in all beings, and who envelops the universe like a subtle film on the top of ghee, one is released.[72] Furthermore, there is also a thought of Śaivism that reflects in this Upaniṣad, *i.e.*, He creates and recreates and maintains his power, sovereignty on all the worlds.[73] Divine Umā, who imparts knowledge of the Brahman to Indra, the chief of the Gods, is mentioned in the *Kena. Up.*[74] In this way, the seeds of later Śaivism can be seen in the Upaniṣads.

Upaniṣads and the Bhagvadgītā

It will not be an exaggeration if it be said that the philosophy of the *Bh. G.* is almost wholly based on that of the Upaniṣads. Many verses of the *Bh. G.*, especially from chapter two, are borrowed from the Upaniṣads. Also, the verse of *Kaṭh. Up.*, that the Ātman is neither killed nor ever kills is reproduced in the *Bh. G.* [75] and so on. Some ideas are borrowed from the Upaniṣads, are transformed and further developed in the *Bh. G.* The *Bh. G.* has developed the philosophy of *karmayoga,* on the same line as that of the *Īśa. Up.*[76] A description of *Viśvarūpa,* in the eleventh chapter of the *Bh. G.* is based on the description of the Cosmic Person in the *Muṇḍ. Up.;* which probably has borrowed the idea from the Puruṣasūkta of the *Ṛv.*[77] it is true that the *Bh. G.* has also incorporated the thoughts of the philosophical systems such as Vedānta, Sāṁkhya, Pātañjala Yoga etc. which were popular in those days. The *Bh. G.* is a wonderful amalgamation of the best of the thoughts of the Upaniṣads, and other philosophical systems. It has presented its own philosophy as was the need of the time.

The Upaniṣads and the Philosophy of the School of Vedānta

The three great schools of the Vedānta philosophy, the schools of Śaṅkara, Rāmānuja, Mādhva interprete the Brahmasūtra-s as well as the Upaniṣads to suit their own way. They fashion their philosophy in the light of these interpretations. For instance, the philosophy of Śaṅkara is based on the fundamental principles of the Upaniṣadic thought that the universe is one, there is no difference within it or without it. Brahman is alike throughout, the substratum of all and the knowledge through and through.

The dualistic school of Mādhva resorts to the passages such as those in the *Muṇḍ. Up. and Kaṭh. Up.* to justify the doctrine of Individual soul being entirely distinct from the universal soul.

The Absolute of Rāmānuja consists of Nature, Soul and God. The doctrine of *antaryāmin* constitutes the fundamental position in his philosophy when he calls God, the soul of Nature.

The quest of the pioneers of the Upaniṣads to comprehend the Ultimate Truth, like many other philosophers, led them to the fact that the world of multiplicity is reducable to one single primary Reality which reveals itself to our senses in different forms. The word used in the Upaniṣads to indicate the Supreme Reality is

Brahman. The following chapter will examine, the Ultimate Reality as conceived in the earlier and the later Upani-ṣads.

REFERENCES

1. Max Müller, Friedrich, quoted by Radhakrishnan, S. and Moore, A. *A Source Book in Indian Philosophy,* New Jersey, 1957, p. 26.
2. Radhakrishnan, S., *The Principal Upaniṣads,* Delhi, 1998, p. 5.
3. Frauwllner, Erich, *History of Indian Philosophy,* Vol. I, Delhi, 1973, pp.33-34. also seeOldenberg Herman, *The Doctrine of the Upaniṣads and the Early Buddhism,* Delhi, 1991, p. 2.
4. *Chānd. Up.* I. 10. 1

   मटचीहतेषु कुरुष्वाटिक्या सह जाययोषस्तिर्ह चाक्रायण इभ्यग्रामे प्रद्रणक उवास।

   Ibid. V. 3. 1[a]

   श्वेतकेतुर्हारुणेयः पञ्चालानाँ समितिमेयाय...।
5. *Bṛ. Up.* III. 1. 1[a]

   जनको ह वैदेहो बहुदक्षिणेन यज्ञेनेजे तत्र ह कुरुपञ्चालानां ब्राह्मणा अभिसमेता बभूवुः।
6. Frauwllner Erich, *op. cit.*, pp. 33-34.
7. Deussen, Paul, *The Philosophy of the Upaniṣadas,* New York, 1966, pp. 8-9.
8. *Ibid.,* p. 33.
9. *Ibid.,* p. 23.
10. Ranade, R.D., A *Constructive Survey of Upaniṣadic Philosophy,* Bombay, 1986, p. 12.
11. Vaidya, C.V., *History of Sanskrit Literature* Vol. II, Delhi, 1986, p. 163.
12. Belvalkar, S.K., Ranade, R.D., *History of Indian Philosophy* Vol. II, Delhi, 1974, pp. 87[ff] also, Deussen, P. *The Philosophy of the Upaniṣads.* N.Y. 1966. pp. 23-25.
13. Desai, S.G., *A Critical Study of the Later Upaniṣads,* Mumbai, 1996, p. xxxiv.
14. Ghosh, Aurobindo, *The Upaniṣads,* Pondicherry, 1972, pp.1-3.
15. *Muṇḍ Up.*, I. 2. 7[a]

प्लवा ह्येते अदृढा यज्ञरूपा अष्टादशोक्तमवरं येषु कर्म।

16. *Bṛ. Up.*, I. 1. 1-2.
17. *Chānd. Up.* V. 19-24.
18. *Kau. Up.*, II.4[a]

    अथात: सांयमनं प्रातर्दनमान्तरमग्निहोत्रमितिचाचक्षते यावद्वै पुरुषो भाषते न तावत्प्राणितुं शक्नोति प्राणं तदा वाचि जुहोति यावद्वै पुरुष: प्राणिति न तावद्भाषितुं शक्नोति वाचं तदा प्राणे जुहोत्येतेऽनन्तेऽमृताहुती जाग्रच्च स्वपंश्च संततमव्यवच्छिन्नं जुहोत्यथ या अन्या आहुतयोऽन्तवत्यस्ता: कर्ममय्यो भवन्ति एतद्वै पूर्वे विद्वांसोऽग्निहोत्रं न जुहवांचक्रु: ॥

19. *Kaṭh. Up.* I. 3. 14[b].

    क्षुरस्य घारा निशिता दुरत्यया दुर्गं पथस्तत्कवयो वदन्ति।

20. Max Müllar, F., *Sacred Books of the East* (*S.B.E.*) Vol. I, Delhi, 1993, p. lxxxxi.
21. Śaṅkara, *Complete Works of Śri Śaṅkarācārya,* Vol. III. *"Kāṭhakopaniṣad"* p. 123.

    सदेधातोर्विशरणगत्यवसादनार्थहयोपनिपूर्वस्य क्विप्प्रत्ययान्तरस्य रूपमिदम् 'उपनिषत्' इति।

    Also, commentary on *Tait. Up.*, p.615.

    उपनिषण्णं वा अस्याम् परं श्रेय इति।

22. Sāyaṇa, q. by Sandal, M., *Philosophical Teachings of the Upaniṣads, The Sacred Book of the Hindus*, Vol.5, ed. Basu., B.D., Allahabad, 1945, pp.4-5.
23. *Chānd. Up.* III. 14. 1[a]

    तज्जलानिति शान्त उपासीत।

24. *Nṛsiṁha. U. Tā. Up., Up. S.* pt. I. p. 234. l. 23

    इति रहस्यम्।

25. *Chānd. Up.* III. 5. 2[a]

    गुह्यादेश: ॥

26. *Kaṭh. Up.* I.3.17[a], also *Śvet. Up.*, VI. 22,

    परमं गुह्यम्।

27. *Mai. Up.* VI. 29.

    गुह्यतमम्।

28. *Chānd. Up.* III. 11. 5

    इदं वाव तज्ज्येदंय पुत्राय पिता ब्रह्म प्रब्रूयात्प्रणाय्याय वाऽन्तेवासिने।

29. *Bṛ. Up.* III. 2. 13[b].

    आहर सोम्य हस्तमार्तभागाऽऽवामेवैतस्य वेदिष्यावो न नावेतत् सजन इति।

30. Oldenberg, H., *op. cit.*, p. 5.
31. Dange, S.A., *Hindū Dharma āṇi Tattvajñāna* (Mar), Pune, 1973, p. 344.
32. Vaidya, C.V., *op. cit.*, vol. II, p. 162.
33. Passmore, Jhon, '*Philosophy*', *Encyclopaedia of Philosophy.* Vol. V., ed. by Edwards, P., U.S.A., 1972, p. 216.
34. *The Concise Oxford Dictionary,* ed. by Thompson, Della, p. 1026.
35. Durant, Will, *Pleasures of Philosophy*, N.Y., 1953, p. 2.
36. Radhakrishnan, S., *Indian Philosophy,* Vol. II, India, 1941, p. 23.
37. Radhakrishnan, S., *The Principal Upaniṣads,* Delhi, 1998, p. 52.
38. *Ibid.*, p. 73.
39. *Bṛ. Up.*, II. 1. (1-20).
40. *Ibid.*, IV. 4. 5.
41. *Chānd. Up.* III. 14.

    Bṛ Up., IV. 4. 5.

    Chānd. Up. VI. 8. 7[f].

    तत्त्वमसि।

    Bṛ Up., I. 4. 10.

    अहं ब्रह्मास्मि।

42. *Chānd. Up.* VI. 2. 1.

    तद्ध एक आहुरसदेवेदमग्र आसीत्।

43. *Kaṭh Up.* I. 1. 20[ab].

    येयं प्रेते विचिकित्सा मनुष्ये अस्तीत्येके नायमस्तीति चैके।

44. *Ibid.*, I. 1. 26[abc].

    श्वोभावा मर्त्यस्य यदन्तकैतत्सर्वेन्द्रियाणां जरयन्ति तेजः। अपि सर्वं जीवितमल्पमेव...।

45. *Bṛ. Up*. IV. 4. 22.

ते ह स्म पुत्रैषणायाश्च वित्तैषणायाश्च लोकैषणायाश्च व्युत्थाय अथ भिक्षाचर्यं चरन्ति।

46. *Ibid.*, III. 2. 13.
47. Hume, R.E., *The Thirteen Principal Upaniṣads*, p. 7.
48. Ranade, R.D., *op. cit.*, p. 134.
49. *Chānd. Up*. VI. 4. 1.

यदग्ने रोहितं रूपं तेजसस्तद्रूपं यच्छुक्लं तदपां यत्कृष्णं तदन्नस्यापागादग्नेरग्नित्वं वाचारम्भणं विकारो नामधेयं त्रीणि रूपाणि इत्येव सत्यम्।

50. *Śvet. Up*. IV. 5[ab].

अजामेकां लोहितशुक्लकृष्णां बह्वीः प्रजाः सृजमानां सरूपाः।

51. *Kaṭh Up*. I. 3. 10-11.

इन्द्रियेभ्यः परा हयर्था अर्थेङ्खभ्यश्चपरं मनः। मनसस्तु परा बुद्धिः बुद्धेरात्मा महान्परः।

महतः परमव्यक्तं अव्यक्तात्पुरुषः परः।

52. *Praśna. Up*. VI. 2.

इहैवान्तः शरीरे सोम्यास पुरुषो यस्मिन्नेताः षोडशकलाः प्रभवन्तीति।

53. Ranade, R.D., *op. cit.*, p 136.
54. *Śvet. Up*. V. 5.

यच्च स्वभावं पचति विश्वयोनिः पाच्यांश्च परिणामयेद्यः।
सर्वमेतद्विश्वमधितिष्ठत्येको गुणांश्च सर्वान्विनियोजयेद्यः।

55. *Ibid.*, VI. 16[c].

प्रधानक्षेत्रज्ञपतिर्गुणेशः।

56. *Ibid.*, IV. 10[ab].
57. *Ibid.*, IV. 9[cd].

अस्मान्मायी सृजते विश्वमेतत्तस्मिंश्चान्यो मायया संनिरुद्धः।

58. *Ibid.*, IV. 5[cd].

अजो ह्येको जुषमाणोऽनुशेते जहात्येनां भुक्तभोगामजोऽन्यः।

59. *Ibid.*, VI. 11[cd].

कर्माध्यक्षः सर्वभूताधिवासः साक्षी चेता केवलो निर्गुणश्च।

60. *Ibid.*, II. 8-15.
61. *Kaṭh Up*. II. 3.12.

तां योगमिति मन्यते स्थिरामिन्द्रियधारणाम्।

62. *Śvet. Up.* I. 14.

ध्याननिर्मथनाभ्यासाद्देवं पश्येन्निगूढवत्।

63. *Chānd. Up.* VIII. 6. 1.

अथ या एता हृदयस्य नाडयस्ताः पिङ्गलस्याणिम्नस्तिष्ठन्ति शुक्लस्य नीलस्य पीतस्य लोहितस्येत्यसौ वा आदित्यः पिङ्ग एष शुक्ल एष नील एष पीत एष लोहितः।

64. *Kau. Up.* IV. 19.

हिता नाम हृदयस्य नाड्यो हृदयात्पुरीततमभिप्रतन्वन्ति।

65. *Bṛ. Up.* IV. 3. 20.

ता वा अस्यैता हिता नाम नाड्यो यथा केशः सहस्त्रधा भिन्नस्तावताऽणिम्ना तिष्ठन्ति शुक्लस्य नीलस्य पीतस्य प्रिङ्गलस्य हरितस्य लोहितस्य पूर्णाः।

66. *Mai. Up.* I. 2.

अस्थिचर्मस्नायुमज्जामांसशुक्रशोणितश्लेष्माश्रुदूषिते विण्मूत्रवातकफपित्तसंघाते दुर्गन्धे निःसारेऽस्मिञ्छरीरे किं कामोपभोगैः।

67. *Kaṭh Up.* I. 2. 9[ab].

नैषा तर्केण मतिरापनेया प्रोक्ताऽन्येनैव सुज्ञानाय प्रेष्ठ।

68. *Mai. Up.* (*Up.* . pt. I) p. 194.

खजाग्नियोगाद्धृदि संप्रयुक्तमणोर्ह्यणुर्द्विरणुः कण्ठदेशे।
जिह्वाग्रदेशे त्र्यणुकं च विद्धि विनिर्गतं मातृकमेवमाहुः।

69. *Bṛ. Up.* II. 1. 19.

अथ यदा सुषुप्तो भवति यदा न कस्यचन वेद हिता नाम नाड्यो द्वासप्ततिः सहस्त्राणि हृदयात्पुरीततमभिप्रतिष्ठन्ते ताभिः प्रत्यवसृप्य पुरीतति शेते स यथा कुमारो वा महाराजो वा महाब्राह्मणो वाऽतिघ्नीमानन्दस्य गत्वा शयीत एवमेवैष एतच्छेते।

70. *Īśa. Up.* 9.

अन्धंतमः प्रविशन्ति येऽविद्यामुपासते। ततो भूय इव ते तमो य उ विद्यायाँ रताः॥

71. *Śvet. Up.* III. 2[a].

एको हि रुद्रो न द्वितीयाय तस्थुः।

72. *Ibid.*, IV. 16[a].

घृतात्परं मण्डमिवातिसूक्ष्मं ज्ञात्वा शिवं सर्वभूतेषु गूढम्।

73. *Ibid.*, V. 3.

एकैकं जालं बहुधा विकुर्वन् अस्मिन्क्षेत्रे सस्हरत्येष देवः।
भूयःसृष्टवा पतयस्तथेषः सर्वाधिपत्यं कुरुते महात्मा॥

74. *Kena. Up.* III. 12.

स तस्मिन्नेवाकाशे स्त्रियमाजगाम बहुशोभमानामुमाँ॰ हैमवतीं तां होवाच।

75. *Kaṭh Up.* I. 2.18.

न जायते म्रियते वा विपश्चिन्नायं कुतश्चिन्न बभूव कश्चित्।
अजो नित्यः शाश्वतोऽयं पुराणो न हन्यते हन्यमाने शरीरे॥

also, *Bh. G.* II.20.

76. *Īśa. Up.* 2.

कुर्वन्नेवेह कर्माणि जिजीवेच्छतँ॰ समाः।
एवं त्वयि नान्यथेतोऽस्ति न कर्म लिप्यते नरे॥

77. *Muṇḍ. Up.* II. 1. 1-10.
also *Ṛv.* X.90.1-16.

CHAPTER II

THE ULTIMATE REALITY

The Ultimate Reality–Brahman

The word ultimate means, 'the final fundamental fact or principle' and the word 'reality' connotes, what is real or existent, or that which underlies appearances. The Upaniṣads deal with the 'Ultimate Reality', that is, the reality which forms the basis of the world of appearances, and to realize it, is the ultimate goal of Individual souls in human bodies, individually as well as in relation to the sentient and insentient beings. The words which the Upaniṣads use to indicate the Ultimate Reality, are the Ātman and the Brahman.

In the *Ṛv*, the word 'Brahman' means a hymn or incantation or a prayer. Gradually, it acquired the meaning – 'the power or potency of prayer.' In the period of the *Av*, the word Brahman signifies a 'magic formula' as distinguished from a 'simple prayer' in the *Ṛv*.[1] During the days of sacrificial texts (Brāhmaṇa-s), the Brahman was identified with various Vedic deities such as Mitra, Vāyu, Bṛhaspati and also with the sacrifice.[2] The priest, the fire, the oblations and all the rituals of sacrifice are identified with the Brahman.[3] He who knows the Brahman, knows and controls the universe. Brahman is the primal principle and the guiding spirit of the universe; and is regarded as omnipotent. There is nothing more ancient and brighter than the Brahman.[4] The Brahman created all the gods and distributed the three regions – earth, space and heaven – to the three gods, Agni, Vāyu, Sūrya.[5] The sacrifice was identified with Viṣṇu, the all pervading entity.[6] Since the sacrifice and Viṣṇu are identified, the Brahman also became all pervading entity.

In the Āraṇyaka-s, the conception of the Brahman has become more or less metaphysical. "One who realizes it becomes emancipated. It is both *Sat* as well as *Asat*. It is described as the truth, the knowledge, the endless. From the Brahman, all animate and inanimate objects have come forth, through whom these exist and wherein they merge."[7]

The word Brahman, which, in the days of the *Ṛv*, simply meant 'prayer'; as the time and the thought progressed gathered various broader meanings and, was used in its ultimate sense in the Upaniṣads.

The Ultimate Reality–Ātman

The term Ātman was never associated with any idea of God. From the very beginning, it seems to have been used in the sense of the Self; of course, the very conception of the Self differed from stage to stage according to the gradual development of human knowledge. In the *Śat. Brā.*, the word Ātman has been used to indicate the middle portion of the physical organism.[8] Again, the *Śat. Brā.*, identifies it with *manas, buddhi, ahaṁkāra,* and *citta.* Also, the word is used to denote the four stages of consciousness.[9]

In the Āraṇyaka-s also the word Ātman has passed through various stages. It is used in the sense of the middle portion of a human being, and the human being himself. It is identified with *manas* and *prāṇa,* and is called *vijñānamaya.* Later, it is called *ānandamaya*, in the *Tait. Āra.* The *Ait. Āra.* says the Ātman is as extensive as the space between Dyu and Pṛthivī. It says that there is nothing but the Ātman in the beginning. This is undoubtedly the conception of the Ātman which is free from all the limitations. Further, the Āraṇyaka says, that the Ātman desired to create the *loka*-s. the *Tait. Āra.* and the *Ait. Āra.* present almost a complete idea of the true nature of the Ātman as found later on in the system of the Upaniṣads. It is also said to be all pervasive, and it manifests itself in the organisms having both *citta* and *rasa*; in human beings alone, it manifests itself fully.[10]

Brahman as Ātman

In the early prose Upaniṣads, the Ātman is the principle of the individual consciousness and the Brahman, beyond place or time; the ground of the cosmos. Soon, the distinction diminishes and the two are identified. There is no duality between the words the Ātman and the Brahman. God is not merely the transcendent 'other', but is also the universal spirit, which is the essence of human personality and its vitalizing power. For the first time, the *Bṛ. Up.* says in clear and definite terms that the Ātman is the Brahman,[11] and that its nature is of consciousness (*prajñāna*) and bliss. It is illustrated by the dialogue between the king Janaka and Yājñavalkya that the light of the Sun and that of the Ātman are one and the same.[12] In the *Chānd. Up.* it is said, "verily this whole world is the Brahman; and this soul of mine, within the heart, this is the Brahman."[13] The individual consciousness can be one with the cosmic existence by entering into the cosmic consciousness.

The seers of the Upaniṣads, who had realized the Ātman, have tried to describe this undescribable Brahman in different ways. These descriptions act as a bright, guiding beacon for the ardent hankering souls.

The seers perceived and realized the inner spring of life and the inmost spirituality of man as he is within himself; and beyond the range of the senses and discursive thought. The description of the nature of the Brahman may be regarded as the states of experience between which the minds of the sages oscillated in attempting the realization of a truth which is beyond speech and thought. There are certain limitations while putting the experiences in words as the 'experience' is beyond words. Their efforts were to make the aspirants with different intellectual levels to be able to share their experiences in a way they would be able to understand; that is from the grossest to the subtlest. It means a gradual ascent in the measure of spiritual values and experience towards the spiritual goal and completion of the same.

The Brahman as the Essence – (An Abstract Entity, the Reality Underlying a Phenomena)

The seventh section of the *Bramhāvallī - adhyāya* of the *Tait. Up.* states that, " non-existent was this world in the beginning, from that, existence was produced. Therefore, it is called well-made (*sukṛtam*), verily, what that 'well formed' is the essence of existence, for truly by obtaining the essence, one becomes blissful."[14] When a man finds his essence, his resting place in the invisible, inexpressible, unfathomable one, then he has attained the peace.

According to a story in the *Chānd. Up.*,[15] when Śvetaketu returned home after twelve years stay in the hermitage, where he studied the Veda-s; he became arrogant and considered himself to be a wise man. His father enquired, "What have you learned that you seem to think yourself so wise?" Do you know that which when once known, everything else becomes known?" When you once know iron, you know all that can be made out of iron, for these are in essence nothing but iron; we can distinguish the iron vessels from iron only by their specific forms and names. But whatever may be their forms and names, the true essence in them all, whether they may be needless pans or handles, is nothing but iron. It is only that there are so many forms and names. What are these names and forms without essence? It is the essence, the iron that manifests itself in so many forms and names. When this iron is known, all that is made of iron is also known. It is the ineffable reality, the Ultimate being, which is the essence of everything else. Continuing the instruction further, the father asked the son to bring a fruit of *nyagrodha* tree and asked him to break it. The son observed fine seeds in the fruit, when broken. Again, the father asked him to break one of those seeds; and then the son observed that there was nothing at all in that seed. Then the father said to him, "My dear, that subtle essence which you do not perceive, from that very essence this great *nyagrodha* tree exists."[16] Through this illustration, the father explains how the world which has names and forms arises from the subtle essence of Pure Being.

The Brahman as Reality (*Satyam*)

The name of the Brahman is the 'True', states the *Chānd. Up.* and explains that, it consists of three syllables *sat, ti, yam* – the *sat* that is the immortal. The *ti* that is the mortal. The *yam*, with it one holds the two together.[17] The three syllables are differently explained in the *Br. Up.*[18] The first and the last syllables are the truth (*satyam*), and in the middle is the untruth (*anṛtam*). This untruth is enclosed on both the sides by truth; it partakes of the nature of truth itself. Him, who knows this, untruth does not injure. The *Bṛ. Up.* states that the Brahman is the Reality of the real (*satyasya satyam*) the source of all existing things. That which alone, in this reality is truly real.[19]

The Brahman as Being (*Sat*)

The Ultimate reality is 'being'. All philosophical quests presuppose the reality of being; there is not merely 'this' but there is also the other, the transcendent one. In the *Tait. Up.*, where the verse says, "Not-being was this in the beginning, from that being arose",[20] it is to be understood that, it is not the absolute not-being, as compared with the later concrete existence. Further, it is said, "after he had created it, he entered into it and when he entered into it, he was the 'being' and 'beyond'."[21]

Consciousness (*Cit*)

"The entire development of philosophy from Plato to Aristotle to the present, with few exceptions has been dominated by the thought that the nature of the soul, and in connection therewith the nature of the God, is to be conceived as something analogous to human thought as reason, spirit or intelligence," opines Deussen, P.[22] for instance, when Uṣasta asks Yājñavalkya, to explain this Brahman, which cannot be perceived directly and "the indweller of all." He explains, "You cannot see the seer of seeing, hear the hearer of hearing, think the thinker of thinking. He is your Self which is in all things." He who breathes in with your breathing, is the Self of yours.[23] The conception of the

Ātman, implies that; the Brahman pervading all, and the Ātman, the essence of a man is knowing subject.

The Brahman as Bliss

In the Upaniṣads, bliss does not appear as the "attribute" of the Brahman, but the Brahman is bliss itself. In the *Chānd. Up.*,[24] it is said that the Brahman is joy (*kam*). Also, in the *Chānd. Up.*, the word pleasure (*sukham*) denotes bliss.[25] *Ānandāvallī* of the *Tait. Up.* treats the Brahman as bliss.[26] Herein, *annamaya, prāṇamaya, manomaya,* and *vijñānamaya* sheaths of the Ātman are described and when they are stripped off as mere husks, the kernel can be perceived as the *ānandamaya* Ātman. This Ātman, consisting of bliss is described as, "love is his head, joy his right side, joyousness as his left side, bliss his trunk, and the Brahman, his base."[27] Here, Brahman is described as the base of the Self consisting bliss. In the passage of the *Bṛ. Up.*, the origin of the doctrine of the Brahman as bliss may be found. Here, the state of deep sleep is described, "that is his real form, in which he is exalted above desire, and is free from evil and fear."[28] He is not affected by good and evil, as all contrasts disappear in the state of deep sleep. This is the state of existence as subject without an object. Further, it is said, "this is his Supreme happiness, and Supreme bliss, by a small measure of this all other creatures live."[29]

Two Forms of the Brahman

The *Mai. Up.* describes beautifully, two forms of the Brahman, as 'time' and the 'timeless'. "That which is prior to the Sun is timeless, without parts; but that which begins with the Sun is time, which has parts. The form which has parts is the year; from the year the creatures are produced, by the year they grow and in the year they disappear."[30] It may be noticed that the time is exalted as the highest principle, as the source of all 'this'. The time abides in itself when one crosses the bridge, and gets to the other shore, the troubles of the world cease, for there is neither virtue nor vice.

Savitṛ, from whom are begotten the moon, stars, planets, the year and from them comes the whole world here. The Sun as the 'Self' of time is the ordainer. *Kaṭh Up.* describes the Brahman as independent of past and future.[31] The *Bṛ. Up.* and *Kaṭh Up.* also describe it as the "lord of the past and future."[32] The *Śvet. Up.* tells us that it is "beyond the three times",[33] "at whose feet time rolls along" explains the *Bṛ. Up.*[34] Thus, from the above descriptions it may be inferred that the Brahman, being both the time and the timeless transcends them both. The Brahman is the bridge. Day and night are the factors of the time, the determinants of morality of all things under the Sun. Over the bridge, the day and night do not cross.[35]

The *Mai. Up.* again, states that there are two forms of the Brahman, the manifest and the unmanifest. "That which is manifest is unreal, and that which is unmanifest is real; that is the Brahman."[36] Radhakrishnan, S. in his commentary on the above verse says that, "the formed is the effect and the formless is the cause."[37] The Brahman being the ultimate Reality, encompassing all–the living and non-living things, at the same time, the very essence of the things, and formless by itself. Radhakrishnan says the Brahman to be the 'cause', which is beyond causality; only in the sense that without which nothing can exist.

The Brahman is beyond causality, and no becoming touches the essential reality. The *Chānd. Up.* teaches that "change (*vikāra*) is merely a matter of words, nothing but a name (changes)."[38] Causality–which means the relation of cause and effect–is the universal rule according to which all changes in the world proceed. Where there is no change, there is no causality. The *Kaṭh Up.* says, "The seer is not born, nor does he die. He does not spring from anything, and becomes anything. He is unborn, eternal, abiding and ancient. He does not perish, for it is the body that perishes".[39] The *Īśa. Up.* explains, that the manifest (*sambhūti*) and the unmanifest (*asambhūti*) are the two aspects of the Supreme.[40] To be absorbed in the world without turning to the principle at the base; and to be absorbed in the contemplation of the unmanifest, indifferent to the material world, are two extremes. Radhakrishnan, S. comments that, "we must centre our thoughts in the eternal remembering that the eternal is the Self of the temporal."[41]

The Brahman is the Supreme

The supremeness of the Brahman is described in the *Kaṭh. Up.* The verse aptly describes that the lustre of everything is dependent upon his lustre.[42] In some Upaniṣads, the Brahman is described as the overlord of all. He is the Supreme lord from whom everything has proceeded and who is the source of all energy.[43] Thus, in the *Ken. Up.*, we find the query, "by whose will and directed by whom does the mind work? By whose command the Prāṇa-s move? At whose direction speech is uttered?" Then comes the answer that, "It is from Him that the organs of speech, eye etc. have all derived their powers. So neither the mind nor the eye etc. can tell us anything about Him, because neither the eye etc. can reach him. He alone is the agent operative through all these organs and making the eye, the perceiver; the ear the hearer etc. But He in his own nature cannot be grasped by any of these."[44]

A story illustrates the greatness of the Brahman, as the Supreme and all powerful lord. All the Gods, once, were jubiliant over the victory, against their fight with the demons. They considered it to be their own greatness, though all the while it was the Brahman alone who was great. The Brahman saw the false conceit of the Gods and appeared before them as the all powerful lord.[45]

The Brahman is all pervading. That infinite is indeed in the east, west, south and north; and above and below, infinite in every direction. From him, indeed the directions exist. He is immeasurable, unlimited.[46] The Brahman is vast and subtler than the subtle; in him are the worlds and the beings established.[47] In *Bṛ. Up.,* he is described as the controller, the lord and the master of all. He is the creator of the universe and the world belongs to

Him. Yet, He is the indweller (*antaryāmin*), inner controller and He is the inmost Self of all living beings. (*sarvabhūtāntarātman*).[48]

The descriptions of the Brahman as the knowing subject within us are usually accompanied by the assertion that this knowing subject, 'knower' of 'knowing' himself remains unknowable;[49] thereby denying objective existence to the Brahman. By the seers of the Upaniṣads, the Brahman is described in negative terms also. Yājñavalkya, in the *Bṛ. Up.,* sums up his dialogue with the king Janaka, "He, however, the Ātman, is not so, not so. He is incomprehensible for he is not comprehended; indestructible for he is not destroyed, unaffected for nothing affects him; he is not fettered, he is not disturbed, he suffers no harm.[50] (It again occurs another three times in the *Bṛ. Up.*) Yājñavalkya describes the Ātman as, unbegotten (*aja*), without decay (*akṣ ara*), without growth (*ajara*), immortal (*amṛta*) fearless (*abhaya*).[51]

A passage in the *Chānd. Up.* also describes the Brahman in negative terms, such as free from old age, free from suffering etc.[52] as is described in the *Bṛ. Up.* Sometimes, the unknowableness of the Brahman is described paradoxically as is described in the *Īśa. Up.* He is described as, "he moves and moves not, he is far away yet so near" etc.[53] The mutually contradictory qualities are ascribed to the Brahman, in such a manner that they only illustrate that the Brahman cannot be conceived by means of empirical descriptions; for it is independent of all limitations, beyond everything.

The Upaniṣads affirm that the Brahman on which all else depends, to which all existence aspire, the Brahman which is sufficient in itself, aspiring to no other, without any need is the source of everything, which is created. The Upaniṣads, either as a whole or individually offer a complete conception of the universe logically developed.

For the philosophers of the Upaniṣads, the primary search was after the origin of things. What is that from which all things spring up, and in which they sustain and into which they are dissolved? The *Tait. Up.* teaches, "that from which the beings are born, by which the born live and into which they are resolved; that alone might be regarded as the Ultimate Reality."[54] The *Chānd. Up.* uses the mystic word *'tajjalān',* to describe the primary substratum.[55] Different Upaniṣads present different theories of creation. (Beginning with the creation of the Universe, and describing the creation of the organic and inorganic matter.)

A beginning for this search was made even at the time of the *Ṛv.* A progress was being made towards the conception of cosmogony; we find evidence in certain hymns of the *Ṛv.* The concept of Being and Not-being is already raised, and the primal existence is declared to be superior to the Being and Not-being in the hymn of creation.[56] A philosophical impulse of the Vedic period, passing through the Brāhmanic period, gathered force at the beginning of the Upaniṣadic period.

Ait. Up. states, "In the beginning, this universe was the Ātman alone. Nothing else whatsoever winked. He thought, "let me now create the worlds." He created these worlds, water, light rays (atmosphere), death (earth), waters.[57] Further, it is said, "He deliberated, how can this exist apart from me." In what way shall I enter into this? Accordingly, he entered through the opening of the skull.[58] The *Ait. Up.* cites the five elements – earth, air, ether, light, and water; which are termed as the five great elements[59] (first time here). Moreover, the Ātman's entering into man by the door of the skull is mentioned. The *Tait. Up.* says, "He desired, let me become many, let me be born. He performed austerities; having performed the austerities, he created all this, whatsoever is here; having created, he entered into it. He became both the actual and the beyond, both the founded and unfounded, the true and untrue. As the real, he became whatever there is here."[60] The *Tait. Up.* also states that the five elements are the proceedings of the Ātman.[61]

The *Chand. Up.* says, "In the beginning, there was only one, without the second. He proposed, I will become many; then he created the heat." From heat, water was produced and from water, food (earth) proceeded.[62] Then he thought, "I will enter into these three, with this living Self and manifest thereupon by name and form."[63] The *Br. Up.*, enumerates, "The universe, earlier was not unfolded; it was then manifested as names and forms... As the fire has entered the wood, the Ātman has entered into the universe upto the finger tips as a knife is hidden in a sheath."[64]

The traditional view; that the primeval being created the universe, and then as the first born, entered into it; appears frequently in the Upaniṣads.[65] The passages earlier illustrated, carry the same thought.

The Upaniṣadic seers also regard the elements as the source of things. The elements as water, fire, space, air are regarded as responsible for the unfoldment of creation. Thus, in the *Bṛ. Up.* it is said that, "In the beginning, the waters alone existed, from the waters was born Truth. Truth produced the Brahman, the Brahman gave birth to Prajāpati, and from him were the gods born. These gods worship truth alone."[66] Raikva puts forth the theory that, "air is the final 'absorbent' of things;"[67] and therefore, probably the origin of them. The *Kaṭh. Up.* tells us that, "the fire having entered the universe assumed all forms."[68] On the contrary the *Chānd. Up.* tells us that fire was the first evolute from the primeval being, and from the fire came water and then the earth.[69] In the *Chānd. Up.* when Pravāhaṇa Jaivali was asked, "what was the final habitat of all things?" He answered, "It was space."[70] Another passage of the *Chānd. Up.*, corroborates this passage, in which it is stated that space is really higher than fire. In space, are all things born.[71]

The *Chānd. Up.* explains the process of *trivṛtkaraṇa*.[72] Each of the three original elements, the fire, water and earth is to be (considered) divided into two equal portions. Again, the half is to be divided into two equal portions, the two quarters of the two other elements, are to be combined with the one half of the original element making up a transformed evolute of the original elements, have three different colours, red, white and black. Further, the Upaniṣad states that, "what really exists is the three different colours or the three different elements."[73] This passage conveys the idea that everything manifested, contains these three elements or the colour. This manifestation is a modifactory appearance of the original elements, and all of them are born from the primeval being. In this theory of the threefold division of the original elements, lies the seed of the later distinction of subtle elements (*tanmātrā*-s) and gross elements. (*sthūlabhūta*-s). This distinction is seen in the *Praśna. Up*. The expressions here used, *Pṛthivīmātrā, āpomātrā* and so on were later comprehended under the term *tanmātrā*.[74] The *Mai. Up.* also mentions these *mātrā*-s.[75] In the Sāṁkhya philosophy, they play an important part. The passages from the *Chānd. Up.*[76] and *Tait. Up.*[77] record the five elements as proceeding forth, first from the Brahman and each in succession from its immediate predecessor. This number of five elements is in consonance with five organs of knowledge and each element has its assigned quality.

The Creation of the Creatures, Animals, Plants

The statement that, "the Brahman is the sole reality," and an emergence of the universe from the Brahman are really contradictory.[78] But when it is said, "after he had created it he entered into it."[79] and "into it that one has entered upto finger-tips"[80] and so on,[81] there remains no contradiction.

In the *Bṛ. Up.* it is said that he created all living creatures as his abode, and into the citadels he entered as a bird; into the citadels as a citizen.[82] The thought that; all living creatures and thereby all plants, animals, men and gods are his abodes into which the Brahman has entered as an individual soul, is expressed in the *Muṇḍ. Up.*[83] The *Ait. Up.* says, "this is the Brahman, this is Indra, Prajāpati, this is all gods; it is the five elements; it is that which is born of an egg, womb, sweat, or shoot; it is horses, cattle, men–all that lives, walks or flies, all that is motionless (also)."[84] The Brahman is also known as *sāman* for he is equivalent to an ant, elephant, to this entire universe.[85] The *Bṛ. Up.* beautifully describes the creation of the beings through a mythical story, according to which, the Ātman originally is neither male nor female, but an undistinguished union of the two. It divides itself into the shape of a man and a woman – and attains to unity in conjugal act. Thereupon, the woman flees and hides herself successively in different species of animals, the horse, cow, goat etc. down to the ant. The Ātman pursues her and thus, begets creatures of each kind. Thus, the creatures are manifested.[86] The myth asserts that all the forms are essentially similar and are the manifestations of the Ātman.

The Concept of the *Hiraṇyagarbha*

Hiraṇyagarbha creates the world according to the Veda-s, which has within itself eternally the primary types of all classes of things. According to the *Ṛv*, *Hiraṇyagarbha* came forth as the first born of creation from the primeval waters, which was created by the first principle. He is the world-soul, the divine creator.[87] As the individual soul is related to its body, so is the world-soul related to the body of the universe. *Hiraṇyagarbha* arises at the beginning of the world and is dissolved at every world ending. He is the intermediary between the Brahman and the creation. He is as though the Brahman personified. This conception of the first-born of creation is seen in the *Śvet. Up*. Here, the Supreme is described as looking upon *Hiraṇyagarbha* while he was being born.[88] He was the first to be created by God and endowed by him all powers.[89]

Deussen stated that, for the metaphysical comprehension of the universe, this idea of the creator, or the first born is indispensable. The entire objective universe is possible only in so far as it is sustained by a knowing subject. This subject as the sustainer of the objective universe is manifested in all individual subjects, but is by no means identical with them. For the individual subjects pass away but the objective universe continues to exist without them; there exists, therefore, the eternal knowing subject also (*Hiraṇyagarbha*) by whom it is sustained. Space and time are derived from this subject. It is itself accordingly, not in space and time.[90] It has no empirical reality, only a metaphysical reality.

Myth of the Universal Egg

In the *Chānd. Up.*, an interesting myth is associated with the philosophy of Not-Being; in which it is told that, "in the beginning, what existed was Not-Being. It then converted itself into Being. It grew and became a vast egg. It lay in that position for a year and then broke open. Its two parts were one of silver and the other of gold. That which was silver, became this earth and that part of gold became the heaven. The thick membrane of the egg became the mountains and the thin membrane – the clouds; the arteries of the egg became the rivers, the fluid in the egg became the ocean. What which was born of out of the egg was, the Sun."[91]

Similarly, the universe also came to be regarded as huge chest in the *Chānd. Up.* The bottom of that huge chest is the earth, and the heaven is the upper lid. The quarters as its corners and the sky as its inside; containing in its inside a rich treasure.[92]

The myth of the Sun coming out of the egg, indirectly indicates further creation; of the earth, the planets, creatures, plants etc.

The alternative conception of the universe as a huge chest, is noteworthy; for the purpose of contrasting it with the universe regarded as a great spherical egg. (though it has got nothing to do with the philosophy of Not-Being).

The sages of the Upaniṣads, as a result of their contemplation, put forth the theories of creation through myths. These may not be precise in describing the order of creation and may not be proved by science; but they are the representations of the evolution of the universe, from the Ātman.

The Brahman as the Sustainer

As the theories of creation are illustrations of evolution of the universe from the Ātman; they also aim to teach the absolute dependence of all existing beings on the Ātman. The sage of the *Śvet. Up.* asks in wonder at the beginning of his treatise, "From whom are we born? In whom do we live and have our being?"[93] "All these creatures my dear, have their roots in the Being. They have the Being as their abode, Being as their support" expresses the *Chānd. Up.* clearly.[94] The Upaniṣad also says, "this whole world is the Brahman, from which he comes forth, within which he will be dissolved and in which he breathes."[95] A passage from the *Kaṭh. Up.* shows how from one Brahman as root the multiplicity of the universe arose.[96] As the rich foliage of a tree is linked to its roots, similarly, the universe is connected to its root, the Brahman. In reality, the Ātman alone exists, and the universe is essentially only the Ātman. The things of the universe are related to the Ātman as the sparks of the fire, when they leap forth, and with which they are essentially 'akin to it.'[97]

The *Ait. Up.* offers elaborate explanation of the generation of all the objects in the universe. After the creation of the worlds, the world governers, the hunger and thirst, the creator created matter as food for them all. He proceeded to create the soul in the human body. Then he thought, "How shall this body sustain without me?" so he entered by the door of division. (*vidṛti*).[98] The myth shows that the sustenance of human body is not possible without the Ātman.

Brahman as the Dissipater

There is ample evidence in the Upaniṣads which proves the return of individual beings into the Brahman. In the *Br. Up.*, 'death and hunger' pose as the creators of the universe. "All that he created he resolved to devour, because he devours everything. Even death is absorbed in the Eternal."[99] The *Bṛ. Up.* also says, Prajāpati creates the *manas*, speech and *prāṇa* as food for himself.[100] The *Kaṭh. Up.* states, "for Him, priesthood and nobility serve as food and death as a sauce."[101] Death leads to the reabsorption into the Supreme of the entire world in which Brāhmaṇa-s and Kṣatriya-s hold the highest place. In the *Chānd. Up.* it is said, "It is from the *ākāśa* that all the creatures proceed and into the *ākāśa* they take resort."[102] In the *Muṇḍ. Up.*, Brahman is compared to a spider, which sends forth threads to weave the web and draws them back again into itself.[103] In the same sense regarding the Ātman the *Muṇḍ. Up.* states, "He is the cradle of the universe; for he is the creation and the end of living beings."[104] The famous mystical name in the *Chānd. Up.*, '*tajjalān*' means (Brahman) out of which the beings arise into which they are resolved and by which they breathe.[105]

Deussen quotes Anaximander, who says, "that from which existing things originate, into it they necessarily also disappear." Therefore, it is natural to assume that the existing things and the universe return into Brahman, from whom they have come forth.[106]

The universe also is taken back into the Brahman. "He (Rudra as a personification of the Brahman) resides in the creatures, and he as the lord destroys all created things."[107] "He regulates all the creatures, until finally the whole is lost in him, who is the beginning." –are the thoughts propounded in the *Śvet. Up.*[108]

The Descriptions of the Brahman in the Later Upaniṣads

In the later Vedānta, Brahman is described as Saccidānanda, by the combination of its three essential attributes as being (*sat*), mind (*cit*), and bliss (*ānanda*). This name does not occur in any of the earlier Upaniṣads, but the steps leading to this celebrated formula can be seen in the earlier Upaniṣads. In the *Bṛ. Up.*, the Brahman is "bliss and knowledge(*vijñānam ānandaṁ Brahma*)"[109] as declared by Yājñavalkya. In the same Upaniṣad, the words *satyam, prajñā* and *ānanda* appear in one passage.[110] Elsewhere, closer to the character of the above formula, which became a characteristic later, appear the words *satyam, jñānam, ānandam* side by side.[111] A combination of the four predicates is found in the *Sarvopaniṣatsāra,* where the Brahman is defined as "true, knowledge, infinite, bliss."[112] The formula, '*Sat, cit, ānanda*' occurs first in the *Nṛsiṁha. U. Tā. Up.*,[113] and is employed in the *Rāma. P. Tā. Up.* and the *Rāma. U. Tā. Up.* and then used frequently in the other later Upaniṣads.[114]

For the later Upaniṣads, whether the Brahman is Being or Not-Being or whether it is thinkable or unthinkable etc., has no significance. These, like all other pairs of opposites are transcended by the Brahman. For *e.g.*, "Unempty, it appears as empty, above emptiness it stands majestically. Nor thought it is, nor thinking; unthinkable yet thinkable. It is all and yet it is nothing, there is nothing higher than it," describes the *Tejobindu Upaniṣad.*[115]

The earlier Upaniṣads describe the Brahman as the light of lights.[116] It means that the Ātman is itself its own light. "There no Sun shines nor the moon and stars, lightnings also do not shine where then could this fire shine? Everything shines after that shining light, His shining illumines all the world."[117] The whole objective universe is illumined by Him, for it cannot illumine itself. Further, in the *Chānd. Up.* and the *Brhmopaniṣad* it is said that the soul in deep sleep is raised out of this body and enters into the purest light, and thereby assumes its original form.[118] This thought reminds Yājñavalkya's conception of the Ātman, in a dialogue with Janaka–as *paraṁ jyotiḥ,* which as the knowing subject is its own light.[119] This idea may be the base of another frequently recurring idea of the eternal day of the Brahman.[120] This idea is echoed in the *Kaṇṭhaśruti Up.* and the *Nādabindūpaniṣad.* Meditation on Oṁ leads in the highest degree to the "eternal day of the Brahman, which is the source of the illuminaries" says the *Nādabindūpaniṣad.*[121] "For him, (the one, who has attained the knowledge of the Ātman) there is no day and no night" states the *Kaṇṭhaśruti Up.*[122]

Brahman is described as 'bliss' in the earlier Upaniṣads. All the later Upaniṣads depend mostly upon the *Bṛ. Up.* and *Tait. Up.* for the description of the Brahman as bliss. For *e.g.* the *M.N. Up.*, the *Tejobindū. Up.* describe the bliss as "the rapture indeed, yet beyond pleasure",[123] The *Sarvasāropaniṣad* describes, "when he remains in the knowledge that he himself is the cause of the four sheaths, (of the Ātman) as the fig seeds of the fig tree, then it is called the sheath consisting of bliss (*ānandamaya*)."[124]

The later Upaniṣads, most of which are sectarian in character, have a major portion devoted to different deities. But they resemble the earlier Upaniṣads in this respect, that they equate their favourite deity with the Brahman, and use the personal aspect of the deity for reaching the impersonal one. The method adopted by the later Upaniṣads is, first the description of the physical aspects of the deity is given for worship. Secondly, the deity is described metaphorically for the purpose of meditation. Through meditation on these different aspects, and discarding the attributes one by one, one reaches the indescribable Brahman. The *Nārāyaṇātharvaśira Up.* describes Nārāyaṇa as eternal, indwelling spirit, and all pervading. "Nārāyaṇa is all this. Brahmā, Śiva, Viṣṇu, Indra, the quarters, the time, above and below, everywhere is Nārāyaṇa. Whatever is the past and future, is Nārāyaṇa. This pure one is the only one without a second."[125] Here, the qualities of the qualitiless Brahman are superimposed on Nārāyaṇa. In the *Gaṇapati Up.*, while praising the deity it is said, "You are the Brahman incarnate. You are the Ātman incarnate.[126] You are the doer (*kartṛ*), you support everything. You are beyond the time, *guṇa*-s, and three *kāla*-s. You alone are Brahmā, Viṣṇu, Rudra; you are *sat, cit, ānanda.* This world proceeds from you, is sustained in you and dissolves in you."[127] Again, the abilities of the Brahman of creating, maintaining and dissolving the world, the nature of Brahman as being *Sat, Cit* and *Ānanda*; the substratum of all things and beings are bestowed on Gaṇapati. Similarly, other deities like Śiva, Rudra, Sūrya, Devī are exalted to the position of the Brahman.

A myth is a tale that narrates a sacred story, or an event that took place in primordial time, or an account of creation and that the actors are super-human beings. It is said that every genuine myth is a myth of observation; the observation of men of a state of primitive culture; of a fact which had struck home to their minds. A myth, though traditional tale like other types of stories; is different from them on account of its being non-artful, fostered by faith in a tradition and which indicates inquisitiveness. Myths are characterised by elements which apparently are most irrational. The irrationality about the myth is due to the mysterious or wonderful experience that lies at the basis of its formation, or due to non-regular problem or situation faced by an inquisitive mind.

A considerable number of myths deal with the problem of creation, first couple, life after death and so on. The couples are seen to represent the aspect of nature, which are deified.[128]

The Views on Creation in the Later Upaniṣads

As regards the creation, the later Upaniṣads describe the theories of creation of the world which are influenced by the various systems of philosophy. According to Gajendragadkar, these may be categorised broadly as follows:

(*i*) Mythical and ritualistic (creation through sacrifice, penance or formula-s),

(*ii*) Creation by the deities (theistic),

(*iii*) Creation through the elements like water, space etc.,

(*iv*) Mythical and partially philosophical, and

(*v*) Philosophical.

Further he says that, "when a satisfactory solution is not found to a problem; the authors of the later Upaniṣads, resort to myths and formulae (*mantra*-s); and relying on them; they try to solve it."[128a] But, it may be said that as the Purāṇa-s adopted a different mode to preach pure, deeper knowledge to the commoners, through the medium of stories it is the mode adopted by the *Mbh.* also and then, the stories became a means to an end, the end was the knowledge; so also, the sages of the later Upaniṣads, while describing the Ultimate Principle described the order of creation through the medium of myths and stories. The psychology behind this was that human mind is always eager for the tales through which the knowledge, philosophy which is otherwise difficult to comprehend is rendered easier. In the *Mudgalopaniṣad,* it is said that "Brahmā willed to create the universe, but he did not know how to create it. He practised penance. The lord (*Īśvara*) in the form of Nārāyaṇa graced him, and asked him to perform a natural sacrifice; considering the summer season as the sacrificial fire; the spring as the sacrificial ghee, and the rainy season as the Soma juice; the senses as the priest (*hotṛ*), the body as the oblations; and Nārāyaṇa as the chief sacrificial deity."[129] Through this sacrifice, Brahmā acquired the power, with which he created the universe.

Creation through the Anuṣṭubh Metre

In the *Nṛsiṁha. P. Tā. Up.*, Prajāpati created the world by means of the Nṛsiṁha formula. After practising penance, he (Prajāpati) saw this royal formula (*mantrarāja*) related to Nṛsiṁha, composed in the *Anuṣṭubh* metre. With it, he created the whole world. Therefore, they say, this whole world is *Anuṣṭubh* "From *Anuṣṭubh,* indeed are born these creatures, having born, they live by the *Anuṣṭubh,* and departing, they again go back to the *Anuṣṭubh.*"[130]

The earth with its oceans, mountains and islands – that one should know as the first line of the formula. The atmosphere populated with the Yakṣa-s, Gandharva-s, Apsaras-s; as the second line; the heaven inhabited by Vasu-s, Rudra-s, Āditya-s and all gods as the third line; and the undefiled, self-essence of the Brahman dwelling "in the highest place" – that one should know as the fourth line of the formula.[131]

Creation by the Deities

All the sectarian Upaniṣads describe their favourite deity as the creator, preserver and dissipater of the universe. Each deity can destroy and create the universe whenever it wills so. There are a few different thoughts in the *Gopālapūrvatāpinī. Up.* and *Mahopaniṣad.* The idea of the *pañcapada*-s is new in the former Upaniṣad, where it has been said that the earth, water, fire, *ākāśa,* vāyu, that is, the five great elements were evolved from the 'five feet' of the Gopālakṛṣṇa.[132] The latter presents the view that, Nārāyaṇa projects out of himself 'the twentyfive fold Puruṣa', *i.e.* the twentyfive principles of the Sāṁkhya-s, substituting *tejas* in place of Prakṛti and Ātman in that of Puruṣa.[133]

Then Nārāyaṇa once more meditated and then the virtues, truth, penance, chastity, austerity, renunciation were created. Again, he meditated and as he stood absorbed in meditation, sweat came out of his forehead. It expanded into these primordial waters. In them was born *tejas* as a golden egg. Therein was born the God Brahmā with four faces. According to Deussen, the form of narration is patterned on the line of the creation – myths of the Brāhmaṇa-s.[134]

These reflections are in nature, but they are the admixtures of myths, for during the period of these Upaniṣads science was not advanced. "This creation was created from the waters" says the *Bṛ. Jābāla. Up.*[135] This Upaniṣad, mentions that "earlier, nothing existed except water, in that water was born Brahmā, floating on a lotus (*puṣkara*) leaf. He willed to create the world; from his mind a seed was formed and from that seed this world was created." Elsewhere, this Upaniṣad says that, "this world is created from the space, in the space it is sustained and in the space it merges."[136]

The description of creation in the *Avyaktopaniṣad*,[137] is partially essential and partially mythical. It says, "Initially only the 'light' existed. There was nothing else whatsoever. It divided itself into two parts; green and red; the Puruṣa and Prakṛti. By them, a golden egg was created and *parameṣṭī* was born from that egg. When he desired to know, from whom was he created and the work that was to be accomplished by him, he heard words, that he was born from the unmanifest, and the work to be accomplished was the manifestation of the world. Then he practised penance for a thousand years. In his penance, he saw the form of Viṣṇu, having the face of a deer and the body of a man. This lustrous form of Viṣṇu asked him to perform a sacrifice; considering the sacrificial deity as Viṣṇu and the Self as the sacrificial fire. When *Parameṣṭī* performed the sacrifice as advised, he gained the power of creation.

The information regarding the creation, given in the *Tvmn. Up.* is also of a mixed type. "When the God in the form of

Nārāyaṇa opens his eyes, the universe is created and when he closes his eyes, the universe is destroyed. Once, when he opened his eyes, 'unmanifest' was created. From that unmanifest (*avyakta*), *mūlāvidyā,* and in succession, *mahat, ahaṁkāra,* five subtle elements, five gross elements were created. From the gross elements, nescience in the form of egg was created. This egg itself is Nārāyaṇa, endowed with the attribute *māyā*. He is Virāṭ Puruṣa; having thousand heads, eyes and hands. He is omniscient, the manifest and the unmanifest. He is the 'knowledge', sacrifice, power and brilliance. After having created these worlds, he has entered in them", narrates the Upaniṣad.[138]

Māyā as the Cause of Creation

"Sarasvatī represents *māyā*, and the universe is created from her" says Sarasvatī. *R. Up.*[139] *Rāmatāpinī. Up.* and *Sītopaniṣad* state that; "Sītā is *māyā* and is the creative power of Rāma."[140] *Gopālapūrvatāpinī. Up.* and the *Nṛsiṁha. P. Tā. Up.* opine that, the Brahman is real and *māyā* is unreal. From this unreal *māyā*, the world of multiplicity is created.[141]

Though these later Upaniṣads state that, *māyā* is the cause of creation; this thought is not justified and explained fully by the authors of these Upaniṣads.

The Brahman as the Creator

Many later Upaniṣads propound that the *Sat* or the Brahman is the cause of creation. *Yogacūḍāmaṇi. Up.*[142] describes the creation as; "From the eternal, pure, untainted, attributeless Brahman, a power like its own form, was created. From the Ātman were created the space, wind, fire, water and the earth. Everything which exists, movable and immovable was created from the Brahman. The *Gopālottaratāpinī. Up.* describes creation in a similar manner.[143] The peculiarity of this Upaniṣad is that it mentions the elements; *mahat, ahaṁkāra,* five subtle elements; of the Sāṁkhya philosophy; while describing the creation.

Dissolution of the Universe

The *Subālopaniṣad* beautifully enumerates the account of dissolution. "At the end he (the same world spirit), becoming Vaiśvānara completely burns all existing things. The earth dissolves in water, water dissolves in fire, fire dissolves in air, air dissolves in the ether, the ether in the senses, the senses in the subtle elements, the subtle elements dissolve in their subtle sources, the subtle sources dissolve in the principle of *mahat,* the principle of *mahat* dissolves in the principle of the unmanifested and the principle of the unmanifested dissolves in the Imperishable. The Imperishable dissolves in the darkness. The darkness becomes one with the transcendent (Brahman). Beyond the transcendent, there is no other existence nor non-existence nor both-existence and non-existence."[144]

Here, the order of dissolution is the reverse of the order of evolution and the account is based on the Sāṁkhya theory.

Taking into consideration this view, it may be said that the later Upaniṣads take a step ahead of the earlier Upaniṣads.

The meaning of the word Māyā

"Māyā, which means an 'illusion, appearance' is a term in the philosophy of Vedānta applied to the illusion of the multiplicity of the empirical universe produced by *avidyā*, when, in reality there is only One, the Brahman, the Ātman."[145(a)]

"The Brahman alone is real (*sat*) the world (together with empirical egos) considered as distinct from the Brahman is illusion (*māyā*)."[145(b)]

"Māyā is a prominent term of Hindu philosophy, the notion that the versatile world is an illusion. Caird says, "religion teaches us that only by looking on the world and the lust thereof; as *māyā*, as illusion, vanity, deceptive appearance; can we get near to God."[145(c)]

Māyā is that, which measures (*mīyate anayā*). It measures the immeasurable; that is, in other words, it sets the limit to the limitless. From this, comes its secondary sense of power of concealment; for unless the vastness of the Infinite is concealed, it becomes impossible to represent it as the small or the finite. Its third sense, trickery or deception or illusion also arises from this, because it deceives all by presenting the Infinite as the finite, the vast as the small, the Eternal as the fleeting and the fleeting as the Eternal.

Māyā acts as an instrument, through which the division between *jīva* and *Īśvara* occurs. It creates the twin selves, the subject and the object; and also the *jagat,* to be enjoyed and ruled by each of them respectively. Thus, the division between the subject (*jīva*) and the object (*Īśvara*) is within the womb of *māyā*, and beyond that, there is undifferenciated unity.

Māyā is, thus, represented as having two functions *viz.* veiling (*āvaraṇa*) and distraction (*vikṣepa*). It puts a veil on the face of the Reality and this is its covering function. This concealment of Truth is referred to again and again in the Upaniṣads. It goes on to make some other things pass for the Reality, and this is its distracting function. In the famous line, "Indra assumes many forms through *māyā*,"[146] it may be noted that the term *māyā* is used in the plural, to make it tally with the plurality of forms assumed thereby. Here, the distracting function can be noted, where, the 'One' appears as 'many.'

Inexplicability of Māyā

Māyā represents the principle of non-Being, and it is the womb of becoming. If the relation between non-Being, becoming (*māyā*) is in identity of the Being, then the immutability of the Being is jeopardised. And if the relation is of difference; there exist two independent principles which cease the doctrine of non-duality (*advaita*). To get out of this dilemma, the Vedāntins call it inexplicable (*anirvacanīya*). Only one, who is beyond *māyā*, knows its nature and to all else with the empirical consciousness its nature remains inscrutable. Nāsadīya Sūkta says, "Even the gods came after it,"[147(a)] which means, the knowledge of its nature is hidden even from the gods. Māyā is neither *sat* nor *asat*. Māyā is not an unreality (*asat*) from our point of view; again it is not a reality (*sat*) from the standpoint of the Absolute.

The concept of *māyā* was not unknown to the pre-Upaniṣ adic period. The *Ṛv* uses the word *māyā* , but the word does not occur there in the same sense, as was used in the later philosophies. There it means; the divine power; as opposed to demoniacal power (*yātu*).[147(b)] The word *māyā* occurs infrequently in the earlier Upaniṣads; to be precise, it occurs thrice-twice in the *Śvet. Up.* and once, in the *Praśna Up.* Radhakrishnan, S. comments on this verse from the *Praśna Up.* as "this use of the word *māyā* has led to the view that the world is deceptive in character."[148]

There are some, who are inclined to think that the doctrine of *māyā* is an invention of Śaṅkara. After refuting each and every idea; examined by Ranade, R.D.; as those which may have led Śaṅkara to elaborate the theory of *māyā*, Chakravarti, S. says, "such words as veil, blindfoldness, knot never did ensnare him. (Śaṅkara). Whatever views he expressed, he did so as the result of his conviction brought about in a different manner. In giving expression to his views, he never allowed himself to be deterred by a word or a phrase. He was the master of dialectics." Further, he concludes, "the ideas that have been expressed there, in the Upaniṣads are quite in keeping with the fundamental doctrines of the Upaniṣads and do not indicate the existence of the theory of illusion. In most cases, we have found that the passages relied upon as indicating the presence of *māyā* refer to the stage of duality and the changes that are constantly going on in this world. Because a thing would change. One is not justified in saying that it is the work of *māyā*. Because change is the order of the universe; because most things are transitory, one cannot say that it is the work of *māyā*".[149]

Though the quotations above reflect the opinion of the author that, the theory of *māyā* is an invention of Śaṅkara; following the reputed scholars, one may definitely say that, the theory of *māyā*, developed by Śaṅkara; is based on the ideas of the Upani-ṣads.[150]

Māyā in the Earlier Upaniṣads

As we know, the Upaniṣads do not present us a developed philosophy; they contain trends of thought which later were developed by different philosophers and the systems were formed. Ranade, R.D. rightly says, "*māyā* is to be found in ideas rather than the words in the Upaniṣads."[151]

The Ideas in the Upaniṣads

The Upaniṣads speak about the terms *vidyā* and *avidyā*. Dange, S.A. opines that; according to Śāṅkara Vedānta, *vidyā* is solely the knowledge of the ultimate, and *avidyā* comprises of works (*karmakāṇḍa*). But according to him, the element of *avidyā* is inclusive of all the things in the world as well as the world of appearances itself.[152] *Īśa. Up.* tells us that, "he who knows this pair of *vidyā* and *avidyā* conjointly, crosses death through ignorance and by the knowledge enjoys immortality."[153] The *Īśa. Up.* puts forth the idea that he who knows both the path of ignorance and the path of knowledge together, by his knowledge of the one, is able to cross the bund of death, and by his knowledge of the other, is able to attain immortality. A man must reconcile the claims of both knowledge and works to be able to soar in the regions of the Infinite.

The *Mūṇḍ Up.* tells us about two kinds of knowledge. The higher knowledge (*parā vidyā*) and the lower knowledge (*aparā vidyā*). The higher knowledge is that by which the Undecaying is apprehended.[154] The lower knowledge is the knowledge of the *Ṛv.* the, Yajurveda, the Sāmaveda, the Atharvaveda and the limbs of the Veda-s phonetics, ritual, grammar, etymology, metrics and astronomy. Radhakrishnan, S. comments that, lower knowledge (*aparā vidyā*); is also a kind of knowledge which aims at the knowledge of the highest reality even though in a partial or imperfect manner.[155] The seer of the Upaniṣad is here distinguishing between the knowledge by description and the knowledge by acquaintance or experience.

Also, aparā vidyā includes ceremonial religion. The Mūṇḍ Up. condemns people, deluded in the midst of ignorance, wise in their own esteem, thinking themselves to be learned. Further, the Upaniṣad asserts the superiority of higher knowledge (parā vidyā) also known as Brahmavidyā.[156]

Again, the Īśa. Up. speaks about two seemingly contrasting principles, the manifest (saṁbhūti) and the unmanifest (asaṁbhūti) and it is said that, he who understands the manifest and the unmanifest both together crosses death through the unmanifest and attains life eternal through the manifest.[157]

The Īśa. Up., invokes the grace of God Pūṣan to lift up the golden lid, and allow the truth to be seen.[158] Here, we have the conception of concealment which prevents the truth from being seen. The *Kaṭh. Up.* says, "widely apart and leading to the divergent ends are these ignorance and wisdom." Further, it is said that the fools, wise in their own esteem, go about like blind men led by one, who himself is blind.[159] Here, it is suggested that people abiding in the midst of ignorance, follow others blindly in search of reality – which they would have easily seen, had they followed the path of knowledge. The *Mūṇḍ. Up.* compares ignorance to a knot, which one has to untie, and only then one can have a glimpse of truth in his own heart.[160] The *Chānd. Up.* tells us that, what one performs with knowledge (and not due to ignorance), indeed becomes more powerful.[161] It further states that, a cover of untruth hides the ultimate truth from us. As the treasure of gold lies hidden under the surface of the earth, and the person treading over it, does not know it, similarly, one cannot reach the Ātman, verily inside ones own heart, for it is covered by the untruth.[162] Here, the idea of *anṛta* gives rise to the concept of *māyā*. In the *Bṛ. Up.*, a devotee prays fervently to God, to lead him from non-Being (*asat*) to Being (*sat*), from darkness to Light and from death to immortality.[163] Here, unreality is compared to darkness, non-Being to death.

The *Śvet. Up.* directly uses the word *māyā* almost in the sense of illusion. There, it is told that, by meditation upon god, by entering into his Being there is freedom from the great world-illusion.[164] The Upaniṣad describes god as a magician (*māyin*), who creates this world by his powers (*māyā*); the other (individual soul) is bound down again by *māyā*.[165] The *Śvet. Up.* also contains a passage, where *māyā* is identified with Prakṛti. She is described as the only one and unborn (*ajā ekā*). She is comprised of three virtues symbolised by red, white and black.[166]

As is rightly pointed out by Dange, S.A. "It may be said that the seed of the doctrine of *māyā*, later propounded by Śaṅkara; lies here."[167]

Māyā, in the Later Upaniṣads

The later Upaniṣads describe *māyā* in more concrete terms. In the *Sarvasāropaniṣad*, she is defined as, one without a beginning and without an end, which behaves alike towards valid means of knowledge and non-valid means of knowledge, which is not existent and yet not non-existent, which is not real yet not unreal, which does not exist but is the cause of created objects undescribable and without any characteristics.[168] The *Nṛsiṁha. U. Tā. Up.* describes the nature and functions of *māyā*. It says, she is of nature of darkness, motionless, illusory, endless void. As the seed of a fig tree same in itself, possesses the potentiality of many fig trees; *māyā* though one, possesses the potentiality of plurality in it. Just as a fig-tree, same in itself, although it is one, brings forth many fig trees stretching out beyond itself, all of which have their seed, and which is full and whole in each of them; similarly *māyā* also manifests many locations (of the soul), stretching beyond itself, existing full and whole, and similarly manifests the individual and the divine soul (*jīva* and *Īśvara*), and doing so it still remains only a deception and ignorance. She is not different from her *guṇa*-s (*sattva, rajas, and tamas*) and is everywhere, as the form of Brahmā, Viṣṇu and Śiva. As explained by Mahadevashastri, A., its character, as the source everywhere, stems from this Ātman alone. The Ātman, having created elements, organs, the *Virāj*, the natural divinities and the sheaths (*Tait. Up.*

II), and having entered in these, remains undeluded, but it appears to be deluded as it were and in activity only through *māyā*.[169]

The *Kaivalya. Up.* says that, "this Self deluded by *māyā*, dwelling in the body strives after works. In the waking state, he finds satisfaction in women, food and drink. In the dream state, tasting joy and sorrow, fashions a world. In deep sleep, shrouded by darkness, he enjoys bliss. And when he perceives the 'Whole' the triad of states come to rest."[170] The *Brahmabindū. Up.* supports the statement and says, "One who is enveloped in world-delusion (*māyā*), remains caught up in the heart-lotus, but when the darkness grows clear, he sees the unity all alone."[171]

The *Garbhopaniṣad* contains contemplation of *jīva*, who says, "If I escape from the mother's womb, I shall meditate on the Brahman." But then, oppressed by the squeezing as he is hardly born, then touched by the *Vaiṣṇava* wind; the wind of the outer world, as against Vāyu in the body; he can no more remember his previous births and deaths and has no knowledge any more, of good and bad deeds.[172] On this basis, one can infer that with the touch of *māyā*, the *jīva* is enveloped in ignorance.

As is seen earlier, the later Upaniṣads maintain that *māyā* is the cause of creation of this universe. *viz.* Sītā is *mūlāprakṛti*, and the creative power of Rāma.[173] In the *Devī. Up.* Durgā's name is accounted for, "Beyond whom there is none is called Durgā. As, she saves one from the crisis, she is called Durgā." She is described as Prakṛti; knowledge as well as ignorance; born as well as unborn. She is one, who bestows enjoyments and also emancipation. She is imperceptible, for she cannot be perceived.[174] The *Gopālottara-tāpinyupaniṣad* says that Rukmiṇī is the creative power of Kṛṣṇa, who creates the world.[175] The Brahman, the one without second, appears fourfold due to *māyā*.[176] The *Ganeśa. U. Tā. Up.* puts forth a Sāṁkhya thought, that indescribable *māyā* is the root of this world. Gaṇeśa is the Pradhāna and she (his power) is the Prakṛti; and she is *māyā*.[177] This *māyā*, the power of Vināyaka creates, maintains and dissolves all this.[178] *Sarasvatī R. Up.* equates *māyā* and Prakṛti, and that *māyā* is the adjunct of the lord under his own control.[179]

As is seen earlier, one can trace the source of the doctrine of *māyā*, in the earlier Upaniṣads. Deussen, P. traces the earliest thought of *avidyā* and explains, how the term *avidyā* was transformed from the negative idea of ignorance; as regards the Brahman; into the positive idea of false knowledge, *i.e.* emperical knowledge, knowledge of sciences etc.; during the period of the earlier Upaniṣads itself.[180] In the *Bh. G.* also, the doctrine of *māyā* is seen rather in ideas than in words. Herein, the term *māyā* is used in the sense of Divine power.[181] Moreover, the *Bh. G.* being a theistic metaphysical treatise there is not much scope for the development of the doctrine of *māyā*.

The development of the doctrine of *māyā* is seen in the *Kārikā*-s of Gauḍapāda; the spiritual ancestor of Śaṅkara. In his doctrine; we find that he regards the world as non-creation; which is known as *ajātivāda*. He maintains that, all this duality is nothing, (there exists) non-duality in reality.[182] Later, in the commentary on Brahmasūtra, Śaṅkara propounded his fulfledged doctrine of *māyā*, based upon the thoughts expressed in the Upaniṣads and the Gauḍapādakārikā. When he uses the expressions such as inexplicability, *rajjusarpa*, superimposition etc.; he indicates that the world is merely an appearance.

Coming to the later Upaniṣads; which were composed during the post Śaṅkara period; we find the concept of *māyā* described in more definite terms. The composers of these Upaniṣads, are seen to be further developing the same.

The Individual Self (*Jīvātman*)

The word *jīva* is derived from the root *jīv*, which means, 'to breathe'. *Jīva* means, 'that which breathes.' This refers to the biological aspect of man's nature. The Upaniṣads do not attempt to seek any direct evidence of the existence of the soul. "By what should one know that by which all this is known?" "By what should one know the knower?" says Yājñavalkya.[183] To the Upaniṣadic sages, the existence of the soul is a necessary assumption. The Upaniṣads contain various suggestions regarding the existence of the soul. It is called Puruṣa, in the sense, that which dwells in the citadel of the body. This means that the biological aspect of a man serves the purpose of another, the soul or psyche. That something, without which the mechanism of the body would be meaningless, is the soul. It is the enjoyer (*bhoktṛ*) and the doer (*kartṛ*). [184] The material body, the principle of breath (Prāṇa) which regulates the unconscious activities of the individual, the mind (*manas*) and the sensory organs, the organs of action, intellect (*buddhi*) are the adjuncts of the soul. Experiences of the senses and the mind assemble together around a centre–'ego'. At the basis of this whole structure is the Universal consciousness, Ātman, which is our real being.

Relation of the Body and the Soul

The bodily senses are dependent on the soul. "As a rich man enjoys his own men, and his own men are of service to the rich man, so does this conscious Self feed with the senses, and the senses feed on the Self." This passage of the *Kau. Up.* tells us that the soul must be regarded as the master of all bodily faculties.[185] Prajāpati Kratu; when approached by the Vālakhilya-s, with a query regarding the mover of the body–answered that the mover of the body chariot is the soul.[186] Thus, Puruṣa is the subjective light of consciousness in the beings.

The second chapter of the *Tait. Up.*, describes the sheaths of the soul. Within the body, which is made up of food, is another body which is made up of vital air, anterior to this body, is another body which consists of mind, more internal than the mental body is the body full of intelligence, still more internal than this body of intelligence is the body consisting of bliss.[187]

The Size of the Soul

In the *Chānd. Up.*, the soul is called as, *prādeśamātra* and *abhivimāna*.[188] After taking into consideration the views; regarding the meaning of these words; by Śaṅkara, Ānandagiri, Amarakośa etc., Ranade, R.D. in conclusion understands the meaning of the words as, "measuring the span's length from the forehead to the chin", and interpretes the passage as, "he who worships the Self as measuring the span's length from the forehead to the chin, and as existing in all men, he enjoys food in all worlds, in all beings, in all Selves."[189]

The *Kau. Up.* tells that the soul occupies the entire body and is hidden in it as the razor hidden in a razor case.[190] In the *Br. Up.,* the soul is understood as, "the intelligent luminous Self in the heart, as small as a grain of rice or barley, and yet the ruler of all, ruling all this and whatever exists.[191] The *Kaṭh. Up.*, tells us that the soul is of the size of the measure of a thumb and dwells in the mid-region of the body.[192] Later, this idea is expressed in the *Bh. G.,* where it is told that this Puruṣa resides in the heart. The Upaniṣads, also speak of the idea, that the soul is not restricted to any part of the body, but is infinite and occupies all the space.[193] The *Mai. Up.* reconciles these contradictory statements and says that, "a man reaches the Supreme state by meditating on the soul, which is smaller than the atom, or of the size of a thumb, or of a span, or of the whole body."[194]

The philosopher of the *Chānd. Up.* says, "my soul in the heart is smaller than the grain of rice, or barley or mustard and yet my soul concealed in the heart is greater than the earth, greater than the sky, greater than all the worlds."[195]

When the soul is in identity with its adjuncts, its identity with the Brahman is forgotten, and then it is ordinarily believed to be finite and therefore distinct from the Absolute.

The Relation of the Self and the Universal Self

The theory of the identity of the human and the Divine spirit is the root of the Vedānta philosophy and finds its first expression in the early Upaniṣads.[196] Lines of thought running in the Upaniṣads; not apparently uniform in nature; gave rise to different systems of philosophy. Different views are held by different schools of thought, while interpreting the relation of the Universal Self and the Individual Selves.

Śaṅkara believes that the Universal soul is identical with the individual Self. The former is omniscient, omnipresent, neither active nor passive, and therefore, free from the very beginning. The latter is limited in wisdom, power and capacity of movement; is active and receptive and therefore, entangled in the rounds of birth and rebirth (*sāṁsāra*), and stands in need of deliverance. Yet, this distinction is said to be apparent, and lasts only till the true knowledge dawns. Each of the Self is a complete measure, the Supreme Ātman himself, as he manifests himself, though his real nature remains concealed by the adjuncts. Rather, it is ignorance (*avidyā*) by which the *upādhi*-s are superimposed on the Ātman, and thus, is regarded as the individual Ātman. Rāmānuja, the propounder of the Viśiṣṭādvaita doctrine maintains that the individual Self is eternally one with, and also different from the Universal Self. According to Mādhva, the individual Self is eternally different from the Universal Self.

In the Sāṁkhya philosophy, the soul is regarded as the fragment (*aṁśa*) of the Divine mind; but is subsequent to the Divine mind for it is the recipient of the Divine idea. Also, the individual Selves are relatively different from one another. The Vaiśeṣika-s recognised the existence of many souls and the reality of the world. Feeling, will and thought are regarded as the functions of the soul.

The later Upaniṣads acknowledge the Self with different names. The *Śāṇḍilya. Up.* gives the etymology of the word Ātman as follows. Ātman is so called because it attains everything, gets everything and eats everything.[197] The soul due to *avidyā* does not realise the Haṁsa. Haṁsa, possessed of eight feet is pure. The soul is described as Haṁsa here. The state of realization of Haṁsa is known as Parama Haṁsa. Kṣetrajña : He is devoid of *āvirbhāva* and *tirobhāva* and is self luminous. The consciousness that shines forth from the subtle body is the Kṣetrajña. He is indicated by *tvaṁ pada*. He is the knower and the witness. The soul is also called Kūtastha, the one pervading the intelligence of all. He is also known as Āntaryāmin. When he is devoid of all adjuncts, he is called Pratyagātman. Satyātman is the one who is unchanged in all times and places, names, things. Standing amongst the perishable, it does not perish. Caitanyātman is of the nature of knowledge and is devoid of origin and destruction. The Anantātman is like the earth in the earthen things, gold in the things of gold. The one, with the nature of unlimited joy and bliss is called Ānandātman. Paramātman is the one who is eternally unchanged and is indicated as *tat pada*.[198]

The States of Consciousness of the Soul

The Upaniṣads take a wider view of life and study the Self under different states of consciousness, *viz.* waking, dream-sleep, sleep, dreamless sleep and *turīya* state. Of these, like waking and dream state come under the study of psychology proper, for in these states the mind functions while the other two, where the mind ceases its functioning are considered with a view to discover the real nature of the soul. Gauḍapāda says that, "It is the one alone who is known in the three states."[199]

In the waking state, a man, without reflections, accepts the universe as he finds it. The soul is conscious only of the external objects and enjoys the gross things and is known as Vaiśvānara. Śaṅkara explains that, he is so called because he leads all creatures of the universe in diverse ways to the enjoyment of various objects.[200] In other words, this state may be called as, waking life of outer moving consciousness.

Analysis of Sleep According to the Upaniṣads

Many theories regarding the nature of sleep are put forth by the seers of the Upaniṣads. The *Bṛ. Up.* tells that, "As a bird or falcon, flying in the sky becomes tired and folding its wings it retires to its nest, so does this person goes to this state, where he desires no more desires and dreams no more dreams."[201] This description of the nature of sleep corresponds to the explanation given by modern physiology. When the body is tired, it goes in the state of sleep. It was imagined by those ancient seers, that in deep sleep the soul moved from the heart by means of the arteries to the *purītata*.[202] This explanation appears almost mythological when compared with modern science. According to the *Praśna Up.*, during sleep, all the senses are collected in the mind.[203] The *Chānd. Up.* says that, the sleep occurs when the mind is merged in vital breath.[204] Again, the *Bṛ. Up.* tells that sleep occurs when the soul goes in the space of the heart to rest.[205] The Upaniṣads also tell us that, in deep sleep the soul is one with the Brahman. A passage in the *Praśna Up.* says, "the mind which is the sacrificer is carried everyday to Brahman."[206] "When a man is asleep, he becomes united with the Brahman" says the *Chānd. Up.* But further the Upaniṣad adds, though the soul is united with the Brahman in deep sleep, it still did not know this. "As people tread over the hidden treasure in the earth again and again and do not know of it, so do all the creatures day after day become merged in the Brahman and yet they do not discover it."[207]

This state of the soul, the dreamless sleep, is described as *suṣupti*, where the senses along with *manas* are quiescent and there is a cessation of empirical consciousness. There is no longer contrasting of one object with another. There is no duality between the subject and the object. Though the individual Self is said to attain a temporary union with the Absolute, *suṣupti* is not identified with the state of release. It only signifies that the consciousness of individuality is absent till the state lasts. The soul, when being centred in itself and being full of knowledge and bliss, feeding on bliss is called Prājña.

The Dream State

The dream state is an intermediate stage between the waking and the deep sleep. This condition is the dream life of inward moving consciousness. The references to dreams in the Upani-ṣads are frequent, suggesting that they attracted a good deal of attention of the thinkers, at the time. The *Bṛ. Up.* tells us that the soul moves away from its nest; guarding with breath the lower nest; to where he can roam at will and creates manifold forms for his own enjoyment, either enjoying with women or food or seeing beautiful sights.[208] This passage analyses that by being in this state, he sees both those states which belong to this and the other world. This state is called *sandhyam,* the joining of the waking and deep sleep state, which Ranade, R.D. aptly terms as, "the twilight state of consciousness."[209] With a beautiful simile of a fish, this passage of the *Bṛ. Up.* describes the Self as, "moving along both the states, the states of waking and sleeping, as a large fish moving along both the banks, the nearer and the farther." The difference between the waking and the dream state is that, the mind in the former receives from outside impressions, which it builds up into ideas in the latter. It fashions a world of forms, unaided and by itself. For this purpose, it uses the material of waking hours, generally visual and auditory.[210] The dreams which are revived impressions are felt as real, for the time being till the state lasts. This subtle analysis of dream experience may be described as, "perception without sensation." In this state of consciousness, the soul is called as *Taijasa*, for the soul is conscious of internal objects, sees things in his own light, and enjoys the subtle things.[211]

Turīya State

There are not merely these three states of consciousness but the *Māṇḍ. Up.* recognises the fourth state, the *turīya* state. Viśva and Taijasa are conditioned by the cause and effect. But Prājña is conditioned by the cause alone. These two, the cause and effect, do not exist in *turīya*.[212] The difference between the deep sleep and the *turīya* state is that; as the name Prājña implies, that he is fully conscious. In it, we have a thinker and a thought. In the *turīya* state, the mind is not simply withdrawn from the objects but becomes one with the Brahman, who is free from fear, and complete illumination.[213] Gauḍapāda says, "The non- cognition of duality is common to both Prājña and *turīya* state, but Prājña is associated with the seed (consciousness) in sleep while this does not exist in the *turīya*."[214] Radhakrishnan, S. comments, "the objective consciousness is present; in deep sleep; in an unmanifested seed form, while it is completely transcended in the *turīya* consciousness.[215] When there is no knowledge of internal objects as well as external objects, nor the two together, when the soul is not a mass of intelligence transcending both consciousness and inconsciousness, then the state is usually recognised as 'superconscious' or 'self-conscious', a word proposed by Ranade, R.D. The indefinable, beyond thought, the peaceful and full of auspiciousness, such is the fourth quarter. He is the Self (Ātman). The attainment of this state is regarded as the culmination of spiritual training.

On the basis of the older Upaniṣads, the later Upaniṣads enumerate and explain the main concepts of the Vedānta-system, for the purpose of teaching and learning. They explain on the basis of the older Upaniṣadic passages yet with an independent attitude. The description of the states of the soul, in the later Upaniṣads is styled in accordance with the older Upaniṣads. The *Nṛsiṁha. U. Tā. Up.* amplifies the four states, where the conception is further refined and the four degrees of the *turīya* are also distinguished as *otā, anujñātṛ, anujñā* and *avikalpa.* The Ātman is similar to the *otā,* which means 'inwoven' as the intellectual element running through the whole world. And the Ātman is similar to the *anujñātṛ*, affirmer of this world because he gives his own Self and thereby makes this world visible like the Sun. The Ātman has *anujña*, because by his very nature, he is pure thought comparable to the fire after he has consumed fuel. The Ātman is 'indifference' (*avikalpa*), the complete eradication of all differences, so that only the pure, objectless subject of perception remains. Each of the first three states; waking, dreaming and deep-sleep, is *caturātman, i.e.* mixed with the three other states so that each of them contains the gross, the subtle, the seed and the spectator. So also in the *turīya*, the first three states have a share in these four determinations through which they flow into the *Turīya*. Only the *avikalpa* is completely real; the first three affected by deep sleep, dreaming and sheer illusion. The fourth of the fourth (*turīya turīya*) is purified from every taint of the world; is beyond all distinctions, and is the pure Absolute thought.[216]

The *Subāla. Up.*[217] states that when the Self is yoked with different chief vital airs, he sees different things. It says, in the centre of the heart is a lump of flesh of red colour. In it, (the *dahara*) the white lotus blooms with its petals spread in different directions like red lotus. There are ten hollows in the heart which are occupied by the chief vital airs. When this soul is yoked with the Prāṇa breath, he sees cities, rivers etc.; when associated with the Vyāna breath, he sees seers and gods; when yoked with the Apāna breath, he sees Yakṣa-s, Rākṣasa-s and Gandharva-s. Joining with the Samāṇa breath, he sees the heavenly world. When yoked with the Vairambha breath, he sees what he has formerly seen. In the ether of the heart, situated in the interior sheath, the soul attains the state of deep sleep, then by resorting to the same course, he leaps into the waking state.[217]

Some of the later Upaniṣads ponder over the places of this Puruṣa in the body in these four states. In the waking state, he dwells in the eye. During dream, he resides in the neck and during deep-sleep in the heart. As *turīya,* he dwells in the head. Though the Upaniṣad states that Puruṣa resides in the eye in the waking state, the Upaniṣad, in its earlier part states that the navel is the place of the soul in the waking state.[218] At these four places, the Brahman shines; in the waking as Brahmā, in the dream as Viṣṇu, in the deep sleep as Rudra and in the *Turīya* as the highest imperishable.[219] The authors of the Upaniṣads mention the places of the soul in body, in different states but they do not elaborate the technical reasons for these different dwellings of the soul *vis-a-vis* the states. Some authors of the later Upaniṣads not only state the four states of the soul but also say that there is a state beyond the *turīya* state which they say is inexplicable, incomprehensible.

The later Upaniṣads clearly bring out the difference between the state of *samādhi* and *suṣupti*. The earlier Upaniṣads, when they say that; in *suṣupti* the soul unites with the Brahman and enjoys its bliss; do not differenciate the bliss enjoyed in the state of deep sleep and bliss enjoyed when in union with the Brahman.

The thinkers of the later Upaniṣads rightly say that, in deep sleep, in which all things disappear, the mind is overcome by the darkness of ignorance, he (soul) experiences happiness. In this state, there is a lack of consciousness, and in *samādhi*–the bliss of Brahman–the mind is calm and tranquil in His light and the soul enjoys the bliss of the Brahman in full consciousness. One may say that the later Upaniṣads go a step ahead of the earlier Upaniṣads when they clearly bring out the differences between the state of *samādhi* and *suṣupti*.

The Doctrine of Transmigration

Belief of people in rebirth has persisted from the time of the Upaniṣads. Macdonell says that the idea of Transmigration is of un-Āryan origin, which was received from the aborigines by the Indian Āryans.[220] But it appears clearly that this idea is a natural development from the views of the Veda-s and Brāhmaṇa-s; developed stage by stage; which was expressed articulately in the Upaniṣads. The doctrine of transmigration in the Upaniṣads, rests on two basic ideas. The original Vedic belief of reward in the heaven or punishment which is later combined with the doctrine of rebirth.

The Indian Āryans believed in the world of the Gods and the world of fathers. They understood that the godly men went to the heaven which is full of honey and the others to the abode of Yama.[221] These verses indicate the belief of continued existence, either with the Gods or under the control of Yama.

The Vedic people believed that the eye of a man at death goes to the Sun, his speech to the fire, his life breath to the wind and his limbs to the different parts of the universe.[222] This idea is echoed in the *Br. Up.*, where it is said that, after a man's death, his speech enters into the fire, his breath into the wind, his eye into the Sun, his mind into the moon, his body into the earth, his Ātman into the space, his blood and seed into the water and so on. But further, question is put forth by Ārtabhāga "then where does a man remain?" Yājñvalkya took him aside, and they conversed with one another, and what they said that was 'work'. In truth, a man becomes good by good works and evil by evil works.[223] The last sentence indicates the motive which lies at the basis of transmigration. It also gives rise to the thought that a man has existed before his birth and that his inborn character is the fruit and the consequence of the previous action. Another passage of the *Bṛ. Up.,* describes "his knowledge and works take him by the hand, and his former experience accompanies him. Just as a caterpillar going to the end of a blade of grass, by undertaking a separate movement collects itself, so this Self after destroying this body, removing ignorance by a separate movement collects itself. Just as a goldsmith, fashions new and fair form from a small bit of gold, so does the soul, after destroying this body, and removing ignorance, fashions a newer and fairer form.[224] According to Dasgupta, S., this doctrine refers to 'desires' as the cause of rebirth and not *karman*.[225] "A man is full of desires. As he desires, so he wills, as he wills, so he works." says the *Bṛ. Up.*[226] When the Self continues to desire and act, it reaps the fruit and comes again to this world for performing acts.[227] Elsewhere it is said, "He who knowingly desires is born by his desires in those places accordingly."[228] Thus, a desire is the root cause of rebirth and *karman* forms the connecting link between desire and rebirth. The Self which is subject to rebirth, is a unity of moral and psychological tendencies and the elements which compose physical world, and the logic of genesis of *karman* and its fruit. But for him, whose desires have been fulfilled, and who has realized himself, all his desires vanish here.[229] The destruction of desires is effected by the right knowledge of the Self.

One interesting idea to note in this connection is, that some Upaniṣads describe the conception of a child; as a result of desire (*kāma*); as the first birth, the birth of a child, that is coming into this world; as the second birth and the next birth elsewhere after death, as the third birth.[230]

The Upaniṣads use the word *kāma*, to indicate any desire, monetary or worldly desire. No special emphasis is given on sex-desire. It is the same as any other desire.

The complexities of the *Karman* doctrine, which we find in the later developments of Hindu thought are conspicuously absent in the Upaniṣads.

At the root of this scheme is the desire. *Karman* is the connecting link, between desires and the actual effects willed and desired by a person.

The Way of Gods (*Devayāna*) and the Way of Fathers (*Pitṛyāna*)

The course followed by the soul after death is described in the Upaniṣads. As regards the destiny of good souls, the Upaniṣads speak of two ways open to mortals. They are, the way of light (*archirmārga, devayāna,* and *uttarāyaṇa*) and the way of smoke. (*dhūmramārga, pitṛyāna,* and *dakṣiṇāyaṇa*). The idea of these two ways is as old as the *Ṛv.*, wherein they are clearly mentioned.[231] Later, under the epithets of *śuklagati* and *kṛṣṇagati*, the *Bh. G.* has immortalised these two paths.[232] The *Chānd. Up.* says that, the souls of those who are adept in the science of five fires (*pañcāgnividyā*), and of those who practise penance in the forest; irrespective of the obsequies performed by people after their death enter the path of light and move successively from light to day, from day to the bright half of the month, then on to the six months of the year during which the Sun moves to the north, then to the year, from the year to the Sun, then to the moon and then to the lightning. From there, he is carried to the Brahman by a person, who is non-human. This path is known as the path of the Brahman or the path of gods. Those who proceed on this path, never return to the cycle of human existence.[233]

Almost similar description of this path is supplied by the *Bṛ. Up.*[234] The *Praśna. Up.* gives a slightly different account. It says, "those who seek the soul; by penance, austerities; by the northern way, win the sun."[235] The *Kau. Up.* makes an interesting development in the conception of the way of Gods. It tells us that when a soul comes to the path of gods, he successively goes to the worlds of fire (*agni*), wind (*vāyu*), Varuṇa, Sun, Indra, Prajāpati and finally to the world of the Brahman. Instead of the posts mentioned in the *Chānd. Up.* and the *Bṛ. Up.*, the *Kau. Up.* substitutes the new ones, recognised as deities. Further, the Upaniṣad says, when such a soul has reached the Brahman, he is received by the attendants of the Brahman, in all the glory which is due to himself alone. As the soul reaches the Ageless river, he can never become old. The celestial damsels decorate the soul with the ornaments, clothes, garlands, perfumes etc. He crosses the Ageless river merely by the motion of the mind. Then he shakes off his good deeds as well as his bad deeds. His loved ones share the fruit of good deeds and his unloved ones partake of bad deeds. Being free from good deeds as well as evils, knowing Brahman, he moves towards the Brahman.[236] Deussen, P. comments, "the meaning of the whole is that, the soul on his way of God reaches regions of ever increasing light, in which is concentrated all that is bright, radiant as stations on the way to the Brahman."[237]

The Way of Fathers

The *Chānd. Up.* describes the path of the fathers, which is traversed by the souls of people who live in towns, indulge in the act of charitable deeds and perform works of public utility. It describes, "from smoke they go to night, from the night to the dark half of the month, then to the six months during which the Sun moves to the south, but they do not reach the year. From these months, they go to the world of fathers, from there to the sky and then to the moon. They dwell there till the time comes for them to fall down. Their descending is way from the moon to the sky, from sky to the wind; having become wind they become smoke, then the mist, and a cloud; having become cloud they rain down. Then they are either born as barley or rice, herbs etc. Whosoever eats the food and discharges the seed, like unto him do they become." The *Bṛ. Up.* gives almost similar account to that of the *Chānd. Up.* while describing the smoky way.[238] The *Kau. Up.* describes that the souls departed from this world go to the moon. In the bright half, the moon thrives on their breathing spirits, in the dark half it causes them to be reborn.[239] The *Praśna. Up.* gives fairly appreciable account of the way of the fathers. It says, "those who worship, thinking that sacrifices and good actions are our work, they win only the lunar world. They indeed return again. Therefore, those seers, desirous of having offsprings, go to the southern way."[240]

In agreement with the scholars, one can say that the path of the Gods and the path of the fathers are symbolic expressions; merely imaginary ways in which the primeval mind tried to express itself in regard to the eschatological idea.[241] The path of the Gods is suggestive of the spiritual elevation of the soul; and that of the fathers speaks of the spiritual degeneration of it. The actual stages of the ascent and descent of the soul; indicative of the upward and downward movements; are not philosophically important. But the idea of the ascent and descent based on a 'moral'[242] foundation throws light on the Upaniṣadic eschatology, a great philosophical value.

The philosophers of the Upaniṣads believed in the dark Sunless regions. Some passages of the Upaniṣads point out that the souls of the persons performing acts of charity for personal gain, the ignorant, unenlightened and the evil souls are destined to enter these dark regions.[243] However, the Upaniṣads do not mention whether the destined stay in this joyless region is temporary or eternal.

While describing the course of the soul after death, most of the later Upaniṣads repeat the thoughts expressed in the earlier Upaniṣads. With a few variations in the description of the *Kau. Up*, the *Tvmn. Up.* describes the course of the soul in a sectarian fashion. It says that, "the soul, after leaving this material body acquires the unending, lustrous, blissful form of Mahāviṣṇu.Then, after having bathed in a river in the world of Sūrya, procuring the form of Nārāyaṇa, he is endowed with the divine emblems and opulence of Viṣṇu. Then he proceeds to the world of Truth, where he is joyously received by Brahmā. He then succeeds to the world of Dhruva and then to Vaikuṇṭha. Here, he unites with the

Brahman; merges into the bliss of the Brahman.[244] The *Subālopaniṣad* says that, in the centre of the heart is a mass of red flesh, in it are four vessels (*nāḍī*-s) called Ramā, Aramā, Icchā and Apunarbhavā. The *nāḍī*-s lead the soul to the worlds of righteousness, unrighteousness, desire and Brahmā successively.[245]

In general, the thoughts in the later Upaniṣads; regarding the transmigration of the soul; are almost the same as those expressed in the earlier Upaniṣads. Even if some Upaniṣads record some new thoughts, they are not philosophically important. However, they justify the prevailing customs. *e.g. Piṇḍopaniṣad* says that when the soul leaves the body, he stays in water, fire and space successively for three days in each of the elements and on the tenth day, he stays in Vāyu.[246] Therefore, these ten days are considered to be impure. (*aśauca*). The ten rice-balls (*daśapiṇḍa*-s) given in his honour in this world, form the organs of his subtle body. Hence, the ceremony of *Śrāddha* should be performed, says the Upaniṣad.[247]

Gajendragadkar, K. opines that the philosophers of the later Upaniṣads did not give much thought to the eschatology. The reason may be that, as the mind of a human being gets involved in the advancing material world, his thinking gets directed towards the achievements in the mortal life, thereby reducing the quest for the search of materially unknown knowledge.[248]

To comprehend the Abstract, the Upaniṣads the earlier ones and the later ones, take recourse to describing the supports (*ālambana*-s), perceptible to the senses or the mind, which will be elaborated in the following chapter.

REFERENCES

1. Belvalkar, S.K. and Ranade, R.D., *op. cit.*, vol. II, pp. 10-14.
2. *Śat. Brā.*, IX. 3.2.4.

   ब्रह्म वै बृहस्पतिः। क्षत्रमिन्द्रो ब्रह्मणा चैवेनेमेतत्क्षत्रेण च सुषुवाणंमुभयतः परिगृह्णाति।
3. N.J. Shende, *'The Religion and the Philosophy of the Atharvaveda'*, Pune, 1952, p. 201.

4. *Śat. Brā.*, IX.3.5.11.
5. *Ibid.*, XI.2.3.1.
6. *Jaim. Br.*, II.68.

   यज्ञो वै विष्णुः।

   also *Yāska, Nirukta,* XII, XVIII, 2.
7. Mishra, Umesh, *History of Indian Philosophy,* Allahabad, 1957, pp. 78, 79.
8. *Śat. Brā.*, VII.1.1.18
9. *Ibid.*,

   स चतस्रः प्राचीरुपदधाति द्वे पश्चात्तिरश्च्यौ द्वे पुरस्तात्।
   तद्याश्चतस्रः प्राचीरुपदधाति स आत्मा। तद्यत्ताश्चतस्रो भवन्ति।
   चतुर्विधो ह्ययमात्मा। अथ ये पश्चात् ते सक्थौ।
   ये पुरस्तात्तौ बाहू यत्र वा आत्मा तदेव शिरः॥

   which is explained by Sāyaṇa as

   स आत्मेति। मध्यदेह इत्यर्थः।

   त्वगसृङ्मांसास्थिभेदेन मनोबुद्ध्यहंकारचित्रैर्वाजाग्रदाद्यवस्थाचतुष्ट्येन वा आत्मनश्चातुर्विध्यम्।
10. *Tait. Āra. & Ait. Āra.* quoted by Mishra, Umesh, *op. cit.*, pp. 77-90.
11. *Bṛ. Up.*, IV.4.5[a],

    स वा अयमात्मा ब्रह्म विज्ञानमयः...।
12. *Ibid.*, IV.3.2[a],

    ...किं ज्योतिः अयं पुरुषः इति। आदित्य ज्योतिः ...।

    and IV.3.6[b],

    आत्मैवास्य ज्योतिर्भवतीत्यात्मनैवायं ज्योतिषास्ते पल्ययते कर्म कुरुते विपल्येतीति॥६॥
13. *Chānd. Up.*, III.14.1[a],
    also, III.14.2[a],

    एष मे आत्माऽन्तर्हृदये...।
14. *Tait. Up.*, II.7.1

    असद्वा इदमग्र आसीत्। ततो वै सदजायत।

तदात्मानँ᳐स्वयमकुरुत। तस्मात्तत्सुकृतमुच्यत इति। यद्वै तत्सुकृतम्।
रसो वै सः। रसँ᳐ ह्येवायं लब्ध्वानन्दी भवति।

15. *Chānd. Up.*, VI.1.1-5.

16. *Ibid.*, VI.12.1-2

न्यग्रोधफलमाहरेतीदं भगव इति भिन्धीति भिन्नं भगव इति किमत्र पश्यसि....धाना भगव इत्यासामङ्गैकां भिन्धीति भिन्ना भगव इति किमत्र पश्यसीति न किञ्चन भगव इति॥ तँ᳐होवाच यं वै सोम्यैतमणिमानं न निभालयस एतस्य वै सोम्यैषोऽणिम्न एवं महान्यग्रोधस्तिष्ठति।

17. *Ibid.*, VIII. 3.4[b]-5

तस्य वा एतस्य ब्रह्मणो नाम सत्यमिति॥ तानि ह वा एतानि त्रीण्यक्षराणि सतीयमिति तद्यत्सत्तदमृतम् अथ यत्ति तन्मर्त्यमथ यद्यं तेनोभे यच्छति यदनेनोभे यच्छति तस्माद्यमहरहर्वा एवथवित्स्वर्गं लोकमेति॥

18. *Bṛ. Up.*, V.5.1[b],

तदेतत्त्र्यक्षरं सत्यमिति स इत्येकमक्षरं तीत्येकमक्षरं यमित्येकमक्षरं प्रथमोत्तमे अक्षरे सत्यं मध्यतोऽनृतं तदेतदनृतमुभयतः सत्येन परिगृहितं सत्यभूयमेव भवति नैवम् विद्वांसमनृतं हिनस्ति॥

19. *Ibid.*, II.1.20[b]

...तस्य उपनिषत्सत्यस्य सत्यमिति...।

also II.3.6[b]

...अथात आदेशो नेति नेति न ह्येतस्मादिति नेत्यन्यत्परमस्त्यथ नामधेयँ᳐सत्यस्य सत्यमिति।...।

20. *Tait. Up.*, II.7.1[a],

असद्वा इदमग्रमासीत्। ततो वै सदजायत॥

21. *Ibid.*, II.6.1[aq],

तत्सृष्ट्वा तदेवानुप्राविशत्। तदनुप्रविश्य सच्च त्यच्चाभवत्॥

22. Deussen, P., *The Philosophy of the Upaniṣads,* p.133.

23. *Bṛ. Up.*, III.4.2[b], 1[a],

न दृष्टेर्द्रष्टारं पश्येर्न श्रुतेः श्रोतारं श्रृणुया न मन्तेर्मन्तारं मन्वीथा न विज्ञातेर्विज्ञातारं विजानीयाः। एष त आत्मा सर्वान्तरः॥

...सर्वान्तरो यः प्राणेन प्राणिति स त आत्मा सर्वान्तरो...।

24. *Chānd. Up.*, IV.10.5[a],

प्राणो ब्रह्म कं ब्रह्म खं ब्रह्मेति।

25. *Ibid.*, VII.23.1[a]

यो वै भूमा तत्सुरवम् नाल्पे सुखमस्ति भूमैव सुखं भूमा त्वेव विजिज्ञासितव्य इति...।

26. *Tait. Up.*, III.6.1[a],

आनन्दो ब्रह्मेति व्यजानात्। आनन्दाद्ध्येव खल्विमानि भूतानि जायन्ते। आनन्देन जातानि जीवन्ति। आनन्दं प्रयन्त्यभिसथ्विशन्तीति॥

27. *Ibid.*, II.5[ff],

तस्य प्रियमेव शिर:। मोदो दक्षिण: पक्ष:। प्रमोद उत्तर: पक्ष:। आनन्द आत्मा। ब्रह्म पुच्छं प्रतिष्ठा॥

28. *Bṛ. Up.*, II.1.19[b]

अतीघ्नीमानन्दस्य गत्वा शयीतैवमेवैष एतच्छेते।

29. *Ibid.*, IV.3.32-33.

30. *Mai. Up.*, VI.15[a].

द्वे वाव ब्रह्मणो रूपे कालश्चाकालश्चाथ य: प्रागादित्यात्सोऽकालोऽकलोऽथ य आदित्याद्य: य काल: सकल: सकलस्य वा एतद्रूपं यत्संवत्सर: संवत्सरात्खल्वेमा: प्रजा: प्रजायन्ते संवत्सरेणेह वै जाता विवर्धन्ते संवत्सरे प्रत्यस्तं यन्ति।

31. *Kaṭh. Up.*, I.2.14[b]

अन्यत्र भूताच्च भव्याच्च यत्तत्पश्यसि तद्वद।

32. *Ibid.*, II.1.12[b],

ईशानो भूतभव्यस्य न ततो विजुगुप्सते, एतद्वै तत्।

also, *Bṛ. Up.*, IV.4.15,

ईशानो भूतभव्यस्य...।

33. *Śvet. Up.*, VI.5[a].

आदि: स संयोगनिमित्तहेतु: परस्त्रिकालादकलोऽपिदृष्ट:।

34. *Bṛ. Up.*, IV.4.16,

यस्मादर्वाक्संवत्सरोऽहोभि: परिवर्तते। तद्देवा ज्योतिषां ज्योतिरायुर्होपासतेऽमृतम्॥

35. *Chānd. Up.*, VIII.4.1,

अथ य आत्मा स सेतुर्विधृतिरेषां लोकानामसंभेदाय नैतँ सेतुमहोरात्रे तरतो न जरा न मृत्युर्न शोको न सुकृतं न दुष्कृतं सर्वे पाप्मानोऽतो निवर्तन्ते ...।

36. *Mai. Up.*, VI.3[a],

द्वे वाव ब्रह्मणो रूपे मूर्तं चामूर्तं चाथ यन्मूर्तं तदसत्यं यदमूर्तं तत्सत्यं तद्ब्रह्म ...।

37. Radhakrishnan, S., *"The Principal Upaniṣads"*, p. 817.

38. *Chānd. Up.*, VI.1.4.

यथा सोम्यैकेन मृत्पिण्डेन सर्वं मृन्मयं विज्ञातँ स्याद्वाचारम्भणं विकारो नामधेयं मृत्तिकेत्येव सत्यम्॥

39. *Kaṭh. Up.*, I.2.18.

न जायते म्रियते वा विपश्चिन्नायं कुतश्चिन्न बभूव कश्चित्।
अजो नित्यः शाश्वतोऽयं पुराणो न हन्यते हन्यमाने शरीरे॥

40. *Īśa. Up.*, 14.

संभूतिं च विनाशं च यस्तद्वेदोभयँ सह।
विनाशेन मृत्युं तीर्त्वा संभूत्याऽमृतमश्नुते॥

41. Radhakrishnan, S., *"The Principal Upaniṣads"*, p. 577.

42. *Kaṭh. Up.*, II.2.15.

न तत्र सूर्यो भाति न चन्द्रतारकं नेमा विद्युतो भान्ति कुतोऽयमग्निः।
तमेव भान्तमनुभाति सर्वं तस्य भासा सर्वमिदं विभाति॥

43. *Bṛ. Up.*, II.5 .15.

स वा अयमात्मा सर्वेषां भूतानामधिपतिः सर्वेषां भूतानाँ राजा तद्यथा रथनाभौ च रथनेमौ चाराः सर्वे समर्पिता एवमेवास्मिन्नात्मनि सर्वाणि भूतानि सर्वे देवाः सर्वे लोकाः सर्वे प्राणाः सर्व एत आत्मानः समर्पिताः॥

44. *Ken. Up.*, I.1 .1-2[a] ,

केनेषितं पतति प्रेषितं मनः केन प्राणः प्रथमः प्रैति युक्तः।
केनेषिता वाचमिमां वदन्ति चक्षुः श्रोत्रं क उ देवो युनक्ति॥
श्रोत्रस्य श्रोत्रं मनसो मनो यद्वाचो ह वाचँ स उ प्राणस्य प्राणः।

45. *Ibid.*, I.3.1-12

46. *Muṇḍ. Up.*, II.2.11.

ब्रह्मैवेदममृतं पुरस्ताद्ब्रह्म पश्चाद्ब्रह्म दक्षिणतश्चोत्तरेण।
अधश्चोर्ध्वं च प्रसृतं ब्रह्मैवेदं विश्वमिदं वरिष्ठम्॥

also *Mai. Up.*, VI.17[a],

ब्रह्म ह वा इदमग्र आसीदेकोऽनन्तः प्रागनन्तो दक्षिणतोऽनन्तः प्रतीच्यनन्त उदीच्यनन्त ऊर्ध्वं चावाङ्च सर्वतोऽनन्तः। एष परमात्माऽपरिमितोऽजः॥

47. *Muṇḍ. Up.*, II.2.2[a],

यदर्चिमद्यदणुभ्योऽणु च यस्मिँल्लोका निहिता लोकिनश्च।

also, *Kaṭh. Up.*, I.2.20[a],

अणोरणीयान्महतो महीयानात्मास्य जन्तोर्निहितो गुहायाम्।

48. *Bṛ. Up.*, IV.4.22[a] ,

स वा एष महानज आत्मा योऽयं विज्ञानमय: प्राणेषु य एषोऽन्तहृदय आकाशस्तस्मिञ्छेते सर्वस्य वशी सर्वस्येशान: सर्वस्याधिपति: स न साधुना कर्मणा भूयान्नो एवासाधुना कनीयानेष सर्वेश्वर एष भूताधिपतिरेष भूतपाल...।

also *Māṇḍ. Up.*, 6,

एष सर्वेश्वर एष सर्वज्ञ एषोऽन्तर्याम्येष योनि: सर्वस्य प्रभवाप्ययौ हि भूतानाम्।

49. *Ken. Up.*, I.2-8.

50. *Bṛ. Up.*, IV.2.4[b],

स एष नेति नेत्यात्माऽगृह्यो नहि गृह्यतेऽशीर्यो नहि शीर्यतेऽसङ्गो नहि सज्यतेऽसितो न व्यथ्यते न रिष्यत्यभयं...।

Ibid., IV.4.22.

Ibid., IV.5.15.

Ibid., III.9.26.

51. *Ibid.*, IV.4.25.

स वा एष महानज आत्माजरोऽमरोऽमृतोऽभयो ब्रह्माभयं वै ब्रह्माभयँ हि वै ब्रह्म भवति।...।

52. *Chānd. Up.*, VIII.1.5.[a]

स ब्रूयान्नास्य जरयैतज्जीर्यति न वधेनास्य हन्यते एतत्सत्यं ब्रह्मपुरमास्मिन्कामा: समाहिता एष आत्माऽपहतपाप्मा विजरो विमृत्युर्विशोको विजिघत्सोऽपिपास: ...।

53. *Īśa. Up.*, 5.

तदेजति तन्नैजति तद्दूरे तद्वन्तिके। तदन्तरस्य सर्वस्य तदु सर्वस्यास्य बाह्यत:॥

54. *Tait. Up.*, III.1.1[g].

यतो वा इमानि भूतानि जायन्ते। येन जातानि जीवन्ति। यत्प्रयन्त्यभिसंविशन्ति। ब्रद्विजिज्ञासस्व तद्ब्रह्मेति॥

55. *Chānd. Up.*, III.14.1[a].

56. *Ṛv*, X.129.

57. *Ait. Up.*, I.1.1-2,

आत्मा वा इदमेक एवाग्र आसीन्नान्यत्किंचन मिषत् स ईक्षत लोकान्नु सृजा इति॥ स इमांल्लोकानसृजत॥ अम्भो मरीचीर्मरमापोऽदोऽम्भः परेण दिवं द्यौः प्रतिष्ठाऽन्तरिक्षं मरीचयः॥ पृथिवी मरो या अधस्तात्ता आपः॥

58. *Ibid.*, I.3.11[a],12[a].

स ईक्षत कथं न्विदं मस्ते स्यादिति स ईक्षत कतरेण प्रपद्या इति।
स एतमेव सीमानं विदार्यैतया द्वारा प्रापद्यत। सैषा विदृतिर्नाम द्वास्तदेतन्नान्दनम्॥

59. *Ibid.*, V. 3.

एष ब्रह्मैष इन्छ प्रजापतिरेते सवङ्ग देवा इमानि च पञ्च महाभूतानि पृथिवी वायुराकाश आपो ज्योतींषीत्येतानीमानि च क्षुद्रमिश्राणीव॥

60. *Tait. Up.*, II.6[m-z]

सोऽकामयत। बहु स्यां प्रजायेयेति। स तपोऽतप्यत।
स तपस्तप्त्वा। इदं सर्वमसृजत। यदिदं किंच। तत्सृष्ट्वा। तदेवानुप्राविशत्।
तदनुप्रविश्य। सच्च त्यच्चाभवत्। निरुक्तं चानिरुक्तं च। निलयनं चानिलयं च।
विज्ञानं चाविज्ञानं च। सत्यं चानृतं च सत्यमभवत्॥

61. *Ibid.*, II.1[f-j].

तस्माद्वा एतस्मादात्मन आकाशः संभूतः। आकाशाद्वायुः। वायोराग्निः। अग्नेरापः। अद्भ्यः पृथिवी।

62. *Chānd. Up.*, VI.2.3[a]-4.

तदैक्षत बहु स्यां प्रजायेयेति तत्तेजोऽसृजत तत्तेज ऐक्षत बहुल्लयां प्रजायेयेति तदपोऽसृजत। ...ता आप ऐक्षन्त बह्व्यः स्याम प्रजायेमहीति ता अन्नमसृजन्त ...।

63. *Ibid.*, VI.3.2.

सैयं देवतैक्षत हन्ताहमिमास्तिस्त्रो देवता अनेन जीवेनात्मनानुप्रविश्य नामरूपे व्याकरवाणीति॥

64. *Bṛ. Up.*, I.4.7[ab].

तद्धेदं तर्ह्यव्याकृतमासीत्तन्नामरूपाभ्यामेव व्याक्रियतासौ नामायमिदँ रूप इति तदिदमप्येतर्हि नामरूपाभ्यामेव व्याक्रियतेऽसौनामायमिदं रूप इति स एष इह प्रविष्टः। आनखाग्रेभ्यो यथा क्षुरः क्षुरधानेऽवहितः ...।

65. Deussen, P., *The Philosophy of the Upaniṣads*, p.183.

66. *Bṛ. Up.*, V.5.1.

आप एवेदमग्र आसुस्ता आपः सत्यमसृजन्त सत्यं ब्रह्म ब्रह्म प्रजापतिं प्रजापतिर्देवाँ स्ते देवाः सत्यमेवोपासते।

67. *Chānd. Up.*, IV.3.1-2,

वायुर्वाव संवर्गो यदा वा अग्निरुद्वायति वायुमेवाप्येति यदा सूर्योऽस्तमेति वायुमेवाप्येति यदा चन्द्रोऽस्तमेति वायुमेवाप्येति।। यदाप उच्छुष्यन्ति वायुमेवापियन्ति वायुर्ह्येवैतान्सर्वान्संवृङ्क्ङ्क्ते।।

68. *Kaṭh Up.*, II.2.9[a].

अग्निर्यथैको भुवनं प्रविष्टो रूपं रूपं प्रतिरूपो बभूव।

69. *Chānd. Up.*, VI.8.4.

तस्य क्व मूलँ स्यादन्यत्रान्नादेवमेव खलु सोम्यान्नेन शुङ्गेनापो मूलमन्विच्छाद्भिः सोम्य शुङ्गेन तेजो मूलमन्विच्छ तेजसा सोम्य शुङ्गेन सन्मूलमन्विच्छ सन्मूलाः सोम्येमाः सर्वाः प्रजाः सदायतनाः सत्प्रतिष्ठाः ।।

70. *Ibid.*, I.9.1,

अस्य लोकस्य गतिरित्याकाश इति होवाच। सर्वाणि ह वा इमानि भूतान्याकाशादेव समुत्पद्यन्त आकाशं प्रत्यस्तं यन्ति। आकाश हि एव एभ्यो ज्यायान् आकाशः परायणम्।।

71. *Ibid.*, VII.12.1[a].

आकाशो वाव तेजसो भूयान्...।

72. *Ibid.*, VI.3.2-3,

सेयं देवतैक्षत हन्ताहमिमास्तिस्त्रो देवता अनेन जीवेन आत्मना अनुप्रविश्य नामरूपे व्याकरवाणीति। तासां त्रिवृतमेकैकां करवाणीति ...।

73. *Ibid.*, VI.4.1-4.

74. *Praśna Up.*, IV.8[a], 7[b].

पृथिवी च पृथिवीमात्रा चापश्चापोमात्रा च तेजश्च तेजोमात्रा च वायुश्च वायुमात्रा चाकाशश्चाकाशमात्रा..। एवं ह वै तत्सर्वं पर आत्मनि संप्रतिष्ठते।

75. *Mai. Up.*, III.2[b].

पञ्चतन्मात्रा भूतशब्देनोच्यन्तेऽथ पञ्चमहाभूतानि भूतशब्देनोच्यन्ते। अथ तेषां यत्समुदयं तच्छरीरमित्युक्तमथ यो ह खलु वाव शरीर इत्युक्तं स भूतात्मेत्युक्तम्।

76. *Chānd. Up.*, VI.2.3-4.

77. *Tait. Up.*, II.1.1.

तस्माद्वा एतस्मादात्मन आकाशः संभूतः। आकाशाद्वायुः। वायोरग्निः। अग्नेरापः। अद्भ्यः पृथिवी। पृथिव्या ओषधयः। ओषधीभ्योऽन्नम्।

78. *Ibid.*, II.6.1[a-d].

असन्नेव स भवति। असद्ब्रह्मेति वेद चेत्। सन्तमेनं ततो विदुरिति।

79. *Chānd. Up.*, VI.3.3.

...अनेनैव जीवेनात्मनानुप्रविश्य नामरूपे व्याकरोत्।

80. *Br. Up.*, I.4.7[b].

आनखाग्रेभ्यो यथा क्षुरः क्षुरधाने...।

81. *Ait. Up.*, I.3.12[a].

स एतमेव सीमानं विदार्यैतया द्वारा प्रापद्यत।

82. *Br. Up.*, II.5.18[b].

पुरश्चक्रे द्विपदः पुरश्चक्रे चतुष्पदः पुरः स पक्षी भूत्वा पुरः पुरुष आविशदिति।
स वा अयं पुरुषः सर्वासु पूर्षु पुरिशयो नैनेन किंचनानावृतं नैनेन किंचनासंवृतम्॥

83. *Muṇḍ. Up.*, II.1.3-7.

84. *Ait. Up.*, V.3

also *Chānd. Up.*, VI.3.1.

85. *Bṛ. Up.*, I.3.22,

एष उ एव साम वाग् वै सामैष सा चामश्चेति तत्साम्नः सामत्वम्। यद्वेद समः प्लुषिणा समो मशकेन समो नागेन सम एभिस्त्रिभिर्लोकैः समोऽनेन सर्वेण तस्माद्वेद सामाश्नुते साम्नः सायुज्यँ सलोकतां य एवमेतत्साम वेद॥

86. *Bṛ. Up.*, I.4.3-4.

87. Radhakrishnan, S., *The Principal Upaniṣads*, p.72.

88. *Śvet. Up.*, V.2.

यो योनिं योनिमधितिष्ठत्येको विश्वानि रूपाणि योनीश्च सर्वाः।
ऋषिं प्रसूतं कपिलं यस्तमग्रे ज्ञानैर्बिभर्ति जायमानं च पश्येत्।

89. *Ibid.*, III.4.

यो देवानां प्रभवोश्चोद्भवश्च विश्वाधिपो रुद्रो महर्षिः।
हिरण्यगर्भं जनयामास पूर्वं स नो बुद्ध्या शुभया संयुनक्तु॥

also, *Ibid.*, IV.12,

यो देवानां...।

90. Deussen, P., *The Philosophy of the Upaniṣads*, p. 201.

91. *Chānd. Up.*, III.19.1-3.

आदित्यो ब्रह्मेत्यादेशस्तस्योपव्याख्यानमसदेवेदमग्र आसीत्। तत्सदासीत्तत्समभवत्तदाण्डं निरवर्तत तत्संवत्सरस्य मात्रामशयत तन्निरभिद्यत ते आण्डकपाले रजतं च

सुवर्णं चाभवताम्। तद्यंजतँ्सेयं पृथिवी यत्सुवर्णं सा द्यौर्यज्जरायु ते पर्वता यदुल्बँ्स मेघो नीहारो या धमनयस्ता नद्यो यद्वास्तेयमुदकँ्स समुद्रः। अथ यत्तदजायत सोऽसावादित्यः ...।

92. *Ibid.*, III.15.1.

अन्तरिक्षोदरः कोशो भूमिबुध्नो न जीर्यति दिशो ह्यस्य स्नक्तयो द्यौरस्योत्तरं बिलं स एष कोशो वसुधानस्तस्मिन्विश्वमिदँ्श्रितम्।

93. *Śvet. Up.*, I.1.

ब्रह्मवादिनो वदन्ति। किं कारणं ब्रह्म कुतः स्म जाता जीवाम केन क्व च संप्रतिष्ठाः॥

94. *Chānd. Up.*, VI.8.4[b].

सन्मूलमन्विच्छ सन्मूलाः सोम्येमाः सर्वाः प्रजाः सदायतनाः सत्प्रतिष्ठाः।

95. *Ibid.*, III.14.1[a].

96. *Kaṭh. Up.*, II.3.1.

ऊर्ध्वमूलोऽवाक्शाख एषोऽश्वत्थः सनातनः। तदेव शुक्रं तद्ब्रह्म तदेवामृतमुच्यते। तस्मिंल्लोकाः श्रिताः सर्वे तदु नात्येति कश्चन एतद्वै तत्।

97. *Ibid., Up.*, II.3.1.

यथा सुदीप्तात्पावकाद्विस्फुलिङ्गाः सहस्त्रशः प्रभवन्ते सरूपाः। तथाक्षराद्विविधाः सोम्य भावाः प्रजायन्ते तत्र चैवापियन्ति॥

98. *Ait. Up.*, III.11-12.

99. *Br. Up.*, I.2.1-5.

नैवेह किंचनाग्र आसीन्मृत्युनैवेदमावृतमासीत्। अशनाययाऽशनाया हि मृत्युस्तन्मनोऽकुरुतात्मन्वी स्यामिति ...।

100. *Ibid.*, I.5.3[a].

त्रीण्यात्मनेऽकुरुतेति मनो वाचं प्राणं... ।

also I.5.1,

यत्सप्तान्नानि मेधया तपसाऽजनयत्पिता। एकमस्य साधारण द्वे देवानभाजयत्। त्रीण्यात्मने कुरुत...।

101. *Kaṭh. Up.*, I.2.25.

यस्य ब्रह्म च क्षत्रं चोभे भवत ओदनः। मृत्युर्यस्योपसेचनं क इत्था वेद यत्र सः।

102. *Chānd. Up.*, I.9.1.

सर्वाणि ह वा इमानि भूतान्याकाशादेव समुत्पद्यन्त आकाशं प्रत्यस्तं यन्त्याकाशो ह्येवैभ्यो ज्यायानाकाशः परायणम्।

103. *Muṇḍ. Up.*, I.1.7.

यथोर्णनाभि: सृजते गृह्णते च यथा पृथिव्यामोषधय: संभवन्ति। यथा सत: पुरुषात्केशलोमानि तथाक्षरात्संभवतीह विश्वम्।

104. *Māṇḍ. Up.*, 6.

एष सर्वेश्वर एष सर्वज्ञ एषोऽन्तर्याम्येष योनि: सर्वस्य प्रभवाप्ययौ हि भूतानाम्।

105. *Chānd. Up.*, III.14.1[a].

106. Anaximander q. by Deussen, P., *The Philosophy of the Upaniṣads*, p. 225.

107. *Śvet. Up.*, III.2.

एको हि रुद्रो द्वितीयाय तस्थुर्य इमाँल्लोकानीशत ईशनीभि:। प्रत्यङ्जनांस्तिष्ठति संचुकोपान्तकाले संसृज्य विश्वा भुवनानि गोपा:॥

108. *Ibid.*, IV.1.

य एकोऽवर्णो बहुधा शक्तियोगाद्वर्णाननेकान्निहितार्थो दधाति। वि चैति चान्ते विश्वमादौ स देव:...।

109. *Bṛ. Up.*, III.9.28[o].

विज्ञानमानन्दं ब्रह्म रातिर्दातु: परायणं तिष्ठमानस्य तद्विद इति॥

110. *Ibid.*, IV.1.2-6.

111. *Tai. Up.*, II.1.1.

सत्यं ज्ञानमनन्तं ब्रह्म॥

112. *Sarvasāropaniṣad.*, 3[c].

सत्यं ज्ञानमनन्तमानन्दं ब्रह्म॥

113. *Nṛsiṁha.U.Tā. Up. Up. S.* p.231.l.28.

चिन्मात्रं सवृद्रष्टारं सर्वसाक्षिणं सर्वग्रासं सर्वप्रेमास्पदं सच्चिदानंदमात्रमेकरसं पुरतोऽस्मात्...।

114. *Rāma. U. Tā. Up. Up. S.* Pt.I, p. 405.l.6.

also *Rāma. P. Tā. Up. Up. S.* Pt.I, p. 400.l.16.

एवंभूतं जगदाधारभूतं रामं वन्दे सच्चिदानन्दरूपम्।

115. *Tejobindūpaniṣad*, I.1.10-11.

अशून्यं शून्यभावं तु शून्यातीतं हृदि स्थितम्। न ध्यानं च न च ध्याता न ध्येयो ध्येय एव॥ सर्वं च न परं शून्यं न परं नापरात्परम्। अचिन्त्यमप्रबुद्धं च न सत्यं न परं विदु:॥

116. *Muṇḍ. Up.*, II. 2.9[b].

तच्छुभ्रं ज्योतिषां ज्योतिस्तद्यदात्मविदो विदुः॥

also, *Bṛ. Up.*, IV. 4.16,

यस्मादर्वाक्संवत्सरोऽहोभिः परिवर्तते। तद्देवा ज्योतिषां ज्योतिरायुर्होपासतेऽमृतम्।

117. *Muṇḍ. Up.*, II.2.10.

न तत्र सूर्यो भाति न चन्द्रतारकं नेमा विद्युतो भान्ति कुतोऽयमग्निः।
तमेव भान्तमनुभाति सर्वम् तस्य भासा सर्वमिदं विभाति॥

Kaṭh Up., II. 2.15.

Śvet. Up., VI. 14.

118. *Chānd. Up.*, VIII. 3.4[a].

अथ य एष संप्रसादोऽस्माच्छरीरात्समुत्थाय परं ज्योतिरुपसंपद्य स्वेन रूपेणाभिनिष्पद्यत एष आत्मेति होवाच।

119. *Br. Up.*, IV.3.6.

अस्तमित आदित्ये याज्ञवल्क्य चन्द्रमस्यस्तमिते शान्तेऽग्नौ शान्तायां वाचि किं ज्योतिरेवायं पुरुष इत्यात्मैवास्य ज्योतिर्भवतीत्यात्मनैवायं ज्योतिषास्ते पल्ययते कर्म कुरुते विपल्येतीति॥

120. *Chānd. Up.*, VIII. 4.2[b].

तस्माद्वा एतँ सेतुं तीर्त्वापि नक्तमहरेवाभिनिष्पद्यते सकृद्विभातो ह्येवैष ब्रह्मलोकः॥

Śvet. Up., IV.18[a].

यदाऽतमस्तन्न दिवा न रात्रिर्न सन्न चासञ्छिव एव केवलः॥

Mai. Up., VI.24.

धनुः शरीरमोमित्येतच्छरः शिखाऽस्य मनस्तमोलक्षणं भित्त्वा तमोऽतमाविष्टमागच्छत्या। थाविष्टं भित्त्वाऽलातचक्रमिव स्फुरन्तमादित्यवर्णमूर्जस्वन्तं ब्रह्म तमसः पर्यमपश्यत्।

121. *Nādabindū. Up.*, 17.

ततः परतरं शुद्धं व्यापकं निर्मलं शिवम्।
सदोदितं परं ब्रह्म ज्योतिषामुदयो यतः॥

122. *Kaṇṭhaśruti. Up.*, q. by Deussen, P., *Sixty Upaniṣads of the Veda*, p. 748.

123. *Tejobindū Up.*, I.8[a].

अनानानन्दनातीतं दुष्प्रेक्ष्यं मुक्तमव्ययम्।

also *M.N. Up.*, I.5.

124. *Sarvasāropaniṣad,* I. 2[d].

एतत्कोशचतुष्टयं स्वकारणाज्ञाने वटकणिकायामिव गुप्तवटवृक्षो यदा वर्तते तदानन्दमयकोश इत्युच्यते।

125. *Nārāyaṇātharvaśira. Up.,* I.2.

अथ नित्यो नारायणः। ब्रह्मा नारायणः। शिवश्च नारायणः। शक्रश्च नारायणः। कालश्च नारायणः। दिशश्च नारायणः। विदिशश्च नारायणः। ऊर्ध्वं च नारायणः। अधश्च नारायणः। अन्तर्बहिश्च नारायणः। नारायण एवेदं सर्वं यद्भूतं यच्च भव्यम्। निष्कलंको निरञ्जनो निर्विकल्पो निराख्यातः शुद्धो देवो एको नारायणो न द्वितीयोऽस्ति कश्चित्॥

126. *Gaṇapatyupaniṣad, Up. S.* pt. I. ll-1-3.

त्वमेव प्रत्यक्षं तत्त्वमसि। त्वमेव केवलं कर्तासि। त्वमेव केवलं हर्तासि। त्वमेव सर्वं खल्विदं ब्रह्मासि। त्वं साक्षादात्मासि नित्यम्।

127. *Ibid.,* I.L-11-19.

त्वं वाङ्मयस्त्वं चिन्मयः। त्वमानन्दमयस्त्वं ब्रह्ममयः। त्वं सच्चिदानन्दाद्वितीयोऽसि। त्वं प्रत्यक्षं ब्रह्मासि। त्वं ज्ञानमयो विज्ञानमयोऽसि। सर्वं जगदिदं त्वत्तो जायते। सर्वं जगदिदं त्वत्तस्तिष्ठति। सर्वं जगदिदं त्वयि लयमेष्यति। सर्वं जगदिदं त्वयि प्रत्येति। त्वं भूमिरापोऽनलोऽनिलो नभः। त्वं चत्वारि वाक्पदानि। त्वं गुणत्रयातीतः। त्वं कालत्रयातीतः। त्वं ब्रह्मास्त्वं विष्णुस्त्वं रुद्रस्त्वमिन्द्रस्त्वमग्निस्त्वं वायुस्त्वं सूर्यस्त्वं चन्द्रमास्त्वं ब्रह्म भूर्भुवःसुवरोम्।

128. Dange, S.A., *Towards Understanding Hindu Myths,* Delhi, 1996, pp. 1-3.

128. a Gajendragadkar, K.V., *Upaniṣadrahasya,* p. 332,

129. *Mudgalopaniṣad, Up. S.,* pt. I. p. 408. ll. 3-9.

स च पादनारायणो जगत्स्रुष्टं प्रकृतिमजनयत्। स समृद्धकायः सन्सृष्टिकर्म न जज्ञिवान्। सोऽनिरुद्धनारायणस्तस्मै सृष्टिमुपादिशत्। ब्रह्मंस्तवेन्द्रियाणि याजकानि ध्यात्वा कोशभूतं दृढं ग्रन्थिकलेवरं हविर्ध्यात्वा मां हविर्भुजं ध्यात्वा वसन्तकालमाज्यं ध्यात्वा ग्रीष्ममिध्मं ध्यात्वा शरदृतुं रसं ध्यात्वैवमग्नौ हुत्वाङ्गस्पर्शात्कलेवरो वज्रं हीष्यते। ततः स्वकार्यान्सर्वप्राणिजीवान्सृष्ट्वा। पश्चाद्याः प्रादुर्भविष्यन्ति। ततः स्थावरजङ्गमात्मकं जगद्भविष्यति॥

130. *Nṛsiṁha. P. Tā. Up.,* I.1.1[b].

स तपस्तप्त्वा स एतं मन्त्रराजं नारसिंहमानुष्टुभमपश्यत्तेन वै सर्वमिदमसृजत यदिदं किंच तस्मात् सर्वमिदमानुष्टुभमित्याचक्षते यदिदं किंचानुष्टुभो वा इमानि भूतानि जायन्तेऽनुष्टुभा जातानि जीवन्ति अनुष्टुभं प्रयन्त्यभिसंविशन्ति॥

131. *Ibid.*, I. 1.2.

ससागरां सपर्वतां सप्तद्वीपां वसुंधरां तत्साम्नः प्रथमं पादं जानीयाद्यक्षगंधर्वाप्स-रोगणसेवितमन्तरिक्षं तत्साम्नो द्वितीयं पादं जानीयाद्वसुरुद्रादित्यैः सर्वैर्देवैः सेवितं दिवं तत्साम्नस्तृतीयं पादं जानीयाद्ब्रह्मस्वरूपं निरञ्जनं परमव्योम्निकं तत्साम्नश्चतुर्थं पादं जानीयात्।

132. *Gopālapārvatāpinyupaniṣad,* I.1.8[a].

तदाहुरेके यस्य प्रथमपदाद्भूमिर्द्वितीयपदाज्जलं तृतीयपदात्तेजश्चतुर्थाद्वायुश्चरमाद्व्योमेति वैष्णवं पञ्चव्याहृतिमयं मन्त्रं कृष्णावभासं कैवल्यसृत्यै सततमावर्तयेदिति।

133. *M. Up.*, I.1.1[d-1].

तस्मिन्पुरुषाश्चतुर्दशा जायन्ते। एका कन्या। दशेन्द्रियाणि मन एकादशं । तेजः द्वादशोऽहंकारःत्रयोदशकः। प्राणा चतुर्दश आत्मा। पञ्चदशी बुद्धिः। पञ्चतन्मात्राणि पञ्चमहाभूतानि। स एष पञ्चविंशकः पुरुषः।

134. Deussen, P, *Sixty Upaniṣads of the Veda,* Vol. II. Delhi, 1995, p. 799.

135. *Bṛ. Jābāla. Up.*, I.1.1.

अपो वा इदमासीत्सलिलमेव। स प्रजापतिरेकः पुष्करपर्णे समभवत्। तस्यान्तर्मनसि कामः समवर्तत इदं सृजेयमिति। तस्माद्यत्पुरुषो मनसाभिगच्छति तद्वाचा वदति। तत्कर्मणा करोति। कामस्तदग्रे समवर्तताधि। मनसा रेतः प्रथमं यदासीत्।

136. *Ibid.*, VI.12[c].

तदेतदृचाभ्युक्तम् अक्षरे परमे व्योमन्यस्मिन्देवा अधिविश्वे निषेदुः।

137. *Avyaktopaniṣad,* I. 1[a].

पुरा किलेदं न किंचनासीन्न द्यौर्नान्तरिक्षं न पृथिवी केवलं ज्योतीरूपमनाद्यनन्तमनण्व-स्थूलरूपमरूपं रूपवदविज्ञेयं ज्ञानरूपमानन्दमयमासीत्। तदनन्यत्तद्वेधाऽभूद्धरितमेकं रक्तमपरम्। तत्र यद्रक्तं तत्पुंसो रूपमभूत्। यद्धरितं तन्मायायाः। तौ समगच्छतः। तयोर्वीर्यमेवमनन्दत्। तदवर्धत। तदण्डमभूद्धैमम्। तत्परिणममानमभूत्। ततः परमेष्ठी व्यजायत।...

138. *Tvmn. Up. Up. S.*, p. 361, L-23.

तथाविधस्याद्वैतपरमानन्दलक्षणस्यादिनारायणस्योन्मेषनिमेषाभ्यां मूलाविद्योदय-स्थितिलया जायन्ते। कदाचिदात्मारामस्याखिलपरिपूर्ण-स्यादिनारायणस्य स्वेच्छा-नुसारेणोन्मेषो जायते। तस्मात्परब्रह्मणोऽधस्तनपादे सर्वकारणे मूलकारणाव्यक्ताविर्भावो भवति। अव्यक्तान्मूलाविर्भावो मूलाविद्याविर्भावश्च। तस्मादेव सच्छब्दवाच्यं ब्रह्माविद्याशबलं भवति। ततो महत्। महतोऽहंकारः। अहंकारात्पञ्चतन्मात्राणि।

पञ्चतन्मात्रेभ्यः पञ्चमहाभूतानि। पञ्चमहाभूतेभ्यो ब्रह्मैकपादव्याप्तमेकमविद्याण्डं जायते। तत्र तत्त्वतो मायोपाधिको नारायण आसीत्। ...तस्मात् स्थूल विराट् स्वरूपो जायते।...

139. *Sarasvat¨. R. Up.*, I.12[a],14.

प्रकृतित्वं ततः सृष्टं सत्त्वादिगुणसाम्यतः। शुद्ध सत्वंप्रधानायां मायायां बिम्बितो ह्यजः। सत्त्वप्रधाना प्रकृतिर्मायेति प्रतिपाद्यते।

140. *S¨topaniṣad,* I.1[a],

मूलप्रकृतिरूपत्वात्सा सीता प्रकृतिः स्मृता।

S¨topaniṣad, I.2[d],

श्रीरामसान्निध्यवशाज्जगदानन्दकारिणी। उत्पत्तिस्थितिसंहारकारिणी सर्वदेहिनाम्॥

141. *Gopālapārvatāpin¨. Up,* I.1[a].

तन्माया चेति सकलं परं ब्रह्मैतद्यो ...।

also, *Nṛsiṁha. P. Tā. Up.*, III.1.

माया वा एषा नारसिंही सर्वमिदं सृजति सर्वमिदं रक्षति सर्वमिदं संहरति॥

142. *Yogacūḍāmaṇyupaniṣad,* I.72,

नित्यं शुद्धं बुद्धं निर्विकल्पं निरञ्जनं निराख्यातमनादिनिधनमेकं तुरीयं यद्भूतं भवद्भविष्यत् परिवर्तमानं सर्वदाऽनवच्छिन्नं परं ब्रह्म तस्माज्जाता पराशक्तिः स्वयंज्योतिरात्मिका। आत्मनः आकाशः संभूतः। आकाशाद्वायुः। वायोरग्निः। अग्नेरापः। अद्भ्यः पृथिवीः।

143. *Gopālottartāpini. Up.*, I.17[c].

तं हि वै पूर्वं ह्येकमेवाद्वितीयं ब्रह्मासीत्तस्मादव्यक्तं व्यक्तमेवाक्षरं तस्मादक्षरान्महान्महतो वा अहंकारस्तस्मादेवाहंकारात्पञ्च तन्मात्राणि तेभ्यो भूतानि तैरावृतमक्षरं भवति।

144. *Subālopaniṣad,* XIV.1,

पृथिवी वान्नमापोऽन्नादा आपो वान्नं ज्योतिरन्नादं ज्योतिर्वान्नं वायुरन्नादो वायुर्वान्नमाकाशोऽन्नाद आकाशो वान्नमिन्द्रियाण्यन्नादानीन्द्रियाणि वान्नं मनोऽन्नादं मनो वान्नं बुद्धिरन्नादा बुद्धिर्वान्नमव्यक्तमन्नादमव्यक्तं वान्नमक्षरमन्नादमक्षरं वान्नं मृत्युरन्नादो मृत्युर्वै परे देव एकीभवति इति ...।

145 (*a*) J. Allan. "*Māyā*", *Encyclopaedia of Religion and Ethics.* Vol. VIII. ed. by James Hastings, Edingburgh, 1953. p. 503.

(*b*) Smart, Ninian "*Indian Philosophy*". *Encyclopaedia of Philosophy*. Vol. III. ed. by Edwards Paul. New York. 1967. p. 159.

(*c*) Caird, *Oxford English Dictionary.* Reissue of a New English Dictionary on Historical Principles. Vol. VI. Oxford, 1993, p. 1880.

146. *Bṛ. Up.*, II.5.19[b].

पश्यन्नवोचद्रूपँ ऽप्रतिरूपो बभूव तदस्य रूपं प्रतिचक्षणाय। इन्द्रो मायाभिः पुरुरूप ईयते।

Sāyaṇa–

यद्रूपं कामयते तद्रूपात्मको भवति नानाविधानि शरीराणि निर्मिमीते।

147. (*a*) *Ṛv,* X.129, 6[c].

अर्वाग्देवा अस्य विसर्जनेन।

(*b*) Dange, S.A., *Hindu Dharma Āni Tattvajñāna,* Pune,1973, p. 181.

148. Radhakrishnan, S., *The Principal Upaniṣads,* Delhi,1998, p. 655.

Praśna. Up., I.16.

तेषामसौ विरजो ब्रह्मलोको न येषु जिह्ममनृतं न माया चेति।

149. Chakravarti, S., *The Philosophy of the Upaniṣads,* Calcutta. 1935. pp.161-208.

150. Ranadem R.D, *op. cit.,* p.162.

Deussen, P., *The Philosophy of the Upaniṣads,* New. York, 1966, pp. 229-236.

Dange, S.A., *Hindu Dharma Aṇi Tattvajñāna,* Pune, 1973, p. 381.

151. Ranade, R.D, *op. cit.,* p.162.

152. Dange, S.A, *Hindu Dharma Aṇi Tattvajñāna,* Pune, 1973, p. 381.

153. *Īśa Up.*, 11.

विद्यां चाविद्यां च यस्तद्वेद उभयँ ऽसह।
अविद्यया मृत्युं तीर्त्वा विद्ययामृतमश्नुते॥

154. *Muṇḍ. Up.*, I.1.4-5.

द्वे विद्ये वेदितव्ये इति ह स्म यद् ब्रह्मविदो वदन्ति परा चैवापरा च॥

तत्रापरा ऋग्वेदो यजुर्वेदः सामवेदोऽथर्ववेदः शिक्षा कल्पो व्याकरणं निरुक्तं छन्दो ज्योतिषमिति।

अथ परा यया तदक्षरमधिगम्यते॥
विनाशेन मृत्युं तीर्त्वा संभूत्याऽमृतमश्नुते॥

155. Radhakrshnan, S., *The Principal Upaniṣads,* Delhi, 1998, p. 672.

156. *Muṇḍ. Up.* I. 2.7-10.
also, *Muṇḍ. Up.*, I.2.13.

157. *Īśa. Up.*, 14.
संभूतिं च विनाशं च यस्तद्वेद उभयँ सह।
विनाशेन मृत्युं तीर्त्वा संभूत्याऽमृतमश्नुते॥

158. *Ibid.*, 15.
हिरण्मयेन पात्रेण सत्यस्यापिहितं मुखम्।
तत्त्वं पूषन्नपावृणु सत्यधर्माय स्पृष्टये॥

159. *Kaṭh. Up.*, I.2.4[a]-5.
दूरमेते विपरीते विषूची अविद्या या च विद्येति ज्ञाता॥
अविद्यायामन्तरे वर्तमानाः स्वयं धीराः पण्डितंमन्यमानाः।
दन्द्रम्यमाणाः परियन्ति मूढा अन्धेनैव नीयमाना यथान्धाः॥
also *Muṇḍ. Up.*, I. 2.8.
also *Mai. Up.*, VII. 9[c].

160. *Muṇḍ. Up.*, II. 1.10.
पुरुष एवेदं विश्वं कर्म तपो ब्रह्म परामृतम्।
एतद्यो वेद निहितं गुहायां सोऽविद्याग्रन्थिं विकिरतीह सोम्य॥

161. *Chānd. Up.*, I. 1.10[b].
नाना तु विद्या चाविद्या च यदेव विद्यया करोति श्रद्धयोपनिषदा तदेव वीर्यवत्तरं भवतीति खल्वेत स्यैवाक्षरस्योपव्याख्यानं भवति॥

162. *Ibid.*, VIII. 3.1-3.

163. *Bṛ. Up.*, I.3.28[b].
असतो मा सद्गमय तमसो मा ज्योतिर्गमय मृत्योर्माऽमृतं गमयेति ...।

164. *Śvet. Up.*, IV. 10-11,
मायां तु प्रकृतिं विद्यान्मायिनं तु महेश्वरम्।
तस्यावयवभूतैस्तु व्याप्तं सर्वमिदं जगत्॥

यो योनिं योनिमधितिष्ठत्येको यस्मिन्निदं स च वि चैति सर्वम्।
तं ईशानं वरदं देवमीड्यं निचाय्येमां शान्तिमत्येति॥

165. *Ibid.*, IV. 9[h].

अस्मान्मायी सृजते विश्वमेतत्तस्मिंश्चान्यो मायया संनिरुद्धः॥

166. *Ibid.*, IV. 5[a].

अजामेकां लोहितशुक्लकृष्णां बह्वीः प्रजाः सृजमानां सरूपाः॥

167. Dange, S.A, *Hindu Dharma Āṇi Tattvajñana,* Pune. 1973, p. 381.

168. *Sarvasāropaniṣad,* 4[c].

अनादिरनन्तर्वन्ती प्रमाणाप्रमाणसाधारणा न सती नासती
न सदसती स्वयमविकाराद्विकारहेतौ निरूप्यमाणेऽसती।
अनिरूप्यमाणे सती लक्षणशून्या सा मायेत्युच्यते॥

169. *Nṛsiṁha. U. Tā. Up.*, IX, I. 3-12.

also, *Ibid.*, Ed. by Mahadevashastri. A, with commentary of Śṛi. Upaniṣad Brahmayogin, *The Vaiṣṇava. Upaniṣads,* pp. 287-291

170. *Kaivalya. Up.*, I.12-14.

स एव मायापरिमोहितात्मा शरीरमास्थाय करोति सर्वम्।
स्त्रियन्नपानादिविचित्रभोगैः स एव जाग्रत्परितृप्तिमेति॥

स्वप्ने स जीवः सुखदुःखभोक्ता स्वमायया कल्पितजीवलोके।
सुषुप्तिकाले सकले विलीने तमोऽभिभूतः सुखरूपमेति॥

पुनश्च जन्मान्तरकर्मयोगात्स स एव जीवः स्वपिति प्रबुद्धः।
पुरत्रये क्रीडति यश्च जीवस्ततस्तु जातं सकलं विचित्रम्।
आधारमानन्दमखण्डबोधं यस्मिँस्ल्यं याति पुरत्रयं च॥

171. *Brhmabindūpaniṣad,* I. 15,

शब्दमायावृतोयावत्तावत्तिष्ठति पुष्करे।
भिन्ने तमसि चैकत्वमेकमेवानुपश्यति॥

172. *Garbhopaniṣad,* 4[g-h].

यदि योन्यां प्रमुच्यामि ध्याये ब्रह्म सनातनम्। अथ जन्तुः स्त्रीयोनिशतं योनिद्वारि संप्राप्तो यन्त्रेणापीडयमानो महता दुःखेन जातमात्रस्तु वैष्णवेन वायुना संस्पृश्य तदा न स्मरति जन्ममरणं न च कर्म शुभमशुभम्॥

173. *S¨topaniṣad, Up. S.* pt. I, p. 337.

श्रीरामसानिध्यवशात् जगदानन्दकारिणी।
उत्पत्तिस्थितिसंहारकारिणी सर्वदेहिनाम्॥

174. *Devyupaniṣad,*18.

यस्याः परतरं नास्ति सैषा दुर्गा प्रकीर्तिता। दुर्गात्संत्रायते यस्माद्देवी दुर्गेति कथ्यते॥१८॥

Ibid., 1[i-j].

विद्याहमविद्याहम्। अजाहमनजाहम्।

Ibid., 10[o].

भुक्तिमुक्तिप्रदायिनीम्।

Ibid., 17[c].

यस्याः ग्रहणं नोपलभ्यते तस्मादुच्यतेऽलक्ष्या।

175. *Gopālottartāpinyupaniṣad, Up. S.* pt. I. p. 597, l.12,

कृष्णात्मिका जगत्कर्त्री मूलप्रकृतिरुक्मिणी।

176. *Ibid.,* p. 597, l.10,

एकमेवाद्वयं ब्रह्म मायया तु चतुष्टयम्॥

also Radhakrishnan, S., *The Principal Upaniṣads,* Delhi, 1998, p. 72.

1. The transcendental universal Being.
2. Causal principle of differenciation.
3. The innermost of the world.
4. The manifest world.

177. *Gaṇeśa. U. Tā. Up. Up. S.,* pt. I, p. 636, l. 27,

अनिर्वचनीया सैव माया जगद्बीजमित्याह।
सैव प्रकृतिरिति गणेश इति प्रधानमिति च मायाशबलमिति॥

178. *Gaṇeśa. P. Tā. Up. Up. S.,* pt. I, p. 631, L.17,

माया वा एषा वैनायकी सर्वमिदं सृजति, सर्वमिदं रक्षति।
सर्वमिदं रक्षति, सर्वमिदं संहरति तस्मान्मायामेतां शक्तिं वेद॥

179. *Sarasvat¨. R. Up.,* 14, 15[a].

शुद्धसत्त्वप्रधानायांमायायां बिम्बितो ह्यजः।
सत्त्वप्रधाना प्रकृतिर्मायेति प्रतिपाद्यते॥
सा माया स्ववशोपाधिः सर्वज्ञस्येश्वरस्य हि॥

180. Deussen, P., *The Philosophy of the Upaniṣads,* N.Y. 1966, pp. 74-76.

181. *Bh. G.*, XVIII, 61[b].

भ्रामयन्सर्वभूतानि यन्त्रारूढानि मायया॥

182. *Gauḍapādakārikā*, I.17.

प्रपञ्चो यदि विद्येत निवर्तेत न संशयः।
मायामात्रमिदं द्वैतं परमार्थतः॥

183. *Bṛ. Up.*, II. 4. 14[d].

येनेदँ सर्वं विजानाति तं केन विजानीयाद्विज्ञातारमरे केन विजानीयादिति॥

184. *Kaṭh. Up.*, I.3.4.

इन्द्रियाणि हयानाहुर्विषयांस्तेषु गोचरान्।
आत्मेन्द्रियमनोयुक्तं भोक्तेत्याहुर्मनीषिणः॥

Praśna. Up., IV.9.

एष हि द्रष्टा स्पष्टा श्रोता घ्राता रसयिता मन्ता बोद्धा कर्ता विज्ञानात्मा पुरुषः।
स परेऽक्षर आत्मनि संप्रतिष्ठते॥

185. *Kau. Up.*, IV. 20[b].

तद्यथा श्रेष्ठी स्वर्भुंक्ते यथा वा स्वाः श्रेष्ठिनं भुञ्जन्त्येवमेवैष प्रज्ञात्मैतैरात्मभिर्भुंक्ते।
एवं वै तमात्मान एतमात्मानं भुञ्जिति।

186. *Mai. Up.*, II.4[b].

अजेनेदं शरीरं चेतनवत् प्रतिष्ठापितम् प्रचोदयिता वैषोऽप्यस्येति॥

187. *Tait. Up.*, II.2 .

तस्माद्वा एतस्मादन्नरसमयात्। अन्योऽन्तर आत्मा प्राणमयः। तेनैष पूर्णः। स वा एष पुरुषविध एव।

Ibid., II. 3.

तस्माद्वा एतस्मात्प्राणमयात्। अन्योऽन्तर आत्मा मनोमयः। तेनैष पूर्णः। स वा एष पुरुषविध एव।

Ibid., II. 4

तस्माद्वा एतस्मान्मनोमयात् अन्योऽन्तर आत्मा विज्ञानमयः। तेनैष पूर्णः। स वा एष पुरुषविध एव।

Ibid., II. 5.

तस्माद्वा एतस्माद्विज्ञानमयात्। अन्योऽन्तर आत्मानन्दमयः। तेनैष पूर्णः। स वा एष पुरुषविध एव।

188. *Chānd. Up.*, V. 18.1,

तान्होवाचैतै वै खलु यूयं पृथगिवेममात्मानं वैश्वानरं विद्वांसोऽन्नमत्थ यस्त्वेतमेवं प्रादेशमात्रमभिविमानमात्मानं वैश्वानरमुपास्ते स सर्वेषु लोकेषु सर्वेषु भूतेषु सर्वेष्वात्मस्वन्नमत्ति।

189. Ranade, R.D. *op. cit.*, pp. 97, 98.

190. *Kau. Up.*, IV. 20[a].

तद्यथा क्षुरः क्षुरधानेऽवहितःस्यात्। ...प्रज्ञ आत्मेदंशरीरमात्मानमनुप्रविष्ट आलोमभ्य आनखेभ्यः।

191. *Bṛ. Up.*, V. 6.1.

मनोमयोऽयं पुरुषो भाः सत्यस्तस्मिन्नन्तर्हृदये यथा व्रीहिर्वा यवो वा स एष सर्वस्येशानः सर्वस्याधिपतिः सर्वमिदं प्रशास्ति यदिदं किञ्च।

192. *Kaṭh. Up.*, II.1.12.

अंगुष्ठमात्रः पुरुषो मध्य आत्मनि तिष्ठति।
ईशानो भूतभव्यस्य न ततो विजुगुप्सते ..॥

also, *Bh. G.*, XVIII. 61[a].

ईश्वरः सर्वभूतानां हृद्देशेऽर्जुन तिष्ठति।

193. *Kaṭh. Up.*, I.2.21[b].

महान्तं विभुमात्मानं मत्वा धीरो न शोचति।

Muṇḍ. Up., I.1.6[b].

...नित्यं विभुं सर्वगतं सुसूक्ष्मं तदव्ययं यद्भूतयोनिं परिपश्यन्ति धीराः॥

194. *Mai. Up.*, VI. 38[c].

शरीरप्रादेशांगुष्ठमात्रमणोरप्यणुं ध्यात्वाऽतः परमतां गच्छति...।

195. *Chānd. Up.*, III. 14.3.

एष म आत्माऽन्तर्हृदयेऽणीयान् व्रीहेर्वा यवाद्वा सर्षपाद्वा श्यामाकाद्वा श्यामाकतण्डुलाद्वा एष म आत्माऽन्तर्हृदये ज्यायान्पृथिव्या ज्यायानन्तरिक्षाज्ज्यायान्दिवो ज्यायानेभ्यो लोकेभ्यः॥

196. Deussen, P, *The Philosophy of the Upaniṣads*, N.Y., 1966, pp. 256-261.

197. *Śāṇḍilya. Up.*, III. 2[c].

अथ कस्मादुच्यते आत्मेति। यस्मात्सर्वमाप्नोति सर्वमादत्ते सर्वमत्ति च तस्मादुच्यते आत्मेति॥

198. *Sarvasāropaniṣad,* I. 2-4.

199. Edited by Karmarkar, R.D, *Gauḍapādakārika*, Pune. 1973, p. 57.

200. Śaṅkara q. by Karmarkar R.D., *Op.cit*., p. 57.

201. *Bṛ. Up*., IV. 3.19.

तद्यथास्मिन्नाकाशे श्येनो वा सुपर्णो वा विपरिपत्य श्रान्तः सँहत्य पक्षौ संलयायैव ध्रियते एवमेवायं पुरुष एतस्मा अन्ताय धावति यत्र सुप्तो न कञ्चन कामं कामयते न कञ्चन स्वप्नं पश्यति॥

202. *Ibid*., II.1.19[a].

अथ यदा सुषुप्तो भवति यदा न कस्यचन वेद हिता नाम नाड्यो द्वासप्ततिः सहस्राणि हृदयात्पुरीततमभिप्रतिष्ठन्ते ताभिः प्रत्यवसृप्य पुरीतति शेते॥

203. *Praśna. Up*., IV. 2.

यथा गार्ग्य मरीचयोऽर्कस्यास्तं गच्छतः सर्वा एतस्मिंस्तेजोमण्डल एकीभवन्ति ताः पुनः पुनरूदयतः प्रचरन्त्येवं ह वै तत्सर्वं परे देवे मनस्येकीभवति॥

204. *Chānd. Up.,* VIII. 6.3[a].

तद्यत्रैतत्सुप्तः समस्तः संप्रसन्नः स्वप्नं न विजानात्यासु तदा नाडीषु सृप्तो भवति ...॥

205. *Bṛ. Up*., II. 1.17.

...यत्रैष एतत्सुप्तोऽभूद्य एष विज्ञानमयः पुरुषस्तदेषां प्राणानां विज्ञानेन विज्ञानमादाय य एषोऽन्तर्हृदय आकाशस्तस्मिञ्छेते तानि यदा गृह्णाति अथ हैतत्पुरुषः स्वपिति नाम॥

206. *Praśna, Up*., IV. 4[b].

मनो ह वाव यजमान इष्टफलमेवोदानः स एनं यजमानमहरहर्ब्रह्म गमयति॥

207. *Chānd. Up.,* VIII. 3.2[b].

यथापि हिरण्यनिधिं निहितमक्षेत्रज्ञा उपर्युपरि संचरंतो न विन्देयुरेवमेवेमाः सर्वाः प्रजा अहरहर्गच्छन्त्य एतं ब्रह्मलोकं न विन्दति अनृतेन हि प्रत्यूढाः॥

208. *Bṛ. Up*., IV. 3.9-18.

209. Ranade, R.D, *op. cit.,* p. 91.

210. *Praüna Up*., IV. 5[b].

दृष्टं च अदृष्टं च श्रुतं चाश्रुतं च अनुभूतं चाननुभूतं च सच्चासच्च सर्वं पश्यति सर्वः पश्यति॥

211. *Māṇḍ Up.*, 4.

स्वप्नस्थानोऽन्तः प्रज्ञः.... प्रविविक्तभुक् तैजसो द्वितीयःद पादः ॥

212. *Gauḍapādakārikā*, I. 11.

कार्यकारणबद्धौ ताविष्येते विश्वतैजसौ।
प्राज्ञः कारणबद्धस्तु द्वौ तौ तुर्ये न सिध्यतः ॥

213. *Ibid.*, III. 35.

लीयते हि सुषुप्ते तन्निगृहीतं न लीयते।
तदेव निर्भयं ब्रह्म ज्ञानलोकं समन्ततः ॥

214. *Ibid.*, I. 13.

द्वैतस्याग्रहणं तुल्यमुभयोः प्राज्ञचतुर्ययोः।
बीजनिद्रायुतः प्राज्ञः सा च तुर्ये न विद्यते ॥

215. Radhakrishnan, S., *The Principal Upaniṣads,* Delhi, 1998. p. 701.

216. *Nṛsiṁha. U. Tā. Up.*, II.2.

217. *Subāla. Up*, IV.1[a] also *Chānd. Up.*, VIII. 1.1.

218. *Brahmopaniṣaḍ Up. S.* pt.I, p.167, l.17-19.

अथास्य पुरुषस्य चत्वारि स्थानानि भवन्ति। नाभिर्हृदयं कण्ठं मूर्धेति।
तत्र चतुष्पादं ब्रह्म विभाति। जागरितं स्वप्नं सुषुप्तं तुरीयमिति।
जागरिते ब्रह्मा स्वप्ने विष्णुः सुषुप्तौ रुद्रस्तुरीयं परमाक्षरं।

219. *Ibid.*, p. 168, l. 24-27.

हृदयं तद्विजानीयाद्विश्वस्यायतनं महत्। नेत्रस्थं जाग्रतं विद्यात्कण्ठे स्वप्नं विनिर्दिशेत्।
सुषुप्तं हृदयस्थं तु तुरीयं मूर्ध्नि संस्थितम्।

220. Macdonell, A.A., *History of Sanskrit Literature,* Delhi, 1958. p. 387.

221. *Ṛv.*, I. 154.5.

तदस्य प्रियमभि पाथो अश्यां नरो यत्र देवयवो मदन्ति
उरुक्रमस्य स हि बन्धुरित्था विष्णोः पदे परमे मध्व उत्सः ॥

222. *Ṛv.*, X. 16.3.

सूर्यं चक्षुर्गच्छतु वातमात्मा द्यां च गच्छ पृथिवीं च धर्मणा। अपो वा गच्छ यदि तत्र ते हितं ओषधीषु प्रतितिचा शरीरैः ॥

223. *Bṛ. Up.*, III. 2.13.

...यत्रास्य पुरुषस्य मृतस्याग्निं वागप्येति वातं प्राणश्चक्षुरादित्यं मनश्चन्द्रं दिश: श्रोत्रं पृथिवीँ शरीरमाकाशमात्मौषधीर्लोमानि वनस्पतीन्केशा अप्सु लोहितं च रेतश्च निधीयते क्वायं तदा पुरुषो भवतीत्याहर सोम्य हस्तमार्तभागाऽऽवामेवैतस्य वेदिष्यावो न नावेतत् सजन इति तौ हौत्क्रम्य मन्त्रयाञ्चक्राते तौ ह यदूचतु: कर्म हैव तदूचतुरथ यत्प्रशँसतु: कर्म हैव तत्प्रशशँसतु: पुण्यो वै पुण्येन कर्मणा भवति पाप: पापेनेति॥

224. *Ibid.*, IV. 4.2^{b}-3-4^{a}.

...सर्वे प्राणा अनूत्क्रामन्ति स विज्ञानो भवति सविज्ञानमेवान्ववक्रामति। तं विद्याकर्मणी समन्वारभेते पूर्वप्रज्ञाच॥ तद्यथा तृणजलायुका तृणस्यान्तं गत्वाऽन्यमाक्रम-माक्रम्यात्मानमुपसंहरत्येवमेवायमात्मेदं शरीरं निहत्याऽविद्या गमयित्वाऽन्यमाक्रम-माक्रम्यात्मानमुपसंहरति॥ तद्यथा पेशस्कारी पेशसो मात्रामपादायान्यन्नवतरं कल्याणतरं रूपं तनुते एवमेवायमात्मेदं शरीरं निहत्याऽविद्यां गमयित्वाऽन्यन्नवतरं कल्याणतरं रूपं कुरुते..॥

225. Dasgupta, S., *The History of Indian Philosophy,* Vol. I, 1922, p. 56.

226. *Br. Up.*, IV. 4.5^{b}.

अथो खल्वाहु: काममय एवायं पुरुष इति स यथाकामो भवति तत्क्रतुर्भवति यत्क्रतुर्भवति तत्कर्म कुरुते यत्कर्म कुरुते तदभिसंपद्यते॥

also *Ibid.*, I. 4.15^{b}.

227. *Muṇḍ. Up.*, III. 2.2^{a}.

कामान्य: कामयते मन्यमान: स कामभिर्जायते तत्र तत्र।

228. *Ibid.*, III. 1.10.

यं यं लोकं मनसा संविभाति विशुद्धसत्त्व: कामयतेयांश्च कामान्। तं तं लोकं जयते तांश्च कामांस्तस्मादात्मज्ञं ह्यर्चयेद्भूतिकाम:।

229. *Ibid.*, III. 2.2^{b}.

पर्याप्तकामस्य कृतात्मनस्तु इहैव सर्वे प्रविलीयन्ति कामा:।

230. *Ait. Up.*, II.1-4.

and, *Br. Up.*, IV. 4.22.

231. *Ṛv,* X.88.15,

द्वे सृती अशृणवं पितृणामहं देवानामुत मर्त्यानाम्।
ताभ्यामिदं विश्वमेजत् समेति यदन्तरा पितरं मातरं च॥

also, *Br. Up.*, VI. 2.2^{b}.

द्वे सृती ...

232. *Bh. G.* VIII. 23-26.

233. *Chānd. Up.*, IV. 15.5.

अथ यदु चैवास्मिञ्छव्यं कुर्वन्ति यदि च नार्चिषमेवाभिसंभवन्त्यर्चिषोऽहरह्न आपूर्यमाणपक्षमापूर्यमाणपक्षाद्यान्षडुदङ्ङेति मासाँ स्तान्मासेभ्यः संवत्सरँ संवत्सरादातित्यमादित्याच्चन्द्रमसं चन्द्रमसो विद्युतं तत्पुरुषोऽमानवः स एनान्ब्रह्म गमयत्येष देवपथो ब्रह्मपथ एतेन प्रतिपद्यमाना इमं मानवमावर्त नावर्तन्ते नावर्तन्ते॥

also, *Ibid.*, V. 10.1-6.

234. *Br. Up.*, VI. 2.15.

235. *Praśna Up.*, I.1.10[a].

अथोत्तरेण तपसा ब्रह्मचर्येण श्रद्धया विद्ययात्मानमन्विष्यादित्यमभिजयन्त...।

236. *Kau. Up.*, I. 1.3.

स एतं देवयानं पन्थानमापद्याग्निलोकमागच्छति स वायुलोकं स आदित्यलोकं स वरुणलोकं स इन्द्रलोकं स प्रजापतिलोकं स ब्रह्मलोकं तस्य ह वा एतस्य ब्रह्मलोकस्य आरो ह्रदो मुहूर्ता येष्टिहा विजरा नदील्यो वृक्षः सालज्यं संस्थानमपराजितमायतन-मिन्द्रप्रजापती द्वारगोपौ।

Ibid., I. 1.4[b].

तत्सुकृतदुष्कृते धुनुते। तस्य प्रिया ज्ञातयः सुकृतमुपयन्त्यप्रिया दुष्कृतं तद्यथा रथेन धावयन्रथचक्रे पर्यवेक्षत एवमहोरात्रे पर्यवेक्षत एवं सुकृतदुष्कृते सर्वाणि च द्वन्द्वानि स एष विसुकृतो विदुष्कृतो ब्रह्म विद्वान्ब्रह्मैवाभिप्रैति॥

237. Deussen, P, *The Philosophy of the Upaniṣads*, N.Y. 1966, p. 355.

238. *Chānd. Up.*, V. 10.3-6.

अथ य इमे ग्राम इष्टापूर्ते दत्तमित्युपासते ते धूममभिसंभवन्ति धूमाद्रात्रिं रात्रेरपरपक्षमपरपक्षाद्यान्षड्दक्षिणैति मासाँ स्तान्नैते संवत्सरमभिप्राप्नुवन्ति॥

मासेभ्यः पितृलोकं पितृलोकादाकाशमाकाशाच्चन्द्रमसमेष सोमो राजा तद्देवानामन्नं तं देवा भक्षयन्ति॥

तस्मिन्यावत्संपातमुषित्वाऽथैतमेवाध्वानं पुनर्निवर्तन्ते यथेतमाकाशम् आकाशाद्वायुं वायुर्भूत्वा धूमो भवति धूमो भूत्वाऽभ्रं भवति॥

अभ्रं भूत्वा मेघो भवति मेघो भूत्वा प्रवर्षति त इह व्रीहियवा ओषधिवनस्पतयस्तिलमाषा इति जायन्तेऽतो वै खलु दुर्निष्प्रपतरं यो यो ह्यन्नमत्ति यो रेतः सिञ्चति तद्भूय एव भवति॥

also, *Bṛ. Up.*, VI. 2.14-16.

239. *Kau. Up.*, I.1.2[a].

स होवाच ये वै के चास्मात्लोकात्प्रयन्ति चन्द्रमसमेव ते सर्वे गच्छन्ति।
तेषां प्राणैः पूर्वपक्ष आप्यायते तानपरपक्षे न प्रजनयति॥

240. *Praśna. Up.*, I.9.

संवत्सरो वै प्रजापतिस्तस्यायने दक्षिणं चोत्तरं च। तद्ये ह वै तदिष्टापूर्ते कृतमित्युपासते ते चान्द्रमसमेव लोकमभिजयन्ते॥ त एव पुनरावर्तन्ते तस्मादेते ऋषयः प्रजाकामा दक्षिणं प्रतिपद्यन्ते॥ एष ह वै रयिर्यः पितृयाणः॥

241. Garg, R.K., *Upaniṣadic Challenge to Science,* Delhi. 1968, p. 60.

also, Ranade, R.D., *op. cit,* p. 115.

and, Deussen. P., *The Philosophy of the Upaniṣads,* N.Y. 1966, p. 315.

242. *Bṛ. Up.*, IV.4.5[b].

...यथाकारी यथाचारी तथा भवति साधुकारी साधुर्भवति पापकारी पापो भवति पुण्यः पुण्येन कर्मणा भवति पापः पापेन।

and, *Chānd. Up.*, III. 14.1[b].

अथ खलु क्रतुमयः पुरुषो यथाक्रतुरस्मिंल्लोके पुरुषो भवति तथेतः प्रेत्य भवति स क्रतुं कुर्वीत।

243. *Bṛ. Up.*, IV. 4.11,

अनन्दा नाम ते लोका अन्धेन तमसाऽऽवृताः।
तांस्ते प्रेत्याभिगच्छन्ति अविद्वांसोऽबुधो जनाः॥

also, *Iśa. Up.*, 3.

असूर्या नाम ते लोका अन्धेन तमसावृताः।
तांस्ते प्रेत्याभिगच्छन्ति ये के चात्महनो जनाः॥

also, *Iśa. Up.* 9[a], and *Bṛ. Up.*, IV. 4.10,

अन्धं तमः प्रविशन्ति येऽविद्यामुपासते॥

244. *Tvmn. Up.*, II. 5.1.

245. *Subālopaniṣad,* XI.1[a].

हृदयस्यमध्ये लोहितं मांसपिण्डं यस्मिंस्तद्दहरं पुण्डरीकं कुमुदमिवानेकधा तस्य मध्ये समुद्रः समुद्रस्यमध्ये कोशस्तस्मिन्नाड्यश्चतस्त्रो भवन्ति रमोरमेच्छाऽपुनर्भवेति तत्र रमा पुण्येन पुण्यं लोकं नयत्यरमा पापेन पापमिच्छया यत्स्मरति तदभिसंपद्यते अपुनर्भवया कोशं भिनत्ति।

246. *Piṇḍopaniṣad,* 3.

त्र्यहं वसति तोयेषु त्र्यहं वसति चाग्निषु।
त्र्यहं आकाशगो भूत्वा दिनमेकन्तु वायुगः॥

247. *Ibid.,* 4-8.

248. Gajendragadkar, K., *op. cit.,* p. 340.

CHAPTER III

THE *ĀLAMBANA*-S IN THE UPANIṢADS

Having dealt with the nature of the Highest Reality, the concept of *māyā* and the individual soul, it will now be appropriate to examine the supports (*ālambana*-s), which are believed to lead one to the Ultimate Reality.

One cannot start one's worship with the abstract, the Brahman; for the human mind is by nature restless and it cannot understand on what to concentrate itself. By way of support, (*ālambana*) it needs some steady object, which is perceptible either to the senses or to the mind. Therefore, the form of the Brahman which has to be taken for the worship; has to be endowed with qualities, which can be comprehended by the mind on account of the difference between the worshipper and the worshipped. Therefore, whenever the worship of the Brahman is prescribed in the Upaniṣads, the worship of the symbolic representation of the Brahman is proclaimed.

The symbol is a thing representing something, especially an idea or a quality. It is a mark taken as a conventional sign of some object, idea, function etc.[1] These emblems are to be regarded collectively as the visible signs of the invisible ideas they represent. The Indian word for a symbol is *pratīka* and it has a similar conception. The word *pratyañc* a denotes, "the side or face turned towards" us, and therefore perceptible of an object which in other respects is imperceptible. It means that, the side or the portion of any particular object which first becomes perceptible to us and because of which we subsequently acquire the whole knowledge of that particular object. In this sense, the propounders of the Vedānta doctrines often speak of the symbols of the Brahman.

The symbols are definite representations of the Brahman, under some form, perceptible by the senses or the mind, which means that, they belong to an order of reality, different from the Reality that they symbolise. They are used to make the Truth intelligible, to make the unhearable, audible. They are meant to be used as tangible supports for contemplation which help us to reach the awareness of the symbolised Reality. The individual is free to select any form of the Supreme–such as Prāṇa, Vāyu, *ākāśa,* mind–endowed with qualities but purely imperceptible symbols. So also he can worship qualitiful perceptible objects such as the Sun, Vaiśvānara etc. This freedom of choice is aptly described by Radhakrishnan, S. as *iṣṭadevatārādhana.*[2] The acceptance of one form does not mean exclusion of the others, but it means that, the different forms are all included in the Supreme.

Deussen, P. defines 'symbols' as, "by symbol, in a wider sense, we understand all the representations conceived with a view to the worship of the Brahman, himself incapable of representation under some one of his phenomenal forms- such as Prāṇa, Vāyu, *ākāśa,* Āditya, and the syllable Oṁ etc."[3]

Prāṇa, Vāyu

These are the symbols of the Brahman. Prāṇa is 'life' from the biological point of view. Prāṇa; the natural phenomenon, the most intimate essence of things; is manifested in the activity of all the organs. But above all, Prāṇa is active in the process of breathing which determines life itself. Thus, Prāṇa; which means 'breath' constitutes the life of a man, became the 'life-principle'. Just as it signifies the life-principle in man, similarly, the life-principle in the universe also was designated as Prāṇa. Prāṇa means the life-force and also the cosmic-force. Thus, Prāṇa is considered as the life-force and the cosmic-force. It is regarded as the very navel of existence.[4] As Prāṇa was considered as the life force and cosmic-force, naturally it becomes the substratum of all the things. For verily, all the beings enter into the Prāṇa and arise from the Prāṇa.[5] In the *Chānd. Up*, Raikva narrates that, air (*vāyu*) verily is the absorbent of all the things; for when the fire is extinguished, it goes into the air, when the Sun sets it goes into the air and when the moon sets it goes into the air. And with reference to the Self, 'breath' (Prāṇa) indeed is the absorbent. For, when one sleeps; the speech, sight, hearing and the mind get absorbed in the breath.[6] Raikva tries to bring out beautifully the harmony between the macrocosm and the microcosm and concludes that; just as air is the life-principle of the universe, breath is the life-principle in man. And thus, there are these two absorbents, one in the macrocosm (air) and the other in the microcosm (Prāṇa).

The supremacy of the Prāṇa to the other vital organs; ear, eye, speech, mind (*manas*) etc., is illustrated by the parable of the rivalry of the organs. In order to decide, which one of them is the most essential, the Prāṇa-s (of the eye, ear, speech etc.) depart from the body, one after another. Still, the body remains intact without them. When the breath (Prāṇa) proposes to depart, they become aware that none of them can exist without breath.[7] The *Bṛ. Up.* relates the story almost in the same manner, where the Brahman substitutes Prajāpati of the *Chānd. Up.*[8] With slight variations, the story is repeated in the *Kau. Up.* and the *Praśna Up.*[9] The philosopher of the *Kau. Up.* seems to acknowledge the 'consciousness' as the higher category of existence distinguished from the 'life'; for there may be forms of life without consciousness; but wherever there is consciousness, there must be life. Here, Prāṇa is identified with the consciousness (*prajñā*). The Upaniṣad describes Prāṇa not merely as the principle of life but as the principle of consciousness also.[10] Again, Prāṇa is directly identified with life (*āyuḥ*).[11] Life (*āyuḥ*) exists as long as Prāṇa exists. Most importantly, the Upaniṣad identifies Prāṇa with the Ātman itself.[12]

Trying to find out the philosophical end of human life, as early as at the time of the *Chānd. Up.*, the evolved idea of inner sacrifice was recognized. There, it is said that making oblations to the Prāṇa within us is our real sacrifice.[13] With development of thought; about the Prāṇa; finally the Prāṇa becomes the Ultimate. Another important thought; which is explained in the *Chānd. Up.* from physiological point of view; is that man consists of sixteen parts, and after a fifteen days fast, only one–the Prāṇa survives.[14] An enumeration of these sixteen parts is found in the *Praśna Up.* The passage declares that the Puruṣa created the Prāṇa, from which the fifteen other parts succeed.[15] Here, the Prāṇa is dependent on the Pururṣa, *i.e* Ātman, at the same time its empirical representative.

Manas

Another important symbol under which the Brahman is to be worshipped is *manas*.

The *Chānd. Up.* instructs, "the *manas* is to be worshipped as the Brahman."[16] In the same Upaniṣad, *manas* is the third symbol. Beyond which there is something which is still higher.[17] To Satyakāma in the *Bṛ. Up.,* the instruction "the mind is the Brahman" is imparted, and is regarded as inadequate.[18] In a dialogue, between Yājñavalkya and Maitreyī, he says, "just as when a drum is being beaten, one is not able to grasp the external sound, but by grasping the drum or the beater of the drum, the sound becomes grasped."[19] The meaning implied here is, in the case of the knowledge of the external world, if one is not able to grasp the external worlds as it is in itself, by grasping the mind, or by grasping the Ātman, the external world becomes grasped. Ranade, R.D. explains the passage as follows. Ātman here is compared to the drum beater or lute player etc. while the mind by which the Ātman perceives is compared to the drum or lute and the external world is compared to the sounds issued forth by these instruments. By grasping the mind, Brahman can be comprehended.[20] Again, it is implied here that the ultimate substratum of all being the Brahman itself, when any part of it is grasped, the whole is known. Also, the mind acts as an instrument for the activity of the Ātman.

Ākāśa

In the passage of the *Chānd. Up.* quoted earlier, along with the *manas,* Ākāśa is also considered as the symbol of the Brahman. It says, "Ākāśa is to be worshipped as the Brahman." It further expounds how the Brahman as *manas* has as its four feet the cosmic organs, speech, breath, eye, ear; similarly, as it has fire, wind, Sun and heavenly regions as the cosmic gods.[21]

When Pravāhaṇa Jaivali was asked what was the final habitat of all things, he answered it was space. "All these beings emerge from space and are finally absorbed in the space. Space is greater than any of these things; space is the final habitat."[22] This passage from the *Chānd. Up.* is corraborated by another passage from the same Upaniṣad where it is said, "in space are all things born. Meditate upon space as the Highest Reality." In this passage the *ākāśa* appears as a mere symbol beyond which there is something else which is greater than it.[23]

Sun

The worship of the Sun as the Brahman is enjoined in the *Chānd. Up.*[24] The Sun is regarded as the first born of creation.

The first eleven sections of the third chapter of the *Chānd. Up* depict the Brahman as the Sun and the Sun as the phenomenal form of this Brahman.[25] Some passages of the Upaniṣads state that the Puruṣa in the Sun and the Puruṣa in the eye are the Brahman.[26] The *Tait. Up.* says that the Puruṣa in the yonder Sun and the Puruṣa in the eye are the same.[27] To Upakosala, his teacher tells, "the Sun, the moon, the lightning are only the uppermost landmarks on the way of the gods by which Puruṣa (who is not a man) (*tatpuruṣo amānavaḥ*) guides the soul to eternal union with the Brahman.[28]

Prāṇa, *manas, ākāśa* and Āditya are the most important symbols under which the worship of the Brahman is prescribed. There is a dominant note vibrating in the Upaniṣads, and that is the famous dictum that, "all this is verily Brahman." Certainly, any object associated with purity, holiness, strength or something sublime could be chosen as a fit object in which the Supreme Deity could be worshipped. The *Chānd. Up.* enumerates the objects such as the *nāman, vāk, manas, saṅkalpa, citta, dhyāna, vijñāna, anna, āpas, tejas, ākāśa, smara,* and *āśā* etc. which may be regarded as the symbols. So also *vāk, cakṣus, śrotra, manas,* and Prāṇa *hṛdaya*; the modes of representation of the Brahman; though treated as inadequate in the *Bṛ. Up,* are not rejected. Even the buzzing in the ear, the warmth of the body, the fire of digestion in the body (*vaiśvānara*) are recognized as the symbols of the Brahman. Among the symbols, the most important and fruitful, later on closely connected with the Yoga practice; which represents the suprasensible Brahman; which leads to the Brahman; and which is considered as the Brahman itself; is the sacred syllable Oṁ. the *Mānd. Up.* exalts the worship of the syllable Oṁ. Also, the *Tait. Up.* says that, "Oṁ is the Brahman, Oma is verily all this."[29] In harmony, Oṁkāra is described as *amātra* and *anatamātra* in the Gauḍpādakārikā[30] which will be studied later.

Vedic Deities Appearing in the Earlier Upaniṣads

The *Ṛv.* belongs to an age when the social stage of the race was profoundly religious and imaginative in its religion. Symbolism and a wide-spread imaginative or intuitive religious feeling go together. The symbol then is of 'something' which man feels to be present behind himself and his life and his activities; the Divine, the Gods, the Vast, the Unnamable, a hidden, living and mysterious nature of things. The Vedic deities are names, powers and personalities of the universal Godhead and they represent each, some essential greatness of the Divine Being. The gods are not simply poetical personalities of abstract ideas. But to the Vedic seers, they are living realities; the cosmic powers which support and embody them. In the *Ṛv*, the Gods; Indra,

Agni, Vāyu etc.; are generally the lords in their soverign right. Each one of them is Supreme in his place, is indeed the whole Godhead; exhibiting a facet of the Supreme Deity; retaining the particular features for his special function and a distinct personality for the purpose. The gods of the *Ṛv.* occupy a relatively subordinate position, as the Upaniṣadic teachings point only to the Ultimate Reality, which is One, without a second.

The gods of the Vedic pantheon; Indra, Vāyu, and Agni are frequently mentioned in the Upaniṣads as having a double function as Nature-power in the universe (*adhidaivatam*), and as the lord of the senses, life, mind and other instruments of the soul within us (*adhyātman*).

At the beginning of their treatise, the Upaniṣads invoke the grace of the gods, to remove the obstacles in the way of attaining spiritual wisdom. Deities like Indra, Varuṇa, Pūṣan, Mitra are invoked to bestow prosperity, to enjoy life alloted by God, and to have strong limbs.

Agni

As a Vedic deity, Agni is the father, mother, leader of all the beings. In the *Īśa. Up.*, Agni is requested to lead the path. It says, "O, Agni, lead us along the auspicious path to prosperity. O, the knower of our deeds, take away from us deceitful sins."[31] In the *Kaṭh. Up.*; for the fulfilment of Naciketa's boon, Yama describes to him the celestial fire; Jātavedas – the knower of all, which is aid to the heaven and which is the beginning (source) of the world.[32]

Pūṣan

Pūṣan was originally a solar deity, representing the beneficent power of the Sun. He is the guardian of roads, removing dangers out of the way and is called 'son of deliverance' (*vimuco napāt*)[33] In the *Īśa. Up.*, Pūṣan is requested to uncover the golden lid which covers the face of the Truth. He is praised as the sole seer, controller, offspring of Prajāpati and is prayed for the vision of God.[34]

The *Ken. Up.*, in an allegory, describes ignorance of the Vedic Gods; as regards the Brahman. The Brahman, once conquered for the gods. They thought that the victory and greatness is indeed their own. The Supreme, by his powers appeared before the Gods, who knew not what the spirit it was. The Jātavedas and Vāyu were unable to find out what that spirit was. Indra obtained the knowledge, that it was the Brahman, through the grace of the, most beautiful, Haimavatī Umā.[35] Here, Umā is the wisdom personified. Prajāpati of the Veda-s appears as the creator of the worlds, in the Upaniṣads. The gods and the demons are the offsprings of Prajāpati. Yama, who was the god of death, the lord of the world of the forefathers in the Veda-s, poses in the *Kaṭh. Up.* as the preacher, who imparts the Knowledge to Naciketas.

Vedic Deities Appearing in the Later Upaniṣads

Some of the Vedic–deities appear in the later Upaniṣads, but they are not specially adored independently or no special cult is seen to have developed in their honour. Many of these appear as the associates of the deities, described in the later Upaniṣads. The Vedic or the epic importance of the god seems to have diminished during this period also, but there are some spells incidentally mentioned in the later Upaniṣads, for their worship.

Agni

Agni is described as red in complexion. His flames are his hands. He is the messenger for sacrificial purpose. He mounts on a goat, and is the guardian of south-east direction.[36] The feminine power of Agni, is Āgneyi having flames as weapons in her hands. She is identified with Durgā.[37] It is advised that one should perform a sacrifice (Āgneyi-Iṣṭi), before taking to renunciation for Agni verily is the Prāṇa.[38] Agni is prayed for the protection of the cattle and persons in the house of worshipper.[39] The Agni-Gāyatrī spell describes him as one who has seven tongues.[40] He is the knower of all, protector of the sacrifices and possessed of hundred powers.[41]

Yama

He is dark blue in complexion. This deity presides over the southern direction.[42] Buffalo is his vehicle. Yamī is mentioned as his wife.[43] The Rudrākṣa bead with ten facets has Yama as the presiding deity and by wearing it on body, one overcomes evil and obtains solace of the mind.[44]

Varuṇa

He is the lord of the west. He is fair in complexion. He has a noose in his hand and is prayed, so that he may not snatch away life. He mounts on a crocodile.[45] The half *morā* of the Praṇava is regarded as that of Varuṇa.[46]

Indra

Indra is worshipped mainly as one of the ten regional guards protecting the eastern direction. He rides the divine elephant of the name Airāvata. He has golden complexion. As his weapons, he holds a thunderbolt and a goad in his hand.[47] He pierces the clouds for a shower of rain, due to which the crops grow. Indrāṇī is his wife, a personified feminine power. The sixth *mātrā*; out of the twelve *mātrā*-s; of the Praṇava is known as Aindri. If the Yogin parts with his life while meditating upon this *mātrā*, he gets *sāyujya* of Indra.[48] He is described as the great drinker of Soma. He resides in the 'world-egg-shell' as well as in the cave of human heart. Indra is omnipresent and supervises and controls the universe. He is the friend, the father and the mother of this universe. He assumes birth in different forms with his miraculous powers. He dwells in the world in thousand different ways and purifies it from all quarters. He is the giver of bounty and protector of the singers (of his praise). He is the one shining god, and goal of aspiration.[49] *Bāṣkalamantra Up.* glorifies Indra in this way and elevates him to the position of the Brahman. The Upaniṣad consists of twenty five verses, which in form and language resemble the Vedic *sūkta*-s. It may be said that, the *Bāṣkala-mantra Up.* may have once formed an integral part of the Bāṣkala recension of the *Ṛv*.[50]

Aśvins

Aśvins are mentioned as adorned with the garland of blue-lotuses and are prayed for obtaining intelligence.[51]

Following the natural tendency of the Indian mind, not to shake the beliefs of common men but to lead them on stage by stage to the understanding of the deeper philosophical meaning behind their beliefs, the Upaniṣads develop the Vedic ideas and symbols and give them wherever necessary, new meanings which relieve them of their earlier character. Thus, *e.g.*, the Brahmanical idea of sacrifice was modulated in the days of the Upaniṣads and was ultimately transformed into a new concept altogether.[52] It may be called as a mental sacrifice, which is helpful in the process of acquisition of spiritual knowledge. In the *Kaṭh. Up.*, it is said that, "he who has lit the Naciketa fire thrice, associating with the three, performs the three acts, crosses over birth and death."[52] Śaṅkara explains the verse as follows : (*i*) the word 'thrice' alternatively means, one who knows about him, (*ii*) one who studies about him and (*iii*) the one who practises what he has learnt. "Associating with the three" means; father; mother and teacher or Veda, Smṛti, and good men. And by "three acts" Śaṅkara suggests sacrifice, study and alms-giving.[54]

Here, it may be seen that the Brahmanical idea of sacrifice has acquired a new meaning leaving back the technicalities of the act. Similarly, the gods of the Vedic pantheon; though they occupy a relatively subordinate position as regards the Brahman; are frequently mentioned. (In the Upaniṣads, they serve a double function, as Nature-power in the universe and as the lords of the senses. It may be seen that the innovations are gradually introduced.) It may be observed that the two tendencies which characterise the thought of the Upaniṣads, *i.e.* loyalty to tradition and the spirit of reform appear here.

All the forms of god or some sign indicating the Brahman are technically called *pratīka*-s. "When the form is kept before the eyes, in the form of an idol, it becomes a *pratimā*."[55] All these are considered as the inferior forms of the Brahman for they are endowed with some qualities. All the Upaniṣads propound that the real form of the Brahman is different, that is, beyond the reach of the senses. The abstract Reality, and the philosophical speculations of the Upaniṣads were beyond the intellect of an ordinary man. For a common man, an adorable object with a more distinct personality of god, was necessary. During the period of the Epics, Purāṇa-s and later–Upaniṣads, gradually a major change took place. Abstract Vedic gods were replaced by the icons, symbols as objects of worship.

The approach to the goal; that is emancipation; is more of an abstract nature in the earlier Upaniṣads. The theistic worship is not detailed in these treatises. However, the later Upaniṣads elaborated these details.

They have a major portion devoted to deities like Śiva, Viṣṇu, Devī, Sūrya, Gaṇapati, Dattātreya and the like. Their importance increased during the period of the later Upaniṣads as different sects arose in honour of these deities.

The tendency of the *Ṛv.* to elevate a particular god, to whom one is offering hymns to the highest position and to look upon them as the manifestations of the same Reality; is resorted to by the writers of the sectarian Upaniṣads. Thus, the god addressed is treated as an independent and Supreme deity who alone is present in the mind of the worshipper. No depreciation of any other god is meant in this exaggerated form of praise.

Viṣṇu

Viṣṇu in the *Ṛv.* : Viṣṇu is a solar deity which occupies a comparatively subordinate position in the *Ṛv.* being celebrated in a few hymns. The anthropomorphic traits mentioned about him are the strides he takes, connected with which are his exclusive epithets wide-going (*ura-gāya*) and wide-striding (*urukrama*). With these steps, he traverses the earth or the terrestrial spaces. Two of his steps are visible to men but the third is beyond the flight of birds, the one none can reach. In the highest step of Viṣṇu, there is a fountain of honey, where men devoted to the god rejoice.[56] Viṣṇu, however, in spite of his comparatively subordinate position in the *Ṛv.* gained importance during the time of the Brāhmaṇa-s. He is identified with the sacrifice in the *Śat. Brā.*[57] During the Epic and Paurāṇic period, he rose to the rank of the Supreme Spirit. The reason for this elevation may be, the reverence for the third step of his, the highest cherished goal, the mysterious domain of Viṣṇu, the world of perpetual light.

Viṣṇu in the Earlier Upaniṣads

In the Āraṇyaka-s and the Upaniṣads, the sacrifice became a symbolic act. Viṣṇu, the solar deity was identified with the Sun and the Sun became the object of meditation to realize the Brahman. In the *Kaṭh. Up.* it is said that, "he who has the 'understanding' (*vijñāna*) as a charioteer, and controls the rein of his mind, completes his journey, that is the supreme abode of the all-pervading one (Viṣṇu)."[58] The name Viṣṇu (all-pervading) is used for the Supreme Self. In the *Mai. Up.*, food is called the form of Bhagavad-Viṣṇu, which sustains the universe.[59] Again, the triad of Brahmā, Viṣṇu, and Śiva is considered as the threefold manifestatin of the Supreme. The part of Him, characterized by goodness (*sattva*) is this Viṣṇu, says the Upaniṣad.[60]

Vaiṣṇavism

In the fourth and the fifth century B.C., Vaiṣṇavism first appeared as a religious reform like Buddhism or Jainism. However, it was based on the theistic principles.[61] Its early name was 'Ekāntika Dharma', or 'the religion of a single minded love and devotion to One. The *Bh.G.*, a philosophical and spiritual discourse, preached by Vāsudeva-Kṛṣna was its foundation. Soon, it assumed a sectarian form and was known as the Bhāgavata or Pañcarātra religion. It was noticed by Megasthenes at the end of the fourth century B.C. as the religion professed by a tribe of Kṣatriya-s named Sātvata. This faith, in the course of time, mingled itself with the existing one, in that of Nārāyaṇa. The idea of Nārāyaṇa had developed in the period of later Brāhmaṇa-s and

Āraṇyaka-s and had risen to the dignity of the Supreme Soul; and to that of Viṣṇu. Soon after the beginning of the Christian era, other elements such as marvellous deeds of Kṛṣna and his amorous dalliances with cowherdesses were incorporated into this system by the Ābhīra-s. Here too, he came to be regarded as a god. Vaiṣ ṇavism, blossomed till about the eight century, till the doctrine of spiritual monism and world-illusion was proclaimed by Śaṅkara and his followers. This was considered as against Bhakti or love which Vaiṣṇavism enjoined. In the eleventh century, Rāmānuja made strenous efforts to restore and spread the religion of Bhakti. He was followed in the north by Nimbārka who prominently advocated the cowherdess element of Vaiṣṇavism and enjoined the worship of Rādhā. In the thirteenth century, Mādhva established the doctrine of pluralism and considered Viṣṇu to be the Supreme God. Rāmānuja laid particular stress on the name of Nārāyaṇa, Mādhva on that of Viṣṇu, Nimbārka on the names of Kṛṣna and Rādhā. Rāmānanda's efforts in the fourteenth century brought in the name of Rāma in Vaiṣṇavism. He was followed by Kabir in the fifteenth century, but he condemned idol worship. In the sixteenth century, Vallabha proclaimed the worship of Kṛṣna and Rādhā. Caitanya, at about the same time enjoined the worship of grown up Kṛṣna and Rādhā, ever together as images of pure love. Popularisation of the faith in Rādhā acquired an exclusive prominence. In Mahārā-ṣṭra, discarding the Rādhā-Kṛṣnism, the saints Nāmadeva (whose date is uncertain) and Tukārāma (early seventeenth century) cultivated a more sober line of devotion. They laid particular stress on the purification of individual heart and moral elevation as a means to acquire eternal bliss. They preached the worship of Viṭhobā, the form of Kṛṣna; as the Supreme God.

Bhandarkar, R.G. points out that, in these various Vaiṣṇava systems, their spiritual elements are essentially derived from the *Bh.G.* and that the name of Vāsudeva as the Supreme Being stands in the background of all. The only difference is that they give prominence to the one or the other of the three elements mingled with Vāsudevism, and accordingly they set up metaphysical theory and the ceremonial which is imposed on their followers.[62]

The Doctrine of the Incarnations

"The Henotheism, fully explained by Max Müller and its ultimate result, the identification of various gods, influenced later thinkers.[63] For instance, Agni is the same as Varuṇa, Mitra, Indra etc. If these several gods are one, one may become several. This led to the conception of Incarnations which play important part in the later religious systems.[64] The basic scheme behind this idea of Incarnation seems to be that whenever any great calamity threatened the life of Gods and men, the Supreme Spirit who is an ocean of boundless grace, kindness, love and generosity assumed various forms and incarnated Himself to do away the wrong, to relieve the burden of the earth. The exact number of Incarnations of Viṣṇu is not definite. There are ten full Incarnations of Viṣṇu. This is the most commonly accepted number. They are Matsya, Kūrma, Varāha, Nṛsiṁha, Vāmana, Paraśurāma, Rāma, Kṛṣṇa, Buddha and Kalki.

The later Upaniṣads adore various forms of Visṇu such as Hari, Nārāyaṇa, Vāsudeva, Veṅkaṭeśa and Rasikānanda and describe them in detail. Some of the later Upaniṣads are specially devoted to the Avatāra-s like Nṛsiṁha, Rāma, Kṛṣṇa but rest of the incarnations are merely mentioned without giving any special details about them.

Description of Viṣṇu in the later Upaniṣads

Viṣṇu is so called because he pervades all the world.[65] The etymological meaning thus, signifies his omnipresence. Viṣṇu has a complexion like blue cloud. He wears a yellow silken garment, a crown and ear-rings. Kaustubha gem shines on his chest. He holds a conch, disc, mace and sword in his four hands. He is adorned by garlands of forest flowers.[66] For his vehicle, he has an eagle named Garuḍa.[67] The *Pāramātmika Up.* in its commentary takes resort of the Viṣṇu, Matsya, Varāha, Garuḍa, Narsiṁha and Padma Purāṇa-s, to describe the deity Viṣṇu.

Viṣṇu resides in the Vaikuṇṭha and this world can be reached by muttering his spell.[68] The *Pāramātmika Up.* mentions the worlds called Āmoda, Pramoda, Samamoda, and Vaikuṇṭha as situated in the ascending order. A world, highly lustrous is above all these worlds, which is the world of Vāsudeva and is covered by twelve coverings. The full moon always shines over there. The devotees of Viṣṇu go to the world of bliss, which is the highest of all the worlds.[69] Viṣṇuloka is situated above Rudraloka and below the Sudarśana discus. It has the expanse of seven crores of Yojana-s.[70]

The Deeds of Viṣṇu

Viṣṇu destroyed Bhīmaka demon.[71] He killed Rāhu and placed his head in the sky.[72] Through his various incarnations[73] he removes the evil on the earth.[74] He assumes form again and again on the earth for the sake of his devotees.[75] These are his benevolent deeds.

Cosmic Deeds

He pervades all the three worlds[76] and having pervaded, he has his form extended beyond it by ten *aṅgula*-s.[77] He supports Brahmā on the lotus springing up from his navel.[78] Viṣṇu rains down water at the time of femine.[79] His three steps are referred to in the *M.N. Up.*[80] *Mudgalopaniṣad* in sectarian fashion, equates the Puruṣa with Nārāyaṇa.[81] Accordingly, the Upaniṣad explains the Puruṣasūkta. Herein, Puruṣa with thousand heads is Nārāyaṇa. He is all that has been and will be. He instructed the creator Brahmā, as to how he should create. He was told that his limbs were the sacrificers, the knot of the heart was the oblation to be offered, the spring season was the fuel and the autumn was the essence (*rasa*). Brahmā created the world by worshipping that fire.

The later Upaniṣads describe Viṣṇu as the form of Vāsudeva, Hari, Nārāyaṇa, and Rāma etc. All are one but with different names.

Viṣṇu as Oṁkāra

The *Nādabindū Up.* describes the *mātrā*-s of the Oṁkāra, where the seventh *mātrā* is described as Vaiṣṇavī-*mātrā*.[82] If a devotee parts with life when in seventh *mātrā*, he obtains Vaiṣṇava-*pada*. The second *pāda* of the Nṛsiṁha-formula is equated with the syllable *'U'* of the Oṁkāra and Viṣṇu.[83] The *Brahmavidyopaniṣad* equates the syllable *'U'* in the Oṁkāra with Viṣṇu.[84] But in the *Pāramātmika Up.* it is told that the syllable *'A'* of the Oṁkāra represents Viṣṇu.[85]

Viṣṇu as the Brahman

The later Upaniṣads attribute all the qualities with which the indescribable Brahman is described to Viṣṇu and thus, Viṣṇu is exalted to the position of the Brahman. It is stated that Viṣṇu is immanent in all things and he abides in the hearts of all.[86] He is described as omniscient and omnipotent, the substratum, the Lord, Creator, Protector and Destroyer of all. He is the Being and non-Being and yet different from them. He is the Knowledge incarnate and yet beyond it. He is all joy and one object to be sought by the aspirant. He is verily the Brahman beyond all the time, action and qualities. He is symbolised by the sacred word Oṁ. He is without a beginning and an end, taintless, changeless, without name and pure. The *turīya* and the state beyond (*turīyātīta*) is Viṣṇu who is the same as Nārayaṇa.[87] Further, it is explained that the Lord is manifest (*sākāra*) and eternal. The contradiction implied in the bodily form of the God and his eternal nature is explained as, "This is all due to the power of the Lord. Both the embodied and unembodied forms of the Lord are real."[88]

Kṛṣṇa

Kṛṣṇa is one of the important incarnations of Viṣṇu, and is considered as the Supreme Being himself. Kṛṣṇa is so called because he destroys sins.[89] He has lotus-eyes and has dark blue complexion like a cloud. He is adorned with a garland of forest flowers. (*vanamālīśvaraḥ*) He wears bracelets on the wrists and the armlets of *mālati* flowers. He has a deep navel and straight nose. His feet are adorned with the anklets (*Sāmarahasya Up. Up. S.* pt. II. p. 265).

Metaphoric Description

The five elements form the conch, the mind becomes the Sudarśana disc, the primordial *māyā*, is the weapon called Śāraṅga, the universe is the lotus. All these things are held in his hands by Kṛṣṇa. The three qualities *sattva, rajas, tamas* and *ahaṁkāra* constitute his four hands. The first lore (*ādyā vidyā*) constitute his mace. Duty, wealth and desire are the divine ornaments. His neck comprises of, 'what is beyond quality' (*nirguṇa*) is adorned by *māyā*, which is difficult to conquer. His head is crowned, in the form of *sattva* quality; and the earrings are of imperishable existence. One who meditates thus, attains salvation.[90]

Deeds of Kṛṣṇa

He is the destroyer of Kaṁsa clan and the killer of the demons Keśin and Cāṇūra. He is the vanquisher of the demon Ahi. He is the destroyer of Pūtanā and Tṛṇāvarta. He lifted the Govardhana mountain. He is the charioteer of Pārtha.[91]

Kṛṣṇa and Oṁkāra

The comparison with the syllables of the Praṇava is beautifully presented in some Upaniṣads. Rāma, the son of Rohiṇī arises from the syllable *'A'*. Pradyumna is the Taijasa Ātman compared to the syllable *'U'*. Aniruddha is the Prajñātman who arises of the syllable *'M'*, and Kṛṣṇa on whom the whole universe depends is the Turīya, that is the *Ardha-mātrā*. Rukmiṇī represents the *bindū*; she is the power of Kṛṣṇa and is the primeval cause of the creative energy of the universe. She has the inseparable association with Kṛṣṇa the Paramātman himself.[92]

Kṛṣṇa as the Brahman

Kṛṣṇa is omnipresent, infinite and ever abiding. He is the

Ātman. He is one of the two birds sitting on the tree without enjoying the fruit of the *pippala* tree, who simply looks on and is strong and luminous. He is the God Kṛṣṇa who is the Supreme Self. Here, Kṛṣṇa is described as the witness (*sākṣin*).[93] He is one, who stands in the solar disc as Virāṭ Puruṣa. Kṛṣṇa is the knowledge incarnate, and he is the form of the transcendental bliss. Kṛṣṇa is the creator. The eighteen universes, the twelve Suns, Rudra-s, Prajāpati, holy places, the ambrosia, water, the Selves; all are born of Kṛṣṇa.[94]

The Upaniṣads describe the deity, the physical form and the personality of a deity. The associates of the deity, the vehicle etc. are described. Also, the metaphoric description is presented. The consort of the deity is described as the creative power, through which the creation of the universe takes place. The deity is compared with the *mātrā*-s of the syllable Oṁ. Finally, the deity is described as the Brahman incarnate. Such is the pattern of the description of deity in the Upaniṣads.

Rāma

This incarnation of Viṣṇu is considered as one of the most important one. Till today the worship of this popular God goes on in different parts of India. The cult of Rāma exists over a pretty wide area in the present days. The cult of Rāma according to Bhandarkar, R.G. must have come into existence about the eleventh century.[95] Vāsudevism has penetrated into most of the Hindu ceremonies. The twenty four names of Viṣṇu are repeated by Hindus at the beginning of every ceremony. However, the name of Rāma is not included in them. At the end of *śrāddha* ceremony, Janārdana, Vāsudeva; who is considered as a form of ancestors is prayed and it is said that, 'May he be satisfied with the act'. At the time of marriage ceremony also, the groom and the bride are identified with Viṣṇu and Lakṣmī respectively and not with Rāma and Sītā. Therefore, it may be said that the cult of Rāma is modern. The later Upaniṣads devoted to Rāma serve as the scriptures of the sect.[96] Viṣṇu as Rāma is specially dealt with in the *Rāma. P. Tā. Up.*, *Rāma. U. Tā. Up.*, and the *Rāmarahasyopaniṣad.* The *Rāma. U. Tā. Up.* may belong to a later date as one can see the passages repeated from the earlier two Upaniṣads.

Personality and Associates of Rāma

According to the later Upaniṣads, Mahāviṣṇu was pure consciousness and was believed to have been born of the king Daśaratha of Raghu clan. By the wise, he was proclaimed as Rāma because; he destroyed the demons; he shone forth in all his splendour and glory and delighted the earth. He is One, in whom the Yogins rejoice.[97]

Having incarnated himself in this world, along with Sītā, he shines like the moon. For ever she is at his side; like Puruṣa, with Prakṛti. Describing the concrete form of Rāma, this Upaniṣad states that he wears a yellow garment, the earrings in his ears and an ornament set with rubies in his neck. He has a charming face, full of grace. He is a great warrior who wields a bow, and with his eight ministers, he is a mighty conqueror. He is the valiant scion of the race of Raghus. Sītā, the Prakṛti incarnate, is conspicuously seated in his lap, decked with jewels and with her complexion like polished gold. Rāma is embraced by her with her hands.[98] It further states that for obtaining release from the bonds of ignorance; the form of Rāma seated on lotus-bed on the banks of the river Śarayū, in the *vīrāsana* posture and *jñānamudrā,* accompanied by Sītā and Lakṣmaṇa should be meditated upon.[99] For the worshippers of the Yantra; the Upaniṣad recommendes the worship of Rāma-*ṣaṭkoṇa yantra* which describes the splendour and glory of coronation ceremony with his entire retinue.[100]

The Deeds of Rāma

The *Rāma. P. Tā. Up.* narrates the story of Rāma's forest exile. The Upaniṣad views Rāvaṇa's character with a different perspective. There, it stated that Sītā was kidnapped by him, in order to obtain the final beatitude and to enjoy the bliss of four kinds of release, when he would be killed by Rāma as destined.

Again, according to this Upaiṣad Rāma's search for Sītā was motivated by a noble purpose, *i.e.* to release Viṣṇu's retinue who were born as demons due to the curse of a Brāhmaṇa.

Rāma and Lakṣmaṇa killed the demon named Kabandha. Rāma killed the ape Vālin and installed Sugrīva in his place, for he was an ideal king. Aided by his perfect devotee Hanumāna, Lakṣmaṇa etc., he conquered the city of Laṅkā, killed Rāvaṇa, Indrajīt, Kuṁbhakarṇa etc. and appointed Bibhīṣaṇa as the king of the city. Rāma as *saguṇa* Brahman is described as having two to eighteen hands. According to Brahmayogin, the commentator of the Upaniṣad, his arms represent Sītā, Lakṣmaṇa and so on.[101]

Metaphoric Descriptions

Rāma is described as the absolute embodiment of the divine Bliss and is said to be the *ardhamātra* of the Oṁkāra.[102] The limbs of Rāma are described to be, the son of the wind, Vāṇī, Durgā, Vighneśa, Kṣetrapālaka, the Sun, the moon, Nārāyaṇa, Nṛsiṁha, wind, Varāha, Sītā, and Praṇava etc.[103]

Rāma as the Brahman

Rāma is the 'form' of infinite existence,[104] resembles fire, due to his lustre and resembles the moon with cool beams pacifying his faithful votaries.[105] Rāma is described as the Brahman and Nārāyaṇa is a part of Rāma. Rāma is the Highest Self and both Rāma and Sītā are the objects of worship. The *Rāma P. Tā. Up.* describes him as the cause of the world. Verily, he who is the great Brahman and the Self of all gods, pervades the whole universe.[106] The identification of Rāma with the inner-Self and with Praṇava is established on the same lines as that of Nṛsiṁha with the same.[107]

Śiva

Śiva is one of the great gods of the Hindu Trinity; Brahmā, Viṣṇu and Maheśa. Śiva represents, "the earliest and the most general impression of Nature on man, the impression of endless and pitiless change, the recurrent ebb and flow of life" according to Lyall.[108]

The worship of Śiva, has its origin in the distant past. Traces of it are found in the Veda-s. Seals discovered at Mohenjodaro are suggestive of the worship of Śiva as Paśupati.[109] Śaivism has flourished in its *pratyabhijñā* form in Kashmir and hence is known as Kashmir Śaivism. This form of Śaivism represents monistic idealism. In Tamilnadu, it has developed as *Śaiva-siddhānta* with strong theistic and pluralistic features. The early hymns of the Veda-s speak of Rudra, not Śiva. But some of the features associated with Śiva in the later times are found in Rudra; such features as Śiva having braided hair, wearing a hide, dwelling in the mountains etc. The dreadful and destructive phenomena are usually powers of nature as seen in the storms and lightning, disease and death. In these, the old Āryans saw Rudra, which means, 'one who howls'. So Rudra is conceived as the personification of the destructive powers of nature. But Āryans believed in appeasing the dreadful phenomena by prayers, worship and offerings. With such efforts, the god becomes Śiva, meaning benignant. Accordingly, the name Śiva occurs in the later portions of the Veda-s.

Narayana Iyer, C.V. does not accept the interpretation of the word Rudra as, howler. He observes that two functions are attributed to Rudra; that of bestowing prosperity and of removing the sufferings. He quotes the English translation given by Muir, which says, "thou art the god so-called, who drive this away." Muir, following Sāyaṇa, interpretes the meaning of the root *rud*; from which the word Rudra is derived as sin or suffering, which causes suffering etc. Iyer says, if this view be correct, it becomes possible to explain how the Rudra of the *Ṛv.* became Śiva in the later period; because the etymological explanation of the word Śiva bears correspondence with that of Rudra. The root *so* means to 'make thin' or to 'attentuate' (*siddhāntakaumudī*). One of the meanings of the word Śiva is 'he who attentuates sin.' Both Rudra and Śiva, therefore, mean, "he who removes sin or suffering."[110]

It is probable that early Āryans connected suffering with sin and invoked the grace of Śiva to overcome sin which is the cause of suffering. Śiva is no more responsible for pain and disease. Sins arise by violation of rules of morality. Likewise diseases occur by violation of rules of hygiene and health. There is a fascinating aspect in this god and there is a terrific aspect also. Beyond both, there is a mysterious aspect. Thus, Rudra or Śiva is not to be viewed exclusively with his terrifying aspect or with his benign aspect. He is characterised by these aspects and yet has many more aspects, such as the accessibility (*saulabhya*), infinite majesty or Supremacy (*paratva*).

Śiva in the Veda-s

Śiva is Rudra of the *Ṛv*. He is celebrated in only three entire hymns, in part of another, and in one conjointly with Soma. He occupies a subordinate position in the *Ṛv.* He is often associated with Maruts; who are considered as his offsprings. Rudra is described as having beautiful lips (*Ṛv.* II.33.5), and a braided hair. (*Ṛv.* I.114.15). He has a healing and cooling hand (*Ṛv.* II.33.7). He is described as ruddy brown whitish bull and is radiant (*Ṛv.* II.33.3). Rudra is easily invoked (*Ṛv*. II.33.6) and is auspicious Śiva. The epithet Śiva is not yet peculiar to any particular deity which became the regular name of Rudra's historical successor in the post-Vedic mythology.[111] In the *Yv.*, he is the god who can do both good and bad. His greatness is specially praised in a chapter called Rudrādhyāya. He is described as the crying Agni and stood as Agni on the altar, longing for food (*Tait. Saṁ.* 1.5.1). The gods then offered the *Śatarudriya* offering to him. By the time of the *Av.*, He was the god Rudra-Śiva. In the *Śatapatha Brāhmaṇa*, he is known as Tryaṁbaka (*Śat. Brā*. 2.6.2.9). Agni, Paśupati, Bhava, Śarva, Īśāna, Mahādeva and Ugradeva are said to be different forms of Rudra and he is identified with Agni who has these forms (*Śat. Brā*. 6.1.3.7). But Bhava and Śarva are treated as two distinct deities and they rule over two-footed and four-footed beings respectively. Śarva is called the archer and Bhava, the king in the *Av.* (*Av.* IV. 28.1), (*Av.* VI. 93.2).

Śaivism

Rudra, the terrible howler who represented the destructive phenomena of the nature, when propitiated became the auspicious Śiva, the benificient Śaṅkara. Subsequently, he was transformed into the god who resides in fire and water and pervades the entire universe. He dwells in all beings, herbs and trees and is the Supreme ruler of all. When he rose to this position, he became the subject of speculation in the Upaniṣad; by meditating on whom and by knowing whose omnipresence; a man attained blissful serenity. The awful and wild side of his nature was not forgotton, but went on developing. And then the religious schools such as that of the Pañcarātra-s were established, a school which regarded Rudra or Paśupati as the God to be adored was set up, its founder being Lakutin or Lakulin meaning, the holder of the club. The work attributed to him was, Pañcāratha and the system he set up was known as Pāśupata. Two extreme schools were developed out of these and also one which was more moderate was known by the name of Śaiva. According to Bhandarkar, R.G., the traces of these schools are found from about the second century of the Christian era, to about twelfth.[112]

The term Paśupati literally means the lord of flocks. *Paśu* refers to all souls; in the state of bondage. *Pāśa* is the threefold cord, by which the souls are bound. *Āṇava, karman,* and *māyā* together constitute the threefold cord. *Āṇava* is the primal impurity (*mūlamala*); coborn, so to say, with the souls. *Karman* and *māyā* are those, which came later. (*āgantuka*). *Āṇava* defiles *karman* and *māyā* which by themselves are neutral. *Pati* the Lord, who is ever free, helps the souls to free themselves from their bondage. It is through Śakti as an auxiliary of cause that Śiva engages in the activities of creation and dissolution. The dissolution is periodic to give rest to the souls. These activities are the sports of the Lord. It has redemptive purpose, having two features *viz.* obscuration (*tirobhāva*) and bestowal of grace (*anugraha*). The term *paśu*, which refers to the souls in bondage, indicate the plurality of the souls. All *āstika-darśana*-s except the Advaita

Vedānta, accept the concept of the plurality of the souls. In the Advaita Vedānta, plurality of the souls is denied only at the transcendental level and not at the empirical level. The knowledge about *paśu, pāśa, pati;* constitutes the first part of the Śaiva system which is known as the *Vidyāpāda.* The second part; *Kriyāpāda*; throws light on the accomplishment of the formula, worship, muttering name of the Lord (*japa*), oblations in the fire etc. In the third part, or the Yoga part; the principles are mentioned. The deities presiding over them, the lords of different worlds, the individual soul and the all ruling soul, the attainment of the *māya* and *mahāmāya*, the attainment of the miraculous powers, methods of restraint of the breath, meditation, *samādhi*, the position of the circles (*cakra*-s) in the body etc. are taught. The last part contains matters complimentary to and explanatory of the actions enjoined in the second part. The doctrines of the Śaiva school are more moderate and rational than those of the Pāśupata school.[113]

The Śaiva school that developed later, holds that Śiva possesses power (*śakti*), consisting of the rudiments of the material world and the individual souls and from that power, the whole world is developed. It may be noticed that both Pāśupata and Śaiva schools treat the individual and the universal soul as different from each other. When the soul is emancipated, the Pāśupata-s hold that it shakes off ignorance and attains boundless knowledge while the Śaiva-s maintain that the soul becomes Śiva himself, but without the power of creation. This doctrine shows resemblance with that of Rāmānuja and may be called as qualified spiritual monism where Śiva, characterized by 'power' creates. The Śaiva school (*āgamika*) comprises of the school of Śaiva-siddhānta, Tamil Śaivas, Kaśmir Śaivas, Vīra-Śaiva (*liṅgāyata*-s) etc.

Rudra-Śiva in the Earlier Upaniṣads

The seeds of the later Śaivism can be seen in the earlier Upaniṣads. Though the concept of Rudra-Śiva was being developed since the days of the *Ṛv.*, we get a fuller doctrine of Śiva in the *Śvet. Up.* Though the Upaniṣad glorifies Śiva, it does not appear to have been composed in a sectarian spirit. But Ranade, R.D. opines, "it may have been written in interest of Śaivism."[114] The speculations about the nature of God, his relations to man and world acquired a living and active personality in the minds of people. This God was Rudra-Śiva. The Upaniṣad is theistic in character and identifies the Supreme Brahman with Rudra who is conceived as the material and efficient cause of the world, and its protector and guide.

The Upaniṣad says that, "It is the God Īśa who supports both mutable and immutable, the manifest and the unmanifest. As contrasted with Him is the powerless Ātman, who is bound on account of his being the enjoyer of the fruits of action; but when this Ātman knows the Īśa, he is relieved of his bonds - (*pāśa*-s)."[115] The philosophy of *Paśu, Pati* and *Pāśa* is, thus, seen in the seed form in the Upaniṣad. "Rudra is the only Lord God, they do not maintain another God. He who rules these worlds by his powers, standing before every man's face and destroying the created world in anger at the time of dissolution."[116] "The Lord Śiva is hidden in all the beings, he is the one, who envelops the world and by whose knowledge alone comes the freedom from the meshes of ignorance."[117] "The God spreads the manifold meshes in his hands and moves along the world. He creates and recreates and maintains his sovereignity over all the worlds."[118] The attributes of the Supreme Soul are given in very general terms and he is referred to by the non-sectarian name Deva, but Deva often is identified with Rudra, Śiva, Īśāna or Maheśvara. But this does not indicate that these names have been selected for the purpose of raising Rudra-Śiva to the Supreme godhead to the exclusion of another god. According to Bhandarkar, R.G., the age in which the *Śvet. Up.* was composed, Rudra-Śiva alone was the Supreme God and the germs of devotion (*bhakti*) and love, which manifested themselves at this time, were directed towards him.[119]

In the *Ken. Up.*, the name of Umā occurs. She is the daughter of Himavat but she is not mentioned as the wife of Rudra or Śiva, though later, she was known to be so.[120]

Though the conception of Rudra-Śiva was being developed from the days of the *Ṛv.* and the *Av.*, it finds expression in the days of the *Śvet. Up.*, where the doctrine of Śiva is seen to have a philosophical foundation for the theistic way of glorification. Along with the trinitarian monism, this Upaniṣad became the pivot of the doctrine of Śaivism.

The tenets of the different Śaiva sects are reflected in the later Śaiva Upaniṣads. The later Upaniṣads refer to the Āgama-s; (4th to 10th Cen. A.D.); the authoritative books of the Tantra-s, while prescribing the worship of Śiva.[121] They are in the form of a dialogue between Śiva and his consort; they comprise instructions concerning the worship of Śiva.

Śiva in the Later Upaniṣads

Description and Personality of Śiva

Śiva is the lord of North-east direction, and has white complexion. His vehicle is the bull.[122] He is *ūrdhvaretas* and has an ugly eye.[123] He resides on a peak of Kailāsa mountain with Umā, his consort. His body is besmeared with ashes. He is said to have five faces with which he smiles with joy.[124] He has the Gaṅgā on his head and his forehead is adorned by the crescent of the moon. Dakṣiṇāmūrti Śiva has the colour of marble or silver. With his one hand he holds a pearl rosary. With another hand, he carries a pitcher, signifying the pitcher of immortal learning.[125]

The tips of his hand are in *jñānamudrā*. He wears a belt of a serpent, has three eyes and wears various ornaments. He is seated under a Nyagrodha tree, having an axe in one hand, and the other is placed on the knee.[126] Also; adorned by the sacred ashes, milky white in complexion, his hands holding a lotus, a rosary, a lute, a book respectively having a *jñānamudrā* and sitting in a Yogic-posture (*Yogapaṭṭa*); he looks attractive.[127] The knowers of the Brahman call him Dakṣiṇāmūrti-Śiva, for his face is turned to gaze at the 'intellect' which is in the southern direction.[128]

Śiva has one thousand feet. He is the soul of this universe.[129] He has Soma, Sūrya, fire as his three eyes which have the lustre of countless suns and moons.[130] He is glorified as the creator of all beings.[131] Elsewhere, while glorifying Śiva, he is identified with *ṛta, satya* and even with Para Brahma.[132]

Associates of Śiva

Umā stands to the north of Śiva and Brahmā to the east. Viṣṇu to the south and Indra to the west. The numberless Gaṇa-s, endowed with weapons, to destroy sin stand in the Southern direction. Śiva resides in the Rudraloka called Śivavaikuṇṭha having the expanse of seven-crores of *Yojana*-s. The sages, the devotees and the worshippers of Paśupati reside in that world.[133]

Śiva in the Liṅga Form

This is the concrete form of Śiva, often worshipped in the temples of Śiva. He is worshipped in the form of idol also. The injunctions regarding the making of a Śiva-*liṅga* are given in detail in the *Śivopaniṣad*. Detailed rules about the measurements from the ground to the altar and above the altar have been given. It is believed that Skanda resides at its bottom, Devī in the middle and Rudra at its top. Also, it is said that the triad of Brahmā, Viṣṇu and Śiva resides in the *liṅga*. These three parts are also identified with the three *guṇa*-s, three worlds and three Veda-s.[134] Śiva-*liṅga* is worshipped by different deities and is accordingly made up of pearl, gold, Vaidūrya, sapphire etc.[135]

The Liṅgāyata-s worship the *liṅga* placed in a silver box and wear it on their body. The later Upaniṣads devoted to the worship of Śiva-*liṅga* appear to have been composed to serve as the authoritative doctrines of the sects engaged in the Liṅga worship.

Prāṇa-Liṅga and Viśva-Liṅga

These *liṅga*-s are of abstract nature. The fivefold character of the *liṅga* is earth, water, lustre, wind and sky and the five sense-organs refer to the five fold character of the *liṅga*. The *liṅga* of the nature of Praṇava is known as Brahma-*liṅga*. Vidyā-*liṅga* is of the form of knowledge.

The Śiva-*liṅga*, is placed inwards, in the cavity of heart, which is of the measure of a thumb. Those who know this reach the highest abode (*para pada*).[136] There is a beautiful metaphor in the *Śivopaniṣad*, where the body is identified with the temple of Śiva. And the lotus of the heart is the altar and the Oṁkāra is the Śiva-*liṅga* which should be meditated upon.[137]

Śiva as Vaṭuka

The Śaivopaniṣads add one more form of Śiva and it is that of the Vaṭuka. The description of this form of Śiva occurs here for the first time. *Vaṭukopaniṣad* is devoted to the description of this god. It describes him, as born from Akṣara.[138] The creation of the world is attributed to Vaṭuka, because when he breathed out, darkness seemed to rise up; from that darkness, water arose, when the water was churned by his fingers, foam was formed, from that foam an egg was formed which gave rise to Brahmā, Oṁkāra, Sāvitrī and Gāyatrī successively. Gāyatrī finally created the worlds.[139] The earth, the mid-region and the heaven are his *Ādi, Madhya* and head respectively.[140] He is omnipresent having different forms in all the directions *viz.* he is Hetuka in the east, Tripurāntaka in the south-east and so on.[141] Vaṭuka is Death. He is subtle. He helps to cross the old age, death and the cycle of births and deaths. When Vaṭuka sleeps, he withdraws the subjects.[142]

Śiva as Śarabha

Śarabhopaniṣad praises god Śiva as the highest and Supreme among all the gods.[143] Śarabha created Brahmā and Viṣṇu. He cut off the fifth head of Brahmā.[144] he defeated Viṣṇu at the time of sacrifice performed by Dakṣa, and bound him by snakes.[145] Śarabha is described as an animal, with eight feet. Four feet below the body and four, above the body.[146] He destroys the three worlds by the fire from his third eye.[147] He gave Brahmā the creative power and Viṣṇu, the power of sustenance from the Brahman through himself. He is formless, changeless and eternal. Śarabha performed many deeds and they are recorded in this Upaniṣad. Śarabha is superior to all the incarnations of Viṣṇu. This form was assumed by Śiva for killing Nṛsiṁha who was destroying everything after killing Hirṇyakaśyipū. The Upaniṣad seems to have been composed to highlight the supremacy of Śiva over Viṣṇu and other gods.

The Śivopaniṣads describe Śiva as Sadāśiva, Mahādeva, Paśupati in detail. They have blended Rudra and Śiva into one. But at times they make distinction between the two. Both the gentle and the formidable forms are described in the Upaniṣads. Thus, the *Jābāla Up.* says that Rudra enlightens a man at the time of death, and makes him free from bondage of rebirth.[148] He saved the people by drinking the poison which came out from the sea, when it was churned. Even though one is low born, with faith and devotion to Rudra, he becomes superior to a Brāhmin. Even a Cāṇḍāla who worships Śiva-liṅga is superior.[149] The *Atharvaśiras Upaniṣad* identifies Rudra with the Brahman. Rudra enters the world and sustains it. He is mysterious in nature. He is omnipresent infinite, subtle.[150] The *Dhyānabindupaniṣad* points out that Brahmā, Viṣṇu and Rudra are the deities which should be meditated upon.[151] The *Nīlarudra. Up.* says that Rudra is one who cures with water (*jalāṣabheṣaja*). He cures the gastric troubles. He is described as the anger incarnate (Bhavabhāma Bhavamanyu). Śambhu in the capacity of granting grace.[152]

The authors of the *Śaivopaniṣads* have propounded Vedānta doctrines through Śiva-worship and have blended Sāṁkhya, Yoga, Saṁnyāsa, Bhakti, *Mantra* and Tantra with a view to enable people to reach the final goal of human life, *i.e.* to realise the Brahman. The rituals are simplified and different modes of worship are beautifully blended together.

The Gods, Viṣṇu and Śiva, are exalted to the highest position by the Vaiṣṇava and the Śaiva Upaniṣads respectively. There is an attempt to reconcile these two great Gods. There are many references found in the Upaniṣads in which Śiva and Viṣṇu are equated. There is no difference between Śiva and Viṣṇu says *Śarabhopaniṣad.*[153] The *Skanda. Up.* says that, the heart of Viṣṇu is Śiva and the heart of Śiva is Viṣṇu indeed.[154] Viṣṇu meditates on Śiva and *vice-versa*. The lotus feet of Maheśa were worshipped by Viṣṇu who in turn was favoured by Śiva.[155] Śiva drank the deadly poison by meditating upon the name of Viṣṇu.[156]

The *Siddhāntaśikhā Up.* is the only Upaniṣad which states that one who considers Śiva as Viṣṇu perishes, because there is no other real truth in the world other than Śiva. But when the knowledge that, Śiva is the Supreme God dawns upon a man, all his sins are burnt and one does not sink down in this worldly ocean. The Upaniṣads identify Viṣṇu with Gaṇeśa, Sūrya, Devī, Brahmā, Oṁkāra etc. Śiva is identified with Viṣṇu, Vaṭuka, Śakti (Devī) etc.

Brahmā : In the Earlier Upaniṣads

Regarding the theories of creation; of the world; one may notice that, except the details of the *Praśna Up.* and the *Tait. Up.*, nowhere else, the creator with a personal existence is brought in for the purpose of creation. The creation proceeds either from the elements, or from Being or Non-Being, or from hunger or even death. The theories are more or less naturalistic accounts of cosmogenesis.

But in the *Praśna Up.* we are told that the creator became desirous of creating and with that aim, he practised penance and first created a pair of Rayi and Prāṇa. Here, Pippalāda, the seer has conceived the notion of a 'duality of primary existence' (the matter and the spirit). It is said that in this way the creator was able to create all the dual existence in the world.[157] The *Tait. Up.* states that, "the creator, at the beginning practised a penance created all things that exist, and having created them, entered into them."[158] From these passages, it may be inferred that the idea of the creator is introduced here.

Brahmā in the Later Upaniṣads

The description of the Trinity of gods is seen in almost all the later Upaniṣads. In consonance with the Purāṇa-s, it is said that Brahmā is the creator of the world of this trinity of gods, Viṣṇu and Śiva are adored and worshipped; and different sects arose in their honour. But Brahmā remains only as the cosmic power personified. No cult is dedicated to Brahmā worship. The God plays a subordinate part, being only the creator of the world. The *Akṣamālika Up.*, *Tvmn. Up.* and *P. Haṁsa. P. Up.* describe him.[159] He is praised and requested to impart knowledge in the *Kalisana Up.*, *Kātyāyana Up.*, *Kaivalya Up.*[160] and many other Upaniṣads.

Description of Brahmā

Brahmā is the superintendent of the upward direction. His complexion is red. He has four faces in four directions. Earlier, he had five but his fifth head was cut off by Śiva. On this account, different legends are narrated in the Purāṇa-s. For his vehicle, he has swan. He holds a wooden pitcher in his hands. His wife is Brahmāṇī.[161] Gāyatrī, the goddess belongs to Brahmā.[162] He is one of the five limbs of the Brahman.[163] The Tulasī plant has Brahmā residing in its middle.[164] The *M.N. Up.* states a Gāyatrī spell in honour of Brahmā. In this spell, he is described as having four faces and holding a water-pot in his hands.[165] In the mental worship, Brahmā is identified with the 'mind'. He is identified with the first morā of the Oṁkāra. He is identified with Rudra. He resides on the left side of a Bilva-tree.[166] Brahmā is seated on a lotus in the region of the heart.[167] There are six Purāṇas devoted to him, namely Brahma P., Brahmāṇḍa P., Brahmavaivarta P., Mārkaṇḍeya P., Bhaviṣya P. and Vāmana Purāṇa.

However, it must be noted that Brahmā did not receive the same recognition in the later Hindu religion. No satisfactory reason can be given as to why he is ignored. It may be said that he has accomplished the task of single act of creation and is adored no more; but even this reason falls short of justification.

Although he is worshipped at other places (Thailand), even today, he is hardly worshipped in India.

Devī

In the Vedic literature, no female deity of predominant power is mentioned. They are the associates of god. Uṣas, Rākā, Aditi, Ilā etc. received offerings in the sacrifice along with the gods. Umā too, was the wife of a God and does not overshadow her male consort. The creative power of the God is deified and then described as Devī. But later on, the male god element is subdued by the female element which became predominant and the deity is considered highest goddess by her devotees. As the development of the idea of power (*śakti*) progressed, the goddesses were worshipped as goddesses in fierce forms, milder forms and sensual forms. *e.g.* Kālī, Sarasvatī and Tripurasundarī respectively. Devī is the object of worship for the school of Śākta-s, who are so called because they are the worshippers of Śakti. She is adored as a deity in the form of the mother of the universe.

In the Bhīṣmaparvan of the *Mbh.*, (*Mbh.*23.6) Durgā is praised by Arjuna under the advice of Kṛṣṇa, for the victory in the forthcoming battle. This verse indicates that, Durgā had already acquired such an importance that she was adored by men as a powerful goddess, able to fulfil their desires.

There is a group of goddesses known as Mahāvidyā-s. They have been known as a group since early medieval period; *i.e.*, around the tenth century.[168] However, some of them predated this development. They continued to be very well-known independently *e.g.* the fierce black goddess Kālī. She is also usually the primary (*ādi*) Mahāvidyā. Kamalā, or popularly known as Śrīlakṣmī is also included in this group. Tārā and Tripurasundarī are lesser known but still far from obscure are other examples of the Hindu goddesses who are popular on their own and as a part of the group. On the other hand, Bagalāmukhī, Chinnamastā, Dhūmāvatī and Mātaṅgī are rarely mentioned apart from the Mahāvidyā-s. Mahākālasaṁhitā enlists fifty one goddesses. Nine out of ten Mahāvidyā-s are mentioned therein. This text is dated as early as the tenth century and may be said to be having the earliest mention of the Mahāvidyā-s as a group.[169] Kālī, Tārā, Mātaṇgī etc. are described in the small sections (*upatantra*-s) in the Samamohatantra which was probably written in the fifteenth century.[170] Winternitz. M. opines, "the fact that the worship of Durgā, which plays so great a part in the Tantra-s harks back to the later Vedic period, does not prove that the Tantrism and the Tantra-s are of an equally venerable age. This goddess and her cult do unite traits of very different deities, Āryan and non-Āryan. The system of Tantra-s adopted many characteristics from the non-Āryan and non-Brahmanical cults. On the other hand, some essential traits of the Tantra-s can be found as far back as in the Atharva Veda. Śāktism was prevalent from the twelfth to the sixteenth century."[171]

An underlying assumption of many Śākta-texts is that the highest Reality is the Great-goddess and this infinitely great being manifests herself in a wide variety of forms. She assumes different forms at different times to maintain cosmic stability. She oversees the three principal cosmic functions; creation, maintenance and dissolution. She is Prakṛti, the inherent or vital principle of creation. The Devī-s or Mahāvidyā-s are the concrete expressions of the idea of many forms.

There are appropriate paths for each type of an aspirant. They are said to be of three types. Divya-s are superior and associated with *Sattvaguṇa*, Vīra-s are mixed type and may engage in left handed Tāntric rites and are associated with *rajoguṇa*. *Paśu*-s are the beastly types associated with *tamoguṇa*. And there are perhaps appropriate goddesses for them to worship.[172]

Alper, H. opines that the Tāntric development supported the return to power, in popular Hinduism, of the figure of the mother Goddess of numerable names – Devī, Durgā, Kālī, Pārvatī, Umā, Satī, and Tripurasundarī etc. whose cult rooted in the Neolithic past, had been overshadowed for a period of about thousand years by male divinities of the patriarchal Āryan pantheon.The goddess began to reassert herself in the period of the later Upaniṣ ads. She is today the important divinity again.[173]

These Devī-s or Mahāvidyā-s are noticed and described in the later Upaniṣads.

Mahādevī

Devī herself describes her form to the gods in the *Devy-upaniṣad.*[174] She is the form of the Brahman. She is the form of five elements and the whole world. Everything is born of her, and she is the ruler of the universe. She alone moves in various forms as Rudra, Vasu-s, Āditya-s and Viśvedeva-s.[175] Devī dwells in the lotus of the heart. She has complexion like that of the rising sun. Her form is attractive. Her hands are in Varada and Abhayamudrā. She has three eyes and she wears red clothes.[176] She is like fire in colour, and dazzling with knowledge. She is the destroyer of the demons and darkness. She supports Soma, Pūṣan, Bhaga, Viṣṇu, Brahmā and Prajāpati.[177]

From the above description, it may be observed that the functions of creation, preservation and dissolution, universal ruler and the inner controller, which are attributed to the Brahman are carried out by Devī. She is praised and is equated with the Higher Self. Here again, one can see the tendency to raise the personal deity to the position of the Brahman.

The nineteen names of Devī are mentioned in the *Bahvṛcopaniṣad Up. S.* (pp. 650-51). They include the names Dhūmāvatī, Bagalā, Mātaṅgī. These are the forms of Devī, described in the ten Mahāvidyā-s also; the sect which prevailed from the tenth century onwards as mentioned earlier. It may also be inferred that, the period of Devī Upaniṣads is parallel to that of the Mahāvidyā-s.

Kālī

Kālī is the concrete form of one of the powers of Śiva, which has terrible and destructive aspect.

The cosmic form of Kālī is described by Śiva to Pārvatī in the *Guhyakālī. Up*. Here, the subtle distinction between Kālī and Pārvatī has been presented where, Kālī has a formidble form and Pārvatī has a milder one. According to the cosmic description, Kālī gave rise to the whole universe. The verses (twenty-seven to eighty-four) which describe this are fashioned exactly like those in the *Śvet. Up*., the only difference being that the word Devī is used in place of the word Deva.

Kālī is described as the undiminishing and the highest lustre of the Sun. She is described as *guhya*, for her form is mystic, concealed in nature. Her form represents both good and evil aspects of the universe. And her eternal form can be known through Sāṁkhya and Yoga.[178]

Guhya Kālī, the mother of the universe is the Haṁsī sporting in the city of nine doors.[179] The *Kālikopaniṣad* describes Kālī as Kālikā with a complexion of a cloud filled with water. She has plump breasts, crooked jaw and a seat of corpse.[180] Her fifteen names enlisted in the *Kālikopaniṣad*, describe her lustrous and formidable form.[181] Kālī is so called, because she is the destroyer of death (*kāla*).[182] Her other eight names like Brāhmī, Vārāhī etc, with reference to the eight-petalled lotus are also mentioned in the Upaniṣad.[183]

The *Haṁsaṣodhopaniṣad* describes her as the beloved of Mahākāla. She is the ruler of the speech and rules over the great Tripura-s. She wears a garland of big skulls, and has a big belly. She crushes the enemy. She holds a rosary and a book in her hands. She removes poverty and laziness and is Mahālakṣmī herself.[184]

Durgā

The earliest passages of the worship of Durgā occur in the

Mbh. (*Mbh.*6.23) as seen earlier. The other names of Durgā in this passage are Kumārī, Kālī, Kāpālī, Mahākālī, Caṇḍī, Kātyāyanī, Karāta, and Vijayā etc.[185] The passage shows how the frightful and mild form of Devī were both known and mingled into one goddess. Bāṇa's '*Caṇḍīśataka*' probably dates back to the seventh century when the emperor Harṣa was in rule. The sect of Durgā was recognized under the form of the sect, the authoritative canon of which are the Tantra-s ranging from 500 to 900 A.D. The right hand school of the Śākta-s has come up from the influence of the *Bhāgavata Purāṇa*. Release is sought through emotional devotion towards the goddess. One of the auxiliary Purāṇa-s, Devī-Bhāgavata is considered as their chief scripture. The left hand school of the Śākta-s is traced even upto the period of 1800 A.D.[186] It may thus, be seen that the Upaniṣads belonging to Śakti belong to quite later period; ranging from 500 to 1600 A.D.

Durgā in the Later Upaniṣads

The etymological meaning of the word Durgā is; the one who saves her devotees from the calamities.[187]

The infinite, unborn and incomprehensible Durgā, lives in the lotus of the heart.[188]

Description

She is described as being seated on a golden lotus. She has three eyes and wears a crescent of the moon on her forehead.[189] She is refulgent like the morning Sun. She has a complexion like fresh Dūrvā grass. She wears many ornaments.[190] Sometimes she is described as sitting on a buffalo or on the corpse of the demon Mahiṣa killed by her. In this form, she holds a conch, a sword, a bow, a quiver, arrows, a trident, a discus and thorns in her hands. She has raised her threatening finger. She wears a yellow garment.[191]

She is also described as, riding on a lion and is dark in complexion.[192] She is encircled by the bright flames coming forth from her eyes. She has awful jaw, teeth and a dreadful face. She has a loud roaring laughter. Apart from her cosmic functions (as Prakṛti), she is the destroyer of the demons like Madhu, Mahiṣ āsura, Śumbha, Niśumbha, Dhūmralocana etc.[193] She is prayed for the cures of bodily ailments like fever, *vāta, pitta* and *apasmāra*. The fevers lasting for one to fifteen days even for a month or for a year are cured by her. She protects from all sorts of poisons. As Aruṇī or Vāruṇī she has been asked to free people from the debts and ward off evil influences of the planets respectively.[194]

If a particular spell is recited for twenty-one days as per the injunctions and then if a leaf or flower charmed with the spell is offered to a man or woman, he or she comes under one's sway. The enemy who torments the mind of a devotee is killed in seven nights from the commencement of the recitation of the formula.[195] The Upaniṣad enlists various formulae to destroy enemies. Atharvaṇic character, of using the spells for the destruction of enemies may be observed herein.

The Upaniṣad follows Advaita doctrines in general and the description of the methods of worship and the formulae are similar to those of Śākta texts and the Tantra-s.

Pītāmbarā

This form of Durgā is treated separately in the *Pītāmbaro-paniṣad*. She is adorned with yellow garments and yellow ornaments. She is seated on a golden throne, hence she is known as Pītāmbarā. She is also Śāmbhavī and Mahāvidyā. She is of glorious form. In her four hands she holds a club, a noose, a thunderbolt and the tongue of the enemy respectively. She has elevated breasts and a digit of the moon shines on her forehead. She is endowed with powers (*siddhā*) and one can obtain her in the *Brahmarandhra*.[196] The synonymns of this deity are Bagalā, Jṛmabhinī, Mohinī Bhogā, Yogikā and many others. These names signify the powers she possesses.[197] Six female goblins such as Dākinī, Rākini, etc. are mentioned with reference to the interior part of the Devī-*yantra*.[198] They are her associates. If a devotee worships her with lights for six months he obtains thirty-six powers of the Devī.

Rājyaśyāmalā

She is the deity worshipped by the left-hand school of the Śākta-s. The Upaniṣad enjoins her worship with a spell, hymns, etc. It lays more emphasis on the worship of the female organ as Devīcakra. Miraculous powers are said to be won by following this strange worship. Friday is considered as the important day of worship.[199] In different seasons, she is worshipped differently. Different worships, to lure a woman and enjoy her, are given in this Upaniṣad. The Upaniṣad exhibits fully Vāmācārī-Tāntric influence. The Śākta-s worship her with offerings of clothes, flowers, unguents, wine, flesh etc. From the descriptions, it is obvious that it is the doctrine of Vāmacarī, lower Śākta-sets. The Śyāmā Upaniṣad also presents descriptions of similar kind and again, is the doctrine of the Vāmacarī school of the Śākta-s

Tripurasundarī

She is also known as Lalitā. She is all pervading and pervades the worlds, space, and time with her limbs. She is the form of bliss and of conscious existence.[200] She can be known by experiencing the oneness of the Self and the Brahman. This knowledge is known as Śrīvidyā.[201] Her name explains the three cities in which she resides. The three cities are the three states-waking, dreaming and deep sleep. The plexuses, between the eyes, throat and heart are also said to be the three cities. The regions; the earth, the heaven, the space and the three virtues are also identified with the cities in the same way. She resides in the syllables from A to Kṣa. The three cities are also compared to the gross, the subtle and the causal bodies.

The lower type of worship consists in consuming wine, cooked food, flesh and worshipping the female organ. The *Tripuratāpinyupaniṣad* exhibits Atharvaṇic and Tāntric influence. Different names of the Devī and different powers that she possesses are enlisted in these Upaniṣads.[202]

Annapūrṇā

This is very adorable and pleasant form of Devī. The *Annapūrṇā. Up.* makes the goddess, the object of its praise. She is described as having large eyes and lotus-like smiling face. She has her hair let loose. She is the form of Mahālakṣmī. Annapūrṇā is ever full of delight and is devoid of any outside support. She is requested to bestow the desired food upon her worshipper, with the belief that she can do so. She is requested to preach the great lore (Mahāvidyā) which leads to a release. She is known as Pārvatī also.[203]

Sarasvatī

Sarasvatī holds an important place from the days of the *Ṛv.* In the *Ṛv.*, she is the river personified. The *Sarasvatī. R. Up.* has described her as extremely fair in complexion who is adorned with golden frangipani (*campaka*) flowers. She has beautiful limbs and elevated breasts.[204] Her hair is adorned with the digit of the moon; and the rays of the moon.[205] In her hands, she holds a rosary, a book, a noose, and a weapon (*aṅkuśa*) She wears a garland of pearls and is adorned with various other ornaments.[206] She resides in the city of Kāśmir, as well as on the tip of tongue of her devotees.[207] She is beginningless and endless.[208] She is the speech (*vāk*), manifest and unmanifest and all the Veda-s abide in her.[209] She is the river of nectar, pacifying the torments of the wordly existence. She bestows poetical power, fearlessness and liberation upon her devotees.[210]

Sarasvatī is indeed, the Brahman and has the nature of the Brahman. The world is created by her by means of Prakṛti. Her nature; *i.e.* the nature of the Brahman is always eternal. She is the form of the Truth, Consciousness and Bliss.[211]

Sarasvatī is identified with Gāyatrī. It is said that she is Gāyatrī in the evening. She is the ancient one and wears black garments. In this form, she has a conch, a discus, a mace in her hands. One of her hands is in *Abhaya Mudrā*. She is established in the heaven and is, of the form of the Sun. The Sāmaveda, the heaven (*svaḥ*), the third libation, the state of *suṣupti*, the Āditya, the Jagatī metre, Virāj and the Brahman belong to her.[212]

Lakṣmī

Lakṣmī is the active power of god Viṣṇu having exceptional charm and beauty. She is the goddess of wealth, of all kinds. The *S.L. Up.* describes this goddess, and the source of this description is the famous Śrīsūkta. A technique by which, she is obtained is Śrīvidyā.

She has golden complexion. For her seat, she has the spells and is surrounded by the deities. Mahālakṣmī is seated on a red-lotus and holds lotuses in her hands. The other two hands exhibit *Varadamudrā* and *abhayamudrā*. Her unique beauty is enhanced by jewelled ornaments. She has eyes like the petals of lotus.[213] Her twenty-four adjectives enlisted in the Upaniṣad, exhibit the auspicious character of Lakṣmī.[214]

The mother of the universe (*mūlaprakṛti*); she is the Devalakṣ mī of gods. Siddhalakṣmī of the Siddha-s, Mokṣa-Lakṣmī for the aspirants of *mokṣa* and so on.

Other goddesses such as Rādhā, Sītā are also praised and described in the Upaniṣads in similar manners. The *Śrī-Rādhā Up.* and *Śrī-Rādhikātāpinī. Up.* describe Rādhā. The *Sītopaniṣad* is devoted to Sītā. The deification of the plant of Tulasī as Devī is worthy of adoration. One complete Upaniṣad, which glorifies the plant is known by her name. The medicinal effects of Tulasī plant are stated in the form of fruit won by the worship of the plant.

Devī is described in various forms in the later Upaniṣads. Some of her forms *viz.* Sarasvatī, Vāk, etc. can be traced back to the Vedic period. Some other forms can be traced back to the period of the epics and the Purāṇa-s. Many forms are new. These Upaniṣads belong to the *Av.*, therefore, this is the contribution of the *Av.*, to the formation of and development of the post-Vedic Paurāṇic Hindu religion. They also contribute to the development of the doctrine of Bhakti. The Vaiṣṇava goddesses like Lakṣmī, Sītā, Tulasī are milder and pleasant in character. The Śaivite deities like Umā, and Devī are milder while, Kālī is awful; whereas some like Durgā show mixed traits. But, though different names, forms and powers they possess, they are one. While preaching unity in diversity of names and forms, the later Upani-ṣads stress the Vedānta-doctrines and for this purpose, they resort to the methods of Tantra, Yoga, Sāṁkhya, Bhakti and *Karman*-s. The worship of Śaktī is open to all. Again, the attitude; of the later-Upaniṣads; to inculcate and accomodate different casts is seen here. The Tāntric influence is seen to a great extent, but the underlying trait is that of unity.

Sūrya (In the *Ṛv.*)

The worship of Sārya existed since very early times in the *Ṛv*. Ten hymns are addressed to Sūrya. Since the name designates the orb of the Sun, as well as god, Sūrya is the most concrete of the solar deities. The eye of Sūrya is mentioned several times. He himself is often called the eye of Mitra and Varuṇa also.[215] He is described as far-seeing, all-seeing, the spy of the whole world. He beholds all beings and the good and the bad deeds of mortals. He is the soul of all that moves or is stationary. He is Āditya, the son of the goddess Aditi. The Dawns reveal Sūrya, and are referred to, as his wife. His father is the heaven (*Dyaus*). He is the rouser of people and rolls up darkness.

In the *Ṛv.,* Sūrya is conceived as a bird, traversing space. He is prayed for the easy travel of the paths and protection.

Bhandarkar, R.G. says that, the cult of the worshippers of the Sun existed from early times. He became the object of sectarian worship some time later. About the third century of the Christian era, another cult of the sun was introduced from Persia. It was rooted in India and prevailed for a long time in North-Western India, evidences of which are beautiful temples erected for his worship from time to time. Megas, is the name for the caste of priests associated with the cult. The masses of the Hindus adopted it; as if it originated naturally in this region.[216]

Sūrya in the Later Upaniṣads

Sūrya is brilliant like gold and is seated on a red lotus or in a chariot driven by seven horses. He has four hands. His two hands are in *Abhayamudrā* and *Varadamudrā* respectively, and in the other two, he holds lotus-flowers.[217] The Sun has palms of his hands made of nectar. He is the great Lord with thousand eyes. Sūrya is perceived directly while other deities are not.[218] Sūrya and Sāvitrī are a divine couple, they are equated with other couples and they represent the male and female power respectively.[219]

Sūrya bestows boon on his devotees and makes them fearless. He sets in motion, the wheel of time. He stimulates the intellect of his worshippers. Sūrya protects his devotees from death. He creates the food, rain and sacrifice.[220]

Sūrya as the Brahman

Sūrya is identified with the Puruṣa and it is said that the Puruṣa assumes the form of the Sun, with thousands of rays and shines for the benefit of the people.[221] He is the holy Haṁsa of the universal form.[222] Fire, water, air, earth and sky proceed from the Sun.[223] He is identified with the five-senses with their objects, the five kinds of breath, with the heart, the mind, the intellect, *Citta* and *Ahaṅkāra*. He is of the nature of bliss and wisdom and knowledge. He is verily the Brahman.[224]

In the later Upaniṣads, we find continued deification of the deity Sūrya. They describe the form of Sūrya, use Vedic hymns in his worship. They enhance the old method of adoration by adding different spells, and the worship of *Yantra*-s. In this manner, they borrow from the Vedic-literature and the Tantra literature, for the methods of worship they prescribe. Supreme glory of the Sūrya is sung in the *Ṛv.;* (*Ṛv.*VII.63ff) sacrificial and worldy importance as giver of rain and wordly pleasures is described in the *Yv.*, power of granting relief from diseases is described in the *Av.* (*Av.* I.3.5). The authors of the later Upaniṣads seem to have been influenced by the above traits of the Sun.[225] These Upaniṣads are said to be the doctrines of the Sūrya sect. However, they do not mention Maga-s, the class of priests and hence are free from any foreign influence.[226]

Gaṇapati

The worship of Gaṇapati, without reference to any sect is practised by nearly all Hindus at the beginning of all religious ceremonies.

The Sect of Gāṇapatya-s

According to Bhandarkar, R.G., Rudra had his hosts of Maruts who were called his Gaṇa-s, and the leader of these, was Gaṇapati. As the name, Rudra was generalised, so was the name Gaṇapati and meant many leaders of the groups (*gaṇa*-s). Soon, another name denoting a spirit also came into use. He mentions that in the *Mahānavagṛhyasūtra*, (II.14), an account of Vināyaka-s is given. They are four in number. In its own nature, the Vināyaka is considered to be an unfriendly and malignant spirit; but is capable of being made friendly and benignant by propitiation to him. In this respect, he resembles Rudra. The Vināyaka-s had come to be the object of faith before the Christian era. Gaṇapati-Vināyaka was introduced in the Hindu pantheon much later. Between the end of the fifth and end of the eighth century, the Gaṇapati cult must have come into practice, opines Bhandarkar, R.G. But when and how the God came to have elephant's head; is difficult to decide. In two caves of Ellora, Gaṇapati has that elephant head. The caves are to be referred to the latter part of the eighth century.

Six varieties of Gāṇapatya sect are mentioned by Ānandagiri in his *Śaṅkaradigvijaya*. The followers of the Ucchiṣṭagaṇapati are said to resort to the left handed path (*vāmamārga*).[227]

Description of Gaṇapati in the Later Upaniṣads

The *Gaṇapatyupaniṣad* describes that Gaṇapati has a big head of an elephant, one tusk and four hands with significant and sharp weapons that destroy the difficulties and sins of his devotees.

He is red in complexion, has a large belly and sharp big ears like the winnowing basket (*śūrpa*). He is anointed with red sandal wood paste, wears red clothes and is worshipped with red flowers. For his vehicle, he has a mouse. Vrātapati, Pramathapati, Śivasuta etc. are the epithets which describe him as the son of Śiva and the leader of the Gaṇa-s.[228]

Eka is *māyā* and Danatin is *māyin*. The union of these two is Ekadanatin. The mouse symbolises the 'ego'; which enjoys the pleasures of the senses like a thief; is kept under control by Gaṇapati.

Gaṇapati as the Brahman

Gaṇapati Up. equates the deity with the Ātman. He is the creator, sustainer and destroyer of the universe. He is omnipresent and transcends the three qualities of the Prakṛti. He is beyond Time and Space. The Yogins always meditate upon him.[229]

The *Gaṇeśapūrvatāpini Up.*, describes Gaṇapati as follows: Gaṇapati is the son of Śiva and Umā. He sleeps in the Milky ocean or he stands under a tree named Kalpa. He is the form of the sky and has strong massive arms. He wears matted hair. He is the giver of the boons, auspicious, quiet and protects his devotees from fear. He has the toe of his foot raised up. He has strong thighs, broad waist and a deep navel. He is embraced by Siddhi and Buddhi. His face is like a lotus, fully blossomed.[230] Gaṇeśa Puruṣa is Śiva, and has the sky as his seed. All these beings are born of the sky and merge in it.[231]

Heramba is the special form of Gaṇapati praised in the later Upaniṣads. He is described as the Lord of all lords. His complexion is red, has the face of an elephant; has four arms. He is assisted by Lakṣmī. He is in the form of Brahmā, Hari, Indra and moon and is the highest Ātman. He is the creator, the holder and the dissipator of the universe. He is the witness of the good and the bad deeds of the beings. He assumes manifold forms through his *māyā*. Unifing with him through meditation and worship, the sages cross the worldly ocean.[232]

Four different stages can be observed in the development of this deity. Gaṇapati is identified with Bṛhaspati, the Vedic god. The dreadful aspect of Vināyaka and the gentle aspects of Gaṇapati are combined into one to form Gaṇapati-Vināyaka. Though their names are different, in reality, they stand for Gaṇeśa only. The association of the elephant head to Gaṇapati is perhaps the indication that the deity was specially adored by the forest-tribes. The description of cosmic form of Gaṇapati is fashioned on the line of that in the Puruṣasūkta (*Ṛv.*, X.90).

Relation of Philosophy and Religion

The term philosophy has been already explained in the light of various definitions presented by different scholars. (*Ibid.*, p. 12) Philosophy is an enquiry into the nature of reality or the Ultimate Reality. It is the quest for the knowledge of what ultimately was real, making the use of reason and argument. This merged into a quest for the comprehension of the ultimate meaning or significance of life.

Philosophy, which is based on assumptions; deals with two aspects, the material and spiritual. Philosophy speculates about the cause of the world, its origin, maintenance and dissolution. Philosophically speaking, man as a self-conscious being craves for rising above the material and the finite and achieving the knowledge of the infinite. Philosophy aims at unfolding the relations between the finite and the infinite and tracing out the process to communion with the infinite and attainment of Eternity.[233]

Religion

"Religion is a universal social phenomenon. Some relate it with the feelings of wonder, awe, ecstacy etc. the feelings the man experienced through the order (*Ṛta*) and phenomena of nature; while, for some it is the outcome of some psychical tendencies. It is based on beliefs in transcendental values – laws, ideals, ideas-and faith in supernatural powers. It indicates the sense of longing, longing for the union with the Ultimate Reality. Religion is characterised by two aspects.

The psychological one in the form of various emotions experienced by man and the physiological one in the form of the manner of approaching that Reality which is revealed in propitiating it. These two together have their impact upon human life. Religion serves as a means to an end.

Religion and philosophy are closely related to each other. Philosophical concepts always form an integral part of religion. It is difficult to know whether philosophy originated from religion or vice-versa. This contraversial issue discussed by Tiele, C.P., is summarised by Bakre, A., as follows :

> "If philosophy or at least its theosophic part is regarded as merely a more precise and scientific form of religious doctrine, it indicates that it would then have sprung from religion and would satisfy those who are more intellectually developed and who desire definite declarations instead of the parables and allegories. Another possibility is that philosophy may have been the parent and religious doctrine the offspring and if so, the religious doctrine would be regarded as a popular philosophy, rendered accessible to the masses and in that case, religion would strive to build its practical system on a theoretical foundation."[234]

This means that the speculations regarding the Highest Reality, the creation and the theories in relation to these form the part of philosophy. The practical aspect of religion, approaching that Reality, culminates into worship.

As stated earlier, (p. 12) Radhakrishnan, S., believed that Indian philosophy is fundamentally a synthesis of both religion and philosophy, of knowledge and conduct, reason and intuition, man and nature. All are brought into harmony, where ethics, psychology, facts, values, etc. are treated as aspects of single comprehensive reality. Further, he has said that, Indian philosophy believes in the intimate relationship of philosophy and life, theory (doctrine) and practice that is, it is for the life and it is to belived.

It may be observed that, as belief system underwent changes, monism was replaced by polytheism. People started adoring and worshipping personified deities. However, it must be noted that even though the later Upaniṣads glorified various deities, all these divinities are considered as the manifestations of the Highest Reality. They are the supports with different names and forms and with the help of which one can realise the Abstract.

REFERENCES

1. Ed. by Thompson, D., *The Concise Oxford Dictionary*, Calcutta, 1995, p. 1411.
2. Radhakrishnan, S., *The Principal Upaniṣads,* Delhi, 1998. p. 138.
3. Deussen, P., *The Philosophy of the Upaniṣads,* New York, 1966. p. 101.
4. *Chānd. Up.* VII.15.1,

   ...यथा वा अरा नाभौ समर्पिता एवमस्मिन् प्राणे सर्वं समर्पितम्...।
5. *Ibid.,* I.11.5

   ...सर्वाणि ह वा इमानि भूतानि प्राणमेवाभिसंविशन्ति प्राणमभ्युज्जिहते ...।
6. *Ibid.,* IV. 3.1-4

   वायुर्वाव संवर्गो यदा वा अग्निरुद्वायति वायुमेवाप्येति यदा सूर्योऽस्तमेति वायुमेवाप्येति यदा चन्द्रोऽस्तमेति वायुमेवाप्येति॥ यदाप उच्छुष्यन्ति वायुमेवापियन्ति वायुर्ह्येवैतान्सर्वान्संवृङ्क्ते इत्यधिदैवतम्॥ अथाध्यात्मं प्राणो वाव संवर्गः स यदा स्वपिति प्राणमेव वागप्येति प्राणं चक्षुः प्राणँ श्रोत्रं प्राणं मनः प्राणो ह्येवैतान्सर्वान्वृङ्क्ते इति॥
7. *Ibid.,* V. 1.6-12.
8. *Bṛ. Up.,* VI.1.7-13.
9. *Kau. Up.,* II.9

   also, *Praśna Up.* II.2.4.
10. *Kau. Up,* III.3[f],

    यो वै प्राणः सा प्रज्ञा या वा प्रज्ञा स प्राणः। सह ह्येतावस्मिञ् शरीरे वसतः सहोत्क्रामतः॥
11. *Ibid.,* III.2[b],

    आयुः प्राणः प्राणो वा आयुः।

12. *Ibid.*, III.8[e],

स एष प्राण एव प्रज्ञात्मा आनंदो ऽ जरो ऽ मृतो न साधुना कर्मणा भूयान्भवति नो एवासाधुना कनीयान्।

13. *Chānd. Up.*, V. 24.1-5.
14. *Ibid.*, VI. 7.1-6.
15. *Praśna. Up.*, VI. 2, 4.

इहैवान्तः शरीरे सोम्य स पुरुषो यस्मिन्नेताः षोडशकलाः प्रभवन्तीति॥ स प्राणमसृजत प्राणाच्छ्रद्धां खं वायुर्ज्योतिरापः पृथिवीन्द्रियं मनोऽन्नमन्नाद्वीर्यं तपो मन्त्राः कर्म लोका लोकेषु च नाम च॥

16. *Chānd. Up.* III. 18.1[a],

मनो ब्रह्मेत्युपासीतेत्यध्यात्मम्...।

17. *Ibid.*, VII. 3.2,

स यो मनो ब्रह्मेत्युपास्ते यावन्मनसोगतं तत्रास्य यथाकामचारो भवति यो मनोब्रह्मेत्युपास्ते...।

18. *Bṛ. Up.* 'V.1.6[a],

यदेव ते कश्चिदब्रवीत्तच्छृणवामेत्यब्रवीन्मे सत्यकामो जाबालो मनो वै ब्रह्मेति...।

19. *Ibid.*, II. 4.7.
20. Ranade, R.D., *op. cit.*, p. 157.
21. *Chānd. Up.* III. 18.1-2,

मनो ब्रह्मेत्युपासीतेत्यध्यात्ममथाधिदैवतमआकाशो ब्रह्मेत्युभयमादिष्टं भवत्यध्यात्मं चाधिदैवतं च॥ तदेतच्चतुष्पाद्ब्रह्म वाक्पादः प्राणः पादश्चक्षुः पादः श्रोत्रं पाद इत्यध्यात्ममथाधिदैवतमग्निः पादो वायुः पाद आदित्यः पादो दिशः पाद इत्युभयमेवादिष्टं भवत्यध्यात्मं चैवाधिदैवतं च॥

22. *Ibid.*, I. 9.1,

अस्य लोकस्य का गतिरित्याकाश इति होवाच सर्वाणि ह वा इमानि भूतान्याकाशादेव समुत्पद्यन्त आकाशं प्रत्यस्तं यन्त्याकाशो ह्येवैभ्यो ज्यायानाकाशः परायणम्॥

23. *Ibid.*, VII. 12.1-2[b],

आकाशो वाव तेजसो भूयानाकाशे वै सूर्याचन्द्रमसावुभौ विद्युन्नक्षत्राण्यग्निराकाशेनाह्वयत्याकाशेन श्रुणोत्याकाशेन प्रतिश्रुणोत्याकाशे रमत आकाशे न रमत आकाशे जायत आकाशमभिजायत आकाशमुपास्स्वेति॥... ...आकाशाद्वाव भूयोऽस्तीति इति।

24. *Ibid.*, III. 19.1[a],

आदित्योब्रह्मेत्यादेश:

Ibid., III. 19.3[a],

अथ यत्तदजायत सोऽसावादित्यस्तं जायमानं घोषा उलूलवोऽनूदतिष्ठन्सर्वाणि च भूतानि...।

25. *Ibid.*, III. 1-11.
26. *Ibid.*, IV. 11.1. *Bṛ. Up.*, V. 5.2.
27. *Tait. Up.*, III. 10.4[b],

    यश्चायं पुरुषे॥ यश्चासावादित्ये॥
28. *Chānd. Up.*, IV. 15.1-5.
29. *Tait. Up.*, I.8.1[a],

    ओमिति ब्रह्म। ओमितीदँ सर्वम्।
30. *Gauḍpādakārikā,* I. 28[a],

    अमात्रोऽनन्तमात्रश्च द्वैतस्योपशम: शिव:॥
31. *Īśa. Up.* 18,

    अग्ने नय सुपथा राये अस्मान्विश्वानि देव वयुनानि विद्वान्।
    युयोध्यस्मज्जुहुराणमेनो भूयिष्ठां ते नमउक्तिं विधेम॥
32. *Kaṭh. Up.* I. 1.14, 15[a],

    प्र ते ब्रवीमि तदु मे निबोध स्वर्ग्यमग्निं नचिकेत: प्रजानन्। अनन्तलोकाप्तिमथो प्रतिष्ठां विद्धि त्वमेतं निहितं गुहायाम्॥ लोकादिमग्निं तमुवाच तस्मै या इष्टका यावतीर्वा यथा वा ॥
33. Macdonell, A., *The Vedic Mythology*, Varanasi, 1963, p. 36.
34. *Īśa. Up.*, 15-16,

    हिरण्मयेन पात्रेण सत्यस्यापिहितं मुखम्। तत्त्वं पूषन्नपावृणु सत्यधर्माय दृष्टये॥
    पूषन्नेकर्षे यम सूर्य प्राजापत्य व्यूह रश्मीन्समूह।
    तेजो यत्ते रूपं कल्याणतमं तत्ते पश्यामि योऽसावसौ पुरुष: सोऽहमस्मि॥
35. *Ken. Up.*, III. 1-12.
36. *Vanadurgopaniṣad. Up. S.* pt. II. p. 439, l. 8

    आग्नेय्यां दिश्यग्निर्देवता। मेषारूढो रक्तवर्णो ज्वालाहस्तोऽग्नि...।
37. *Ibid.*, p. 449, ll. 23,

    नमो भगवति आग्नेयि ज्वालाहस्ताभ्यां...।

38. *Jābālopaniṣad. Up. S.* pt. I. p. 145, l. 16,
तदु यथा न कुर्यादाग्नेयीमेव कुर्यात्। अग्निर्ह वै प्राणः प्राणमेवैतया करोति...॥
39. *M.N. Up.* II.10,
मा नो हिंसीज्जातवेदो गामश्वं पुरुषं जगत्।
40. *Ibid.,* III. 6-7,
वैश्वानराय विद्महे लालेलाय धीमहि॥
पावकाय विद्महे सप्तजिह्वाय धीमहि॥
41. *Ibid.,* XXV.
42. *Vanadurgopaniṣad Up. S.* pt. II, p. 439, l. 18,
याम्यां दिशि यमो देवता। महिषारूढो नीलवर्णो कालदण्डो यमो बध्नातु यममण्डलम्।
43. *Ibid.,* p. 450. l. 6.
44. *R. Jābāla. Up. Up. S.* pt. I. I. 12,
दशवक्त्रं तु रुद्राक्षं यमदैवत्यमीरितम्। दशाप्रशान्तिजनकं धारणान्नात्र संशयः॥
45. *Vanadurgopaniṣad. Up. S.* pt. II. p. 440, l. 15,
वारुण्यां दिशि वरुणो देवता। मकरारूढः श्वेतवर्णः पाशहस्तो वरुणो बध्नातु वरुणमण्डलम्॥
46. *Nādabindūpaniṣad,* 6[b],
परमा चार्धमात्रा या वारुणीं तां विदुर्बुधाः।
47. *Vanadurgopaniṣad, Up. S.* pt. II. p. 438,
प्राच्यां दिशीन्द्रो देवता। ऐरावतरूढो हेमवर्णो वज्राङ्कुशहस्त इन्द्रो बध्नातु इन्द्रमण्डलम्।
48. *Nādabindūpaniṣad,* 10[a], 15[a]
पञ्चमी नामधेया तु षष्ठी च चैन्द्र अभिधीयते।
15a,
षष्ठ्यामिन्द्रस्यसायुज्यं यदि प्राणैर्वियुज्यते।
49. *Bāṣkalamantropaniṣad,* 4-25.
50. Belvalkar, S.K., and Ranade, R.D., *op. cit.,* pp. 132-170.
51. *M.N. Up.* XVI. 5[b],
मेधां मे अश्विनावुभावाधत्तां पुष्करस्त्रजौ।
52. *Chānd. Up.* V. 24.1-5

also, *Kau. Up.* II. 5.

53. *Kaṭh. Up.* I. 1.17[a],

त्रिणाचिकेतस्त्रिभिरेत्य सन्धिं त्रिकर्मकृत्तरति जन्ममृत्यू॥

54. Śaṅkara, quoted by Radhakrishnan, S., *The Principal Upaniṣads,* Delhi, 1998, p. 602.

55. Tilak, B.G., *Gitārahasya,* (Vol. I), Pune. 1935. p. 284.

56. *Ṛv.,* 1.154.4,

विष्णो: पदे परमे मध्व: उत्स:।

57. *Śat. Brā.* 14.1.1.10,

यज्ञो वै विष्णु:।

also, *Yajurvedasaṁhitā,* VI. 5, "the wise always perceive the all pervasive highest position of Viṣṇu." quoted by Mishra Umesh, *op. cit.,* p. 77.

58. *Kaṭh Up.* I.3.9,

विज्ञानसारथिर्यस्तु मन: प्रग्रहवान्नर:।

सोऽध्वन: पारमाप्नोति तद्विष्णो: परमं पदम्॥

Śaṅkara's commentary on *Kaṭh Up.* I.3.9.,

तद् विष्णो: व्यापनशीलस्य ब्रह्मण: परमात्मनो वासुदेवाख्यायस्य।

59. *Mai. Up.* VI. 13[a],

अथान्यत्राप्युक्तं विश्वमृद्वै नामैषा तनूर्भगवतो विष्णोर्यदिदमन्नम्।

60. *Ibid.,* V.2,

अस्य सात्विकोंऽशोऽसौ स ब्रह्मचारिणो योऽयं विष्णु:।

61. Bhandarkar, R.G., *Vaiṣṇavism Śaivism and Minor Religious Systems,* Bombay. 1913. pp. 100, ff.

62. Bhandarkar, R.G., *op. cit.,* p. 101.

63. Max Müller quoted by Bhandarkar, R.G., *op. cit.,* p. 2.

64. Bhandarkar, R.G., *op. cit.,* p. 2.

65. *Pāramātmika, Up. S.* pt II, p. 86.

विश्वव्यापनशीलत्वाद्विष्णुरित्युच्यते बुधै:॥ व्याप्नोति इति विष्णु:॥

66. *Nārāyaṇa. P. Tā. Up. Up. S.* pt. II. p. 76.

नीलजीमूतसंकाशं पीतकौशेयवाससम्।
किरीटकुण्डलधरं कौस्तुभोद्भासितोरसम्॥
शङ्खचक्रगदाङ्गधारिणं वनमालिनम्।
वामभागे महालक्ष्म्यालिङ्गितार्धशरीरिणम्॥

67. *Pāramātmika. Up. Up. S.* pt. II. p. 199.
गरुडो वाहनं चापि विष्णोर्देवस्य कीर्तितः॥

68. *Nārāyaṇātharvśira. Up.* 4[c].
ॐ नमो नारायणायेति मंत्रोपासको वैकुण्ठभुवनं गमिष्यति॥

69. *Pāramātmika. Up. Up. S.* pt. II. V. 10, p. 154.
आमोदश्च प्रमोदश्च संमोदस्तदनंतरम्।
वैकुण्ठमिति विज्ञेयास्तेऽन्योन्यमुपरि स्थिताः॥
अतः परं चतुर्थः स्यात्सेकः परमभास्वरः।
वासुदेवस्य सुमहत्तद्दीप्तमजरावृतम्।
...आनन्दं नाम तं लोकम् परमानन्दमद्भुतम्।

70. *Rādhopaniṣad. Up. S.* pt. II. p. 208. l. 10-12,
दशकोटियोजनविस्तीर्णो रुद्रलोकः। तदुपरि विष्णुलोकः। सप्तकोटियोजनविस्तीर्णो विष्णुलोकः। तदुपरी सुदर्शनचक्रम् त्रिकोटियोजनविस्तीर्णम्॥

71. *Vanadurgopaniṣad, Up. S.* pt. II. pp. 448-49,
अवान्तरस्यां दिशि विष्णुः सपरिवारो देवता प्रत्यधिदेवता। तद्दिक्षु भीमको नाम राक्षसः ... इदं विष्णुर्विचक्रमे त्रेधा निदधे पदम्।

72. *Pāramātmikopaniṣad, Up. S.* pt II.VIII. 5. p. 184
सो वा स्वरूपः समदृक समग्रो विधुदं तुदन् यो विदधत्पदं वा वियति प्रकाशं बृहते गुहेन तं बिम्बवन्तं समदं समयं स्वाहा। *commentary,*
...राहुममृतपानवेलायां तुदन् हिंसां कुर्वन् तस्य राहोः।

73. *Rāma. P. Tā. Up.* I.1[a],
चिन्मये अस्मिन्महाविष्णौ जाते दशरथे हरौ।

74. *Ibid.,* I. 2[b],
राक्षसा येन मरणं यान्ति स्वोद्रेकतोऽथवा।

75. *Ibid.,* I. 7[b],
उपासकानां कार्यार्थं ब्रह्मणो रूपकल्पना।

76. *Śarabhopaniṣad,* I. 24,

एको विष्णुर्महद्भूतं पृगग्भूतान्यनेकशः। त्रिलोकान्व्याप्य भूतात्मा भुङ्क्ते विश्वभुगव्ययः॥

77. *Mudgalopaniṣad,* I. 1[b],p. 407

अनन्तयोजनं प्राह दङ्गुलवचस्तथा॥

78. *Pāramātmika Up.* VII. 8, p. 180

यः पुण्डरीकः परमान्तरात्मा कम्राङ्गरूपं कमलं दधार सासिष्वसन्तं सरसे रसाय स्वाहा॥

79. *Ibid.,* III. 1,

यस्त्वं भूत्वा पर्जन्यो बिभेति रन्ध्रे प्रजाभिराकृष्यमाणः सत्यं कालं व्रतेन पालयन् ह्यदयिष्यसे स्वाहा॥

80. *M.N. Up.* II. 4[b],

त्रीणि पदा निहिता गुहासु यस्तद्वेद..।

81. *Mudgala, Up. Up. S.* pt. I. p. 408.

82. *N~dabindū. Up.* 10[b], 15[a],

सप्तमी वैष्णवी नाम अष्टमी शांकरीति च॥

षष्ठ्यामिन्द्रस्य सायुज्यं सप्तम्यां वैष्णव पदम्।

83. *Nṛsiṁha. U. T~. Up. Up. S.* pt. I. p. 229, l. 22,

द्वितीयाऽन्तरिक्षं स उकारः स यजुर्भिर्यजुर्वेदो विष्णुः ...।

84. *Brahmavidyopaniṣad,* I. 5[b],

विष्णुश्च भगवान्देव उकारः परिकीर्तितः॥

85. *Pāramātmikopaniṣad Up. S.* pt. II. p. 99.

अकारेणोच्यते विष्णुः सर्वलोकेश्वरो हरिः। उद्धता विष्णुना लक्ष्मीरुकारेण तथोच्यते। मकारस्तु तयोर्दास इति प्रणवलक्षणम्।

86. *Vāsudevopaniṣad, Up. S.* pt. I. p. 406, L. 16,

एको विष्णुरनेकेषु जङ्गमस्थावरेषु च। अनुस्यूतो वसत्यात्मा भूतेष्वहमवस्थितः॥

87. *Tvmn. Up. Up. S.* pt. I. p. 361. ll. 16-17.

तद्वत्परब्रह्मणः सर्वात्मकस्य साकारनिराकारभेदविरोधो नास्त्येव विविध-विचित्रानन्तशक्तेः परब्रह्मणः स्वरूपज्ञानेन विरोधो न विद्यते।

also, *Nārāyaṇāthrvaśira. Up,* p. 151

88. *Tvmn. Up. Up. S.* pt. I. p. 358, 360.

also, *Nārāyaṇārtharvaśira. Up*. p. 151

89. *Gopālpārvatāpinyupaniṣad,* I. 1,1.

कृषिर्भूवाचकः शब्दो नश्च निर्वृत्तिवाचकः। तयोरैक्यं परं ब्रह्म कृष्ण इत्यभिधीयते। ...पापकर्षणो गोभूमिवेदविदितो वेदिता गोपीजनाविद्याकलाप्रेरकः।

90. *Gopālottaratāpinyupaniṣad, Up. S.* pt. I. p. 597. ll. 26-32,

91. *Gopālapārvatāpinyupaniṣad,* II. 5, 6[a], 8,

कंसवंशविनाशाय केशिचाणूरघातिने। वृषभध्वजवन्द्याय पार्थसारथये नमः॥ वेणुवादनशीलाय गोपालायाहिमर्दने। ... नमः पापप्रणाशाय गोवर्धनधराय च। पूतनाजीवितान्ताय तृणावर्तासुहारिणे॥

92. *Gopālottaratāpinyupaniṣad, Up. S.* pt. I. p. 597, ll. 10-13,

रोहिणीतनयो रामो अकाराक्षरसंभवः। तैजसात्मकः प्रद्युम्न उकाराक्षरसंभवः। प्राज्ञात्मकोऽनिरुद्धो वै मकाराक्षर संभवः। अर्धमात्रात्मकः कृष्णो यस्मिन्विश्वं प्रतिष्ठितम्। कृष्णात्मिका जगत्कर्त्री मूलप्रकृतिरुक्मिणी॥

93. *Ibid*., I. 6,

अयं हि कृष्णो यो वो हि प्रेष्ठः शरीरद्वयकारणं भवति द्वौ सुपर्णौ भवतो ब्रह्मणोंऽशभूतस्तथेतरो भोक्ता भवति। अन्यो हि साक्षी भवतीति॥

94. *Śrīkṛṣṇapuruṣottamasiddhāntopaniṣad, Up. S.* pt. II. p. 217, l-1-10.

95. Bhandarkar, R.G., *op. cit.,* p. 47.

96. Desai, S.G., *op. cit.,* p. 65.

97. *Rāma. P. Tā. Up.* I.1-6,

चिन्मयेऽस्मिन्महाविष्णौ जाते दशरथे हरौ।
रघोः कुलेऽखिलं राति राजते यो महीस्थितः॥
स राम इति लोकेषु विद्वद्भिः प्रकटीकृतः।
राक्षसा येन मरणं यान्ति स्वोद्रेकतोऽथवा॥
रमन्ते योगिनोऽनन्ते नित्यानन्दे चिदात्मनि।
इति रामपदेनासौ ब्रह्माभिधीयते॥

98. *Ibid.,* III. 7-9,

प्रकृत्या सहितः श्यामः पीतवासा जटाधरः
द्विभुजः कुण्डली रत्नमाली धीरो धनुर्धरः॥

प्रसन्नवदनो जेता धृष्ट्यष्टकविभूषितः।
प्रकृत्या परमेश्वर्या जगद्योन्याऽङ्किताङ्कभृत्॥

हेमाभया द्विभुजया सर्वालंकृतया चिता।
श्लिष्टः कमलधारिण्या पुष्टः कोसलजात्मजः॥

99. *Rāmarahasyopaniṣad,* II. 3^{b}-4,

सरयूतीरमन्दारवेदिकापङ्कजासने॥
श्यामं वीरासनासीनं ज्ञानमुद्रोपशोभितम्।
वामोरुन्यस्ततद्धस्तं सीतालक्ष्मणसंयुतम्॥

100. *Rāma. P. Tā. Up.* VI, 7-16,

101. *Ibid.,* $I.8^{b}$, 9^{a}, The Verse Commented by Brahmayogin, *Vaiṣṇava-Upaniṣadaḥ*, p. 308.

द्वि चत्वारि षडष्टाऽऽसां दशद्वादश षोडश॥
अष्टादशामी कथिता हस्ताः शङ्खादिभिर्युताः।
सहस्रान्तास्तथा तासां वर्णवाहन कल्पना॥

102. *Rāma. U. Tā. Up.* 2^{b},

अर्धमात्रात्मको रामो ब्रह्मानंदैकविग्रहः।

103. *Rāmarahasyopaniṣad,* I. 7^{b},

वायुपुत्रं विघ्नेशं वाणीं दुर्गां क्षेत्रपालकं सूर्यं चन्द्रं नारायणं नारसिंहं
वायुदेवं वाराहं ...सीतां लक्ष्मणं शत्रुघ्नं भरतं विभीषणं सुग्रीवमङ्गदम्
जाम्बवन्तं प्रणवमेतानि रामस्याङ्गानि जानीथाः।

104. *Ibid.,* I. 6^{b},

राम एव परं ब्रह्म राम एव परं तपः। राम एव परं तत्त्वं श्रीरामो ब्रह्म तारकम्॥

Rāma. P. Tā. Up. I.7,

चिन्मयस्याद्वितीयस्य निष्कलस्याशरीरिणः।
उपासकानां कार्यार्थं ब्रह्मणो रूपकल्पना॥

105. *Ibid.,* III. 5^{b}, 6^{b},

अत्र रामोऽनन्तरूपरतेजरा वह्निना समः॥
उत्पन्नः शीतया भाति चन्द्रश्चन्द्रिकया यथा॥

106. *Ibid.,* II. 1-5,

107. *Rāma. U. Tā. Up. Up. S.* pt. I. p. 401, ll-18-21,

अकाराक्षरसंभूतः सौमित्रिर्विश्वभावनः।
उकाराक्षरसंभूतः शत्रुघ्नतैजसात्मकः॥
प्राज्ञात्मकस्तु भरतो मकाराक्षर संभवः।

108. Lyall, quoted by Desai, S.G., *op. cit,* p. 90.
109. Devasenapathy, V.A., "*Basic Concept of Śaiva Siddhānta.*" *Indian Philosophical Annual.* Vol. 14. Ed. by Balasubramanyam, R. and Raghavan, V.K.S.N. Madras, 1982. p. 39.
110. Iyer, Narayana C.V., *Origin and Early History of Śaivism in South India,* Madras. 1974. p. 4.
111. Macdonell, A. *The Vedic Mythology,* Varanasi, 1963. p. 77.
112. Bhandarkar, R.G., *op. cit.,* pp. 117-120.
113. Devasenapathy. V.A., *op. cit.,* pp. 39-81.
114. Ranade, *op. cit.,* p. 20.
115. *Śvet. Up.,* I. 8,

     संयुक्तमेतत्क्षरमक्षरं च व्यक्ताव्यक्तं भरते विश्वमीशः।
     अनीशात्मा बध्यते भोक्तृभावाज्ज्ञात्वा देवं मुच्यते सर्वपाशैः॥
116. *Ibid.,* III. 2,

     एको हि रुद्रो न द्वितीयाय तस्थुर्य इमान्लोकानीशत ईशनीभिः।
     प्रत्यङ्जनांस्तिष्ठति संचुकोपान्तकाले संसृज्य विश्वा भुवनानि गोपाः॥
117. *Ibid.,* IV. 16,

     घृतात्परं मण्डमिवातिसूक्ष्मं ज्ञात्वा शिवं सर्वभूतेषु गूढम्।
     विश्वस्यैकं परिवेष्टितारं ज्ञात्वा देवं मुच्यते सर्वपाशैः॥
118. *Ibid.,* V. 3,

     एकैकं जालं बहुधा विकुर्वन्नस्मिन्क्षेत्रे संहरत्येष देवः।
     भूयः सृष्ट्वा पतयस्तथेषः सर्वाधिपत्यं कुरुते महात्मा॥
119. Bhandarkar, R.G., *op. cit.,* p. 111.
120. *Ken. Up.,* III. 12,

     ...बहुशोभमानामुमाँ हैमवतीं तां होवाच।
121. Devasenapathy, V.A. *op. cit.,* p. 139.
122. *Vanadurgopaniṣad, Up. S.* pt. II. p. 442. l. 1,

     ईशान्यां दिशीशानो देवता। वृषभारूढः श्वेतवर्णस्त्रिशूलहस्त ईशानो ...।
123. *Jābāla. D. Up.,* IX. 2,

     ऊर्ध्वरेतं विश्वरूपं विरूपाक्षं महेश्वरम्। सोऽहमित्यादरेणैव ध्यायेद्योगीश्वरेश्वरम्॥
124. *Bhasmajābālopaniṣad, Up. S.* pt. I. p. 561,

कैलासशिखरावासमोंकारस्वरूपिणंमहादेवमुमार्धकृतशेखरं... भस्मोद्धूलितविग्रहं.. स्मितसंपूर्णपञ्चविधपञ्चाननम्...।

125. *Dakṣiṇāmūrtyupaniṣad,* I. 3,

स्फटिकरजतवर्णं मौक्तिकीमक्षमालाममृतकलशविद्यां ज्ञानमुद्रां कराग्रे।
दधतमुरगकक्षं चन्द्रचूडं त्रिनेत्रं विधृतविविधभूषं दक्षिणामूर्तिमीडे॥

126. *Ibid.,* I. 5,

मुद्रां भद्रार्थदात्रीं स परशुहरिणं बाहुभिर्बाहुमेकं जान्वासक्तं दधानो भुजगबिलसमाबद्धकक्ष्यो वटाधः॥

127. *Ibid.,* I. 8,

भस्मव्यापाण्डुराङ्गः शशिशकलधरो ज्ञानमुद्रामक्षमालावीणा-पुस्तैर्विराजत्करकमलधरो योगपट्टाभिरामः॥

128. *Ibid.,* I. 19,

शेमुषी दक्षिणा प्रोक्ता सा यस्याभीक्षणे मुखम्। दक्षिणाभिमुखः प्रोक्तः शिवोऽसौ ब्रह्मवादिभिः॥

129. *Atharvaśikha. Up., Up. S.* pt. I. p. 174. l. 15,

सहस्त्रपादेकमूर्धा व्याप्तं स एवेदमावरीवर्ति भूतम्।

130. *Bhasmajābālopaniṣad, Up. S.* pt. I. p. 561, l. 2,

...सोमसूर्याग्निनयनमनन्तेन्दुरविप्रभम्...।

131. *Siddhāntaśikhopaniṣad, Up. S.* pt. II. p. 381, l. 7-8.

132. *Mṛtyulāṅgulopaniṣad, Up. S.* pt. II. p. 307, l. 13-20.

133. *Bhasmajābālopaniṣad, Up. S.* p. 566,

तत्र पूर्वस्यां दिशि ब्रह्मा कृताञ्जलिरहर्निशं मामुपास्ते। दक्षिणस्यांदिशि विष्णुः...। प्रतीच्यामिन्द्राः ...। उदीच्यामग्निकायमुमानुरक्ता हेमाङ्गविभूषणा हेमवस्त्रा मामुपासते...। तत्र गणा रौद्रानना नानामुखा नाना शस्त्रधारिणो...। तत्रानेकगणाः ...। ऋषयः शांभवाः पाशुपता महाशैवा... मोदमानास्तिष्ठन्ति॥

134. *Śivopaniṣad,* II. 5, 6.

अधोभागे स्थितः स्कन्दः देवी च मध्यतः।
ऊर्ध्वं रुद्रः क्रमाद्वापि ब्रह्माविष्णुमहेश्वराः॥

एत एव त्रयो लोका एत एव त्रयो गुणाः।
एत एव त्रयो वेदा एतच्चान्यत्स्थितं त्रिधा॥

135. *Siddhāntaśikhopaniṣad, Up. S.* pt. II. p. 382, l. 18, ff
ऐन्द्रनीलं पूजितं विष्णुनासील्लिंगं वैडूर्यं विधिना पद्मरागम्॥
शक्रेण हैमं यक्षराजेन विश्वेदेवै रौप्यं वसुभिः कांस्यकं च।
आदित्यैस्ताम्रं मौक्तिकं देवतैम्रंतैरनन्ताद्यैः फणिभिश्च प्रवालम्।
दैत्यैर्जालं राक्षसैश्च त्रिलोहं गणैः शैलं सैकतं मातृकाभिः॥

136. *Sadānandopaniṣad,* I., pt. II., p. 378. V.1.ff

137. *Śivopaniṣad,* I.24,
हृद्यन्तःकरणं ज्ञेयं शिवस्यायतनं परम्।
हृत्पद्मं वेदिका तत्र लिङ्गमोङ्कारमिष्यते॥

138. *Vatukopaniṣad, Up. S.* pt. II. p. 317,
अक्षराज्जायते कालः कालाद्व्यापक उच्यते।

139. *Ibid.,* p. 317,
उच्छ्वासिते तमो भवति तमस आपोऽप्स्वङ्गुल्या मथिते मथितं शिशिरे शिशिरं मंयमानं फेनं भवति फेनादण्डं भवत्यण्डाद्ब्रह्मा भवति ब्रह्मणो वायुर्वायोरोंकार ओङ्कारात्सावित्री सावित्र्या गायत्री गायत्र्या लोकाः भवन्ति॥

140. *Ibid.,* p. 315,

141. *Vanadurgopaniṣad, Up. S.* pt. II. p. 430,
हेतुकं पूर्वपीठे तु ह्याग्नेय्यां त्रिपुरान्तकम्। दक्षिणे चाग्निवेतालं नैर्ऋत्यां यमजिह्वकम्॥

142. *Vatukopaniṣad, Up. S.* pt. II. p. 317,
व्यापको हि भगवान्वटुको भोगायमानो यदा शेते रुद्रस्तदा संहरते प्रजाः॥

143. *Śarabhopaniṣad.* 4.
स एकः श्रेष्ठश्च सर्वशास्ता स एव वरिष्ठश्च। यो घोरं वेषमास्थाय शरभारव्यं महेश्वरः॥

144. *Ibid.,* 7[b].
यो ब्रह्मणः पञ्चमवक्त्रहन्ता तस्मै रुद्राय नमो अस्तु॥

145. *Ibid.,* 11.
यो दक्षयज्ञे सुरसङ्घान्विजित्य विष्णुं बबन्धोरगपाशेन वीरः।

146. Desai., S.G., *op. cit.,* p. 109.

147. *Śarabhopaniṣad,* 8[a].
यो विस्फुलिङ्गेन ललाटजेन सर्वं जगद्भस्मसात्संकरोति। पुनश्च सृष्ट्वा पुनरप्यरक्षदेवं स्वतंत्रं प्रकटीकरोति॥

148. *Jābālopaniṣad,* I. 1[d],

अत्र हि जन्तोः प्राणेषूत्क्रममाणेषु रुद्रस्तारकं ब्रह्म व्याचष्टे येनासावमृतीभूत्वा मोक्षी भवति...।

149. *Rudropaniṣad,* pt. II. p. 308. ll. 3, 5.,

अधमश्चाण्डालोऽपि शिवभक्तोऽपि ब्राह्मणाच्छ्रेष्ठतरः।
...शिवलिङ्गार्चनयुतश्चाण्डालोऽपि स एव ब्राह्मणाधिको भवति।

150. *Atharvaśira. Up. Up. S.* pt. I. p.171. ll. 1-10.

151. *Dhyānabindūpaniṣad,* I. 21-31.

ब्रह्मा पूरक इत्युक्तो विष्णुः कुम्भक उच्यते।
रेचो रुद्र इति प्रोक्तः प्राणायामस्य देवताः॥ .... विचिन्तयेत्।

152. *Nīlarudropaniṣad,* I. 3[a],

एष एत्यवीरहा रुद्रो जलासभेषजीः।

Ibid., I. 4[a],

नमस्ते भवभामाय नमस्ते भवमन्यवे।

Ibid., I. 5[a],

यामिषुं गिरिशन्त हस्ते बिभ्यर्षस्तवे।

Ibid., II. 6[a],..,

निशीर्य शल्यानां मुखा शिवो नः शंभूराभर...। शम्भुः-सुखहेतुः ...।

153. *Śarabhopaniṣad,* I. 29,

यत्परात्परं ब्रह्म यत्परात्परतो हरिः। परात्परतो हीशस्तस्मात्तुल्योऽधिको न हि॥

154. *Skandopaniṣad,* I. 8,

शिवाय विष्णुरूपाय शिवरूपाय विष्णवे। शिवस्य हृदयं विष्णुर्विष्णोश्च हृदयं शिवः॥

155. *Śarabhopaniṣad,* I. 16,

यत्पादाम्भोरुहद्वन्द्वं मृग्यते विष्णुना सह.. भक्त्या नम्रतनोर्विष्णोः प्रसादमकारोद्विभुः।

156. *Pārmātmikopaniṣad, Up. S.* pt. II, P. 95,

अच्युतानन्तगोविन्दमन्त्रानुष्टुभं परम्। ओम् नमः संपुटीकृत्य जपन् विषधरो हरः।
यन्नजीर्णं च गरळं कण्ठे स्तब्धं कपालिनः। अन्तरात्मधृतस्तस्य हृदये गरुडध्वजः॥

Siddhāntaśikhopaniṣad, I. 1,

विश्वाधिकं शङ्करं ये प्रमूढा हीनं विष्णोर्ब्रह्मणो वा वदन्ति। न संसारात्प्रमुच्यन्ते कदाचिच्छतैः कल्पैः कोटिभिर्वाऽथ दोषैः।

157. *Praśna. Up,* I. 4,

तस्मै स होवाच प्रजाकामो वै प्रजापतिः स तपोऽतप्यत स तपस्तप्त्वा स मिथुनमुत्पादयते। रयिं च प्राणं चेत्येतौ मे बहुधा प्रजाः करिष्यत इति॥

158. *Tait. Up,* II. 6.1

सोऽकामयत। बहु स्यां प्रजायेयेति। स तपोऽतप्यत। स तपस्तप्त्वा। इदँ सर्वमसृजत। यदिदं किञ्च। तत्सृष्ट्वा। तदेवानुप्राविशत्।

159. *Tṛmn. Up.* I. 1[a], *Akṣamālikā. Up.* I.1[a].

160. *Kaivalya. Up.,* I.1[a].

... अथाश्वलायनो भगवन्तं परमेष्ठिनमुपसमेत्योवाच। अधीहि भगवन्ब्रह्मविद्यां वरिष्ठां...।

also, *Kātyāna. Up.* 1, *Kalisaṅ. Up.*1.

161. *Vanadurgopaniṣad, Up. S.* pt. II. p. 442,

ऊर्ध्वायां दिशि ब्रह्मा देवता। हंसारूढो रक्तवर्णः कमण्डलुहस्तो ब्रह्मा बध्नातु ब्रह्ममण्डलम्...।

also *Ibid.,* 452,

ऊर्ध्वायां दिशि ॐ नमो भगवति ब्रह्माणि स्त्रुक्स्त्रुवकमण्डल्वक्षसूत्रहस्ताभ्यां..।

162. *Gāyatrīrahasyopaniṣad, Up. S.* pt. II. p. 405, ll. 3-4.

163. *Gopūlpārvatāpinyupaniṣad, Up. S.* pt. I. p. 592. l. 17.

164. *Tulasī. Up.* II 6[cd],

यन्मूले सर्वतीर्थानि यन्मध्ये ब्रह्मदेवताः।

165. *M.N. Up.,* II. 18,

चतुर्मुखाय विद्महे कमण्डलुधराय धीमहि। तन्नो ब्रह्मा प्रचोदयात्।

166. *Atharvaśikhopaniṣad,* I. 1-2[a],

पूर्वाऽस्य मात्रा पृथिव्यकारः स ऋग्भिर्ऋग्वेदो ब्रह्मा वसवो गायत्री गार्हपत्यः। प्रथमा रक्ता ब्राह्मी ब्रह्मदेवत्या ...।

...सर्वाञ्जयति ब्रह्माऽबृहत्सर्वकारणानि संप्रतिष्ठाप्य ध्यानाद्विष्णुर्मनसि नादान्ते परमात्मनि..

also, *Bilvopaniṣad, Up. S.* pt. II. p. 304,

वामदक्षिणमध्यस्थं ब्रह्मविष्णुशिवात्मकम्।
इन्द्रादयश्च यक्षान्ता वृन्तभागे व्यवस्थिताः॥

167. *Dhyānabindūpaniṣad,* I. 31,

कुम्भकेन हृदि स्थाने चिन्तयेत्कमलासनम्।
ब्रह्माणं रक्तगौराभं चतुर्वक्त्रं पितामहम्॥

168. Kinsley, David, *Tāntric Visions of the Divine Feminine (The Ten Mahāvidyās),* Delhi. 1998. p. 1.

169. *Mahākālasaṁhitā, Kāmakala khaṇḍa,* Allahabad. 1947. pp. 65, 66.

170. Prabodhachandra, Bagchi, *Studies in the Tantrs-s*, Calcutta. 1975. p. 101.

171. Winternitz, Maurice, *A History of Indian Literature*, Vol. I, Delhi. 1981. p. 569.

172. Banerji, Sureshchandra, *Tantra in Bengal : A Study of its Origin, Development and Influence,* Delhi. 1996. pp. 155-156.

173. Ed. by Alper Harvey, P., *Understanding Mantras,* p. 568.

174. *Devyupaniṣad, Up. S.* pt. I. p. 542, l. 2,

साब्रवीदहं ब्रह्मस्वरूपिणी।

175. *Ibid.,* p. 542, l.1-9.

176. *Ibid.,* p. 543, l. 8-9

हृत्पुण्डरीकमध्यस्थां प्रातःसूर्यसमप्रभाम्। पाशाङ्कुशधरां सौम्यां वरदाभयहस्तकाम्।
त्रिनेत्रां रक्तवसनां भक्तकामदुधां भजे॥

177. *Ibid.,* p. 542-(V. 1),

अहं रुद्रेभिर्वसुभिश्चराम्यहमादित्यैरुत विश्वेदेवैः।
अहं मित्रावरुणावुभौ बिभर्म्यहमिन्द्राग्नी अहमश्विनावुभौ।
अहं सोमं त्वांरं पूषणं भगं दधाम्यहम।
विष्णुमुरुक्रमं ब्रह्माणं उत प्रजापतिं दधामि॥

4a - तामग्निवर्णां तपसा ज्वलन्तीं वैरोचनी..॥

178. *Guhyakālyupaniṣad, Up. S.* pt. II, I. 71^{cd},

तत्कारणं सांख्ययोगाधिगम्यं ज्ञात्वा देवीं मुच्यते सर्वपाशैः॥

179. *Ibid.,* I. 50,

नवद्वारे पुरे देवी हंसी लीलायतां बहिः।

also, I. 32

नवद्वारं पुरं कृत्वा गवाक्षाणीन्द्रियाण्यपि।
सा पश्यत्यत्ति वहति स्पृशति क्रीडतीच्छति॥

180. *Kālikopaniṣad, Up. S.* pt. II. p. 401,
अभिनवजलदसंकाशा घनस्तनी कुटिलदंष्ट्रा शवासना कालिका ध्येया।

181. *Ibid.,* p. 401,
...काली कपालिनी कुल्ला करुकुल्ला विरोधिनी विप्रचित्ता उग्रा उग्रप्रभा दीप्ता नीला घना बलाका मात्रा मुद्रा ऽमिता...।

182. *Guhyaṣodhānyāsopaniṣad. Up. S.* pt. II. p. 420.
कालसंकलनात् काली।

183. *Kālikopaniṣad, Up. S.* pt. II. p. 401.
ब्राह्मी नारायणी माहेश्वरी कौमारी अपराजिता वाराही नारसिंहिका...।

184. *Hamasaṣodhopaniṣad, Up. S.* pt. II. p. 474,
...महामुण्डमालाधारिणी महाकालप्रिये मां रक्ष रक्ष।
षट्चक्रवासिनि वागीश्वरी जिह्वाग्रे वस।
...महात्रिपुरभैरवी पुस्तकाक्षमालाधारिणि शत्रुमुखस्तंभनं कुरु...।
...महामारि मारहारिणि दारिद्र्यं हर...। लम्बोदरि मातर्महामंगलप्रिये मम जाड्यं छेदय...।

185. Bhandarkar, R.G., *op. cit.,* p. 142

186. Desai, S.G., *op. cit.,* pp. 131-134.

187. *Devyupaniṣad,* I. 18,
...दुर्गात्संत्रायते यस्माद्देवी दुर्गेति कथ्यते।

188. *Ibid.,* I.15,
हृत्पुण्डरीकमध्यस्थां प्रातःसूर्यसमप्रभाम्।
पाशाङ्कुशधरां सौम्यां वरदाभयहस्तकाम्। त्रिनेत्रां रक्तवसनां..।

189. *Vanadurgopaniṣad, Up. S.* pt. II. p. 427. l. 11,
सौवर्णाम्बुजमध्यगां त्रिणयनां सौदामिनीसन्निभां। शङ्खं चक्रवराभयानि दधतीमिन्दोः कलां ब्रिभ्रतीम्।

190. *Ibid.,* p. 426, l. 14,
...महिषोत्तमाङ्गसंस्थां नवदूर्वासदृशी श्रियेऽस्तु दुर्गा।
Ibid., p. 427. l. 3,
उद्यत्भास्वत्समाभां विधृतनवजपामिन्दुखण्डावबद्धां।
हारग्रैवेयभूषां मणिगुणवलयाद्यैर्विचित्राम्बराढ्याम्॥

191. *Ibid.*, p. 426, L.10-13,

अरिशङ्खकृपाणखेटबाणान् सधनुश्शूलकतर्जनीर्दधानाम्।
...हेमाब्जस्थां पीतवस्त्रां प्रसन्नां देवीं दुर्गां दिव्यरूपां नमामि।

192. *Ibid.*, p. 427, l.15,

सिंहारूढां श्यामकान्तिं शङ्खचक्रधराम्।

193. *Ibid.*, p. 431, l.11-15,

घोरघोरानने नयनोज्ज्वलज्वालासहस्त्रपरिवृते महाट्टहासधवलीकृतदिगन्तरे...
मधुकैटभ महिषासुरधूम्रलोचनचण्डमुण्डप्रचण्डरक्तबीजशुम्भनिशुम्भदैत्यनिकृन्तके।...

194. *Ibid.*, p. 433, l. 17-22,

ऐकाहिकं द्व्याहिकं... सांवत्सरिकं वातिकं पैत्तिकं आपस्मारिकं ब्राह्मिकं ... सान्निपातिकं संततज्वरं .... विषमज्वरं ... आदि सर्व रोगान् सर्वविषं जहि जहि।

Ibid., p. 458, l.15-16,

अरूणी वारुणी रक्षेत् सर्वग्रहनिवारणी।
सर्वदारिद्र्यशमनी सर्वराजवशङ्करी॥

195. *Ibid,* p. 459, L. 1-5,

एकविंशतिवाराणि परिजप्य शुचिर्भवेत्।
पत्रं पुष्पं फलं दद्यात् स्त्रियो वा पुरुषस्य वा।
अवश्यं वशमित्याहुरात्मना च परेण वा॥

महाविद्यावतां पुंसां मन:क्षोभं करोति य:।
सप्तरात्रौ व्यतीतायां स च शत्रुर्विनश्यति॥

196. *Pītāmbaropaniṣad, Up. S.* pt. II. P. 421, l. 1-9,

...पीतवाससं पीतालङ्कारसंपन्ना ...।
...स्वर्णसिंहासनमध्यकमलसंस्थां ...।
ब्रह्मास्त्रांमहाविद्यां शाम्भवीं सर्वस्तम्भकरीं सिद्धां..
स्ढीभूतपीनोन्नतपयोधरयुग्माढ्यां..
चतुर्भुजां दक्षाभ्यां कराभ्यां मुद्गरपाशौ वामाभ्यां शत्रुजिह्वाव्रजे..
ललाटपट्टोस्सत्पीतचन्द्रार्ध..
अथ हैनां ब्रह्मरन्ध्रे सुभगां ब्रह्मास्त्रस्वरूपिणीमाप्नोति।

197. *Ibid.*, p. 422, l.1-11, 8,

ब्राह्मी माहेश्वरी कौमारी वैष्णवी, वाराही नारसिंही चामुण्डा etc. and

मोहिनी वश्या अचला चला ... मदगमना ... भोगा योगिका कल्पना कालकर्षिणी ..

भ्रमरिका शींल.

198. *Ibid.*, p. 422, l. 11-12,

षड्योनिगर्भांता डाकिनी राकिनी लाकिनी काकिनी शाकिनी हाकिनी...।

199. *Rājaśyāmalārahasyopaniṣad Up. S.* pt. II. P. 423, ll. 8-11

मन्त्रजपाधिकरणन्यासाधिकरणस्त्रोत्राधिकरणपूजाधिकरणमैथुनाधिकरणै: पञ्चाभिब्राह्मणो भोगमोक्षमाप्नोति। ...शुक्रवारे भार्याजगन्मोहनचक्रे त्रिशतं मन्त्रजपेन मन्त्रसिद्धि:।

200. *Bahvṛcopaniṣad, Up. S.* pt. I. pp. 651, 650.

सत्यमेकं ललितारव्यं वस्तु तदद्वितीयमरवण्डार्थं परं ब्रह्म।

...सैव पुरत्रयं शरीरत्रयं व्याप्य बहिरन्तरवभासयन्ती

देशकालवस्त्वन्तरसङ्गान्महात्रिपुरसुन्दरी वै प्रत्यक् चिति:।

201. *Ibid.*, p. 651, L. 3-5,

अयमात्मा ब्रह्मेति वा ब्रह्मैवाहमस्मीति वा योऽहमस्मि वा सोऽहमस्मीति वा... या भाष्यते सैषा षोडशी श्रीविद्या।

202. *Tripuratūpinyupaniṣad,* I.

203. *Annapūrṇopaniṣad,* I. 5, 9[b], 8[a], 3.1[a]

नित्यानन्दा निराधारा विख्याता विलसत्कचा॥

विष्टपेशी महालक्ष्मी: कामस्तारो नतिस्तथा॥

अन्नपूर्णा विशालाक्षी स्मयमानमुखाम्बुजा॥

नमो भगवत्यन्नपूर्णे ममाभिलषितमन्नं देहि स्वाहा॥

तां मे ब्रूहि महाविद्यां मोक्षसाम्राज्यदायिनीम्।

निदाघो नाम योगीन्द्र ऋभुं ब्रह्मविदां वरम्॥

204. *Sarasvatī R. Up. Up. S.* pt. I. p. 645. ll. 2-3,

नीहारहारघनसारसुधाकराभां कल्याणदां कनकचम्पकदामभूषाम्

उत्तुंगपीनकुचकुम्भमनोहराङ्गीं वाणीं नमामि मनसा वचसा विभूत्यै॥

205. *Ibid.*, p. 646, l. 27,

नमामि यामिनीनाथलेखालंकृतकुंतलाम्।

206. *Ibid.*, p. 646, ll. 22-24,

अक्षसूत्राङ्कुशधरा पाशपुस्तकधारिणी।

मुक्ताहारसमायुक्ता वाचि तिष्ठतु मे सदा॥

कम्बुकण्ठी सुताम्रोष्ठी सर्वाभरणभूषिता।

207. *Ibid,* p. 646, l. 21,

नमस्ते शारदे देवि काश्मीरपुरवासिनि।

l. 25,

भक्तजिह्वाग्रसदना॥

208. *Ibid.*, p. 645, l. 15,

अनादिनिधनानन्ता सा मां पातु सरस्वती।

209. *Ibid.*, p. 646, ll. 8-9,

व्यक्ताव्यक्तगिरः सर्वे वेदाद्या व्याहरन्ति याम्।

210. *Ibid.*, p. 646, ll. 26-27,

भवानीं भवसंतापनिर्वापणसुधानदीम्।
यः कवित्वं निरांतङ्कं भुक्तिमुक्ती च वाञ्छति।
सोऽभ्यर्च्यैनां दशश्लोक्या नित्यं स्तौति सरस्वतीम्।

211. *Ibid.*, p. 647, l. 5

ब्रह्मत्त्वं मे सदा नित्यं सच्चिदानंदरूपतः।

212. *Gāyatrīrahasyopaniṣad, Up. S.* pt. II. P. 406

सायं संध्या सरस्वती वृद्धा कृष्णांङ्गी कृष्णवासिनी कृष्णगंधमाल्यानुलेपना शंखचक्रगदामयहस्ता गरुडारूढा विष्णुदैवत्या सामवेदसहिता आदित्यपथगामिनी स्वर्गलोकव्यवस्थिता॥

213. *S. L. Up. Up. S.* **pt.** I. P.653 L3, 12-13.

...सवार्वेत्कटां सर्वमन्त्रासनगतां पीठोपपीठ देवतापरिवृतां..।
अरुणकमलसंस्था तद्रजःपुञ्जवर्णा करकमलधृतेष्टाऽभीतियुग्माम्बुजा च।
मणिकटकविचित्रालंकृताकल्पजालैः सकलभुवनमाता संततं श्रीः श्रियै नः।

Ibid, p. 653, ll. 19-21

भूयाद्भूयो द्विपद्माभयवरदकरा तप्तकार्तस्वराभा।...

... रक्तौघाबद्धमौलिर्विमलतरदुकूलार्तवालेपनाढ्या पद्माक्षी पद्मनाभोरसि कृतवसतिः पद्मगा श्रीः श्रियै नः।

214. *Ibid.*, p. 654, L. 2-6,

श्रीलक्ष्मीर्वरदा विष्णुपत्नी वसुप्रदा हिरण्यरूपा स्वर्णमालिनी रजतस्रजा स्वर्णप्रभा स्वर्णप्राकारा पद्मवासिनी पद्महस्ता पद्मप्रिया मुक्तालंकारा चन्द्रसूर्या बिल्वप्रिया ईश्वरी भुक्तिर्मुक्तिर्विभूतिर्ऋद्धिः समृद्धि कृष्टिः पुष्टिर्धनदा धनेश्वरी श्रद्धा भोगिनी भोगदा सावित्री धात्री विधात्री ...।

215. *Ṛv.,* VII. 63.1[a,c,d], 4[b].

उद्वेति सुभगो विश्वचक्षाः।
चक्षुः मित्रस्य वरुणस्य देवः।
चर्मेव यः समविव्यक्तमांसि।
दूरे अर्थस्तरणिर्भ्राजमानः।

216. Bhandarkar, R.G., *op. cit.,* p.157.

217. *Sūryopaniṣad, Up. S.* pt. I. p. 509. ll. 9-10,

...रक्ताम्बुजसंस्थितं। सप्ताश्वरथिनं हिरण्यवर्णं चतुर्भुजं पद्मद्वयाभयवरदहस्तं कालचक्रप्रणेतारं श्रीसूर्यनारायणं य एवं वेद स वै ब्राह्मणः...

218. *Sūryatāpinyupaniṣad, Up. S.* pt. II. p. 55. ll. 21,

प्रत्यक्षदैवतं भानुः परोक्षं सर्वदेवताः।

219. *Sāvitryupaniṣad,* I. 6,

कः सविता का सावित्री आदित्य एव सविता द्यौः सावित्री स यत्र आदित्यस्तत्र द्यौर्यत्रवा द्यौः तदादित्यस्ते द्वे योनी तदेकं मिथुनम्।

220. *Sūryopaniṣad, Up. S.* pt. I. p. 509,

सूर्याद्यज्ञः पर्जन्योऽन्नमात्मा नमस्ते आदित्य।

221. *Akṣyūpaniṣad, Up. S.* pt. I. p. 511. L.1-2,

सहस्त्ररश्मिः शतधा वर्तमानः पुरुषः प्रजानामुदयत्येष सूर्यः।

222. *Ibid.*, p. 510, l. 24,

हंसो भगवाञ्छुचिरूपः प्रतिरूपः।

223. *Sūryopaniṣad, Up. S.* pt. I. p. 509. ll. 17-18,

आदित्याद्वायुर्जायते। आदित्याद्भूमिर्जायते। आदित्यादापो जायन्ते। आदित्या-ज्योतिर्जायते आदित्याव्द्योम दिशो जायन्ते।

224. *Ibid.*, p. 509, l. 17, p. 510, l. 3

आदित्योन्तःकरणमनोबुद्धिचित्ताहंकाराः...। आनन्दमयो ज्ञानमयो विज्ञानमय आदित्यः... असावादित्यो ब्रह्म।

225. Desai, S.G., *op. cit.*, pp. 81-82.

226. *Ibid.*, p. 88.

227. Bhandarkar, R.G., *op. cit.,* pp.147-148.

228. *Gaṇapatyupaniṣad, Up. S.* pt. I. p. 571, ll. 5-8,

एकदन्तं चतुर्हस्तं पाशमङ्कुशधारिणम्।
अभयं वरदं हस्तैर्बिभ्राणं मूषकध्वजम्॥
रक्तं लम्बोदरं शूपकर्णकं रक्तवाससम्।
रक्तगन्धानुलिप्ताङ्गं रक्तपुष्पैः सुपूजितम्॥

...नमो व्रातपतये नमो गणपतये नमः प्रमथपतये
नमस्तेऽस्तु लम्बोदरायैकदन्ताय विघ्ननाशिने शिवसुताय
श्री वरदमूर्तये नमो नमः॥

229. *Ibid.*, p. 571, l. 8,

अविर्भूतं च सृष्टयादौ प्रकृतेः पुरुषात्परं।
एवं ध्यायति यो नित्यं स योगी योगिनां वरः।

230. *Gaṇeśa P. Tā. Up., Up. S.* pt. I. p. 631, ll. 25-28, p. 632, ll. 1-3,

क्षीरोदार्णवशायिनं कल्पद्रुमाधःस्थितम् वरदं व्योमरूपिणं प्रचण्डदण्डदोर्दण्ड़ं वक्रतुण्ड़स्वरूपिणं पार्श्वार्धः स्थितकामधेनुं शिवोमातनयं विभुम्। रुक्मांबरनिभाकाशं रक्तवर्णं चतुर्भुर्जम्। कपर्दिनं शिवं शान्तं भक्तानामभयप्रदम्॥ उन्नतप्रपदांङ्गुष्ठम् गूढगुल्फं सपार्ष्णिकं। पीनजंघं गूढजानुं स्थूलोरुं प्रोन्नमत्कटिम्। निम्ननाभिं कम्बुकण्ठं लम्बोष्ठं लम्बनासिकं। सिद्धिबुद्धिउभयाश्लिष्टं प्रसन्नवदनाम्बुजम्॥

231. *Ibid.*, p. 632, ll. 11-12,

सर्वाणि ह वा इमानि भूतान्याकाशादेव जायन्ते जातानि जीवन्त्याकाशं प्रयन्त्यभिसंविशन्ति। तस्मादाकाशबीजं शिवो विद्यात्।

232. *Herambopaniṣad, Up. S.* II. p. 390.5^{b}-7,

प्रभुः प्रभूणामपि विघ्नराजः सिन्दूरवर्णः पुरुषः पुराणः॥
लक्ष्मीसहायोऽद्वयकुञ्जराकृतिश्चतुर्भुजश्चन्द्रकलाकलापः।
मायाशरीरो मधुरस्वभावस्तस्य ध्यानात् पूजनात्तत्स्वभावाः॥
संसारपारं मुनयोऽपि यान्ति स वा ब्रह्मा स प्रजेशो हरिः स।
इन्द्रः स चन्द्रः परमः परात्मा स एव सवार्वे भुवनस्य साक्षी॥

233. Dikshit, S.H., *Bhāratīya Tattvajñāna,* Kolhapur, 1990, pp. 1-13.

234. Bakre, A.B., *op. cit.* p. 24.

CHAPTER IV

THE WAY TO THE SUPREME REALITY

Having discussed the *ālambana*-s in the Upaniṣads, it would be interesting to focus attention on the virtues one has to imbibe while treading the path of spirituality and the learning of *vidyā*-s which lead to the goal.

Preparation

The Upaniṣads have unanimously stated that the realization of the Ātman or the Brahman will not be possible unless someone who has already realized, shows the correct way. The first necessity to get on the way of knowledge is to have an ideal guide who can lead and direct; as the path of knowledge is hard to traverse and is as sharp as the edge of a razor.

An initiation in the path of Self-realization by a worthy spiritual guide was considered to be imperative and its significance lies in the fact that only that teacher who himself has reached the other shore can take his aspiring disciple to the other shore. Thus, the *Kaṭh. Up.* has mentioned that, unless one has a spiritual teacher of a superior calibre, spiritual knowledge would be hard to attain. Likewise, unless the initiation comes from a spiritual teacher who has realized his identity with the Self, there can be no knowledge regarding the subtle path which transcends all power of logic and argumentation. "Let us not divert our intellect towards wrong ways by mere logic. For how can we hope to attain the knowledge of the Ātman unless we are initiated by another?"[1] Another passage of the Upaniṣad instructs, "Arise, awake and learn from those who are better than you."[2]

These and other such passages from the Upaniṣads make it very clear that only an experienced soul can generate the experience in the aspiring soul, only the burning lamp can light another lamp. Without the grace of a spiritual teacher, one is bound to wander astray.

Deussen, P. has explained the term Upaniṣad as, 'confidential secret sitting' (session); meant for imparting secret instruction.[3] The seeker, on getting a worthy teacher would naturally want to have all his problems; regarding knowledge; solved by the teacher because he would not like to lose this opportunity as he sits face to face with the profoundly illumined teacher. In the *Kaṭh. Up.*, we find that Naciketas; who is a true seeker; rejects all tempting offers made to him by Yama and adheres to his original quest about the ultimate nature of the things because he knows that he would not have such a teacher to reveal the Supreme mystery. In the benedictory verse of the *Kaṭh. Up.*, we find a prayer for the protection and enjoyment of both, the teacher and the disciple whose joint endeavour makes the study all the more luminous.[4] Here, the teacher is conceived as forming one part, and student the other part.[5] Both of them conjointly make a whole, and their conjoint endeavour is more radiant. For this, the disciple had to become an *antevāsin*, *i.e.*, he had to confine himself to the family of a teacher and stay there for a long time to learn and serve. Only then one could expect the knowledge to dawn. The fourth chapter of the *Chānd. Up.* narrates a story of Upakosala, who stayed with his teacher, tended the sacrificial fire with faith, perseverance and patience, and served his master for twelve years. Only then he could become a worthy recipient of the knowledge.[6]

In a parable of the *Chānd. Up.*, a teacher is regarded to be as essential as the remover of a bandage of a blindfolded man who wishes to find his way home. While commenting on this passage, Śaṅkara has stated that our real home is *sat,* our eyes are bandaged with worldly desires. When a person; the knower of the Self; is met and when a way is pointed out, then the bonds are broken down and one is released.[7]

Monier Williams tried to trace the origin of personified human gods. He believed that the origin of such gods was influenced by the preaching of Buddha. According to him, Buddha's religion which emphasized the importance of charity, liberty, equality and fraternity attracted the masses and after his death, Buddha was deified by his followers. This marked the beginning of a new phase of religion. From that time onwards, Indian people felt the need to revere personal and human gods.[8]

The Upaniṣads have stressed upon the necessity of a worthy, enlightened *guru* again and again. For, according to them, the subtle and mystic knowledge could not be attained by one's own individual effort. The *Śvet. Up.* stated that, whose devotion for his teacher is as intense as that for the God, only to him the objects are revealed.[9] "The *Śruti* has said that the *guru* indeed is the Hari incarnate" says the *Brahmavidyopaniṣad.*[10] While praising the greatness of a *guru,* the *Śuka. R. Up.* stated that, to him I propitiate, who is the form of eternal Bliss, beyond duality, the bestower of the highest Bliss, the one always steady, pure, resembling the sky, beyond existence (*bhāva*), devoid of the three *guṇa*-s.[11]

The *Dvayopaniṣad*, which is devoted to the praise of the two syllables of the word '*guru*', has stated that the former syllable in the word represents the ignorance of a student and the latter means the destruction of the same.[12] Thus, one who removes the ignorance of a student and brings about the union of the *jīva* with Śiva; of the finite with the infinite; is a real preceptor. The *Śivopaniṣad* says, "*Guru* is the father, the mother and the Highest Śiva. One who has such fixed notion, emancipation is not far off from him."[13]

Thus, the later Upaniṣads considered *guru* as the Highest divinity, as he is considered as the Brahman incarnate. Doubt has been expressed by some people regarding the necessity of having a spiritual teacher. To the query that, can it not be attained by reference books? Ranade, R.D. answers, stating an apt quotation of Plato. Plato has said about the comparative value of knowledge to be obtained from books and the knowledge to be obtained from a teacher by a word of mouth. The former is entirely lifeless and the latter is the outcome of full-fledged life of the master. For, the books cannot solve the actual difficulties in the path of Self realization, while a *guru* who himself has treaded the path, knows the difficulties of the aspirant, solves them and leads the aspirant to the path of spirituality step by step.[14]

About the method of approaching a teacher, there is one essential formality recorded in the Upaniṣads. While approaching the teacher, the student was expected to take sacrificial fuel in his hands. However, on several occasions, Yājñavalkya taught persons, including his own wife informally, without insisting on prior initiation. (*Bṛ. Up.* II. 4).

This custom of carrying sacrificial fuel symbolised the duty of the seeker to collect sacrificial fuel (*samidhā*), to beg alms and to serve his teacher humbly. This symbolic act also suggested a real flame of aspiration-of uniting with the God-burning in the heart of the seeker, who approached the teacher to burn ignorance and dispel darkness; the aspirant desired to have a deep and comprehensive knowledge of the Supreme Reality.

The Qualities that are to be Imbibed for Self-Realization

Brahmacarya

When students aspiring to have sacred knowledge approached teachers and when they were accepted as disciples of the system, they had to undergo rigorous training. Along with learning the lores, they had to inculcate and develop many virtues. The Upaniṣads used the term *brahmacarya*, which denotes the period of rigorous training. This was the period for the conservation of forces or channelizing forces towards the achievement of the goal. This method was followed by the sages of the Upaniṣads as they knew that without proper conservation of the energy, the imparted knowledge cannot be retained. According to the *Praśna Up.*, "The Ātman is to be sought after by penance, celibacy etc."[15] Thus, Upakosala observed celibacy before he obtained knowledge.[16] Indra and Virocana also spent thirty-two years in celibacy before they were initited.[17]

The *Muṇḍ. Up.* warns that, this Ātman cannot be attained by one who is devoid of strength, ... and then assures that he who strives by these means, enters the abode of the Brahman.[18] Hence, along with the observance of celibacy, physical fitness was also required so as to hold the Supreme essence.

The *Tait. Up.* begins with *śīkṣāvallī*, wherein we find a prayer as follows. "May my body be strong. May I be fit to hold the immortal essence."[19] Again, in the *Ken. Up.*, a prayer is recited to strengthen all the limbs and different senses with the divine strength.[20] Prayers like these, reinforce the thought mentioned above.

Radhakrishnan, S., commented on the verse of the *Tait. Up.* (I. 4.1). He has stated that this is a prayer for acquiring retentiveness, and for physical and moral health.[21]

Purity of the Being (*Sattvaśuddhi*)

To obtain constant remembrance, the Upaniṣads prescribed purity of the whole being, *i.e.* the purity of the body and mind. According to the Upaniṣads, this purity depends on the nature of the things we take in and assimilate. To keep the body healthy, pure food must be consumed; because "Its middle portion builds the body and its subtlest portion forms the mind."[22] This is an *āhāraśuddhi*, a primary step leading to *sattvaśuddhi*. Later, the term *āhāra* conveyed a wider connotation. It did not merely restrict itself to eating. It also implied *āharaṇa* or gathering. *Āhāra*, according to Śaṅkara means the knowledge of sense-objects (*śabdādiviṣayajñāna*).[23] Hence, the seeker must discriminate between good and bad; and resolve to discard bad. This act of taking in is performed by different senses. Śaṅkara interpreted the word *sattva* as the *antaḥkaraṇa*.[24] So, all the senses are to be cleansed for they are conducive to spiritual health and well-being. In the prayer of the *Praśna Up.*, it is said, "Let us hear by our ears, good and beneficial. Let the eyes behold the good alone."[25] Training of the senses to behold just good, leads to tranquility, which in its turn results into an equilibrium of all senses. The Upaniṣads have termed this equilibrium of senses as the Yoga,[26] and the training which leads to this equilibrium is called *brahmacarya*. The Upaniṣads have looked upon *brahmacarya* to be a sacrifice. Different periods of a man's life are considered to be the oblations offered. Thus, the *Chānd. Up.* has stated, "Verily this is a *yajña*."[27]

The purity of the being results into constant remembrance *i.e. dhṛvāsmṛti*, which was believed to be leading to the final release. Maintenance of continuous flow of constant remembrance was believed to be destroying knots (*granthī*-s).[28] According to Śaṅkara, these knots represent desires, passions of many lives, formed due to *avidyā*.[29] The later Upaniṣads, especially those pertaining to Yoga, stress the importance of pure and measured food, beneficial in the study of Yoga and to avoid the food which causes obstacles. During the practices of Yoga, leading to the purity of the being; (*sattvaśuddhi*), one is advised to take a diet of milk and ghee and avoid spicy, oily, hot, sour and bitter food.(*Y.T. Up.* I. 28^b, 47,48). Thus, the meaning of the word *āhāraśuddhi* is elaborated in the later Upaniṣads.

Resolution (*Kratu*)

Kratu primarily means a resolution and secondarily, a *yajña*. A man is made up of a resolution. Whatever purpose a man has in this world, so does he become.[30] The *Īśa. Up.* expected man to remember what he had resolved and what he had done;[31] because only the thing he had passionately desired would determine his future embodiment. The Upaniṣads laid down injunctions to follow the truth, perform penance etc. and mentioned the prohibitory actions, that are to be avoided. A right resolve makes a right man. The perseverence of the right resolve or vow is called as '*śirovrata*' in the *Muṇḍ. Up.*[32]

Truth

In the *Tait. Up.*, the very first instruction is, "Speak the truth."[33] By adhering to truth, one gradually stabilizes one's own reason. By cultivation of truth, the mind is purified. It becomes candid and honest. According to the *Bṛ. Up.*, "The abode of truth is this heart, for by the heart this truth is known."[34] Truth was considered to be the Supreme quality essential for a disciple. The importance of the value of truth can be known through the story of Satyakāma Jābāla. When Satyakāma approached his spiritual teacher for initiation, the teacher asked him from which family he hailed. In a straightforward manner, Satyakāma replied that he knew nothing about his family except his mother's name. He also informed that she herself also did not know who his father was, as she had led a wanton life in her youth. The teacher Gautama then initiated him, as he had not swerved from the truth.[35] This story indicates that even the son of a wanton girl cherishing the value of truth must be the son of a Brāhmin. Again, in the same Upaniṣad, it is told that truth has a power; it even saves one from death; for truth is merely a counterpart of the Reality. The story also states that a burning axe cannot cause harm to a man who covers himself with truth. On the contrary, if he lies, the burning axe would bring about his destruction.[36] The story reflects an unshakeable belief in the power of truth. Even the *Praśna Up.* has stated, "He who speaks untruth gets totally dried up, one should not dare speak untruth.[37] The *Muṇḍ. Up.* has stated that, this Self within the body, of the nature of light and pure, is attainable by truth, austerity by right knowledge and practice of chastity."[38] The truth alone conquers, not the untruth. By truth is broadened the path leading to the Gods; by which travel the sages who have all their desires fulfilled, wherein lies the supreme abode of the Truth" declares the *Muṇḍ. Up.*[39] The practice of truth as a moral virtue was believed to be enabling one to reach the Absolute. In a dialogue between Nārada and Sanatkumāra, Sanatkumāra told Nārada, "Truth is to be found only in the attainment of Reality; what people call truth, is no Truth at all."[40]

Ranade, R.D. believed that truth is the ultimate moral correlate of the realization of the Absolute.[41]

In consonance with the Earlier Upaniṣads, the Supreme virtue, 'truth' is glorified by the later Upaniṣads. The speech, in harmony with body mind and actions, the words of real nature, that are beneficial to the beings, is 'truth' according to the *Śāṇḍ. Up.*[42] The *Jābāla. D. Up.* stated that whatever is seen by eyes, heard by the ears, *i.e.* whatever is experienced by the senses, that knowledge is expressed in the same manner, and not otherwise, is the truth. However, the knowledge that all this is verily the Brahman is the highest Truth. This Upaniṣad also stated that the truth and the Ultimate are just the same.[43] The practice of 'truth' which is a virtue is a means to the Self realization. If one takes into consideration the broader connotation of the word 'truth', which also is another name of the Brahman,[44] one may say that the 'truth' is the realization of the fact that all this is the Brahman.

Tapas

There is a frequent occurence of the term *'tapas'* in the Upaniṣads. *Tapas* primarily means heat. The penance practised by Prajāpati before he created the universe is frequently mentioned in the Upaniṣads. Thus, *tapas* here means the conservation of the supreme force or energy, the primal heat which produces the universe; or the energy at the root of creation. Later, *tapas* meaning heat, Supreme force or energy came to mean the endurance of Self-imposed afflictions, that is penance. This was considered to be one of the means for the realization of the Self. Thus, the *Bṛ. Up.* says, "The Brāhmaṇa-s seek Him by practising *tapas,* by fasting, by performing sacrifices, by giving away gifts etc."[45] The *Chānd. Up.* states that those who observe penance, faith etc. in the forests, travel by the path of gods after death and attain the Brahman.[46] Self-inflicted afflictions were believed to be generating heat, force or energy. According to the *Bh. G., tapas* led to the purification of the body, mind and soul.[47] This primary work of cleansing was performed through *tapas.*

The later Upaniṣads defined penance as "wearing away of the body with hardships."[48] Taking a wider view, the *Jābāla. D. Up.*, stated that the *tapas,* in fact, meant the contemplation upon the idea of release from the chain of births and rebirths.[49]

Charity (*Dāna*)

There are ample illustrations of *dāna* throughout the Upaniṣads. In the *Kaṭh. Up.,* which begins with the theme of charity; it is pointed out that the gift of bad or useless things carries a person to the joyless worlds.[50] The *Tait. Up.*, explains in detail the right manner of offering gifts. It states that the Brāhmins who are superior to us should be comforted and should be offered a seat. The gifts that are to be given should be given with faith, should not be given without faith. The gifts should be given in plenty and should be offered with modesty, fear and sympathy.[51] Thus, the Upaniṣads point out the nature of gifts to be given and how they are to be offered. In one of the stories of the *Bṛ. Up.,* it is stated that gods, men and demons went to the father Prajāpati and requested him to impart the knowledge. He cryptically instructed them with a single syllable '*Da*'. The gods understood the meaning of '*Da*' as self-control (*dāmyata*), demons understood it as a practice of compassion (*dayadhvam*) and men understood it as charity (*dāna*). Further, it is told that, when the celestial voice, the thunderbolt repeats, *Da, Da, Da,* it intends to communicate these three sets of virtues, to be followed.[52]

Simplification of the Concept of *Dāna*

The concept of *dāna* is as old as the *Ṛv.* It is seen to be undergoing changes over the years. The sacrificial texts and the Purāṇa-s also stressed the importance of *dāna.* However, many a time they reflect selfish motive of the priestly class.

At times, the earlier Upaniṣads record the gifts of a hundred or thousand cows.[53] However, the Upaniṣads being philosophical portion (*jñānakāṇḍa*) of the Vedic literature, are never seen to be expecting people to give away or pay sacrificial fees with any selfish motive in view.

The period of the later Upaniṣads runs parallel to that of the Purāṇa-s.[54] The Purāṇa-s extolled the act of *dāna*, and proclaimed that with such and such type of *dāna*, one yould obtain a number of material and non-material benefits.[55] Though not many accounts of *dāna* are found in the later Upaniṣads, the *Śivopaniṣad*, in consonance with the Purāṇa-s, emphasizes the importance of various types of offerings made to Śiva, *guru*, Śiva-*yogins*, temples and the type of fruit attained thereby. Thus, the Upaniṣad says that he who offers a ripe pomegranate to Śiva or *guru*, is honoured in the world of Śiva, in relation to the number of seed in the fruit.[56] "He who offers a ripe fig, enjoys a number of pleasures for one lakh years in the world of Śiva."[57] From simple gifts like flowers, leaves, fruits, needle, nail-cutter etc. to expensive gifts like gems, corals, pearls, chariots, gardens, land, decorative and useful objects, cows, buffaloes could be offered to the devotees of Śiva, temples of Śiva etc.[58] "He who supports the life of a widow, an orphan and old men enjoys greatness in the world of Śiva" says the Upaniṣad.[59]

These accounts of charity throw light on the fact that masses could take part in the act of charity, and thereby follow religion. Consequently, it seems that the later Upaniṣads opened the doors of religion and knowledge to common people.

Reverence for Parents and Respect for Guests

The whole aim of Brahmavidyā is to seek the Divine in every form. He is more easily grasped in the living and concrete form of parents. Parents are to be looked upon as the Divine incarnates.[60] The primary virtues such as truth are first imbibed from the parents. The tradition of Brahmavidyā was also handed down from the father to the son (*smaprati, sampradāna*).[61] As the father entrusted to the son; the son also should regard his father as the Divine or the spiritual teacher. A guest too, is to be looked upon as a god and worshipped as such.[62] Hospitality to be shown to him is to be considered as a worship and not a duty. The roots of this tradition are to be found in the *Ṛv.*, where Agni is are looked upon as an *atithi*-s.[63] In the *Kaṭh. Up.*, Naciketas stayed in the house of Yama, whereupon Yama stated that, when a Brāhmin guest enters the house, one must regard it as the entry of Agni himself.[64] "The absence of the worship of a guest spoils the Agnihotra sacrifice", stated the *Muṇḍ. Up.*[65]

Dharma

The word *dharma*, ordinarily translated as 'religion' or 'virtue' connotes different senses in different schools and religious traditions of Indian thought. With the changing time, connotation of the term '*dharma*' underwent various changes.

Artha, kāma, dharma, mokṣa are the four *puruṣārtha*-s, which were considered to be the goals of human life. The former two were secular values and the latter two were the spiritual ones. *Dharma* was given utmost importance as it was the means to the goal, the supreme ideal, *i.e. mokṣa*. *Dharma* was that which was conducive to *mokṣa*.

During the age of sacrificial texts, '*dharma*' stood for sacrifices, performed for securing material benefits such as health, wealth and progeny. They were performed in order to collect merit (*apārva, puṇya*) and enjoy pleasures in the heaven after the fall of this material body. The aim in view was the attainment of the heaven and the like. The Mīmāṁasāsātra begins with an enquiry regarding the nature of *dharma*. It was defined as, that good which is determinable only by the Vedic commands-[66] which means only those desirable results which are attainable by operation (sacrifice) which are performed strictly in accordance with the Vedic injunctions.

Hence, *dharma* in this sense had nothing to do with the God, or with ordinary or customary morality or any kind of mystical or religious fervour as it is understood now. It simply stood for the Vedic rituals and the fruits acquired through their performances. *Dharma* had a sway over all kinds of emotions, feelings and exercises, of intellect. There was no slightest trace of any internal spiritual law, or rational will or loyalty to God's will. It was only a strict loyalty to external spiritual commands.

During the period of the *Smṛti*-s, *dharma* no longer remained restricted to the Vedic commands. Manu defined *dharma* as that, which is always followed by the learned who are devoid of attachment and antipathy and that which appeals to the heart.[67] This means *dharma* included the following of the customary practices of good people and the performance of beneficial actions that may produce mental satisfaction.

Dange, S.A. has stated that each *yuga* had its own ideal *dharma* for *e.g.* performing sacrifices was the most ideal *dharma* of *dvāpāra yuga* and *dāna* was that of *kali.* He has defined the term *dharma* as a tradition of customs, beliefs, duties of a particular group of society for protecting and supporting themselves, which leads to a firm bondage. This bondage binds different components of society. It protects and supports the society. Dange, S.A. observed that though Hindu *dharma* was based on traditions, it was not characterised by traditionality. It underwent several changes along with the changing conditions and customs. In the changing times, the Vedic religion accepted several non-Vedic ideas and customs; prevalent then; and the synthesis of these two brought about transformation of the Vedic religion into Hinduism and soon it was evolved into a religion of the masses.[68] The term *dharma* is also defined as that which protects, sustains, supports and uplifts society.[69]

In the earlier Upaniṣads, there are many evidences that throw light on how *dharma* was conceived in those days. The *Tait. Up.* contains a passage where a disciple is advised to follow good actions of his spiritual teacher who has balanced views, who has known the Brahman, who is cautious, gentle...[70] This statement indicates that, one should always mould one's conduct on the pattern of the conduct of persons who are better disposed and who can be ideal.

This statement also supports the above quoted definition of *dharma* in the *Mbh.* and shows how certain behavioural pattern gets rooted, is transformed into a 'rule' and then becomes a part and parcel of the tradition.

In the *Bṛ. Up., dharma* and truth are equated. The Upaniṣad states, "What is *dharma* is verily the truth; therefore, when one speaks the truth he is said to be speaking about *dharma;* or when one speaks about *dharma* he is said to be speaking about the truth,"[71] *i.e.* if one knows the truth. he must act in the right manner; when action and thought (of truth) are in harmony, *dharma* will be established. *Dharma* is thus an actualisation of truth. The *Tait. Up.* (I. 1.11) has ordained, "Follow religion (*dharmaṁ cara*)." Here, *dharma* is not religion as it is generally understood; rather it is a basic or inherent nature of a thing which sustains it. It also is an inspiration (*codanā*) to all actions.[72] Every action should have an inspiration as its base and that too, for a noble purpose–is the significance of the command. It can also mean righteous conduct (*sadācāra*).

According to the scriptures, *dharma* is comprised of *abhyudaya* and *niḥśreyas.*[73] It enables one to grow, to prosper and then to have complete freedom from the fetters of life and birth and obtain bliss thereby.

Hence, *dharma* in the Upaniṣads is a means of achieving the Supreme Truth.

Faith

Faith is the most important value for a seeker. Faith protects the seeker like a mother. It initiates the quest and sustains the seeker till the end of his spiritual journey. Faith induces one to enquire. In the *Kaṭh. Up.,* in case of Naciketas, faith entered into him and induced him to reflect. He insisted that Yama should expound on the Supreme Truth as he was endowed with faith.[74]

In the story of Śvetaketu, his father taught him that the imperceptible and the subtle Brahman is the cause of visible world through the illustration of a fig fruit. The father explained; when the finest seed is broken into minute particles, nothing can be seen in the minutest particle. Still a large tree grows out of that seed. Similarly, the Brahman which is subtle is the cause of visible manifestation. Even here, the father expected the son to have faith (*śrāddhasva*).[75] Śaṅkara has commented that the most subtle things are hardly apprehended without deep faith, if one is fascinated by external objects. With faith, the mind can focus its attention on the object desired to be known, which at a later stage is known.[76] The *Bh.G.* emphasizes on *śraddhā* and says that he who is full of faith attains Knowledge; and on the contrary, one devoid of it is lost to the spiritual path.[77] When Nārada went to Sanatkumāra for instruction, he told that when one has faith, he thinks. Only he who has faith, contemplates.[78] Śaṇakara commented that, belief in the Being and contemplation on that is *śraddhā*.[79] According to the *Bṛ. Up.*, (*Bṛ. Up.* III. 9.21) "the abode of faith is the heart; for through the heart one knows faith." Thus, according to the Upaniṣads, *śraddhā* which resides in the heart, initiates the quest, induces one to contemplate, leads one to the knowledge of the Self. Hence, the *Muṇḍ. Up.* has stated, "those who practise austerity and faith... depart through the door of the Sun, where dwells the immortal Person.[80]

The later Upaniṣads also stressed the importance of observance of *brahmacarya,* truth, penance, *dharma śraddhā* etc. but they do not elaborate, or describe profusely these virtues, probably because they were already grasped and accepted.

The Pleasant and the Beneficial

The seekar has to be ever alert and conscious while choosing between the pleasant and the beneficial. Naciketas of the *Kaṭh. Up.*, is a true seeker because he refused to be tempted by the offers of *preyas* made by Yama and exhibited his steadfast attention on *śreyas* alone.[81] He who falls prey to the allurement of pleasant things loses his purpose, while he who chooses the beneficial is wise. Śaṅkara in his exposition on the Brahmasūtra (I. 1.1) pointed out that the discrimination between the eternal and non-eternal (*nityānityavastuviveka*) is one of the prerequisites after which deliberation on the Brahman can proceed.[82]

The later Upaniṣads, while disclosing the path of spirituality for the masses, do not disregard the *preyas.* On the contrary, they point out the aim, *i.e.* the Brahman to be reached, and promise a number of material gains that may be secured by a *sādhaka* while performing his *upāsana*. Thus, one who studies the *Śaṇk. Up.*, gets the fruit of sacrifice, obtains peace, purity of mind, the fruit of visiting all sacred places. Saṅkarṣaṇa is the bestower of release.[83] One who knows the *anuṣṭubh* royal spell with reference to Gaṇeśa, obtains wealth and attains to immortality.[84] The worship of *Rāmayantra* leads to release. It bestows good health, life and sons to those, who do not have any.[85]

One who mutters *'haṁsa, haṁsa'* does not suffer from diseases, old age and death. He obtains *siddhi*-s like *aṇimā* and finally attains Īśvara.[86]

Thus, both the beneficial and the pleasant are combined in the *upāsanā*-s of the later Upaniṣads, probably to induce the masses to follow the path of spirituality.

Ahiṁsā

It may be noted that non-violence does not occupy a privileged position in the earlier Upaniṣads. It is mentioned just once along with other virtues in the *Chānd. Up.*[87] The stress on non-violence might have come along with the origin and popularity of Buddhism.

However, the later Upaniṣads laid great emphasis on the principle of *ahiṁsā*. Especially the Upaniṣads that propounded the doctrine of Yoga glorified *ahiṁsā*. The *Śāṇḍ. Up.* stated that, *hiṁsā* means afflicting others with activities performed by mind, speech and body.[88] As against it, *ahiṁsā* means not to cause harm in any way to any living being.[89] Again, the Upaniṣad says that, the knowledge that the Ātman is omnipresent and uncut is *ahiṁsā*.[90] Banerjee, S. has stated that in the system of Yoga, the ethical percepts are comprised in the *yogāṅga*-s called *yama* and *niyama*. Of these, *ahiṁsā* is the principal virtue from which arise all other virtues. Further he says, "*Ahiṁsā* of the philosophy of Yoga is universal and cannot be compromised under any circumstances. Certain groups of people commit *hiṁsā* on certain occasions or in compliance with a practice pertaining to their communities or professions. But *yama* of *Yogaśāstra* requires its observance irrespective of caste, religion, time and custon.[91]"

The later Upaniṣads also laid due stress on the inculcation of virtues while treading the path of realization. Ranade, R.D. has opined, "It is undoubtedly true that in the discussion of the practical side of ethics, the Upaniṣadic period is surpassed by the neo-Upanisadic period."[92] The later Upaniṣads tried to give due importance to ideal thought, firm belief (*niṣṭhā*) and an attempt was undertaken to turn the extrovert tendency of mind inwards. At the same time, giving due importance to ethical and moral aspect, they stressed the importance of qualities such as compassion (*dayā*), purity (*śauca*) etc. following which the society as a whole was benefitted.

Yama

Yama is tenfold which comprises of the virtues such as; non-violence, truth, non acceptance of another person's possessions (*asteya*), celibacy, compassion (*dayā*), straightforwardness or rectitude of conduct (*ārjava*), forgiveness (*kṣamā*), steadfastness (*dhṛti*), measured acceptance of food (*mitāhāra*), purity of being (*śauca*).[93]

Asteya

It is a state of being non-covetous of others' wealth. The *Īśa. Up.* has expressed the same thought.[94] Ghosh, Aurobindo's commentary on the verse of the *Īśa. Up.* clarifies the underlying idea. He has stated, "... the terms of this liberation are freedom from egoism and consequently freedom from personal desire. Practically, this renunciation implies that one should neither regard anything in the universe as a necessary object of possession, nor as possessed by another...nor as an object of greed in the heart or the senses. This attitude is founded on the perception of unity for all souls are one possessing Self; and although the Lord inhabits each object as if separately, yet all objects exist in the Self."[95]

The other Upaniṣads reiterated the same points. Thus, the *Śāṇḍ. Up.* stated that the absence of desire for wealth of others is, *asteya.*[96] According to *Jābāla. D. Up.*, the actions performed in ignorance, without the discrimination between the Self and the non-Self is *asteya.*[97] For, when everything is seen as the form of the Ātman, theft is not possible. Thus, one may say that with the adornment of the virtue *asteya*, illusion of the separate ego-sense (*ahaṁkāra*) which makes each being conceive of itself as an independent personality diminishes and one proceeds towards the concept of unity.

Compassion

The highest compassion, to regard all the beings as one's own Self is *dayā.*[98]

Rectitude of Conduct (Ārjava)

Is to treat a friend, wife, son and even an enemy as one's own Self.[99]

Forgiveness

Forgiveness is to treat pleasant and unpleasant alike or to be tranquil, calm in the bodily and mental torture, or to remain calm even if others speak harsh words is 'forgiveness'.[100]

Steadfastness (Dhṛti)

Dhṛti is the state of being calm and undisturbed in any calamity like that of the loss of wealth or death.[101] It is also a conviction that the knowledge of the Veda would lead to the release from the bondage of *saṁsāra.*[102]

Mati

Mati is a firm belief in the actions enjoined by the Veda-s.[103] It is also the knowledge in the form of, I am the Ātman not other than it, is called as *mati.*[104]

Consuming light, nutritious and agreeable food in measured amount is known as *mitāhāra*.[105] The *R. Jābāla. Up.* lays down that the sour, pungent, salty food and also garlic, onion should not be eaten.[106]

Śauca

The body, when washed with mud and water is cleansed. This is termed as external purity. With the study of philosophy and meditation, the mind gets purified and this is called as real *śauca*.[107] The knowledge that, I am pure, is *śauca* as is proclaimed by the wise.[108]

Tenfold Niyama-s

Penance, contentment, belief in God (*āstikya*) charity, worship of God, modesty (*ṛhi*), understanding (*mati*), *japa*, vow, listening to the established view of the Reality (*siddhānta*) are the virtues enlisted under the heading *niyama*-s.[109] The virtues as the devotion for the Guru, an interest in the path of the Truth, isolation, the *karman*-s that are performed without any desire etc. are enumerated in the *Maṇḍala Brā. Up.* under the heading *niyama*-s.[110]

Santoṣa

To be pleased with whatever one gets is known as *santoṣa*. Real *santoṣa* is to be desireless for all the worldly pleasures.[111]

To have firm belief in the *karman*-s enjoined by the Veda-s is known as *āstikya*.[112]

Feeling shy to act against the injunctions of the Veda-s and the feeling of shame to act against the worldly ways is known as '*rhï* '.[113] The belief in the injunctions of the Veda-s is known as *mati*.[114]

Repeated utterance of the spell as advised by the Guru, either in the mind or with speech is known as the *Japa*.[115]

Vrata

The adherence to the vow to perform the actions following the injunctions of the Veda-s and to abandon the actions prohibited by the Veda-s is known as a *vrata*.[116]

Tyāga

It is a renouncement of the phenomenal world, after introspecting of the ever existing essence of consciousness, the Ātman.[117] This is capable of giving instantaneous liberation from bondage, says the *Tejobindū Up.*[118]

Quietitude (*Mauna*)

This is of two types. The lower one refers to the word of mouth and is for the ordinary men.[119] The *yogin* observes quietitude by curbing all his outgoing senses and turning them inwards.[120]

Taking into consideration the principles of psychology, all these virtues are again divided into three groups in the *Śārīrakopaniṣad*. This description is similar to the description of the virtues; possessed by the persons endowed with *sāttvika*, *rājasa* and *tāmasa* qualities; in the *Bh. G.* The virtues such as non-violence, the truth, *asteya*, celibacy, non-acceptance are the *sāttvika* virtues. The feeling of self-importance, ego is associated with the *rajoguṇa*. The vices, lethargy, sleep, delusion etc. are associated with the *tamoguṇa*. It is also said that a person endowed with the qualities of goodness attains the heaven. A person possessing the evil qualities goes to the dark world and a person with the *rājasa* qualities stays in the mid-position; which means he is reborn on this earth again. The truth, adherence to duty and ignorance are his special qualities.[121]

The worship of the deities like Rudra, Viṣṇu etc. is considered to be a lower type of worship. But the real worship is; "not to hurt anyone by harsh words, not to hurt anyone with one's own behaviour and to be pure in the heart and speech."[122]

Repeated hearing and contemplaton of the Vedāntic thought; *i.e.* the Brahman is the truth, the consciousness and the bliss, is the Ultimate Reality; is known as the *siddhānta śravaṇa.*[123]

Condemnation of Immoral Acts

The *Chānd. Up.* warns that, "he who steals gold, he who drinks wine, he who has a desire for the wife of a teacher, he who kills a Brāhmin and also he who associates in these sins, suffers from eternal damnation."[124] This passage states that these were considered; by the Upaniṣadic seers; as five chief different kinds of sins. These were condemned and prohibited.

The Upaniṣads also discourage too much of learning as it amounts to mere play of words. 'One should not absorb oneself in many words, for that only tires the speech' says the *Bṛ. Up.*[125] It is possible that too much of learning leads to distraction and builds up an ego and arrogance. Only in a heart free from all prejudices and bias, the truth is revealed. That is why the innocence and simplicity of a child is sought to the exclusion of all outward scholarship and learning. The Upaniṣad says, "after fully exploring knowledge, one should desire to remain as a child."[126]

The *Śivopaniṣad* lays down the following taboos for the students who are in the company of their preceptors. "One should not laugh, yawn, speak loudly, spread his legs or sing in presence of the teacher."[127] A student should not wear shoes, use umbrellas, bed clothes etc. which were once worn by his Guru.[128] He should not talk to his teacher with his mind fascinated by something else, or while eating, standing and while sleeping.[129] One should not disobey his teacher. A student violating these rules goes to hell.[130] One should not find fault with his preceptor and should not discuss about the instructions of his preceptor and so on.

Views of Śaṅkara on Ethics[131]

Antarkar, W.R. has elucidated Śaṅkara's ethics comprehensively. He stated, "Among the means of liberation, Śaṅkara makes a distinction between internal (*aṅtaraṅga*) means and external (*bahiraṅga*) means. Direct knowledge of the Self is an internal and direct means while all others are external and indirect means." Further, he says that; according to Śaṅkara, qualification for knowledge is fourfold. (1) Discrimination between eternal and non-eternal, (2) Non attachment for the enjoyment of fruit-temporal or heavenly, (3) Rigorous discipline in the form of the control of the mind, bodily senses etc. (4) Desire for liberation. Quoting *Gītābhāṣya,* he says that, *Karman*-s such as sacrifice, *tapas, dāna, agnihotra* purify the mind when they are performed without any desire for fruit and with a spirit of dedicating them all to god.[132] *Karman*-s, therefore, are only indirectly useful for liberation. But they have to be given up after purification. Śaṅkara enjoins (1) listening to the Vedāntic expositions (*śravaṇa*), (2) meditating on what is heard and contemplation on the true nature of the Self (*manana, nididhyāsana*). (*Bṛ. Sū.Śā. Bh.* I. 4). In conformity with his own times, Śaṅkara insisted on observance of the caste rules and of the order and rules of *āśrama*-s. He believed that the gates of Eternal knowledge were open to all true aspirants. The real qualification was internal and anyone who had it could attain the goal. Ethics, according to Śaṅkara, has a meaning during the state of ignorance only. Once the individual soul cuts the knot of *avidyā*, realises his own nature truly and transcends the limits of the body with which he had identified himself so far due to *avidyā*, ethical ruies cease to exist for him. This, however, does not mean that he becomes a licentiate in practising immorality. On the contrary, he becomes super-normal; moral behaviour becomes his nature and whatever he does becomes a law and an ideal unto others. Every act of his; grounded as it is in the Self-knowledge; is rather an expression of Reality itself. Such souls work for the upliftment of the people.

Recapitulating on these values enumerated in the Earlier and the later Upaniṣads ardently, one may sum up the observations as follows :

Ahiṁsā which is just mentioned once in the earliėr Upaniṣ ads (*Chānd. Up.* III.14.4) gained importance in the later period and is glorified on the lines of the *Bh. G.* in the later Upaniṣads. This change might have been due to the spread of Buddhism. Moreover, though the earlier Upaniṣads laid stress on *tapas, svādhyāya* etc., yet they nowhere mentioned any form of offering of the fruit of all actions to god (*Īśvarapraṇidhāna*) during the preparatory stage, which later was propounded by the *Bh. G.* and followed by the works such as later Upaniṣads.

The basic principle underlying the inculcation of these values is to achieve, as Śaṅkara has said, purity of the physical being and of the mind (*sattvaśuddhi*) by training all the senses.[133] Consequently, the state of equilibrium may be attained which is conducive to the state of Bliss. There seems a marked change in the elaboration of virtues in later times as per the transition in social conditions. Due stress is laid on these moral values in the later Upaniṣads which bring about purity of oneself as well as harmony of society. They help to grow and to prosper, and then lead to complete freedom from the fetters of life and death.

Radhakrishnan, S. has rightly said, "when it is said that the Upaniṣads adopt a spiritual view of life, it does not mean that they despise body, life and mind. The values are the conditions or instruments for the life of spirit in man. They are not ends in themselves but are means or opportunities for the expression of the Universal Spirit in us. Spirit and life are not to be separated."[134]

Through a rigid discipline and strenuous endeavour, in the first stage of preparation, the purity of the being is sought. This purity, as said earlier, is not an end in itself, but it is to be acquired in order to qualify for the Brahmavidyā proper– which is an *upāsanā* or contemplation; and which accompanies the seeker all along. The injunctions 'speak' (*vada*) and act (*cara*) involve more or less the body and the will. But the unjunction '*upāsīta*' involves the mind. The word *upāsanā* which literally means 'to get near to' or to contemplate indicates the participation of the mind. The inner being is to grow from within, so it is necessary to let the flow of consciousness move without interruptions towards that goal, to be achieved.

Upāsanā

Śaṅkara defines *upāsanā* as the incessant wholehearted devotion for a particular object in the way sanctioned by the scriptures, uninterrupted by any other consciousness apart from it.[135] *Upāsanā* involves three factors.

(*i*) *Upāsaka* is the subject who contemplates (*viṣayin*).

(*ii*) *Upāsanā* is the act of contemplation.

(*iii*) *Upāsya* is the object, the support (*ālambana*), (*viṣaya*).

Thus, the act of contemplation is the link between the subject and the object. The aim of *upāsanā* is to ultimately merge one (subject) into another (object), through a gradual process of identification. To make the identification possible, the subject must be calm and tranquil.[136] The object too, must not be something imaginary but must be as sanctioned by the scriptures – as pointed out by Śaṅkara. If the object is of one's own fancy or imagination, there is a danger that one only moves in a world of imagination rather than getting anywhere near concrete realization.

Right knowledge (*vidyā*), faith (*śraddhā*) and mystic insight (*Upaniṣad*) are the three factors which contribute to the act of *upāsanā*. With the combination of these three, the *upāsanā* proceeds in a more appropriate and forceful way; than an act which is performed mechanically. "*Upāsanā* is not a mechanical act but an act illumined by right knowledge, sustained by faith and crowned with a mystic faculty" says Mukhopadhyaya, G.G.[137]

Upāsanā literally means, "to come near to." The sentences like "He is to be sought, he is to be enquired about" indicate the Ātman or the Brahman; as the object to be sought.[138] Here, the object to be approached is the very Self of the seeker, and nothing is external. Though it is always in us, one has to approach it. "Just as those who do not know, walk the field again and again over the hidden treasure of gold and do not find it, even so all creatures here go day after day into the world of the Brahman and yet do not find it, for they are carried away by untruth" says the *Chānd. Up.*[139] It is the purpose of *upāsanā* to restore the lost contact. This is brought about in two ways. With the help of *upāsanā*, the veil of ignorance is lifted and consequently the vision is extended and the gap between the subject and the object is narrowed. The purpose of *upāsanā* is to approach the object, to get near to the very Self of it and lastly to identify oneself with it.

Element of Karman in *Upāsanā*

Upāsanā is a process, which depends upon the subject. Consequently, there are gradations in it. It does not lead to an immediate and complete revelation. As it is the link between the subject and the object, the incomplete manifestation of Reality in the subject gradually grows clearer and more complete; the span of time depends upon the efforts of a person who contemplates. *Upāsanā* rests with the agent alone, because here things are moulded according to the thoughts. "As he thinks, so he becomes."[140] This becoming or transformation signifies the element of *karman* in *upāsanā*. Until one gets identified with the Reality of the object (the thing contemplated), one should go on thinking over it. One should always maintain a continuous flow of consciousness. It thus, requires uninterrupted effort by the subject, to get established in the Divine Consciousness. Thereafter, the thing contemplated becomes firlmly established and the smooth flow of consciousness becomes ensued.

The division in consciousness, *viz.* the waking, the dream, the deep-sleep states, is brought about by the *rajoguṇa* (*i.e.* the aimless thoughts) and the inconscience (*tamas*). The aim of *upāsanā* is to remove the split in consciousness. "By constant thinking, the thing contemplated sinks into the subconscious and continues to be revealed even in the dream state. This effort required, to contemplate constantly also refers to the element of *karman* in *upāsanā*.

Jñāna and *Upāsanā*

In *jñāna*, there is no process nor any hierarchy. It is a

revelation which is immediate and complete in itself. Also, it does not depend upon the efforts of the seeker, because it is not a product brought about by endeavours of an individual. It purely rests with the object itself. If the object reveals itself, only then it is revealed.[141]

The Path of Knowledge

The Brahman, though imperceptible and formless is described as having qualities for the purpose of *upāsanā. viz.*, in the *Chānd. Up.* (VIII. 7.1.), the Brahman imperceptible (to the mind) is said to be *satyasaṅkalpa.* The seeker of the Brahman contemplates, upon these points.

Element of Devotion in *Upāsanā*

A feeling of sincere attachment and deep adoration for the object are necessary for the act of contemplation. With deep attachment, the object intrudes on the mind even when one is engaged in performing other distracting activities. The element of feeling plays an important part in the act of contemplation. Taking into consideration this fact; the leading exponents of the *bhakti* school of thought like Rāmānuja laid their whole emphasis on the *dhṛvā smṛti* (*anusadhāna*) as the Supreme means of *sādhanā.*[142]

Thus, the Upaniṣadic *upāsanā* is neither purely emotional nor merely intellectual in nature. But it is an illumined act of the mind suffused with adoration. This is clearly indicated by the terms *vidyayā, śraddhayā* and *upaniṣadā.*[143]

"The Self, though hidden in all beings does not shine forth but can be seen by those subtle seers, through their sharp and subtle intelligence."[144] This sentence of the *Kaṭh. Up.* indicates the element of intelligence required for *upāsanā*. Feeling and devotion are also the components of *upāsanā*. The *Muṇḍ. Up.* says, "Pierce that goal by stretching the bow with the mind suffused by that feeling."[145] Again, *Kaṭh. Up.* says that, "not within the field of vision, stands this form. No one sees Him with the eye. By heart, by thought and by mind He can be apprehended, they who know this become immortal."[146] These sentences point out that the elements which constitute our psychic being have its share in the act of *upāsanā*. It is not one way approach either from the heart or the intellect but an integral seeking of the whole being. Hence; knowledge, action, love, and feeling–all are involved in the act of *upāsanā*.

Grades of *Upāsanā*

Contemplation, being dependent on the agent and being a function of the intellect differs in nature from person to person. According to Mukhopadhyaya, G.G., the grades of *upāsanā* are necessitated by the difference in the levels of intellect.[147] Further, he enumerates the grades as follows :

I. Symbolic (*pratīka*)

(*i*) Wealth (*sampat*) : Wealth of qualities added to otherwise insignificant or small things. *e.g.* the mind called as the Infinite.

(ii) Attribution (*āropa*) : Relation of the whole with a particular thing is attributed to the parts as well, *e.g.* *udgīthopāsanā*.

Attribution of a particular virtue to a particular thing only because it is ordained by scriptures, *e.g.* *Pañcāgnividyā*.

II. Subjective (*Āhaṁgraha*)

(*i*) *Saguṇa*, in which some qualities are bestowed upon the Self and contemplation goes on in that manner.

(*ii*) Abstract (*nirguṇa*) : Identification with the very essence of the being, *e.g.* the *upāsanā* of the *Oṁkāra* has a double aspect, both *saguṇa* and *nirguṇa*.[148] In the *Praśna. Up.*, the Oṁkāra signifies both the higher and the lower Brahman, and with this support the wise man reaches either of these two.[149] In the

> commentary upon this verse, Radhakrishnan, S. says that the verse distinguishes between the Unqualified Absolute (Brahman) and the qualified Personal Īśvara.[150] So, one who performs *upāsanā* of the Oṁkāra attains to any one of the two phases, the higher and the lower Brahman, *i.e. saguṇa* or *nirguṇa* Brahman.

Tilak, B.G. stated that the imperceptible Īśvara (*i.e.* the Brahman) is considered to be superior to the perceptible one. Further, he described this imperceptible Īśvara in three ways–

(*i*) that endowed with qualities,

(*ii*) that endowed with qualities, still devoid of qualities, and

(*iii*) that which is bereft of qualities.[151]

One need not always have a visible icon before oneself for the purpose of worship. It is also possible to worship a 'form' which is formeless (*nirākāra*). It means that, though the form is not visible to the eyes and is not perceptible to the senses, it must be perceptible to the mind. When the mind perceives some quality or the other contemplation is possible. As the mind is able to comprehend the form endowed with qualities, *upāsanā* must proceed in that direction. This is the first step. According to him, the dual (2nd) form may be looked upon as a step between *saguṇa* and *nirguṇa*, because one can realise the *nirguṇa* form only after realising the *saguṇa* form and then omitting qualities one after the other. In this ascending order, the worship of the symbols of the Brahman is described in the Upaniṣads. For instance, in the *Tait. Up.*, initially food is thought of as the Brahman and thereafter in gradual ascending order the forms of the Brahman; namely vital-force (*prāṇa*-s), mind (*manas*), knowledge (*vijñāna*) and joy (*ānanda*); are explained.[152]

The ability of the mind to comprehend the qualities of Īśvara again depend upon the merit of the worshipper. Therefore, different qualities of the Imperceptible Brahman, that are to be worshipped have been described in the Upaniṣads in accordance with the difference in the spiritual merit of the worshipper. Many forms of worship have been described in the Upaniṣads such as Śāṇḍilyavidyā (*Chānd. Up.* III.14), Puruṣavidyā (*Chānd. Up.* III.16.17) etc. which are dealt with in the third section of the third chapter of the Vedāntasūtra-s.

Some Prominent Vidyā-s Described in the Upaniṣads

The portion of the Upaniṣads, in which the qualities of Brahman are described for the purpose of worship is technically called *vidyā*. *Vidyā* means the path (in the form of worship) of reaching Īśvara. The Upaniṣadic term denoting such a path is seen to be ending with the word *vidyā*.[153]

The purpose of *upāsanā* is to know the Ātman or the Brahman. The whole enquiry is conducted in two spheres in the subject (Individual Self) as well as in the object (Universal Self), which means the contemplation may be carried on in two ways–synthetically and analytically.

The way towards synthesis is a process of building up separate elements or ideas into a collected whole, with which the union between the outer and inner spheres is sought. It essentially seeks the centre, where all the divergent lines merge. In the Upaniṣ ads, the three principal centres where the synthesis may be realized easily; are mentioned as the heart (*hṛdaya*) life (*prāṇa*) and the Sun (*Āditya*).[154] These are the symbols or the mediums which the Ātman may be sought.

Daharavidyā

Imagery of the City of the Brahman

As the city of a king has his subjects, attendants, who obey his orders, similarly this body is the city of the Brahman containing several senses, mind, the intellect, all serving the purpose of the master. The body is considered as the temple of God (*devasadana*).[155] The *Śvet. Up.* refers to the city of nine gates of the embodied Self.[156] The *Kaṭh. Up.* mentions the city of eleven gates of the Unborn Self.[157] The *Chānd. Up.* says, "Now in this city of the Brahman, is the subtle abode of lotus, within it is a small space. That which is within it should be sought, for that is what one should desire to understand."[158]

The heart is said to be the abode of the Ātman in numerous statements such as, "In the heart is the Ātman."[159] This Ātman inside the heart is smaller than a grain of a millet. This is my Self within the heart, greater than the earth... greater than the sky..."[160] "The inner Self, who is the Puruṣa, of the size of a thumb ever abides in the heart of all."[161] Further, this thought of the *Kaṭh. Up.* is echoed in the *Bh. G.*, where it is said that "the Lord resides in the region of the heart."[162] The *Chānd. Up.* has presented the etymological explanation of the word heart as, "This one (Ātman) is in the heart (*hṛdi ayam*), therefore, it is called a heart."[163] Thus, these sentences indicate the importance of the heart as it is the place where the Ātman is to be found.

The heart is the support, uniting place of all forms of knowledge.[164] The Supreme Virtues like the truth, faith etc. are rooted in the heart. "In what is truth found? In the heart, for by heart alone, the truth is known. In what is faith rooted? In the heart because through the heart is the faith known."[165] In the *Br. Up.*, Yājñvalkya says, "The heart verily is the Supreme Brahman."[166] Thus, the heart here, is identified with the Brahman. Therefore, all *vidyā*-s, all virtues, all the meanings and values; in fact, everything is rooted in the heart.

The imagery of the lotus; the inner abode of the Self is a subtle lotus of the heart (*Chānd. Up.*, VIII.1.1); also points out that it is the centre of the intellect. The *Tait. Up.* describes the nature of the Brahman and asks, "Who knows it as hidden in the cave founded in the Supreme Space?"[167] The *Ait. Up.* makes it clear by saying that the heart, the mind (*manas*) and all different functions of the intellect are only different names of intellect or *prajñāna* such as – *saṁjñāna, ajñāna,* and *vijñāna, prajñāna.*[168]

Inside this, is the subtle *ākāśa*. As pointed out by Śaṅkara, this is not a physical space but it signifies the name of the Brahman alone. "The Brahman is so called because of its subtleness, bodilessness and all-pervasiveness."[169] Thus, *ākāśa* is a symbol of the Brahman. The Brahman or the Ātman which is subtler than this space is to be sought herein. Thus, from the outer ranges of the city of Brahman, the seeker is led inwards, first into the inner abode-heart, and further to the subtle *ākāśa*.

The *Daharavidyā* (*Chānd. Up.* VIII. 1.1-6) further proceeds to show the harmony between the microcosm and the macrocosm by stating that "the earth and the heaven, all elements, gods, planets, whatever exists and does not exist all are to be found in the heart."[170] This may mean that, through the heart which is the real centre, a synthesis can be sought. Śaṅkara, in his commentary on the *Bra. Sū.* explains this concept and concludes, "It is understood that the small Space, seated in the lotus of the heart, is spoken of as the entity to be known together with earth etc., as well as the true desires (*satyasaṁkalpa*) included within It. And in accordance with the reasons adduced, this must be the Supreme Lord."[171]

The inner symbol–the centre of intellect is concentrated upon in the *Daharavidyā*; and through that the Ātman, who dwells in the subtle space of the heart is sought. Thus, this centre (the heart) is utilized uniquely for the realization of the Ātman.

The Pure being devoid of all determinations, may be conceived as non-Being (*asat*), because ordinary people find it difficult to conceive of the Real as out of space and time. Therefore, they are taught to think of it as an object endowed with qualities.[172] Herein, the symbol of 'the lotus of the heart' with the subtle space contained within, is stated to be the means with which Ātman can be sought after.

Udgīthopāsanā

The *Chānd. Up.* unfolds the *Udgīthopāsanā* and shows its importance from various points of view. In this *upāsanā*, the seeker first has to get hold of the Supreme Principle within himself through Prāṇa and then proceed to know it even outside himself through the symbol of Āditya. Thus, the process of building up seperate elements into a connected whole is carried out in this *upāsanā*. The seeker aims at knowing that Prāṇa and Āditya are just the two aspects of the same Supreme Principle and that there is no difference between the inner and the outer manifestation. The *Udgīthopāsanā* is first to be conducted through Prāṇa.

Initially, the Udgītha is identified with the syllable Oṁ. It is said that, "One should meditate on this syllable, the Udgītha, for one sings the loud chant beginning with Oṁ."[173] The syllable Oṁ, with which every recital of the Vedic chant begins, is here represented as the symbol of the Supreme and therefore the means of the meditation of the Supreme.[174]

The comments of Radhakrishnan, S., on this verse are worth considering. He stated that before one attains to the supreme vision of God, the contemplative realization, one has to resort to prayer and meditation. By singing and chanting with devout mind, fervour of spirit, with an inmost longing and with pure soul, the attention is directed lovingly and continuously towards the God. In meditation a symbol is furnished on which is concentrated the imagination and reasoning. Further, he concludes that one starts with a prayer and then resorts to meditation.[175]

Next, it is said that *Udgītha* is the ultimate essence of all things, by tracing the different sources of things step by step.[176] *Udgītha* is composed of speech (*ṛc*) and breath (*sāman*) which are again identified with *vāk* and Prāṇa respectively, and *Udgītha* is equated with the syllable Oṁ.[177] With the fusion of these two parts comes the fulfillment of desires. This syllable is of assent and assent is said to be fulfillment.[178] The speech (*vāk*) signifies reason and the breath (*prāṇa*) signifies movement-action.[179] Thus, *Udgītha* is a combined product of reason and action. And whatever is performed with knowledge as well as faith, together with the meditative knowledge (*upaniṣadā*), becomes more powerful.[180] In an allegory of rift between the gods and the demons, the gods by resorting to the *mukhya* Prāṇa, lifted themselves up from the sphere of death, and from the attacks of the demons.[181] 'Gods' stand for such functions of the senses as are regulated by scriptures and demons stand for such functions of the senses as affinity for all sensual objects and are of the nature of darkness.[182] Here, by the expression '*mukhya* Prāṇa' is indicated the universal principle and not the vital breath. (*mukhya* Prāṇa is also known as *āsya* as it exists in mouth. (*Chānd.* I.2.12). Now, the Upaniṣad describes the identity between what is inwardly called Prāṇa and outwardly expressed as the Āditya. In the Upaniṣads, many a time, Āditya is identified with Prāṇa. Thus, the *Praśna. Up.* says, "Āditya is verily Prāṇa."[183] "Āditya is the outer Prāṇa"[184] and so on. Here, the identification becomes distinct in the light of the similarity between their action, quality and effect. Both the Prāṇa and the Āditya are called as '*svara*' and *pratyāsvara* respectively, which denote, the 'coming and going of the Prāṇa' and 'rising and setting of the Sun.'[185] Thus, their names which signify their actions are similar.[186] Secondly, the Āditya rises for the benefit of people and sustains the entire creation. Prāṇa being the universal principle also sustains the beings. Thirdly, Prāṇa removes all sins and the Āditya destroys entire darkness and fear.

The name *Udgītha*, which is composed of the syllables *ud, gī, tha,* carries a hidden significance and by meditating on it, one can attain the fruit of contemplation.[187] Śaṅkara explained this as, "Even through the contemplation of the letters of the name, the named itself is contemplated."[188] This means that even the letters of a word may become a symbol; for the realization of the Reality; which are filled with deep significance. The Upaniṣad describes the significance of the word *Udgītha* and indicates the all pervasive nature of the three components of the word. Also, according to the Upaniṣad, each syllable is charged with a divine power. Hence, the right method of pronounciation is enjoined to avoid faults.[189]

Now, a deeper approach is made through the Udgītha. Through meditation upon Āditya, an attempt to penetrate deeply is made. "One begins with white lustre, then finds the deep dark blue and finally one views the Supreme Self within the Sun."[190] As in the Sun, so in the eye, this Supreme Self may be sought.[191] Thus, a seeker realizes the Universal Principle running through all and pervading all.

As in the *Daharavidyā*, the aim was to find the Ātman within the heart through synthesis, here too, the ultimate end is the vision of Puruṣa within the Sun or in the eye of the subject.

Madhuvidyā

The *Madhuvidyā* occupies a unique place in the *upāsanā*-s of the Upaniṣads due to its significance and mystic presentation. There are two different versions – one in the *Chānd. Up.* and another in the *Bṛ. Up.*

The *Chānd. Up.* has worked out a detailed imagery of the honey on the basis of the symbol of the Sun. Here, the Sun is considered as the honey (*devamadhu. Chānd. Up.* III.1.1), the atmosphere as the honeycomb and the heaven as the support or the cross beam from which the honeycomb hangs. The rays of the Sun are compared to bees that are engaged in producing, through this bee-hive, the celestial honey. The Upaniṣad then goes on to show how the Sun is the store of all wisdom and all effect. "The eastern rays of the Sun are its eastern honey cells. The *ṛc*-s are the producers of honey. The *Ṛv.* is a flower. Waters constitute the nectar and those very *ṛc*-s indeed are the bees."[192] Upon this Śaṅkara comments that just as the bees produce honey by extracting the juices of flowers, so do the *ṛc*-s make honey by extracting the juices of actions prescribed in the *Ṛv.*[193] The Upaniṣ ad further states that "these brooded on the *Ṛv.*, from it issued forth as its essence fame, splendour, virility (of senses) food and health." "It flowed forth; it went towards the Sun and that is the red appearance of the Sun."[194] In other words, the red form of the Sun is an embodiment of the fruits of action that follow from the *Ṛv.* Similarly, the southern rays are connected with the *Yv.* and through a similar process, honey is drawn which is the white form (*śuklaṁ rūpam. Chānd. Up.* III.2.3) of the Sun. The western rays are taken to be connected with the *Sāmaveda* and its ultimate form is the dark appearance of the sun. (*kṛṣnaṁ rūpam. Chānd. Up.* III.3.3) Again, the northern rays are connected with the *Av.* from which, honey when drawn, takes the deep dark hue. (*Paraṁ kṛṣnam. Chānd. Up.* III.4.3) But drawing of the honey is yet not complete, for though the Veda-s cover all existence do not exhaust the whole reality. The Supreme essence lies beyond existence. Now, the search is conducted in a different sphere. The upward moving rays are considered as the higher channels of honey. Here, the secret teachings are the bees and the flower from which honey is to be drawn is the Brahman itself.[195] This is the form of the Brahman – the Śabdabrahman – when brooded over will yield out the Supreme essence. Here, the essence or honey, is imagined to be devoid of any colour, because it is beyond all manifestations. The honey here is recognized only as if heaving at the centre of the Sun.[196] Śaṅkara says that one whose vision is calm and collected can behold this.[197] The Upaniṣad concludes by saying that, he who gains this knowledge, upon him drawns the eternal day".[198] Thus, the freedom from darkness is sought through the symbol, Āditya.

The version of *Madhyavidyā* in the *Bṛ. Up.* "depicts a long series of causes and effects, showing their mutual interdependence and finally mentions the Ātman to be the Supreme source of everything. The two versions of the text do not differ in the ultimate result although the approaches are different. It is said that the earth is the essence of all beings and the beings are also in turn its essence. This mutual production of one from the other becomes possible because of the presence of an identical principle in both. This principle is the effulgent immortal Puruṣa which inhabits both - the effect and the cause. This principle is inherent in the whole series of causes and effects, and yet beyond all this. Thus, finally one finds the Supreme Brahman, which has neither a beginning nor an end, which is neither in nor out, and which experiences all."[199] And this Brahman is the Ātman – the very Self of the seeker. Thus, step by step the Upaniṣad establishes complete identification of the Self with the Brahman. When the knowledge dawns upon the aspirant, he reaches the sphere of the eternal day as envisaged in the *Chānd. Up*. This is the consummation of the search for the essence (*madhu*).

The Analytic Way of Search

The analytic method discards all outer symbols through which the Ātman reveals itself. It tries to grasp the Ātman more directly by getting rid of all vestures or symbols, whereby one is able to view the Ātman, as the same single unity.

The Five Sheaths (*Bhārgavī Vāruṇī Vidyā*)

The constituent parts of the embodied Self are critically analysed and examined in order to find out the ultimate ground of the Self. These sheaths are as if the coverings of the Ātman, so the veils are to be lifted one after another, in order to apprehend the true nature of Reality. As Mukhopadhyaya, G. has explained, these sheaths are like so many bodies which are taken up by the Self in order to function at different levels or spheres of consciousness.[200] As the material sphere needs a material form, so the other subtler spheres demand similar forms constituted of subtler stuffs, which make it possible for the Self to function freely at those levels. Every level has its appropriate body, *i.e.* the instrument for making contacts with that particular sphere. The final aim is the realisation of the Reality which is beyond all those forms.

The *Brahmāvallī* of the *Tait. Up.* opens with an assertion that the knower of the Brahman attains the Supreme. Then it expounds the nature of the Brahman by defining it as Truth, Consciousness and Infinite. It lies hidden in the cave (heart) established in the supreme ether.[201]

The personality, of which we are conscious is purely material (*puruṣo annarasamayaḥ. Tait. Up.* II. 1). It is the last outcome of the spirit's downward movement which begins with the ether and ends with the earth.[202] So, the movement for release too, must begin from this level.

(*i*) **The Self Dependant on Food (*Annamaya Ātman*) :** It is the Ātman in the human body and in material nature, the bodily organs are its constituent parts. (*Tait. Up.* II.2.1[n]).

(*ii*) Within this is contained the 'Self dependant on the vital breath' (*prāṇamaya ātman*) the Ātman as the principle of natural life. The physical body is sustained by life. Its constituent parts are the vital breaths in man. And in a cosmical sense the whole of space is its body, the earth its foundation. By stripping off this Ātman as a sheath (*kośa*), one reaches the mental Self.

(*iii*) The Self dependant on *manas* or 'the mental Self' (*manomaya*)whose constituent parts are stated to be the four Veda-s with the Brāhmaṇa-s (*Tait. Up.* II.3.1[a]). According to Deussen. P., "By this definition, we are to understand; by it, the principle of the will (*manas*) embodied both in men and gods, *i.e.* of purpose directed to selfish ends. For it is this that on the human side is expressed in the Vedic sacrificial ritual."[203] According to Mukhopadhyaya, G., the mental Self is constituted of desires (*saṁkalpa, vikalpa*) and hence it is sometimes called subtle body (*liṅgadeha*). Until this body is transcended, an embodiment in the material plane is inevitable, for *manomaya* is at the root of desires. He has further stated that, this body which is constituted of the four Veda-s etc. signifies that it is wholly constituted of the principle of knowledge or consciousness.[204] When this is transcended;

(*iv*) deeper still is found 'the Self full of knowledge' (*vijñāna-maya* Atmaṇ), Radhakrishnan, S., with reference to these two *kośa*-s– *viz. manomaya* and *vijñānamaya* – has stated "*manas* is the faculty of perception. At the stage of *manas* we accept the authority which is external; at the stage of *vijñāna,* internal growth is effected. The Veda-s are our guide at the former level; at the intellectual we must develop faith, order, truthfulness and establish union with the Supreme."[205]

(*v*) *Ānandamaya Ātman* is the innermost kernel of man and is of the nature of the 'Whole'. This Ātman is full of Bliss "before whom words and thought recoil, not finding him."[206] is no longer an object of knowledge.

Interpretations Regarding the Sheaths

1. The *Tait. Up.* says that *yoga* is the very soul of *vijñāna-maya* (*Tait. Up.* II.4.1). According to Mukhopadhyaya, G., for this very reason, *vijñānamaya* is the link principle that connects the Absolute and the relative, Uncreated and the created, the Infinite and the finite. It is in the central position joining the upper and the lower hemispheres and its footing or pedestal has been indicated as 'vast' (*mahaḥ puccharn pratiṣṭhā. Tait. Up.* II. 4.1) Further, he has stated that the sphere of the 'vast' stands in the middle position of the seven spheres that embrace the whole creation. Below it are the three, *bhūḥ, bhuvaḥ, svaḥ* and above it the other three *jana, tapas* and *satya*. Below is the sphere of darkness, *i.e.* ignorance and above is the sphere of eternal light. Hence, those who seek a synthesis of the two contradictory principles of light and darkness lay their whole emphasis on this plane of *vijñāna*. To support this view, he has quoted the views of Ghosh, Aurobindo and has said that, "Aurobindo, being essentially imbued with a spirit of synthesis, makes his philosophy move on this central principle of *vijñāna*; which he has chosen to call 'supermind' in his own terminology. He believes that with the descent of this higher faculty of supermind, a total transformation and regeneration of the ordinary man is inevitable. Through the agency of supermind, the higher light will illuminate the lower spheres of matter, life and mind. Hence, to get in touch

with the sphere of light that lies beyond and then to bring it down to the earth-consciousness one must rend this veil of supermind (*vijñāna*). This will unravel the mystery of creation, solve the riddle of the universe."[207]

2. Śaṅkara thinks that our real Self is beyond the beautific consciousness (*ānandamaya*) though in his commentary on the *Tait. Up.* III.6 he stated that Bhṛgu identified the Ultimate Reality with the spirit of *ānanda*. Śaṅkarācārya on Brahmasūtra. I. 1.12-19, has identified *ānandmaya* with the absolute Brahman and not with a relative manifestation. The objection that the suffix *mayat* is generally used for the modification is set aside on the ground that it is also used for abundance. (*prācūryāt. Br. Sū. Śā. Bh.* I.1.13-14).

Ranade, R.D., presented another interpretation of modern theosophists and the importance that has been attached to the conception of these "bodies of man" by them. Corresponding to these bodies, the theosophists have also recognised seven different planes, on which the several bodies of man keep functioning. Thus, the various planes which they recognise may be said to be respectively the physical, the astral, the mental, the intuitional, the spiritual, the monadic and the divine. Ranade, R.D., tried to find justification for such a view in the light of the theory that the Upaniṣad advanced. The *Tait. Up.* has stated that, "within this physical body which is made up of food, is another body which is made up of vital air; the former is filled with the latter which is like the shape of man" ... and so on. (*Tait. Up.* II. 2-5) Here, it is told that various bodies are pent up within this physical body. Further, he concludes that the 'bodies' of man in the Upaniṣads are nothing more than mere allegorical representations of certain psychological conceptions. Man is made up of physical body, of vital air, of mind and intellect, and of the faculty which is of the nature of bliss and enjoys bliss, and this is what is meant by the passage (*Tait. Up.*, II.2-5) quoted above. To support this view, he quotes Śaṅkara, who did recognize the *kośa*-s but understood them as having merely an ideal existence. According to Śaṅkara they are to be discriminated in thought and one has to find the true Self beyond all these bodies and beyond the beautific consciousness. He insisted that the *kośa*-s have no real existence, and that a theory which is built upon the conception of the sheaths is a theory which is built upon ignorance."[208]

One of the later Upaniṣads, relates the five sheaths with the 'bodies' as follows. "What is brought into being only by the essence of food, what grows only by the essence of food, that which finds rest in earth full of the essence of food, that is the sheath made of food. That alone is the gross body. The five vital airs along with the organ of action constitute the sheath made of vital principle. Mind along with the organs of perception is the sheath made of mind. The understanding along with the organs of perception is the sheath made of intelligence. These three sheaths (of life, mind and intelligence) form the subtle body. The knowledge of one's own form is of the sheath made of bliss. That is the causal body."[209] These are the various interpretations regarding the sheaths. One may say that whatever be the interpretations, through the analysis of all these, discarding the possibilities one by one, one may reach the final aim which is the realization of the Reality beyond all forms – in its purity.

The third chapter of the *Tait. Up.*, discusses the ultimate source of the things, through the teachings of the father Varuṇa to his son Bhṛgu. Bhṛgu, by an analysis, rules out the theories that matter, life, mind, intellect could be regarded as the principle of things and comes to the conclusion that "intuitive Bliss" alone deserves to be regarded as the source of Reality.[210] Thus, it may be said that the world and the individual spring from the same source and hence, the Brahman is the Ātman and *vice-versa*.

Another example of the analytic way of approach is, the analysis of different states of consciousness of the soul, which have been discussed earlier. (*Ibid.*, pa. 74-80). An approach to the Reality by adopting the use of symbols has a drawback; one may say that it is the drawback of one's own mind. Being accustomed to view the Reality through a symbol, there may be a failure to apprehend the Reality fully when the symbol is withdrawn. The superiority of the analytic way of search, and the drawback of the symbolic approach are clearly shown in the famous Gārgya and Ajātaśatru episode in the *Bṛ. Up.*[211] Dṛptabālāki worshipped the Brahman as the Sun, the moon etc. His knowledge was limited till the collective apprehension of the Brahman as the Puruṣa in the Self or Ātman (*ātmanvi*).[212] But Ajātaśatru had an advanced knowledge of the Brahman, he knew Brahman as the Self (of everything). To make the Reality truly known to Gārgya, the king took him towards a sleeping man who inspite of being called by different names did not wake up. Finally, striking him by hand, he awakened him. Thereafter, the king enlightened Gārgya regarding the dream state and the state of profound sleep.

The king explained that the Self resides in itself during sleep; it goes to itself and comes again from itself. These two states of waking and sleeping must be watched carefully in order to know the Self. This is the Supreme significance of the instruction imparted here through the illustration of a sleeping man. As one must pass beyond the state of waking, so also one must go beyond the state of sleep, for both are the states of the mind, and the Ātman is not a state but an unchanging entity which remains the same in all the states and conditions.

According to Ranade, R.D., the four chief states of individual consciousness; described in the *Māṇḍ. Up.*, namely the *Vaiśvānara, Taijasa, Prājña* and *Ātman* have influenced a vast portion of the later Vedānta. Thus, the later Vedānta, mentions the Cosmic Self, that passes through its four states, namely Virāj, Hiraṇyagarbha, Īśa and Brahman which correspond to the four aspects of microcosm. The cosmic consciousness is to be regarded as corresponding state by state to the individual consciousness, and what is in the individual is to be found also in the world. Further, he has said that the *Māṇḍ. Up.* does not mention the four corresponding states of the cosmic Self and even though this idea of relation between the microcosm and macrocosm is not fully brought out in the Upaniṣads, one can trace the tendency towards that view.[213]

Broadly speaking, so far, two approaches *viz* approach by synthesis and by analysis are discussed. There are many other different methods of approach (*vidyā*-s) in the Upaniṣads. The Nārada-Sanatkumāra episode of the *Chānd. Up.* (VII.1-23) concerns itself with what is called as *Bhūmāvidyā*.[214] The discipline aims at the realization of the Infinite Self. In the story, Nārada, well versed in the Veda-s and the limbs of the Veda-s and different sciences approached Santkumāra to have the knowledge of the Self. To him, Santkumāra said, "Whatever you have learned is only a name. Meditate on the name." Further, Nārada asked whether anything was greater than the name. In answer to this question he was told that speech assuredly was greater than the name; for speech makes know the Veda-s. Nārada then was instructed to meditate on the speech as the Brahman. Those who meditate on speech as Brahman become independent so far as speech reaches. Further, Santkumāra told Nārada that mind was greater than speech and one has to meditate upon it as the Brahman. For, *manas* is an internal organ (*antaḥkaraṇa*) endowed with reflection.[215] It has for its function determination, decision, choice. It is said to be the Self because the Self as the character of the doer and the enjoyer only when the mind functions.[216] It is told that he who meditates on mind as Brahman becomes independent so far as the mind reaches. In this way, Nārada was told to meditate upon will, thought, contemplation, understanding, strength, food, water, heat, ether (*ākāśa*), memory, hope, life, truth, thought and understanding, faith, steadfastness (*niṣṭhā*), activity and happiness successively. Lastly, Nārada is told that, the Infinity is the happiness. There is no happiness in anything small (finite). It is the highest, the Infinite that can be reached. There is no happiness in the small, for it produces craving (*tṛṣ ṇā*), which is the seed of sorrow.[217] Śaṅkara comments that the empirical dualities are absent in the experience of the Infinite, and all empirical objects are subject to the law of change.[218] The greatness of the Infinite is rooted in its own greatness while things which are in region of small (*alpa*) are rooted not in themselves but in others.[219]

It may be inferred from the teachings of Santkumāra that spiritual freedom is at the basis of all actions. Spiritual freedom can be reached by stages. The Ātman is the source of all things, may it be a hope, memory, space, light, water etc. It is the source of all power, all happiness.

Oṁkāropāsanā

The *Māṇḍ. Up.* which belongs to the *Av.*, is an exposition of the principle of *A, U, M,* which refers to the three states of waking, dream and profound sleep. The Supreme Self is manifested in the universe in its gross, subtle and causal aspects. Corresponding to the four states of consciousness, wakefulness, dream, profound sleep, transcendental consciousness (*turīya*), there are aspects of the Godhead, the Supreme alone being all inclusive and ultimately Real.[220] The Upaniṣad; by itself, it is said in the *Muktiopaniṣad*, is enough to lead the aspirant to liberation.[221] In this Upaniṣad; fundamental approach to the attainment of Reality; by way of introversion and ascent from the changing, through mind which dreams and thinks, to the divine within; is found.

The syllable Oṁ, which is the symbol of the Brahman stands for the manifested world, the past, the present and the future as well as the unmanifested Absolute.[222] The Self is but One, but is viewed upon as having four quarters because in association with various limiting adjuncts, it functions in different ways in different states. Thus, He resides in the body in the right eye, is known as *Viśva*, experiencing the gross world by means of sense organs and the mind in the waking state. *Taijasa* resides in the mind and experiences the subtle in the dream state. *Prājña*, residing in the ether of the heart experiences bliss in the state of deep sleep. The fourth quarter, the *turīya* is all-pervading, immutable, non-dual. *Viśva* and *Taijasa* are bound by relation of cause and effect, perceiver and perceived, subject and object etc., under the influence of duality. *Prājña* is conditioned by cause alone. These two do not exist in the *Turīya*. The realization of non-duality can be achieved by the worship of the Oṁkāra. Corresponding to the three states are the three quarters of the Ātman and these can be regarded as resembling with or as equivalent with *A, U, M*, the three *mātrā*-s of the Oṁkāra. For the purpose of *upāsanā,* the symbol Oṁ is very useful, as it enables an aspirant to get a proper idea of the Self. Thus, *A* is equated with the *Viśva, A* is the first of the alphabet and *Viśva* deals with the gross which is first perceived and thus resembles *A*. As *A* is all pervading (*vyāpti*) *Viśva* also experiences all outer world. By meditating upon '*A*' as *Viśva,* the aspirant obtains preeminence and fulfills all his desires. The syllable *U* represents superiority and it is the joining link between *A* and *M*. Similarly, *Taijasa* is also superior, for it experiences the subtle and is also the link between the two states, namely the waking and deep sleep. By meditating on this syllable *U* as equated with *Taijasa,* the *sādhaka* secures excess and equanimity. The syllable *M* represents 'measuring' and 'merging', for *M* represents the limit of Oṁ and *M* merges into *A* and *U* to give a complete idea of Oṁ. In a similar way, *Prājña* lays down the limits of the *viśva* and *Taijasa* and after deep sleep comes again to the waking state. By meditating upon *M* as equated with the *Prājña,* one secures omniscience and the idea about merging (*laya*) into the highest. However, the meditation on these three *mātrā*-s of Oṁ as equated with the three quarters of the Self does not lead one to the highest knowledge – which is to realize *Turīya* or the Ātman without any quarters. This would correspond to Oṁ as a whole. The meditation on the *mātrā*-less Oṁ makes one free from fear for Oṁ is the Brahman itself.[223] To know Oṁkāra as a whole, one must know its parts (*mātrā*-s) equated with the quarters of the Ātman. There is no necessity of meditating upon anything else.[224]

The Oṁkāra and the *Praṇava* are one and the same.[225] A Vedic passage is expected to begin and end with Oṁ. Besides the *Māṇḍ. Up.* many Upaniṣads refer to the Oṁkāra and the Praṇava, identify it with the Brahman and glorify it as useful for meditation. The *Kaṭh. Up.* tells that "this is the best support, this support is the highest. Knowing this support, one becomes great in the world of Brahmā."[226] In the *Praśna Up.*, it is said that Oṁ is verily the higher and the lower Brahman.[227] The *Muṇḍ. Up.* imagines the syllable Oṁ to be the bow, one's own Self as an arrow and the Brahman is spoken to be the target of that. It is to be hit without making a mistake. Thus, one becomes united with it as the arrow becomes one with the target.[228] The *Mai. Up.* describes Oṁ as follows : This Oma is the sound form of this Self. Feminine, masculine and neuter; this is his sex form. The fire, wind and the Sun, this is his light form. Brahmā, Rudra and Viṣṇu; this is his lordship form. Gārhapatya Dakṣiṇāgni, Āhavanīya fires constitute his mouth form. The *Ṛg, Yajus* and *Sāman* (Veda-s) constitute his knowledge form. The earth, atmosphere and sky, this is his world form and so on. Therefore, by the utterance of the syllable Oṁ all these forms of the Self are praised and worshipped. Thus, it is said that the syllable Oṁ is verily the higher and the lower Brahman.[229]

The Upaniṣads repeatedly recommend the meditation by means of this supreme symbol to bring about the desired effect. The *Kaṭh. Up.* declares it to be the means of meditation as well as the goal to be reached by it.[230] The symbol in short, stands for both the means and the end of spiritual life.

The Oṁkāra in the Later Upaniṣads

Most of the Upaniṣads unanimously exalt the worship of Oṁkāra. The aim of the Upaniṣads is a practical one. Throughout the Upaniṣads, certain hints for the practical realization of the God by means of Yoga are found. The *Brahmavidyopaniṣad* describes the body of the Oṁkāra as follows. The *Ṛv.*, the Gārhapatya fire, Brahmā form the first *mātrā A*. The midregion, the Dakṣiṇāgni and the deity Viṣṇu form the *mātrā U.M.* is represented by the Īśvara.[231] The three *mātrā*-s should be known as the form of the moon, Sun and fire.[232] Above the symbol of the Oṁ, the tuft of light should be known as half the *mātrā* of Oṁ.[233] Oṁkāra represents the triad of gods; *'A'* being the abode of Brahmā, *U* the place of Viṣṇu and *M* the adode of Rudra, beyond that is the highest Ātman.[234] The Praṇava is described in this Upaniṣad as an esoteric doctrine of Viṣṇu (*Viṣṇurahasya*). Imperishable (*dhruva*) is a characterization of the highest essence (*dhruvaṁ viṣṇusajñitam. Mai. Up.* VI.8) and thereby that of the sound Oṁ also.[235] The *Dhyānabindūpaniṣad* describes the colours of the *mātrā*-s of the Oṁ. Thus, the first *mātrā A* is of yellow colour which represents *rajoguṇa*. The *mātrā U* is of white colour and denotes *sattvaguṇa*, *mātrā M* is of black colour indicating *tāmasaguṇa*.[236] The *Atharvaśikhopaniṣad* describes the colours of the *mātrā*-s as red, white and black respectively.[237] The *Turīyopaniṣad* describes the Praṇava as endowed with qualities (*saguṇa*) without qualities (*nirguṇa*) and the *praṇava* as the creation (*utpatti praṇava*).[238]

Again the *Turīyopaniṣad* describes *praṇava* as possessed of sixteen *mātrā*-s, namely; *A, U, M, ardhamātrā, nāda, bindū, kalā, śakti, śānti, samānā, ātmanā, manonmanā, vaikharī, madhyamā, paśyantī* and *parā*. All these *mātrā*-s are again fourfold with reference to the four states of the soul thus, forming sixtyfour *mātrā*-s. When considered as belonging to each the Prakṛti and Puruṣa, they become double in number forming one hundred and twenty eight *mātrā*-s. Having acquired these different forms, the (*upāsanā*) of the *saguṇa* Oṁ proceeds to the *nirguṇa* Oṁ which is just One and the same as Brahman.[239] Here, a verse of Gauḍapāda may be well remembered which says, "A person who knows Oṁkāra to be portionless, possessed of infinite portions, the cause of cessation of duality and auspicious is a seer."[240] The *Nābindūpaniṣad* describes Oṁkāra as possessed of twelve *mātrā*-s. The Upaniṣad states the names of the *mātrā*-s and the fruit of meditating upon these *mātrā*-s. For *e.g.* it is said that if a person dies while meditating upon the first *mātrā*, he is born as an emperor.[241]

The *Y.T. Up.* describes all comprehensiveness of the Oṁ, so also the place of mind in the heart. It says that, the three worlds, the three Veda-s, the joining times, the three sounds, three fires, the three *guṇa*-s all take resort in these three syllables.[242] The *manas* resides in the middle of the pericarp of the lotus of the heart. By meditation on the Oṁkāra in the lotus of the heart, a *yogin* obtains the highest abode. The Upaniṣads which predominently deal with the exposition of Saṁnyāsa also recommend the meditation on the Oṁkāra. Thus, Oṁkāra is the essence of all the Upaniṣads. The Oṁkāra stated in the earlier Upaniṣads, may be said to be more of an abstract nature, while the later Upaniṣads describe this symbol in a concrete manner. The colour, the names, the number of the *mātrā*-s is described mainly for the purpose of meditation; to let the wandering mind get dissolved in whichever quality that appeals to it.

Sacrificial Symbolism

Singh, S.P., in his 'Sacrificial symbolism in the Upaniṣads' has said that symbolism is a device by means of which the unknown is sought to be made understandable in terms of the known, the abstract in terms of the concrete... and the new in terms of the old. Accordingly, he furnishes the illustration of the horse-sacrifice (*aśvamedha*) in the *Bṛ. Up.* (I.1.1-2) and explains how the refinement through symbolic usage led to the transformation of the act of sacrifice into a philosophical concept, giving cosmogonic dimensions to the political ritual. Due to this, the purpose of sacrifice was elevated and ennobled. Further, he has said that, "if the horse-sacrifice symbolizes the course of cosmic process *vis-a-vis* the Creator, the sacrifice of five fires symbolizes the course, the destiny the individual takes in the cosmos."[243] Through the symbolisation of the five sacrifices (*Pañcāgnividyā*) the vissititudes of the soul are made known. This *vidyā* appears in the *Bṛ. Up.* and with a slight variation also in the *Chānd. Up.*[244] In an answer to the question; in which oblation does the water assume the form of a person; the king Pravāhaṇa Jaivali of Pañcāla himself provides the answer to Gautama. That, the other world is considered to be the fire, the Sun its fuel, the rays the smoke, the day the flame, the directions the embers, the intermediate directions the sparks. In this fire, the gods offer the faith (*śraddhā*). The resultant product of the sacrifice is the *soma*. Singh, S.P., opines that this is a grand cosmic sacrifice comparable to one in which the primeval Puruṣa offers himself as an oblation (*ṚV.* X. 90).[245] While offering himself, Puruṣa produces cosmos. Here, the offering of 'faith' produces the first bearer of life, *i.e. soma.* In the next symbolic sacrifice of this series, *parjanya* is considered as the fire, year as the fuel, cloud as the smoke..., and *soma* is offered as an oblation. The product of this sacrifice is the rain.[246] The dependency of life on the rains the caues and circumstances of it are conceived together as a sacrifice performed on the atmospheric plane. In the third sacrifice, the world is conceived as the sacrificial fire and an offering of rain is oblated by the gods, through which food is produced.[247] Again, at the fourth stage, man serves as the fire... and food is offered as an oblation, of which, semen is a product.[248] Transformation of the same semen into a person through the act of procreation is conceived as the last sacrifice in this order. This symbolic sacrifice gives the notion of the real through representative substitutes. The *Pañcāgnividyā* covers five sacrifices which are concerned with the transformation of the 'waters' into Puruṣa. The process of transformation is a natural act and it is called *vidyā* as it is made understandable through the sacrificial symbolism. The reward of this *vidyā* is declared as follows: Those who know this as such, and those too who meditate with faith in the forest on the truth, pass into the light, from the light into the day. Successively, they are led to the world of Brahmā, from where there is no return.[249]

These are some of the Prominent *vidyā*-s stated in the Upaniṣads. The special feature of each of these *vidyā*-s is the approach with which the Ultimate Reality; *viz.*, the Ātman or the Brahman; full of features or devoid of them is to be viewed. The aspirant may choose any approach as advised by his *guru.* In the ultimate analysis, all these approaches lead to the same goal. One can envisage the Truth as pure existence (*sat*) and discover the road to reach it; or one may also conceive it as *asat* and find an appropriate path. Also, one may even begin with the idea that the entire creation is nothing but just names and forms. It is false (*mithyā*). Thus, by emptying the mind full of ideas, names and forms one may arrive at the acme of perfection, through a negative way by reducing or renouncing the activities of life and discarding thought (like not this, not this, *neti, neti*). However, most of these *vidyā*-s have advocated the positive method of choosing one aspect or the other of the Truth to start with, which would culminate into the attainment of the Brahman, *sampad* as it is called in the Brahmasūtra-s (*Bra. Sū*. IV. 4.1).

There is a feature common to all the *vidyā*-s. For, there is no mention of the actual procedure of the particular *vidyā* that is expounded; and there are no details recorded at all. The *vidyā* was given through initiation to the pupil and this accounts for the absence of details or elaborate explanations.

It must be noted that any kind of *upāsanā* in the Upaniṣad is seen to be remaining incomplete in the absence of proper guidance from the preceptor proficient in metaphysical knowledge.

REFERENCES

1. *Kaṭh. Up*. I.2.8-9[a],

   न नरेणावरेण प्रोक्त एष सुविज्ञेयो बहुधा चिन्त्यमानः।
   अनन्यप्रोक्ते गतिरत्र नास्त्यणीयान्ह्यतर्क्यमणुप्रमाणात्।
   नैषा तर्केण मतिरापनेया प्रोक्ताऽन्येनैव सुज्ञानाय प्रेष्ठ॥

2. *Ibid.*, I. 3.14[a].
3. Deussen, P., *The Philosophy of the Upaniṣads,*. New York, 1966, p. 13.
4. *Kaṭh Up*. I.

   ॐ साह नाववतु॥ सह नौ भुनक्तु॥
   सहवीर्यं करवावहै॥ तेजस्विनावधीतमस्तु मा विद्विषावहै॥

5. *Tait. Up*. I. 3.2[b]-3,

   आचार्यः पूर्वरूपम्। अन्तेवास्युत्तररूपम्। विद्या संधिः।

6. *Chānd. Up,* IV. 14.1-3.
7. *Śaṅkarabhāṣya* on *Chānd. Up.*, VI.1.1.3, p. 535

कश्चित्सद्ब्रह्मात्मविद विमुक्तबन्धनं ब्रह्मिष्ठं यदा आसादयति तेन च ब्रह्मविदा कारुण्याद्दर्शितसंसारविषयदोषदर्शनमार्गो विरक्तः संसारविषयेभ्यो नासि त्वं संसार्यमुष्य पुत्रत्वादिधर्मवान्किं तर्हि सद्यतत्त्वमसि-इत्यविद्यामोनहपटाभिहननान्मोक्षितो गन्धारपुरुषावच्च स्वं सदात्मानमुपसंपद्य सुखी निर्वृतः स्यादिति॥

8. Monier Williams, M., *Brahmanism and Hinduism*, London 1887, pp. 41-42.
9. *Śvet. Up.* VI.23.

   यस्य देवे परा भक्तिर्यथा देवे तथा गुरौ।
   तस्यैते कथिता ह्यर्थाः प्रकाशन्ते महात्मनः प्रकाशन्ते महात्मन इति॥
10. *Brahmavidyopaniṣad*, I. 31,

    गुरुरेव हरिः साक्षान्नान्य इत्यब्रवीच्छ्रुतिः।
11. *Śuka. R. Up., Up. S.*, p. 258, ll. 9-12,

    नित्यानन्दं परमसुखदं केवलं ज्ञानमूर्तिं
    द्वन्द्वातीतं गगनसदृशं तत्त्वमस्यादिलक्ष्यम्।
    एकं नित्यं विमलमचलं सर्वधीसाक्षिभूतं
    भावातीतं त्रिगुणरहितं सद्गुरुं तं नमामि॥
12. *Dvayopaniṣad, Up. S.*, pt. II, I. 4,

    गुशब्दस्त्वन्धकारः स्यात् रुशब्दस्तन्निरोधकः।
    अन्धकारनिरोधित्वात् गुरुरित्यभिधीयते॥
13. *Śivopaniṣad, Up. S.*, pt. II, VII. 38,

    गुरुरेव पिता माता गुरुरेव परः शिवः।
    यस्यैव निश्चितो भावस्तस्य मुक्तिर्न दूरतः॥
14. Ranade, R.D., *op. cit.*, p. 243.
15. *Praśna. Up.* I. 10[a],

    अथोत्तरेण तपसा ब्रह्मचर्येण श्रद्धया विद्ययात्मानमन्विष्यादित्यमभिजयन्त ...।
16. *Chānd. Up.* IV. 10.1[a].
17. *Ibid.*, VIII. 7.3[a].

    तौ ह द्वात्रिंशतं वर्षाणि ब्रह्मचर्यमूषतुः ...।
18. *Muṇḍ. Up.* III. 2.4,

    नायमात्मा बलहीनेन लभ्यो न च प्रमादात्तपसो वाप्यलिङ्गात्।
    एतैरुपायैर्यतते यस्तु विद्वांस्तस्यैष आत्मा विशते ब्रह्मधाम॥

19. *Tait. Up*. I. 4.1[c,d,e],

स मेन्द्रो मेधया स्पृणोतु। अमृतस्य देव धारणो भूयासम्। शरीरं मे विचर्षणम्।

20. *Ken. Up*. I. 1,

आप्यायन्तु ममाङ्गानि वाक्प्राणश्चक्षुः श्रोत्रमथो बलमिन्द्रियाणि च।

21. Radhakrishnan, S., *The Principal Upaniṣads,* Delhi, 1998, p. 530.

22. *Chānd. Up*. VI.5.1,

अन्नमशितं त्रेधा विधीयते तस्य यः स्थविष्ठो धातुस्तत्पुरीषं भवति यो मध्यमस्तन्मा सं योऽणिष्ठस्तन्मनः॥

23. *Śāṅkarabhāṣya* on *Chānd. Up.,* (VII. 26.2),

अह्रियत इत्याहारः शब्दादिविषयविज्ञानं भोक्तुर्भोगाह्रियते। तस्य विषयोपलब्धि-लक्षणस्य विज्ञानशुद्धिराहारशुद्धीरागद्वेषमोहदोषैरसंसृष्टं विषयविज्ञानमित्यर्थः।

24. *Ibid.,*

तस्यामाहारशुद्धौ सत्यां तद्वतोऽन्तःकरणस्य सत्त्वस्य शुद्धिर्नैर्मल्यं भवति।

25. *Praśna. Up*, I. 1[a]

ॐ भद्रं कर्णेभिः शृणुयाम देवा भद्रं पश्येमाक्षभिर्यजत्राः।
स्थिरैरङ्गैस्तुष्टुवान्सस्तनूभिर्व्यशेम देवहितं यदायुः॥

26. *Kaṭh. Up,* II. 3.11[a],

तां योगमिति मन्यन्ते स्थिरामिन्द्रियधारणाम्।

27. *Chānd. Up*., III. 16.1-7,

पुरुषो वाव यज्ञस्तस्य यानि चतुर्विंशतिवर्षाणि तत्प्रातः सवनं...।

28. *Ibid.,* VII. 26.2[b],

...आहारशुद्धौ सत्त्वशुद्धिः सत्त्वशुद्धौ ध्रुवा स्मृतिः स्मृतिलम्भे सर्वग्रन्थीनां विप्रमोक्षः...।

29. *Śāṅkarabhāṣya* on *Chānd. Up.* (VII. 26.2),

अविद्याकृतानर्थपाशरूपाणां अनेकजन्मान्तरानुभवभावनाकठिनीकृतानां हृदयाश्रयाणां ग्रन्थीनां विप्रमोक्षः।

30. *Chānd. Up*., III. 14.1[b],

अथ खलु क्रतुमयः पुरुषो यथाक्रतुरस्मिँल्लोके पुरुषो भवति तथेतः प्रेत्य भवति स क्रतुं कुर्वीत।

31. *Īśa. Up*., I. 17[b],

क्रतो स्मर कृतं स्मर क्रतो स्मर कृतं स्मर।

32. *Muṇḍ. Up.*, III. 2.10[b],

तेषामेवैतां ब्रह्मविद्यां वदेत शिरोव्रतं विधिवद्यैस्तु चीर्णम्।

Śāṅkarabhāṣya on *Muṇḍ. Up.*, (II. 2.10),

शिरोव्रतं, शिरस्याग्निधारणलक्षणम्।

33. *Tait. Up.*, I. 11.1[a].

34. *Bṛ. Up*, III. 9.23.

...कस्मिन्नु सत्यं प्रतिष्ठितमिति हृदय इति होवाच हृदयेन हि सत्यं जानाति हृदये ह्येव सत्यं प्रतिष्ठितम्...।

35. *Chānd. Up.*, IV. 4.1-5.

36. *Ibid.*, VI.16.1-3.

37. *Praśna. Up.*, VI. 1[d],

समूलो वा एष परिशुष्यति योऽनृतमभिवदति।

38. *Muṇḍ. Up.*, III. 1.5[a],

सत्येन लभ्यस्तपसा ह्येष आत्मा सम्यग्ज्ञानेन ब्रह्मचर्येण नित्यम्।

39. *Ibid.*, III. 1.6,

सत्यमेव जयति नानृतं सत्येन पन्था विततो देवयानः।
येनाक्रमन्त्यृषयो ह्याप्तकामा यत्र तत्सत्यस्य परमं निधानम्॥

40. *Chānd. Up.*, VII. 16-17.

41. Ranade, R.D., *op. cit.*, p. 229.

42. *Śāṇḍ. Up.*, I.1[m],

सत्यं नाम मनोवाक्कायकर्मभिर्भूतहितयथार्थाभिभाषणम्।

43. *Jābāla. D. Up.*, I .1, 9-10.

चक्षुरादीन्द्रियैर्दृष्टं श्रुतं घ्रातं मुनीश्वर।
तस्यैवोक्तिर्भवेत्सत्यं विप्र तन्नान्यथा भवेत्॥
सर्वं सत्यं परं ब्रह्म नचान्यदिति या मतिः।
तच्च सत्यं वरं प्रोक्तं वेदान्तज्ञानपारगैः॥

44. *Chānd. Up.*, VIII. 3.4[b],

तस्य ह वा एतस्य ब्रह्मणो नाम सत्यमिति।

also, *Bṛ. Up.*, V. 5.1[b], II. 1.20[b], II. 3.6[b].

45. *Bṛ. Up.*, IV. 4.22[a],
...तमेतं वेदानुवचनेन ब्राह्मणा विविदिषन्ति यज्ञेन दानेन तपसाऽनाशकेनैतमेव विदित्वा मुनिर्भवति।
46. *Chānd. Up.*, V. 10.1-2,
ये चेमेऽरण्ये श्रद्धा तप इत्युपासते...ब्रह्म गमयत्येष देवयानः पन्था इति।
47. *Bh. G. Up.*, XVIII. 5[b],
यज्ञो दानं तपश्चैव पावनानि मनीषिणाम्।
48. *Śāṇḍ. Up.*, p. 410, l. 4,
तत्र तपो नाम विध्युक्तकृच्छ्रचान्द्रायणादिभिः शरीरशोषणम्।
also, *Jābāla. D. Up.*, II. 3[b];
शरीरशोषणं यत्तत्तप इत्युच्यते ...।
49. *Jābāla, D. Up.*, II. 4
को वा मोक्षः कथं तेन संसारं प्रतिपन्नवान्।
इत्यालोकनमर्थज्ञास्तपः शंसन्ति पण्डिताः॥
50. *Kaṭh Up.*, I. 1.3,
पीतोदका जग्धतृणा दुग्धदोहा निरिन्द्रियाः।
अनन्दा नाम ते लोकास्तान्स गच्छति ता ददत्॥
51. *Tait. Up.*, I. 11.3[b-j],
ये के चास्मच्छ्रेयाँसो ब्राह्मणाः। तेषां त्वयाऽऽसनेन प्रश्वसितव्यम्।
श्रद्धया देयम्। अश्रद्धयाऽदेयम्। श्रिया देयम्। ह्रिया देयम्।
भिया देयम्। संविदा देयम्।
52. *Bṛ. Up.*, V. 2.1-3.
53. *Ibid.*, III.1.1, IV. 1.4.
also, *Chānd. Up.*, IV. 2.1-5. *Kaṭh. Up.*, I. 1[a]. etc.
54. Macdonell, A., *A History of Sanskrit Literature,* 1958, p. 238.
also, Winternitz, M., *op. cit.*, p. 222.
55. For more details see Bakre, A.B., *op. cit.*, pp. 237ff.
56. *Śivopaniṣad, Up. S.* pt. II VI. 8-9,
यः पक्वं दाडिमं चैकं दद्याद्विकसितं नवम्।
शिवाय गुरवे वापि तस्य पुण्यफलं श्रुणु॥

यावद्बीजसंख्यानं शोभनं परिकीर्तितम्।
तावदष्टायुतान्युच्चैः शिवलोके महीयते॥

57. *Ibid.*, VI. 7,
एकं वटफलं पक्वं यः शिवाय निवेदयेत्।
वर्षलक्षं महाभोगैः शिवलोके महीयते॥

58. *Ibid.*, VI. 86, 58, 3-22, 233-236, 98, 100, 200, etc.

59. *Ibid.*, VI. 227,
विधवानाथवृद्धानां प्रदद्याद्यः प्रजीवनम्।
आभूतसंप्लवं यावच्छिवलोके महीयते॥

60. *Tait. Up.*, I. 11.3,
मातृदेवो भव। पितृदेवो भव।

61. *Bṛ. Up.*, I.5.17.

62. *Tait. Up.*, I.11.3,
अतिथिदेवो भव।

63. Macdonell, A., The *Vedic Mythology*, Varanasi, 1963, p. 19.

64. *Kaṭh Up.*, I. 1.7[a],
वैश्वानरः प्रविशत्यतिथिर्ब्राह्मणो गृहान्।

65. *Muṇḍ. Up.*, I. 2.3[b],
अहुतमवैश्वदेवमविधिना हुतमासप्तमांस्तस्य लोकान्हिनस्ति।

66. *Jaiminisūtra.*, I. 1.1-2,
अथातो धर्म जिज्ञासा।
चोदना लक्षणार्थो धर्मः।

67. *Manusmṛti.* II. 6
वेदोऽखिलो धर्ममूलं स्मृतिशीले च तद्विदाम्।
आचाराश्चैव साधूनां आत्मनश्चतुष्टिः एवं च॥

68. Dange, S.A., *Hindu Dharma āṇi Tattvajñāna*, Pune, 1973, pp. 1-15.

69. *Mbh. Śanti.*, 109-11,
धारणात् धर्ममित्याहुः धर्मेण विधृता प्रजाः।

70. *Tait. Up.*, I. 11.3-4.
अथ यदि ते कर्मविचिकित्सा वा वृत्तविचिकित्सा वा स्यात्।

ये तत्र ब्राह्मणाः संदर्शिनः....।

71. *Bṛ. Up.*, I.4.14[b],

यो वै स धर्मः सत्यं वै तत्तस्मात् सत्यं वदन्तमाहुधर्मं वदतीति धर्मं वा वदन्तं सत्यं वदतीत्येतध्द्येवैतदुभयं भवति॥

72. *Jaiminisūtra.*, I. 1.2.

73. *Vaiśeṣika. Sū.*, I. 1.2, q. by Bakre, A.B., *op. cit.*, p. 5,

यतोऽभ्युदयनिःश्रेयससिद्धिः स धर्मः।

74. *Kaṭh. Up.*, I. 1.2,

तँ ह कुमारँ सन्तं दक्षिणासु नीयमानासु श्रद्धाविवेश सोऽमन्यत।

Ibid., I. 13[a],

स त्वमग्निं स्वर्गमध्येषि मृत्यो प्रब्रूहि त्वं श्रद्दधानाय मह्यम्।

75. *Chānd. Up.*, VI. 12.2,

तं होवाच यं वै सौम्येतमणिमानं न निभालयस एतस्य वै सोम्येषोऽणिम्न एवं महान्न्यग्रोधस्तिष्ठति श्रद्धत्स्व सोम्येति।

76. *Śaṅkara* on *Chānd. Up.*, VI. 12.2,

अत्यन्तसूक्ष्मेष्वर्थेषु बाह्यविषयासक्तमनसः स्वभावप्रवृत्तस्यासत्यां गुरुतरायां श्रद्धायां दुरमगत्वं स्यादित्याह श्रद्धत्स्वेति। श्रद्धायां तु सत्यां मनसः समाधानं बुभुत्सितेऽर्थे भवेत्ततश्च तदार्थावगतिः। 'अन्यत्रमना अभूवम्' इत्यादिश्रुतेः।

77. *Bh. G.*, IV. 39[a], 40,

श्रद्धावाँल्लभते ज्ञानम्...।

अज्ञश्चाश्रद्दधानश्च संशयात्मा विनश्यति।

नायं लोकोऽस्ति न परो न सुखं संशयात्मनः॥

78. *Chānd. Up.*, VII. 19.1,

यदा वै श्रद्दधाति अथ मनुते... श्रद्दधदेव मनुते।

79. *Śaṅkara* on *Chānd. Up.*, VII. 19.1,

मन्तव्यविषये आदरः अस्तिक्यबुद्धिः श्रद्धा।

80. *Muṇḍ. Up.*, I. 2.11,

तपःश्रद्धे ये ह्युपवसन्ति... सूर्यद्वारेण ते विरजाः प्रयान्ति यत्रामृतः स पुरुषो..।

81. *Kaṭh. Up.*, I. 1.23-29.

82. *Bra. Sū. Śā. Bh. on*, I. 1.1,

नित्यानित्यवस्तुविवेकः इहामुत्रार्थभोगविरागः।

83. *Saṅk. Up., Up. S.* pt. II. p. 219,
एतदधीयानः सर्वक्रतुफलं लभते। शान्तिमेति।
मनश्शुद्धिमेति। सर्वतीर्थफलं लभते। स एष मोक्षप्रदः।

84. *Gaṇeśa. P. Tā. Up.*, I.3.2,
... एतमानुष्टुभं मन्त्रराजं... यो जानाति स भूतिमान् भवति सोऽमृतत्वं च गच्छति।

85. *Rāma. P. Tā. Up.*, I. 9.12[b], 13[a],
सेवकानां मोक्षकरमायुरारोग्यवर्धनम्। अपुत्रिणां पुत्रदं च...।

86. *Brahmavidyā. Up.*, I.23[b]. 24,
हंस हंसेति यो जपेत्। जरामरणरोगादि न तस्य भुवि विद्यते।
एवं दिने दिने कुर्यादणिमादिविभूतये॥

87. *Chānd. Up.*, III. 17.4[a],
अथ यत्तपो दानमार्जवमहिँसा सत्यवचनमिति...।

88. *Śāṇḍ. Up.*, I. 1.1[m],
तत्र हिंसा नाम मनोवाक्कायकर्मभिः सर्वभूतेषु सर्वदा क्लेशजननम्।

89. *Jābāla. D. Up.*, I. 1.7[b],
कायेन मनसा वाचा हिंसाऽहिंसा न चान्यथा।

90. *Ibid.*, I. 1.8,
आत्मा सर्वगतोऽच्छेद्यो न ग्राह्य इति मे मतिः।
सा चाहिंसा वरा प्रोक्ता वेदान्तवेदिभिः॥

91. Banerji, Sureshchandra, *A Companion to Indian Philosophy,* Delhi, 1966, pp. 89-90.

92. Ranade, R.D., *op. cit.*, p. 212.

93. *Jābāla. D. Up.*, I.6,
अहिंसा सत्यमस्तेयं ब्रह्मचर्यं दयार्जवम्।
क्षमा धृतिर्मिताहारः शौचं चैव यमा दश॥

94. *Īśa. Up.*, 1[b],
तेन त्यक्तेन भुञ्जीथा मा गृधः कस्य स्विद्धनम्।

95. Gosh, Aurobindo, *Īśa.Upaniṣad,* Pondicherry, 1993, p. 13.

96. *Śāṇḍ. Up. S.* pt. 1. p. 409,
अस्तेयं नाम मनोवाक्कायकर्मभिः परद्रव्येषु निःस्पृहता।

97. *Jābāla. D. Up.*, I. 12,
आत्मन्यनात्मभावेन व्यवहारविवर्जितम्।
यत्तदस्तेयमित्युक्तमात्मविद्भिर्महामते॥

98. *Ibid.*, I.15,
स्वात्मवत्सर्वभूतेषु कायेन मनसा गिरा।
अनुज्ञा या दया सैव प्रोक्ता वेदान्तवेदिभि:॥

99. *Ibid.*, I. 16,
पुत्रे मित्रे कलत्रे च रिपौ स्वात्मनि संततम्।
एकरूपं मुने यत्तदार्जवं प्रोच्यते मया॥

100. *Ibid.*, I. 17,
कायेन मनसा वाचा शत्रुभि: परिपीडिते।
बुद्धिक्षोभनिर्वृत्तिर्या क्षमा सा मुनिपुङ्गव॥
also *Śāṇḍ. Up. S.*, pt. I. p. 409, l. 20
क्षमा नाम प्रियाप्रियेषु सर्वेषु ताडनपूजनेषु सहनम्॥

101. *Ibid., Up. S.*, Pt. I. p. 410. l.1,
धृतिर्नामार्थहानौ स्वेष्टबन्धुवियोगे तत्प्राप्तौ सर्वत्र चेत:स्थापनम्।

102. *Jābāla. D. Up.*, I. 18,
वेदादेव विनिर्मोक्ष: संसारस्य न चान्यथा।
इति विज्ञाननिष्पत्तिर्धृति: प्रोक्ता हि वैदिकै: ॥

103. *Śāṇḍ. Up. S.*, pt. I. p. 410. l. 10,
मतिर्नाम वेदविहितकर्ममार्गेषु श्रद्धा।

104. *Jābāla. D. Up.*, I. 18[c],
अहमात्मा न चान्योऽस्मीत्येवमप्रच्युता मति:।

105. *Ibid.*, I.19,
अल्पमृष्टाशनाभ्यां च चतुर्थांशावशेषकम्।
तस्माद्योगानुगुण्येन भोजनं मितभोजनम्।
also *Śāṇḍ. Up. S.*, pt. I. p. 410. l. 1,
मिताहारो नाम चतुर्थांशावशेषकसुस्निग्धमधुराहार:॥

106. *R. Jābāla. Up.*, I. 17,
मद्यं मांसं च लशुनं पलाण्डुं शिग्रुमेव च। श्लेष्मातकं विड्वराहमभक्ष्यं वर्जयेन्नर:॥

107. *Śāṇḍ. Up. S.*, pt. I. p. 410. L. 2,
शौचं नाम द्विविधं बाह्यं आन्तरंचेति। तत्र मृज्जलाभ्यां बाह्यं। मनःशुद्धिरान्तरम्। तदध्यात्मविद्यया लभ्यम्॥

108. *Jābāla. D. Up.*, I. 20[c],
अहं शुद्ध इति ज्ञानं शौचमाहुर्मनीषिणः॥

109. *Ibid.*, II. 1,
तपः संतोषमास्तिक्यं दानमीश्वरपूजनम्।
सिद्धान्तश्रवणं चैव ह्रीर्मतिश्च जपो व्रतम्॥

110. *Maṇḍala. Brā. Up.*, I. 1f,
गुरुभक्तिः सत्यमार्गानुरक्तिः सुखावगतवस्त्वनुभवश्च तद्वस्त्वनुभवेन तुष्टिर्निसंःगता एकान्तवासो मनोनिवृत्तिः फलानभिलाषो वैराग्यभावश्च नियमाः।

111. *Jābāla. D. Up.*, II. 5,
यदृच्छालाभतो नित्यं प्रीतिर्या जायते नृणाम्। तत्संतोषं विदुः प्राज्ञाः परिज्ञानैकतत्पराः।
also *Ibid.*, II. 6[b],
सर्वत्र विगतस्नेहः संतोषं परमं विदुः।

112. *Ibid.*, II. 6[c],
श्रौते स्मार्ते च विश्वासो यत्तदास्तिक्यमुच्यते।

113. *Ibid.*, II. 10[ab],
वेदलौकिकमार्गेषु कुत्सितं कर्म यद्भवेत्।
तस्मिन्भवति या लज्जा ह्रीः सैवेति प्रकीर्तिता॥

114. *Ibid.*, II. 10[c],
वैदिकेषु च सर्वेषु श्रद्धा या सा मतिर्भवेत्।

115. *Ibid.*, II. 11,
गुरुणा चोपदिष्टोऽपि तत्र संबंधवर्जितः।
वेदोक्तेनैव मार्गेण मन्त्राभ्यासो जपः स्मृतः॥

Ibid., II.13,
जपस्तु द्विविधः प्रोक्तो वाचिको मानसस्तथा।

116. *Śāṇḍ. Up. S.*, pt. I, p. 410, 1.13,
व्रतं नाम वेदोक्तविधिनिषेधानुष्ठाननैयत्यम्॥

117. Desai, S.G., *op. cit.*, p. 321.

118. *Tejobindūpaniṣad.*, I. 19,

त्यागो हि महता पूज्यः सद्यो मोक्षप्रदायकः।

119. Desai, S.G., *op. cit.*, p. 321.

120. *Tejobindūpaniṣad*, I. 20,

यस्माद्वाचो निवर्तन्ते अप्राप्य मनसा सह।
यन्मौनं योगिभिर्गम्यं तद्भजेत्सर्वदा बुधः॥

121. *Śārīrakopaniṣad*, I. 1-5.

also, *Bh. G.*, XIV, 5-18.

122. *Śāṇḍ. Up., Up. S*, pt. l. 8, p. 410,

ईश्वरपूजनं नाम प्रसन्नस्वभावेन यथाशक्ति विष्णुरुद्रादिपूजनम्।

also *Jābāla. D. Up.*, II. 8,

रागाद्यपेतं हृदयं वागदुष्टानृतादिना। हिंसादिरहितं कर्म यत्तदीश्वरपूजनम्।

123. *Ibid.*, II. 9,

सत्यंज्ञानमनन्तं च परानन्दं परं ध्रुवम्। प्रत्यगित्यवगन्तव्यं वेदान्तश्रवणं बुधाः।

124. *Chānd. Up.*, V. 10.9,

स्तेनो हिरण्यस्य सुरां पिबंश्च गुरोस्तल्पमावसन् ब्रह्महा च एते पतन्ति चत्वारः पंचमश्चाचरन्स्तैरिति।

125. *Bṛ. Up.*, IV. 4.21,

तमेव धीरो विज्ञाय प्रज्ञां कुर्वीत ब्राह्मणः। नानुध्यायाद्बहूञ्छब्द्वान्वाचो विग्लापनँ हि तदिति।

126. *Ibid.*, III. 5.1[c],

तमात्मानं विदित्वा ब्राह्मणाः पुत्रैषणायाश्च वित्तैषणायाश्च लोकैषणायाश्च व्युत्थायाथ भिक्षाचर्यं चरन्ति... तस्मात् ब्राह्मणः पण्डित्यं निर्विद्य बाल्येन तिष्ठासेत्।

127. *Śivopaniṣad, Up. S.* pt. II.VII. 13.

हास्यनिष्ठीवनास्फोटमुच्चभाष्यविजृम्भणम्। पादप्रसारणं गीतं न कुर्यात् गुरुसन्निधौ॥

128. *Ibid.*, VII. 12,

उपानच्छत्रशयनं वस्त्रमासनभूषणम्।
पात्रदण्डाक्षसूत्रं वा गुरुसक्तं न धारयेत्॥

129. *Ibid.*, VII. 16,

अन्यासक्तो न भुञ्जानो न तिष्ठन्पराङ्मुखः। न शयानो न चासीनः संभाष्येद्गुरुणासह॥

130. *Ibid.*, VII. 28,

गुरोर्न खण्डयेदाज्ञामपि प्राणान् परित्यजेत्।
कृत्वाज्ञां प्राप्नुयान्मुक्तिं लङ्घयन् नरकं व्रजेत्॥

131. Antarkar, W.R., *Śaṅkara-vijayas–A Comparative and Critical Study*, Mumbai, 2003, pp. 284-287.

132. *Śaṅkara, Gītābhāṣya,* q. by Antarkar, W.R., *op. cit.*, p. 286,

अभ्युदयार्थोऽपि यः प्रवृत्तिलक्षणो धर्मो वर्णाश्रमांश्चोद्दिश्य विहितः सः देवादिस्थान प्राप्तिहेतुरपि सन् ईश्वरार्पणबुद्ध्याऽनुष्ठीयमानः सत्त्वशुद्धये भवति फलाभिसन्धिरहितः।

133. Śaṅkara's commentary on *Chānd. Up.*,VII. 26.2[b].

134. Radhakrishnan, S., *The Principal Upaniṣads,* 1998, p. 111.

135. Vidyāvāchaspatipanoli, *Upaniṣads in Śaṅkara's own Words.*, Vol. III, p. 9.

उपासनं तु यथाशास्त्रसमर्थितं किञ्चिदालम्बनमुपादाय तस्मिन्समानचित्तवृत्तिसंतान-करणम्॥

136. *Chānd. Up.*, III. 14.1[a],

137. Mukhopadhyaya, G.G., *op. cit.*, pp. 172-196.

138. *Chānd. Up.*, VIII. 7.1,

य आत्मा अपहतपाप्मा विजरो...
सोऽन्वेष्टव्यः स विजिज्ञासितव्यः।

139. *Ibid.*, VIII. 3.2,

अथ ये चास्येह जीवा ये च प्रेता यच्चान्यदिच्छन्न लभते सर्वं तदत्र गत्वा विन्दतेऽत्र ह्यस्यैते सत्याः कामा अनृतापिधानास्तद्यथापि हिरण्यनिधिं निहितमक्षेत्रज्ञा उपर्युपरि संचरन्तो न विन्देयुरेवमेवेमाः सर्वाः प्रजा अहरहर्गच्छन्त्य एतं ब्रह्मलोकं न विन्दन्त्यनृतेन हि प्रत्यूढाः।

140. *Ibid.*, III. 14.1[b],

अथ खलु क्रतुमयो पुरुषो...

141. *Kaṭh. Up.*, I. 2.23,

नायमात्मा प्रवचनेन लभ्यो न मेधया न बहुना श्रुतेन।
यमेवैष वृणुते तेन लभ्यस्तस्यैष आत्मा विवृणुते तनूँ स्वाम्॥

142. *Śrībhāṣya of Rāmānuja,* (I. 1.1-para 14),

उपासनं स्यात् ध्रुवा स्मृतिः दर्शनान्निर्वचनाच्च।

143. *Chānd. Up.*, I.1. 10[b],
नाना तु विद्या चाविद्या च यदेव विद्यया करोति।
श्रद्धयोपनिषदा तदेव वीर्यवत्तरं भवति इति॥

144. *Kaṭh. Up.*, I. 3.12,
एष सर्वेषु भूतेषु गूढोत्मा न प्रकाशते।
दृश्यते त्वग्रयया बुद्धया सूक्ष्मया सूक्ष्मदर्शिभिः॥

145. *Muṇḍ. Up.*, II. 2.3,
धनुर्गृहीत्वौपनिषदं महास्त्रं शरं ह्युपासानिशितं संधयीत। आयम्य तद्भावगतेन चेतसा लक्ष्यं तदेवाक्षरं सोम्य विद्धि।

146. *Kaṭh. Up.*, II. 3.9,
न संदृशे तिष्ठति रूपगरय न चक्षुषा पश्यति कश्चनैनम्।
हृदा मनीषी मनसाऽभिक्लृप्तो य एतद्विदुरमृतास्ते भवन्ति॥

147. Mukhopadhyaya, G.G., *op. cit.,* pp. 188-189.

148. *Ibid., op. cit.,* pp. 188-189.

149. *Praśna Up.*, V. 2[b],
परं चापरं च ब्रह्म यदोंकारस्तस्माद्विद्वानेतेनैवायतनेनैकतरमन्वेति।

150. Radhakrishnan, S., *The Principal Upaniṣads,* India, 1998, p. 604.

151. Tilak, B.G., *op. cit.,* pp. 282, 286.

152. *Tait. Up.*, III. 1-6.

153. Tilak, B.G., *op. cit.,* pp. 283.

154. Mukhopadhyaya, G.G. *op. cit.,* p. 198.

155. Śaṅkara's commentary on *Chānd. Up.*,VIII. 1.1,
राज्ञोऽनेकप्रकृतिमद्यथा पुरं, तथेदमनेकेन्द्रियमनोबुद्धिभिः स्वाम्यर्थकारिभियुक्तमिति ब्रह्मपुरम्।

156. *Śvet. Up.*, III. 18,
नवद्वारे पुरे देही हंसो लेलायते बहिः।

157. *Kaṭh. Up.*, II. 1.1[a],
पुरमेकादशद्वारमजस्यावक्रचेतसः।

158. *Chānd. Up.*, VIII.1.1,
अथ यदिदमस्मिन्ब्रह्मपुरे दहरं पुण्डरीकं वेश्म दहरोऽस्मिन्नन्तराकाशस्त-
स्मिन्यदन्तस्त-दन्वेष्टव्यं तद्वाव विजिज्ञासितव्यमिति।

159. *Praśna Up.*, III. 6[a],
हृदि ह्येष आत्मा।

160. *Chānd. Up.*, III. 14.3,
एष म आत्माऽन्तर्हृदयेऽणीयान्व्रीहेर्वा यवाद्वा सर्षपाद्वा श्यामाकाद्वा श्यामाकतण्डुलाद्वा एष म आत्माऽ न्तर्हृदये ज्यायान्पृथिव्या ज्यायानन्तरिक्षाज्ज्यायान्दिवो ज्यायानेभ्यो लोकेभ्यः।

161. *Kaṭh. Up.*, II. 3.17[a],
अङ्गुष्ठमात्रः पुरुषोऽन्तरात्मा सदा जनानां हृदये सन्निविष्टः।

162. *Bh. G.*, XVIII. 61[a].

163. *Chānd. Up.*, VIII. 3.3. (a),
स वा एष आत्मा हृदि तस्यैतदेव निरुक्तं हृदयमिति।

164. *Bṛ. Up.*, II. 4.11,
...सर्वासां विद्यानां हृदयमेकायनमेवम्...।

165. *Ibid.*, III. 9.23[b],
कस्मिन्नु सत्यं प्रतिष्ठितमिति हृदय इति होवाच हृदयेन हि सत्यं जानाति हृदये ह्येव सत्यं प्रतिष्ठितं भवति।
also III.9.21[b],
हृदयेन हि श्रद्धां जानाति हृदये ह्येव श्रद्धा प्रतिष्ठिता भवतीत्येवमेवैतद्याज्ञवल्क्य॥

166. *Ibid.*, IV. 2.7,
हृदयं वै सम्राट् परमं ब्रह्म..।

167. *Tait. Up.*, II. 1.1[b],
सत्यं ज्ञानमनन्तं ब्रह्म। यो वेद निहितं गुहायां परमे व्योमन्।

168. *Ait. Up.*, V.2,
संज्ञानमाज्ञानं विज्ञानं प्रज्ञानं मेधा दृष्टिर्धृतिर्मतिर्मनीषा जूतिः स्मृतिः संकल्पः क्रतुरसुः कामो वश इति सर्वाण्येवैतानि प्रज्ञानस्य नामधेयानि भवन्ति॥

169. Śaṅkara on *Chānd. Up.*,VIII. 1.1,
अन्तराकाश आकाशाख्यं ब्रह्म।
आकाशइवाशरीरत्वात् सूक्ष्मत्वसर्वगतत्वं-सामान्याच्च॥

170. *Chānd. Up.*, VIII. 1.3,

यावान्वा अयमाकाशस्तावानेषोऽन्तहृदय आकाश उभे अस्मिन् द्यावापृथिवी अन्तरेव समाहिते उभावग्निश्च वायुश्च सूर्याचन्द्रमसावुभौ विद्युन्नक्षत्राणि यच्चास्येहास्ति यच्च नास्ति सर्वं तदस्मिन्समाहितमिति॥

171. *Bra. Sū. Śā. Bh.* on I. 3.14, p. 109,

दहर उत्तरेभ्यः।

172. Śaṅkara on *Chānd. Up.*, VIII. 1.1, introductory,

दिग्देशगुणगतिफलभेदशून्यं हि परमार्थसदद्वयंब्रह्म मन्दबुद्धीनामसदिव प्रतिभाति। तदधिगमाय हृदयपुण्डरीकदेश उपदेष्टव्यः।

173. *Chānd. Up.,* I. 1.1.

ओमित्येतदक्षरमुग्दीथमुपासीत ओमिति ह्युभ्द्गायति तस्योपव्याख्यानम्॥ (उद्गीथ ॐ कार इत्यर्थः)

174. Śaṅkara's commentary on *Chānd. Up.,* I. 1.1,

अर्चादिवत् परस्यात्मनः प्रतीकं संपद्यते। एवं नामत्वेन प्रतीकत्वेन च परमात्मोपासनसाधनं श्रेष्ठमिति सर्ववेदान्तेष्वगतम्।

175. Radhakrisnan, S., *op. cit.,* p. 337.

176. *Chānd. Up.,* I. 1.2-3,

एषा भूतानां पृथिवी रसः पृथिव्या आपो रसोऽपामोषधयो रस ओषधीनां पुरुषो रसः पुरुषस्य वाग्रसो वाच ऋग्रस ऋचः साम रसः साम्न उद्गीथो रसः॥ स एष रसांनां रसतमः परमः पराध्योऽष्टमो युदुद्गीथः॥

177. *Ibid.,* I.1.5,

वागेवर्क् प्राणः सामोमित्येतदक्षरमुद्गीथः। तद्वा एतन्मिथुनं यद्वाक् च प्राणश्चर्क् च साम च।

178. *Ibid.,* I.1.6,

तदेतन्मिथुनमोमित्येतस्मिन्नक्षरे संसृज्यते यदा वै मिथुनौ समागच्छत आपयतो वै तावन्योन्यस्य कामम्॥

Ibid., I. 1.8[a],

तद्वा एतदनुज्ञाक्षरम्।

179. Mukhopadhyaya, G., *op. cit.,* p. 207.

180. *Chānd. Up.,* I. 1.10,

Śaṅkara on *Chānd. Up.* I. 1.0.

उपनिषदा - योगेन युक्तः चेल् इत्यर्थः।

181. *Ibid.*, I. 1.2.1-6,

182. Śaṅkara's commentary on *Chānd. Up.*, II. 1.1,
देवा दिव्यतेर्द्योतनार्थस्य शास्त्रोद्भासिता इन्द्रियवृत्तयः असुरास्तद्विपरीताः स्वेष्वेवासुषु विष्वग्विषयासु प्राणनक्रियासु रमणात्स्वाभाविक्यस्तम आत्मिका इन्द्रियवृत्तयः एव।

183. *Praśna. Up*, I. 5[a],
आदित्यो ह वै प्राणो....।

184. *Ibid.*, III. 8,
आदित्यो ह वै बाह्यः प्राणः...।

185. *Chānd. Up.*, I. 3.2,
समान उ एवायं चासौ चोष्णोऽयमुष्णोऽसौ स्वर इतीममाचक्षते स्वर इति प्रत्यास्वर इत्यमुं तस्माद्वा एतमिमममुं चोद्गीथमुपासीत।

186. *Ibid.*, I. 3.1,
...य एवासौ तपति तमुद्गीथमुपासीतोद्यन्वा एष प्रजाभ्य उद्गायति उद्य ँस्तमोभयमपहन्त्यपहन्ता ह वै भयस्य तमसो भवति...।

187. *Ibid.*, I. 3.6[a],
अथ खलु उद्गीथाक्षराण्युपासीत...।

188. Śaṅkara's Commentary on *Chānd. Up.*, I.3.6,
नामाक्षरोपासनेऽपि नामवत एवोपासनं कृतं भवेत्।

189. *Chānd. Up..*, I. 3.12,
ध्यायन् अप्रमत्तोऽभ्याशो...।

190. *Ibid.*, I. 6.6,
अथ यदेवैतदादित्यस्य शुक्लं भाः सैव साऽथ यन्नीलं परः कृष्णं तदमस्तत्सामाऽथ य एषोऽन्तरादित्ये हिरण्मयः पुरुषः दृश्यते...।

191. *Ibid.*, I. 7.1-4.

192. *Ibid.*, III. 1.2,
तस्य ये प्राञ्चो रश्मयस्ता एवास्य प्राच्यो मधुनाड्यः। ऋच एव मधुकृत ऋग्वेद एव पुष्पं ता अमृता आपस्ता वा एता ऋचः॥

193. Śaṅkara on *Chānd. Up.*, III. 2.1,
यतो रसानादाय मधु कुर्वन्ति, तत्पुष्पमिव पुष्पमृग्वेद एव।... ऋग्वेद शब्देनात्र ऋग्वेद विहितं कर्म।

194. *Chānd. Up.*, III. 1.3-4,
एतमृग्वेदमभ्यतपँस्तस्याभितप्तस्य यशस्तेज इन्द्रियं वीर्यमन्नाद्यँ रसोऽजायत॥
तद्यक्षरत्तदादित्यमभितोऽश्रयत्तद्वा एतद्यदेतदादित्यस्य रोहितं रूपम्॥

195. *Ibid.*, III. 5.1,
अथ येऽस्योर्ध्वा रश्मयस्ता एवास्योर्ध्वा मधुनाड्यो गुह्या एवादेशा मधुकृतो ब्रह्मैव पुष्पं ता अमृता आपः॥
Śaṅkara on *Ibid.*, Brahman according to Śaṅkara signifies the Praṇava, *i.e.* the syllable *aum*.
ब्रह्मैव शब्दाधिकारात् प्रणवाख्यं पुष्पम्।

196. *Chānd. Up.*, III. 5.3,
तद्यक्षरस्तदादित्यमभितोऽश्रयत्तद्वा एतद्यदेतदादित्यस्य मध्ये क्षोभत इव।

197. Śaṅkara on *Ibid.*, III. 5.3,
समाहितदृष्टेर्दृश्यते सञ्चलतीव।

198. *Chānd. Up.*, III. 11.3,
न ह वा अस्मा उदेति न निम्लोचति सकृद्दिवा हैवास्मै भवति।

199. *Bṛ. Up.*, II.5.1-19.

200. Mukhopadhyaya, G.G., *op. cit.*, p. 234.

201 *Tait. Up.*, II.1, 1[a,c,d].
ब्रह्मविदाप्नोति परम्। सत्यं ज्ञानमनन्तं ब्रह्म। यो वेद निहितं गुहायां परमे व्योमन्।

202. *Ibid.*, II.1.1,

203. Deussen, P., *The Phiosophy of the Upaniṣads*, New York, 1996, p. 98.

204. Mukhopadhyaya, G.G., *op. cit.*, p.238.

205. Radhakrishnan, S., *The Principal of Upaniṣads.*, 1998, p.545.

206. *Tait. Up.*, II. 4.1[a],
यतो वाचो निवर्तन्ते। अप्राप्य मनसा सह।

207. Ghosh, Aurobindo q. by Mukhopadhyaya, G.G., *op. cit.*, pp. 240-241,
Śaṅkara's commentary on *Tait. Up.*, III.6,
तत्र चानन्दमयो विशिष्ट आत्मा प्रदर्शितः।

208. Ranade, R.D., *op. cit.*, pp. 102-103.

209. *Paiṅgala. Up., Up. S.* I. pp. 422, ll. 7-11,

अन्नरसेनैव भूत्वाऽन्नरसेनाभिवृद्धिं प्राप्यान्नरसमयपृथिव्यां यद्विलीयते सोऽन्नमयकोश:। तदेव स्थूलशरीरम्। कर्मेंद्रियै: सह प्राणादिपञ्चकं प्राणमयकोश:। ज्ञानेंद्रियै: सह मनो मनोमयकोश:। ज्ञानेंद्रियै: सह बुद्धिर्विज्ञानमय कोश:। एतत्कोशत्रयं लिङ्गशरीरम्। स्वरूपज्ञानमानन्दमयकोश:। तत्कारणशरीरम्॥

210. *Tait. Up.*, III.6.1,

आनन्दो ब्रह्मेति व्यजानात्। आनन्दाद्ध्येव खल्विमानि भूतानि जायन्ते। आनन्देन जातानि जीवन्ति। आनन्दं प्रयन्त्यमभिसंविशन्ति। सैषा भार्गवी वारुणी विद्या।

211. *Br. Up.*, II.1.1-20,

212. *Ibid.*, II.1.13.

Śaṅkara on *Bṛ. Up.* II.1.13.

आत्मनि प्रजापतौ बुद्धौ हृदि चैका देवता तस्या: आत्मन्व्यात्मवानिति विशेषणम्। फलं...आत्मन्वी ह भवत्यात्मवान्भवति।

213. Ranade, R.D., *op. cit.*, p.101.

214. *Chānd. Up.*, VII. 1.23,

215. Śaṅkara's commentary on *Chānd. Up.*, III. 18.1,

मनो मनुतेऽनेनेत्यन्त:करणं तद्ब्रह्म परमित्युपासीतेति।

216. *Ibid.*, commentary on *Chānd. Up.*, VII. 3.1,

मनो ह्यात्मा आत्मन: कर्तृत्वं भोक्तृत्वं च सति मनसि नान्यथेति।

217. *Ibid.*, commentary on *Chānd. Up.*, VII. 23.1,

अतस्तस्मिन्नल्पे सुखं नास्ति। अल्पस्याधिकतृष्णाहेतुत्वात्। तृष्णा च दु:खबीजम्॥

218. *Ibid.*, commentary on *Chānd. Up.*, VII. 24.1,

यद्यन्यदर्शनाद्यभावमात्रमित्युच्यते तदा द्वैतसंव्यवहारविलक्षणो भूमेत्युक्तं भवति।

219. *Ibid.*,

स्वे महिम्नि - स्वे आत्मीये महिम्नि माहात्म्ये विभूतौ प्रतिष्ठितो भूमा।

220. Radhakrishnan, S., *The Principal of Upaniṣads,* India, 1998, p. 63.

221. *Muktikopaniṣad,* I. 26[b],

माण्डूक्यमेकमेवालं मुमुक्षूणां विमुक्तये।

222. *Māṇḍ. Up.*, I.1,

ओमित्येतदक्षरमिदँ सर्वं तस्योपव्याख्यानं भूतं भवद्भविष्यदिति सर्वमोङ्कारमेव॥

223. *Gauḍapādakārika,*. ed. by Karmarkar, R., pp. x-xii.

224. *Ibid.*, I. 24.

ओंकारं पादशो विद्यात्पादा मात्रा न संशयः।
ओंकारं पादशो ज्ञात्वा न किञ्चिदपि चिन्तयेत्॥

225. *Chānd. Up.*, I. 5.1

अथ खलु य उद्गीथः स प्रणवो यः प्रणवः स उद्गीथ इत्यसौ वा आदित्य उद्गीथ एष प्रणव ओमिति ह्येष स्वरन्नेति।

226. *Kaṭh. Up.*, I. 2.17,

एतदालम्बनं श्रेष्ठमेतदालम्बनं परम्।
एतदालम्बनं ज्ञात्वा ब्रह्मलोके महीयते॥

227. *Praśna. Up.* V. 2,

एतद्वै सत्यकाम परं चापरं च ब्रह्म यदोङ्कारस्तस्माद्विद्वानेतेनैवायतनेनैकतरमन्वेति॥

228. *Muṇḍ. Up.*, II. 2.4,

229. *Mai. Up.*, VI. 5,

230. *Kaṭh. Up.*, I.2, 15-17,

सर्वे वेदा यत्पदमामनन्ति तपांसि च सर्वाणि यद्वदन्ति। यदिच्छन्तो ब्रह्मचर्यं चरन्ति तत्ते पदं संग्रहेण ब्रवीम्योमित्येतत्। एतद्ध्येवाक्षरं ब्रह्म एतद्ध्येवाक्षरं परम्। एतद्ध्येवाक्षरं ज्ञात्वा यो यदिच्छति तस्य तत्॥

231. *Brahmavidyopaniṣad,* I. 4-6

ऋग्वेदो गार्हपत्यं च पृथिवी ब्रह्म एव च।
अकारस्य शरीरं तु व्याख्यातं ब्रह्मवादिभिः॥
यजुर्वेदोऽन्तरिक्षं च दक्षिणाग्निस्तथैव च।
विष्णुश्च भगवान्देव उकारः परिकीर्तितः॥
सामवेदस्तथा द्यौश्चाहवनीयस्तथैव च।
ईश्वरः परमो देवो मकारः परिकीर्तितः॥

232. *Ibid.*, I. 8[b]

तिस्त्रो मात्राः तथा ज्ञेयाः सोमसूर्याग्निरूपिणः॥

233. *Ibid.*, I. 9

शिखा तु दीपसंकाशा तस्मिन्नुपरि वर्तते।
अर्धमात्रा तथा ज्ञेया प्रणवस्योपरि स्थिता॥

234. *Ibid.*, I.71[cd], 72[ab]

अकारे संस्थितो ब्रह्मा उकारे विष्णुरास्थितः।
मकारे संस्थितो रुद्रस्ततोऽस्यान्तः परात्परः॥

235. *Ibid.*, I.1
अथ ब्रह्मविद्योपनिषदुच्यते। प्रसादाद्ब्रह्मणस्तस्य विष्णोरद्भुतकर्मणः।
रहस्यं ब्रह्मविद्याया ध्रुवाग्निं संप्रचक्षते॥

236. *Dhyānabindūpaniṣad.*, I.12[b], 13[a],
अकारः पीतवर्णोस्याद्रजोगुण उदीरितः॥
उकारः सात्त्विकः शुक्लो मकारः कृष्णतामसः॥

237. *Atharvaśikhopaniṣad*, I. 1
प्रथमा रक्ता ब्राह्मी ब्रह्मदेवत्या द्वितीया शुभा शुक्ला रौद्री रूद्रदेवत्या तृतीया कृष्णा विष्णुमती विष्णुदेवत्या...

238. *Turīyopaniṣad*, *Up. S.* pt. II. p. 26,
सगुणो विराट् प्रणवः। संहारो निर्गुणप्रणवः। उभयात्मक उत्पत्तिप्रणवः।

239. *Ibid.*, *Up. S.* pt. II. p. 26.

240. *Gauḍapādakārikā*, I. 29,
अमात्रोऽनन्तमात्रश्च द्वैतस्योपशमः शिवः।
ओंकारो विदितो येन स मुनिर्नेतरो जनः॥

241. *Nādabindūpaniṣad.*, I.9-17.

242. *Y.T. Up.*, I. 134[b], 135,
त्रयो लोकास्त्रयो वेदास्त्रयः स्वराः।
त्रयोऽग्नयश्च त्रिगुणाः स्थिताः सर्वे त्रयाक्षरे।
Ibid., I. 137-140[ab].

243. S.P. Singh, *"Sacrificial Symbolism in the Upaniṣads"*, *Sacrifices in India Concept and Evolution*, ed. Dange, S.S., Aligarh, 1987, pp. 73-75.

244. *Bṛ. Up.*, VI. 2.9,
असौ वै लोकोऽग्निर्गौतम तस्यादित्य एव समिद्रश्मयो धूमोऽहरर्चिर्दिशोऽङ्गारा अवान्तरदिशो विस्फुङ्गास्तस्मिन्नेतस्मिन्नग्नौ देवाः श्रद्धां जुह्वति तस्या आहुत्यै सोमो राजा संभवति।

245. Singh, S.P. *op. cit.*, p. 76.

246. *Bṛ. Up.*, VI. 2.10,

पर्जन्यो वावग्निर्गौतम तस्य संवत्सर एव समिदभ्राणि धूमो... विस्फुलिङ्गास्त-स्मिन्नेतस्मिन्नग्नौ देवा: सोमं राजानं जुह्वति तस्या आहुत्यै वृष्टि: संभवति।

247. *Ibid.*, VI. 2.11.

248. *Ibid.*, VI. 2.12.

249. *Ibid.*, VI. 2.15.

CHAPTER V

PATHS OF THE LATER UPANIṢADS

The authors of the later Upaniṣads keen on including the masses, propounded different paths such as Bhakti, Jñāna, Yoga, Saṁnyāsa, and Tantra etc. for the attainment of salvation. They have, however, mostly tried to amalgamate these different paths.

Bhakti

According to the *Bh. G.,* the realisation of the identity between the Ātman and the Brahman or the perception that there is nothing in the world which is as holy as knowledge (*jñāna*) is the only reality.[1] Just as the mental contemplation of the subject matter is wholly dependent on the equability of the reason; so is the path or the manner of acquiring it. In this connection a question may be asked, "How can one acquire that high intelligence with which the nature of the path may be fully known?" Moreover, if one's intelligence is not high one may not be successful. It is true that even the knowers of the Brahman have to say 'not this', 'not this' while describing that indescribable Brahman. The *Kaṭh. Up.* and the *Bh. G.* stated that though there are many who being struck by wonder, describe their experience of the Ātman, and though there are few others who listen to that description, yet no one knows the true nature of the Ātman.[2] Again, in the *Kaṭh. Up.* the sages declare that sharp as the edge of a razor and difficult to traverse is that path.[3] Similarly, the *Bh. G.* also says that the strain is greater for those who have their minds attached to the Unmanifest, for atonement with the Unmanifest is attained with difficulty by those who are centred in the body."[4]

It is obvious that a man possessing an ordinary intellect cannot traverse this path of knowledge. There is a majority of people in the world, having ordinary intellect because highly intelligent people are always a few. It necessarily follows that the path of faith or belief is open for acquiring this knowledge in addition to the path of reason. Tilak, B.G. has stated, "Really speaking, it will be seen that knowledge is not complete or fruitful without religious faith." Further, he has explained that certain philosophers believe in inferencial reasoning and think that knowledge is acquired only by intelligence and no other mental faculties are required for this purpose. Moreover, he has pointed out that the knowledge must be made to permeate the heart and the bodily organs by means of intense practice and consistent habit; and that the realization of the Ātman or the Brahman must become inherent nature, by means of constant behaviour in consonance with the idea. The only way of achieving that result is to imbibe the nature and the form of the highest Lord by love and faith and to make one's mind uniform with the Lord. This method has been in vogue in our country from the times immemorial and is known as worship or devotion.[5]

Bhakti and Jñāna

While following the path of devotion, one concentrates on the concrete form. The followers choose their paths in accordance with their abilities to focus their minds on. The path of knowledge presupposes intellectual ability, and that of devotion begins with love and faith. The first step towards the path of knowledge is intelligence and the first step on the path of devotion is love and faith, though apparently different, one following these paths, attains the same goal, has the same kind of realization and secures the same release. One is ultimately able to stabilise one's own reason by following any one of these paths. While following the path of knowledge it is both a means as also an end. Devotion, however is just a means leading to knowledge, and is not a goal in itself.

Bhakti and Yoga

If the vision of the Infinite is obtained by pursuing the more activistic or intellectualistic methods such as fixed postures, penances and meditation, it leads to the 'Yoga'. If that vision or experience is realised in emotional frame of mind, the result is *bhakti*.[6] This means that, *bhakti* is predominantly emotional while Yoga is predominantly intellectual. This *bhakti* is a disciplinary means, particularly appropriate to theism with a belief in a personal God. The *Bh. G.*, aptly describes, "with their minds fixed on Me, with their lives surrendered to Me, enlightening one another about My greatness and speaking of Me, My devotees ever remain contented taking delight in me."[7] The devotees find spiritual exaltation in the company of others who are similarly inclined. This points out to a social element included in *bhakti* while the *yogins* are inclined to seek the Absolute singly.

The Meaning of the Word Bhakti

The word *bhakti* is derived from the root *bhaj,* – to adore, to resort to etc. and therefore, has the primary meaning of adoration, devotion or worship. Śāṇḍilya defines *bhakti* as the most intense love towards Īśvara. (*Sā parmānuraktiḥi Īśvare – Śāṇḍilya sūtra* I. 2). In the Nārada bhaktisūtra, Nārada considered three definitions given by three sages – Vyāsadeva, Garga, and Śāṇḍilya (*N. Bh. Sū.* II.16-18) and his own opinion. He stated that, *bhakti* consists of offering every act to the Supreme Lord, and feeling extremely distressed in forgetting Him. Nārada has defined the highest form of *bhakti,* which is the culmination of all views.[8]

It may be said that, loving devotion (*bhakti*) for the deity conceived as a person, involves constant endeavour on the part of the individual to rise above the bonds of individuality and seek communion with the Infinite. Offering works which are pure, to the Supreme serve as a means of *bhakti.* It may also be said that *bhakti* begins with faith and culminates in total surrender.

The Origin and Development of Bhakti

According to Velankar, H.D., the root and the manifestation of the idea of *bhakti* is found in the Vedic literature. The word *bhakti* connotes the meaning 'devotional service' or the 'highest love' to the superior one, with or without any expectation of fruit. Accordingly, he stated that there would be different types of *bhakti* – the highest, the medium and the lower type of *bhakti.* As the form of *bhakti* rests solely with the *bhakta*-s depending upon the expectation of fruit, the *bhakta*-s also would be of these three categories.

The word *bhakti* represents the relation of the heart of a human being to the God. As the human thought and emotion are manifested in more or less different manner in different times, the nature of *bhakti* also may be found to be manifesting differently in different times.

The nature of *bhakti* is dependant upon the aim to be achieved. When the idea that progeny, wealth, heaven etc. are the aims to be achieved is prevalent, and when the thought that this type of gain is not eternal but transitory is predominant, the nature of *bhakti* would naturally differ. While elaborating this point, further he has stated that the former idea is inclusive of the feeling that any path other than devotion is difficult and there is no certainty of achieving the desired goal. The latter idea inculcates the thought that eternal peace and bliss would not be obtained by fulfilling the desires of the senses.[9]

The seers of the *Ṛv.* did not back away from mundane worldly goals. They desired to lead prosperous, happy and affluent life. Hence, their concept of *bhakti* was not based on the feeling of denouncement and total surrender to the deities. Moreover, the elevated type of *bhakti, i.e., bhakti* without entertaining any desire is not reflected in the *ṛc*-s of the *Ṛv.* The concept of *bhakti* is linked with the feeling of total surrender. These two can develop only when one can have some concrete symbol before oneself. Probably in the absence of these two, the highest type of *bhakti* element was lacking in the *Ṛv.*

The idea of the goal of human life (*puruṣārtha*) differed from time to time. Initially during the period of the *Saṁhitā*-s, the deities in the universe were worshipped predominantly and the path of *bhakti* was initiated. During the period of the sacrificial texts, ritualistic activities attained supreme importance. During the period of the Upaniṣads, the knowledge of the Brahman as the Supreme Reality was of paramount importance. In this way, the element of *bhakti*, which had its roots in the *Ṛv*. was sidelined during the later Vedic period. The reasons for this, as described earlier, may be found in the total transformation in the basic ideology regarding the supreme achievements in life and the means to achieve the same.[10]

According to Belvalkar S.K., and Ranade, R.D., the tendencies that are inherent in primitive speculations such as ritualistic magic, animism, totemism, ascetism etc. which are generally looked into for the beginnings of Yoga philosophy are also to be considered as germs, out of which the later fulfledged philosophy of *bhakti* evolved. A passionate craving of the soul tormented by the woes of the *saṁsāra* (*trividhatāpa*-s), the urge to seek rest, solace and communion with the power above, howsoever inadequately and divergently conceived, is the root principle of *bhakti*. Moreover, the emotion of *bhakti* does not require the monistic power felt and believed in. Accordingly, polytheistic nature-power worship of the Vedic period, as also the primitive non Āryan spirit worship provided ample scope for such a passionate longing after the 'Divine'. There are some Vedic hymns addressed to deities like Varuṇa, Savitṛ and Uṣas wherein the presence of the feeling of true *bhakti* is felt.[11]

Again, in the hymns we often come across epithets like 'father' prefixed to the names of gods which indicate that a certain intimacy of relation was felt by the worshipper between himself and the deity which he thus addressed. For instance, in a hymn of the *Ṛv*. the attitude of mind towards the godhead Agni is expressed. "O, Agni be easy of access to us as a father is to his son."[12] Another verse of the *Ṛv*. describes the deity Indra as a father and mother.[13] The deity worshipped is also considered as a dear friends *e.g.* "I always think of Agni as my father, a close relative, a brother and a friend"[14] also, "Having become ever dear to you, O, Indra, with strong sons (we) would utter divine worship."[15] "He who is dear to us, may we become dear to him (Indra)."[16] Many are such hymns which express the intimate feelings of the worshipper, wherein the seed of *bhakti* may be found.

The Racial and Social Factors

Each society has its own social structure with several components such as norms, values, belief systems etc. Society and religion are always seen to be interacting with each other. The racial and social factors prevalent then might have contributed towards the origin and the development of the doctrine of *bhakti*.

(*i*) Rudra known as Śiva (beneficent) is generally regarded as an Āryanised form of some local deity worshipped by the non-Āryan predecessors of the Āryans in India. The Veda-s and the Brāhmaṇa-s in particular raised him to the position that he enjoys at a later date. Some of the later Brāhmaṇa-s even draw him into the net of their ritualism. The infusion of Rudra or Śiva worship and their presence in the texts of the Brāhmaṇa-s is significant as indicating the anxiety of the Brāhmaṇa-s to admit and assimilate into their own system.

(*ii*) The connection of Kṣatriya-s of the name Sātvatas with their Kṛṣṇa worship is well-known. This faith which was noticed by Magasthenes in the fourth century B.C., later mingled with the then existing faith of Nārāyaṇa.[17]

Bhakti as seen in the Earlier Upaniṣads

The idea of love towards what was held to be the Highest can be traced in the earlier Upaniṣads. Though the earlier Upaniṣads expound knowledge and propound the *jñānamārga*, they also contain elements of *bhakti* in latent form. Thus, the

Kaṭh. Up. states that, "Knowing the Self, formless among the forms, stable among the unstable all pervading, the great, a wise man does not grieve."[18] In the *Kau. Up.*, like Kṛṣṇa in the *Bh. Gītā*, Indra proclaims himself as the true object of knowledge and worship. Indra, in this passage, speaks in the name of the Supreme Being. "Understand me alone. That is what I deem most beneficial for the mankind. One should understand me."[19] Further it is said, "I am the breathing spirit, meditate upon me as the intelligent Self, as life, as immortality."[20] The *Muṇḍ. Up.* has stated that unless the disciple has performed the task of carrying fire over his head, the spiritual teacher should not impart the spiritual knowledge to him.[21] Here, carrying fire over the head signifies devotion and dedication. Similarly, the *Chānd. Up.* has stated that the mystic knowledge may be imparted to the eldest son or a worthy pupil and to none else.[22] From these passages it may be inferred that devotion and dedication towards one's preceptor was a necessary prerequisite to acquire the knowledge. In these passages the idea of *bhakti* can be traced.

A passage from the *Śvet. Up.* introduces the word *bhakti* for the first time in the Upaniṣadic literature, where it is said, "These subjects which have been declared, shine forth to the high-souled one who has the highest devotion for God and for his spiritual teacher as for God."[23] The Upaniṣad uses the very word *bhakti* which connotes the meaning 'highest devotion' not only towards the God but also for the spiritual teacher who is the channel through which the knowledge of God dawns upon us.

Bhakti-According to the Later Upaniṣads

As is seen in the Purāṇa-s and the epics, *bhakti* is evident in great measure in the later Upaniṣads. As is rightly pointed out by Tiele, C.P., a religious man longs for something more than the vague feelings and abstract philosophical ideas. He has the desire to see his God either personally or through mental vision. It is essential for him to feel his nearness to God. His faith rests and develops on the experience of his senses.[24] The later Upaniṣads prominently glorify the five deities; Śiva, Viṣṇu, Devī, Gaṇapatī, and Sūrya; and a host of other deities are praised by these Upaniṣ ads, finally preaching that all other deities are one with the deity the aspirant chooses to worship. The later Upaniṣads adopt polytheistic worship of the Veda-s and replace the worship of the formless with the worship of the 'formed' or personified divinity. But the later Upaniṣads do not deviate from following the path of monotheism, in exalting the deity to be worshipped to the position of the Brahman and the attitude of finding oneness amongst the many is advocated. As a matter of fact, a fine blend of both these types of worship is observed in these Upaniṣads. Accordingly, the Highest Lord who is unmanifest, kind to the devotees manifests himself for the sake of his devotees.[25]

While glorifying one deity, the worship of other deities is not prohibited. As a matter of fact all the deities are considered to be different forms of the deity to be worshipped.[26] Adopting a liberal outlook, the Upaniṣads include even common people in the act of worship.

The final aim of each path; Yoga, Saṁnyāsa etc. is to reach the Brahman. The Upaniṣads have tried to synthesize teachings of different paths for the benefit of the aspirants. For instance, when a devotee is asked to concentrate his mind and contemplate on the deity of his adoration, the principles of Yogamārga have been synthesized with those of the path of *bhakti.* Also, while worshipping the deity, one is expected to surrender everything to the god one adores.[27] Thus, the spirit of renunciation is considered as a means while following the path of *bhakti.* While laying down the principles of the path of *bhakti,* the Upaniṣads have advanced a number of methods like those of worshipping the deity with the *mantra, tantra,* sixteenfold ritual of worship, mental worship etc. It is noteworthy that there is no conflict discernible in the principles of these different paths that have been recommended.

According to the *Tvmn. Up., bhakti* is the most essential element without which the knowledge of the Brahman cannot be secured. It says that for both; *i.e.* for those who wield some authority and for those who do not wield any; the path of *bhakti* is praised. There is no calamity in this path, because warding off the difficulties the God himself looks after his devotees and frees them from the bondage of births and deaths.[28] Faith (*śraddhā*) is a necessary prerequisite for *bhakti.* One who is adorned with faith and devotion obtains the fruit. The *Sarasvatī R. Up.,* says that he who desires wisdom, enjoyment and release, he who always worships Sarasvatī with the ten verses (cited in the Upaniṣad) with faith and devotion, obtains the fruit within six months.[29] Respect also is a component of *bhakti.* One should meditate on Śiva with respect, and a feeling of 'I am that'.[30] In the *Vāsudevopaniṣad*, Hari himself declared "There is no doubt that one who meditates with concentrated thought on Me as immutable Hari, and as the Self in the lotus of the heart, is released." Further, it is stated "One who knows Me to be the Brahman, which is One without a second, without a beginning and without an end, self lustrous, as Consciousness and the Bliss, understands me to be Imperishable and Effulgent; with devotion."[31]

According to the authors of the Upaniṣads, devotion was the easiest, simplest and the highest means by which one can reach the goal. These authors replaced ritualism by devotion, a simple feeling with which the God is pleased. Accordingly, a devotee could bestow anything right from a fruit, a flower, a leaf, a needle, vessels, clothes, cows, books, land, chariot etc. as gifts upon Śiva or his devotees, gain merit and enjoy pleasures in Śiva's world for a number of years.[32] Even those who just see the chariot procession of Śiva, with devotion go to the world of Śiva.[33] Offering of any gift to the devotees of Śiva in a sacrifice in honour of Śiva would enable a person to secure the fruit which is obtained by performing a sacrifice.[34] A person desirous of obtaining the fruit should give away to the devotees of God one's own favourite things.[35] Thus, the worship with sixteenfold ritual might have come into vogue. In this ritual, the deity is invoked, a seat is offered, with pure water feet are washed, water is offered for sipping (*ācamana*), the deity is bathed, sandalwood paste is applied and is adorned with beautiful clothes, jewellery, garlands. Incense (*dhūpa*) is offered, a lamp is lit (*dīpa*), *naivedya* is placed before the deity and hymns of praise and prayer are recited.[36]

Thus, it was the easiest way to approach the divinity. The favour of the deity was believed to be enabling the worshipper to reach the abode of the deity worshipped.

Even as this *saguṇa* worship came in vogue, the old custom of abstract worship was still prevalent. It was also followed in the form of mental worship (*mānasapūjā*). In this form of worship, concrete offerings were to be visualized by the devotee and were imagined to have been offered to the deity. If any material for ritual worship is not available, the devotee is asked to perform the worship just with water. Even if water is not available, the devotee is expected to perform just mental worship.[37]

The *Ātmapūjopaniṣad* beautifully describes mental worship of the Self. The Upaniṣad says, "The state of being free from thought is his meditation. Expelling all the *karman*-s is (His) invocation. Firm knowledge is the seat (for Him). The state of transcending the mind is water for washing the feet. Desirelessness is the *arghya*. Brilliancy of beauty (*sadādīpti*) is the water for sipping. The accomplishment of the best is (His) bath. Cessation of duality is the *gandha*... the radiance of the Consciousness is the flower... the feeling that, 'I am That', is the propitiation. Quietitude itself is the hymn of praise. This is the worship of the Ātman, performed by a perfect *rājayogin*. All this Pure, Perfect is me. This is the accomplishment of release for the aspirants."[38]

Respect, faith, love towards one's own spiritual teacher are indispensable while treading the path of devotion. One attains knowledge through the devotion for *guru* and *jñāna* leads to release.[39]

While following this path, *japa* was considered to be the easiest method of pleasing the gods. It was believed that by simply muttering the name of one's favourite deity, one would win favours of that deity. It could be practised at any time, at any place and by any one irrespective of the distinctions of the caste and creed. Thus the *Kalisan. Up.* stated that one could cross the ocean of *saṁsāra* in Kaliyuga just by muttering his name.[40]

The later Upaniṣads have declared that following these simple methods and means; as a fruit of the worship; the devotees are assured of the worlds where they would reside after leaving this world.

Presenting fanciful mythological accounts, the Upaniṣads, have described different worlds of different deities. Thus, the *S. Sāra. Up.* describes the Kailāsa mountain, the abode of Śiva. "The highest Oneness is verily the Kailāsa. Those, who are of mature intellect, know this secret." says the Upaniṣad.[41] Further, it says that there are six mountains in succession (*āvaraṇa*-s) namely, Brahmānanda, Chidānandācala... and Kailāsa. The Brahmānandācala is surrounded by beautiful forests of delight. There are desire – yielding trees of Rudrākṣa. The Rudrākṣa-s are as if the joy of Self-realization solidified. The 'Supreme Bliss,' is the ripple on the river Brahmānanda. There are Bilva trees, branches of which are the meanings of the *mahāvākya*-s. They have the 'highest joy' as their flowers and 'release' as their fruit. On the mountain, shines forth a bright flame in the midst of which there is an altar called Cinmaya and Ānanda. All these mountains are metaphorically described in a similar way.[42]

The *Rādhopaniṣad* describes the world of Kṛṣṇa as follows. The God Śeṣa engrossed in the meditation of Kṛṣna, has thousands of hoods on which the world of Viṣṇu is situated. Above that is the Sudarśana disc, three crores of *yojana*-s in extent and above that is Gokula, the land of Kṛṣna. There dwells Govinda with Rādhā in a thousand petalled lotus.[43] There are forests of a variety of trees created as eternal places by Kṛṣna and there he sports in various ways. There is no sorrow, no happiness, no old age and no death. At this place spring is the eternal season.[44] Mental worship, muttering, *dhyāna, kīrtana,* praise are the means by which one secures this eternal place, says the Upaniṣad.[45]

The fourteen worlds mentioned in the *Guhyakālī Up.*, which are imagined to be limbs of Devī are *bhūḥ, bhuvaḥ, svaḥ, mahaḥ, janaḥ, tapaḥ, atala, vitala, pātāla, sutala, rasātala, talātala*, and *mahātala* etc.[46]

Rasa-Mārga

The *Sāma. R. Up.*, also known as *Rasikānanda Upaniṣad* propounds *rasamārga* and discards all other ways. It says that the performers of the Vedic sacrifices, the worshippers of *pitṛ*-s, those of the Gāyatrī, the followers of Kaivalyadharma, Jainism and Buddhism, the Cārvāka-s, Mimāṁsaka-s, the followers of Vedānta, Nyāya, Patañjali, also those who follow the path of knowledge and renunciation do not know Rasikānanda.[47] Thus, the Upaniṣad criticises all other paths. A devotee of *rasamārga,* should avoid their company. The Upaniṣad states that the devotees of other deities reach those respective worlds but are unable to reach the sporting place of Rasikānanda.

The ninefold devotional service; which consists of hearing about the Lord, chanting his glories, remembering him, serving and meditating upon his lotus feet, worshipping him, praying him, thinking oneself as his eternal servant, being his friend and surrendering everything to him,[48] is mentioned in the Upaniṣad.[49]

According to this Upaniṣad *upāsanā* is threefold.

(*i*) *Dhyānamaya :* The devotee should meditate upon Rasikānanda and Rādhā in his heart. He should take keen interest in the *rasa*-sport. In fact, every bower, every tree, the place and the act of *rasa*-sport should be meditated upon.

(*ii*) *Idol Worship :* A stone or metal idol of the divinities Rasikānanda and Rādhika, should be worshipped by offering all rituals of worship by faith.

(*iii*) *Service :* Serving and worshipping the ardent devotees of the divinities. This service is said to be a rare opportunity. By selecting and practising any one of these methods, one becomes worthy of enjoying the *rasa-līlā.*[50]

The Philosophy of the Sect

(*i*) Puruṣottama is existence (*sat*), sentient (*cit*) and Bliss (*ānanda*). *Sat* is omnipresent, *Cit* is full of lustre and *ānanda* is the lord Puruṣottama.[5]

(*ii*) The twenty six elements – ten organs, the mind, five subtle elements, three *guṇa*-s, the individual soul, Mahāviṣṇu all proceed from the Puruṣottama.

(*iii*) The individual soul is the form of *sat, cit* and *ānanda.* The individual soul, where *sat* is predominant, performs many deeds and follows castes and creeds. The *jīva* of the nature of *cit,* is a *yogin* who performs deeds without selfishness.[52] The individual soul, of the form of *ānanda* is of the nature of *rasa* and is the enjoyer of the great sport (*mahālīlā*).[53] All other *dharma*-s are abandoned by him. The individual soul is caught in the fetters of *māyā*, which is *anādisiddhā.* The soul may be freed from the clutches of *māyā* by the rise of great fortune, or by the will of god or by the grace of a spiritual teacher or by being merged sincerely in the *rasamārga.*[54] The follower of this *rasamārga* obtains *rasamārgatva* which is higher than mere bliss. This is the secret doctrine of *Sāma* according to the Upaniṣad.[55] In this Upaniṣad, Rādhā has been glorified to the best and the devotees aspire to become one with Rādhā so that they can enjoy the sport with Rasikānanda. The idea seems to be that the devotee should be ardently attached to the God as a beloved to her lover.

It is noteworthy that many of the characteristics of this sect are similar to that of Vallabhācārya. Vallabha has defined *bhakti* as a great firm feeling of love, associated with a sense of God's superiority and greatness. Accordingly, it places the devotee in a subordinate position.[56] This idea of seeking protection and special grace with a sense of God's supreme superiority, and finding oneself happy in thinking of His greatness is seen everywhere in the later sectarian Upaniṣads. This kind of *bhakti* associated with the doctrine of 'taking refuge in God' (*prapatti*) is found among many classes of *Vaiṣṇava*-s esspecially the followers of Rāmānuja. (eleventh century A.D.) Rāmānuja has defined devotion as a contemplation of God unbroken as the ceaseless flow of oil. Such a contemplation necessarily implies the love of God as its basis.[57]

The highest kind of *bhakti* according to *Nārada Bhaktisūtra* is the devotion without motive of any kind. It is the love of God proceeding directly from the heart and not prompted by any reason. A true devotee does not love God because he seeks something from Him, but he loves Him freely and spontaneously. It is believed that God is attracted by such love and always abides with such a devotee. All distinctions of caste, creed or social status vanish for those who are filled with this true and sincere devotion to God. The true devotee feels that all beings are just the manifestations of the power of God and they are all equal. In the development of devotion, there comes a stage where the bonds of individuality are transcended and communion with the Infinite occurs.

The word *bhakti* implies a participation in the Life Divine, which is possible only when the feeling of one's own identity with the Divine has dawned upon the individual. The later Upaiṣ ads propound that through devotion, communion with the Infinite is possible.

Yoga

As the devotion to God is one of the several other ways of attaining the final Beautitude, the Yoga also is a way, a discipline for the purification of body, mind and soul which prepares them for the beautific vision. The Yoga is a means by which, one can attain the end with an intense contemplation.

A Brief Survey of Yoga Philosophy

In the earlier works, Yoga principles appear along with the Sāṁkhya ideas. Patañjali systematised the conceptions of Yoga and set them forth on the background of the metaphyics of the Sāṁkhya, with slight variations. Yoga has accepted twenty five principles of the Sāṁkhya-s. Accordingly, the universe is uncreated and eternal; it undergoes changes. Prakṛti is the first cause of the universe; of everything except only spirit which is uncaused; and accounts for whatever is physical, both matter and force. Out of it, the whole variety of the universe evolves. Space and time are the aspects of Prakṛti which do not have separate existence. Prakṛti is associated with the *guṇa*-s, namely *sattva, rajas* and *tamas.* Yoga admits plurality of the souls, which by nature are pure, eternal and immutable. But through the association of the universe, they indirectly experience joys and sorrows and assume many embodied forms in the course of *saṁsāra.*[58] Regarding the development of Prakṛti, Yoga holds that there are two parallel lines of evolution starting from *mahat.* On one side, it develops into *ahaṁkāra, manas* and five senses of cognition and the five of action, and on the other, develops into five gross elements through the five subtle elements. The Yoga brings three internal organs of the Sāṁkhya under *citta.* It does not recognise *ahaṁkāra,* and *manas* separate from *buddhi.* It also looks upon sense-organs as material in character and so finds no need for a subtle body. The Yoga accounts for the creation by the two agencies *viz.* God and *avidyā.*[59] The ever revolving energy of Prakṛti transforms itself into modifications as the material and mental world. God, remaining beyond Prakṛti removes the obstructions caused by Prakṛti. God is the intelligence who controls the changes caused by Prakṛti and is the end of individual souls (Puruṣa-s). The individual soul is involved in the matter and this leads to his fall from his purity. Like other systems, the Sāṁkhya and Yoga systems believe in *karman* and transmigration. Birth and death according to them are just modifications of gross body. The individual with the help of God can effect his deliverance. The liberation is the isolation of Puruṣa from Prakṛti, to be attained through the knowledge of discrimination between the two. The Sāṁkhya-s hold that knowledge is a means of liberation while Yoga propounds the methods of concentration and action associated with duty.

The *Bh. G.* mentions the same.[60] Yoga discusses the nature of devotional exercises and mental discipline.

The Meaning of the Yerm Yoga

The word Yoga comes from the root *yuj* which means 'to join', and is used in a variety of senses. It is often used in the sense of yoking. In its spiritual sense, Yoga is that process by which a human spirit is brought into conscious communion with, or is merged into the Divine Spirit. In the Upaniṣads and the *Bh. G.*, the soul in its worldly and sinful conditions is said to live separately and is alienated from the Supreme Soul. To get rid of sorrow and sin-caused due to this estrangement-one must attain spiritual union. The union of consciousness of the soul and the Supreme Soul is Yoga.[61]

In Pātañjala Yoga, it does not mean 'union' but 'effort' for separation between Puruṣa and Prakṛti. It is the search for 'our transcendental me', the divine and eternal part of our being. It is used for the system; the science of restraint of the senses and the mind. It signifies effort, strenuous endeavour. It also indicates, the Supreme Powers possessed by God. Yoga, according to Patañjali, is a methodical effort to attain perfection, through the control of the different elements of human nature, physical and psychical. The physical body, the active will and the understanding mind all are to be brought under control. So, Yoga is the study of body, mind and soul and also, it denotes a process; a process towards the aim of the Yoga, *i.e.* the separation of Puruṣa and Prakṛti (*kaivalyam*).[62]

Yoga in the Earlier Upaniṣads

Many physical and mental powers; which are not found in ordinary men; can be secured by means of a discipline. The restraint of bodily and mental activities, is a means to a release from suffering. Ascetic practices were regarded as a means of attaining various supernatural powers. In ecstatic moods, it is said that the gods have entered into men (*Ṛv.* X. 86.2). Crude conceptions of the value of ecstasy and hypnotic trance are to be met with in the *Ṛv.*, (*Ṛv.* X. 136.4-5). In the *Av.* the idea is very common that the supernatural powers can be obtained through various austerities.[63]

The roots of later Yoga system are found in the earlier Upaniṣads. The rudiments of the practice and philosophy of Yoga doctrine; the rudiments of the study of physiology are also found in the earlier Upaniṣads.

The *Kaṭh. Up.,* mentions certain Sāṁkhya ideas. According to Radhakrishnan, S., the account in the *Kaṭh. Up.,* is different from the classical Sāṁkhya in many respects.

(*i*) He has said that there is no mention of self-sense (*ahaṁkāra*) and further, he has added that, "it is true that the distinction between intellect (*buddhi*) and individuation (*ahaṁkāra*) is not a material one."

(*ii*) The Sāṁkhya identifies *buddhi* and *mahat*, the Upaniṣad distinguishes them.

(*iii*) Puruṣa of the dualistic Sāṁkhya theory is not beyond the *avyakta* or Prakṛti, but is a co-ordinate principle.

(*iv*) The Upaniṣadic account gives certain Sāṁkhya ideas in a theistic setting.[64]

But, it also may be remembered that the Sāṁkhya philosophy was also in precursory stages.[65] for *e.g.* the idea of *liṅga-śarīra* of the Sāṁkhya philosophy is based on the conception of the person with sixteen parts, in the *Praśna Up.*[66] Only the *Śvet. Up.* which was a later composition furnishes the fuller and detailed account of Sāṁkhya philosophy as understood in those days. The *Kaṭh. Up.* recalling the Sāṁkhya ideas, lays down that speech and mind shall be restrained in the intellect (*buddhi*), the intellect in *mahat;* which is still distinguished from it; and *mahat* in the *avyakta.*[67] The Upaniṣad mentions some of the elements specified by the Sāṁkhya – Yoga philosophy.[68] The compeer systems, Yoga and Sāṁkhya are mentioned by name in the *Śvet. Up.*[69] The restraint (*yama*), and the self-restraint (*niyama*) of later Yoga are not enumerated in the earlier Upaniṣads. In justification of this, Deussen, P. has stated that it was so, possibly because they are implied without being stated and were assumed to be universal duties-objective and subjective.[70]

Earliest theory of Yoga practice can be observed separately in the Upaniṣads; but no elaborate scheme of *āsana*-s is furnished, which formed the principal theme of the later Upaniṣads, esspecially of those pertaining to Yoga. In the *Śvet. Up.*, stress is laid on the choice of right locality. It is said that, the place should be pure, free from stones and sand, free from fire, smoke and water conservoires. One should select a cave, protected from the wind and there should be no distraction for the mind and the eye.[71] The *Mai. Up.* suggests 'a pure region' for the practice of Yoga.[72] The *Śvet. Up.* has prescribed holding erect the breast, neck and head, in a straight line, at the time of meditation.[73] Again, one is advised to control one's own senses by means of mind;[74] a process equivalent to the later *pratyāhāra*. One is told to regulate the breath implying that it should be made rhythmical, which indicates the later *Prāṇāyāma* at a preliminary stage.[75] Also, one is informed of the harbingers of a spiritual dawn.[76] Then, the physiological effects produced by the 'fire of Yoga' are stated. The Upaniṣad states that one who practises Yoga, becomes ageless and immortal. One feels his own body to be healthy and light.[77] The state of *samādhi* is the fruit obtained by the practice of Yoga, where the individual Self sees the Universal Self[78] and unites with him; a fact indicated by a famous *Yogasūtra*[79]. Here, *dhyāna* and *dhāraṇā* are not mentioned as the preparatory stapes leading to *samādhi*. However, the earlier chapter of this Upaniṣ ad mentions *dhyāna* where one is asked to meditate upon the God and see the God concealed as it were.[80] The *Kaṭh. Up.* mentions *dhāraṇā* as, "the continued equipoise of the senses, mind and intellect; which itself is Yoga."[81]

After the period of the earlier Upaniṣads, the practice of Yoga was developed into a formal system with its own textbook.

The *Yogasūtra* of Patañjali is the oldest textbook of the Yoga school, which is assigned to the second century B.C.,[82] though according to some, it belonged to the fourth and fifth century A.D.[83]

Yoga in the Later Upaniṣads

The theistic modification of the Sāṁkhya system, is presented in the *Mantrika.Up. Up.* to suit the doctrine of Yoga. Which commences from the twenty-five principles of the Sāṁkhya-s. The Sāṁkhyavādins rank Īśvara with these elements purely on external grounds as the twenty-sixth and insert the Ātman as the twenty seventh one.[84] Later Upaniṣads also incorporate the principles of Yoga philosophy. However, their main interest is not that of metaphysical theorising. It is a practical one, *i.e.* to lead the aspirant to the path of salvation through a disciplined activity. This system, therefore, lays chief stress on the external means (*sādhanā*).

The Yogic practices were followed by different schools of thought. Hence, they had undergone changes in accordance with their own doctrines. Thus, for *e.g.* the Yogic practices which developed in accordance with the doctrines of the Śaiva-s and Śākta-s assumed a peculiar form as the *mantrayoga.* The influence of Yoga in the development in the Tantra and other methods of worship was also very great. The descriptions of the plexuses (*cakra*-s) and the serpent-power (*kuṇḍalinī śakti*), the methods to arouse it are found in the Tantra as well.

Different types of Yoga

The *Y.T. Up.* and the *Y.R. Up.* speak of four kinds of Yoga– *mantrayoga, layayoga, haṭhayoga* and *rājayoga.*[85]

Mantrayoga

Mantrayoga consists of the recitation of spells and muttering of the name of the God. The meditation with the help of the name of the God is sufficient to lead a man to final emancipation, says the *Kalisan. Up.*[86] The *Y.R. Up.* says "through the recitation of the spells; with reference to Brahmā, Viṣṇu and Śiva, this Yoga is successfully accomplished by the learned ones."[87] However, the *Y.T. Up.* states that, by muttering the spell, one obtains the knowledge endowed with virtues like *aṇimā* etc. It also states that the aspirants of lower type resort to this Yoga.[88] It may be said that *mantrayoga* marks the beginning of the spiritual life.

Layayoga

Layayoga is the dissolution of *citta.* It is of many kinds.

One should meditate upon the digitless Īśvara while doing all the activities like standing, going, enjoying and sleeping.[89]

The *Kṣuri. Up.* says that, "having burnt all the actions, a Yogin should attain *laya.*"[90]

Through Yogic practices, one may hear *anāhatanāda.* The *Nādabindūpaniṣad* describes various types of *nāda*-s and states that one should concentrate one's mind on any *nāda,* towards which it is attracted, for having done so mind gets merged into it.[91] The mind which is always attached to the *nāda* does not crave for the desires of the senses.[92] The *nāda* is linked with the Praṇavabrahman which is of nature of light.[93] The place into which the mind gets merged, is said to be the highest place of Viṣṇu.[94]

Layayoga is that portion of *Haṭhayoga* in which creative and sustaining *Śakti* of the whole body is actually and truly united with the Lord's consciousness. The *yogin* makes, this *Śakti* introduce him to her Lord and enjoys the bliss and union through her. Though it is he who arouses her, it is she who imparts 'knowledge', for she herself is 'That'.[95] In the *Y.R. Up.*, it is said that this Yoga was practised by Kṛṣṇa Dvaipāyana and others.[96] He who concentrates on the nine plexuses, one by one, achieves *siddhi*-s and emancipation.[97] Due to *layayoga,* one attains comfort and bliss of one's own Ātman.

Haṭhayoga and Rājayoga

Both *Haṭhayoga* and *Rājayoga* aim at the attainment of the

Reality through control of the senses, but the methods recommended for the same are different. According to Haṭhayoga bodily activities can be mastered. It begins with the purification of nervous system (*nāḍīśuddhi*) through the practice of postures, *bandha*-s and *mudrā*-s. It is believed that the realization of the Brahman can be attained by rousing the serpent-power by means of control of the breath (*prāṇāyāma*).

Rājayoga predominantly is a practical study in psychology since it deals at length with the process of stilling the mind and attaining *samādhi.* Patañjali propounded this kind of Yoga, though bodily control also forms a part of Patañjali's Yoga. The later Upaniṣads follow the usual eight fold scheme (*aṣṭāṅgayoga*). While some adopt a sixfold scheme (*ṣaḍāṅgayoga*); excluding the *yama* and *niyama,* may be because they are assumed to be imperative, as a part of the Yoga. In addition to the usual eight *aṅga*-s, the *Tejobindū. Up.* adds seven more and explains the fifteenfold Yoga. They are, *Yama, niyama, tyāga, mauna, deśa, kāla, āsana, mūlabandha, dehasāmya, dṛksthiti, prāṇāyāma, pratyāhāra, dhāraṇā, ātmadhyāna, samādhi.*[98] Roughly speaking it may be said that, these four processes involving spiritual activities, such as meditation, devotion, communion with the God are included in the *Rājayoga.* Though classified into four categories, the Yoga is essentially one and may be known as *mahāyoga.*

The Choice of Locality

With a view to sharpen the concentration of mind, the stress is laid, in the first place on the choice of the right place. In consonance with the requirements stated in the earlier Upaniṣads (*Śvet. Up.*, II.10, *Mai. Up.*, VI.30), the later Upaniṣads also maintain that the place should be secluded,[99] free from noise,[100] with even surface of the ground, pleasant and devoid of faults.[101] According to the *Y.T. Up.*, the monastery (*maṭha*) should have a small door and no windows. It should be kept pure by cleansing it daily with cow-dung or by whitewashing it. It should be made fragrant with incense (*dhūpa*) or *guggula.*[102] One should have a seat made of *kuśa* grass, covered with a cloth or by the skin (of a deer). It should be neither too high nor too low.[103] Elsewhere, it is said that a wooden seat should be covered with *darbha*, and the skin of black antelope.[104] Yoga should be practised in a *maṭ ha* which is built either on the top of a mountain or on the bank of a river or under the shade of a *bilva* tree or in any region that is pure and beautiful.[105] All these preliminaries are to be observed for a successful practice of Yoga.

The Rules to be Observed by a Yogin

The *Y.T. Up.*, states that one practising Yoga should take a limited quantity of food. He should not eat salt, mustard, sour and pungent eatables.[106] Fear, anger, lithargy (*ālasya*) excessive sleeping, keeping oneself awake for a long time, excessive eating and fasting should be avoided.[107] The sincerity and the zeal of the seeker are important for the aspirant which carry him towards his goal within six months.[108]

The Eight Limbs of Yoga

Abstentions (*Yama*-s)

Yama is a control over the senses through knowledge that all this is the Brahman. One should practise it frequently.[109] Yama, which is an absolute control over the senses is fourfold,

(*i*) the conquest of cold and heat, craving for food and sleep,

(*ii*) control of the senses functioning on the object of their desire,

(*iii*) being tranquil under all circumstances and iv) non-swaying of mind.[110]

Observances (*Niyama*-s)

The observances are purification – external and internal, contentment, austerity and devotion to the God.[111] The accounts of different virtues constituting *niyama* differ slightly in the different Upaniṣads. Generally speaking, both *yama* and *niyama* lay stress on ethical preparation necessary for the practice of Yoga. The cultivation of virtues to be inculcated under the *yama*-s and *niyama*-s have been discussed in the earlier chapter (*Ibid.*, pp. 173-180). As a matter of fact they are to be cultivated by all, but those who practise Yoga have to practise them regularly. This practice leads to the state of detachment (*vairāgya*)[112], either for the things of the world or for the pleasures of heaven.

Posture (Āsana)

Yoga realises that the body has a dignity of its own as much as the mind. *Āsana* is a physical posture which facilitates perfect concentration.[113] The body can be a means to secure divine strength. The Yoga expects to control body. If intellectual life and moral activity are considered to be the true ends of man, then the bodily needs should be subordinated to them. At later stages, Yoga demands great powers of physical endurance and Yoga (especially *Haṭhayoga*), aims at perfecting the instrument *i.e.* body, freeing it from its liability to fatigue and curtailing its tendency to wane with age. According to Yogasūtra, beauty, grace, strength and hardness lead to perfection of body.[114] For this purpose, later Upaniṣads have recommended a number of postures. According to the Upaniṣads an *āsana* enables man to sit in the same posture for a long time, without any undue pressure, without causing discomfort to any organ till one is indulged in meditation.

The *A. Nāda. Up.* has recommended three modes of sitting. *viz.* the lotus seat (*padmāsana*), the *svastikāsana* and the auspicious seat (*bhadrāsana*). This Upaniṣad lays stress upon facing the north while sitting.[115] The reason may be, it is the region of the way towards the gods. The *Triśikhi. Brā. Up.* enumerates sixteen yogic postures such as *svatika, gomukha, vīra, yoga, padma, baddhapadma kukkuta, uttānakūrmaka, dhanu, siṁharūpaka, bhadra, mukta, mayūra, matsya, siddha, paścimottāna* and *sukha.*[116] The Upaniṣad explains the process of performing them and says, "One who has obtained control over the posture has conquered the three worlds."[117] The *Yogaśikhā. Up.* directs the choice of lotus posture with the attention focussed on the tip of the nose and with the hands and feet firmly joined.[118] While practising Yoga, one should not see upwards, downwards and horizontally. He should have a firm foothold without tremour.[119] The *Kṣuri. Up.* lays stress on the right mode of sitting and describes the upliftment of chest, head, hips and neck.[120] The *Y.T. Up.* stresses the importance of invert position (*śīrṣāsana*) in which a person is required to stand on his head. The Upaniṣad declares that the wrinkles on the body of a person would disappear, grey hair would disappear in three months of time and he can even conquer death if he resorts to this posture, three hours a day.[121] The *Yoga. K. Up.* regards only two (*padma* and *vajra*) *āsana*-s to be important.[122] The main purpose behind the practice of these *āsana*-s is to control mind by imposing deliberate fixity upon the body and its limbs. The Upaniṣad warns that a weak person should resort to *sukhāsana.*[123]

Prāṇāyāma

It is the process of controlling the breath. It purifies the body as well as the nervous system. One should begin *prāṇāyāma* under the direct supervision of and guidance of a teacher, who is well-versed in it. The regulation of breath is distinguished into *recaka, pūraka* and *kumbhaka.*[124]

Recaka is exhalation, which ought to be prolonged.[125] *Pūraka* is inhalation effected either through one nostril the other being closed with the finger,[126] or through the mouth pointed like a stalk of a lotus.[127]

Recaka should be accompanied with the thought of Śiva, *Pūraka* with that of Viṣṇu, and *kumbhaka* with that of the Brahmā.[128] According to the *Jābāla. D. Up.* and the *Śāṇḍ. Up.* three *mātrā*-s of the Oṁkāra, representing Gāyatrī, Sāvitrī and Sarasvatī. should be the objects of meditation.[129] The stipulated time for these exercises is 16:64:32, *i.e.* the time for maintaining the breath inside should be four times that of the inhalation and the time for exhalation should be twice that of inhalation.[130] These three exercises are regarded as necessary for the purification of the vessels.

It is stated that *prāṇāyāma* effects the destruction of all diseases.[131] One can cure any disease by concentrating Prāṇa on the affected part. *Prāṇayāma* has the moral efficacy in destroying all the sins.[132] The regulation of breath receives considerable emphasis in the Upaniṣads. Serenity of mind may be attained by cultivation of virtues or regulation of breath. So the choice is left to the people who have faith in any of them. Breath-control is regarded as having a steadying influence on the mind. Respiratory exercises are even at the present day looked upon as highly beneficial to health. Though, if undertaken by physically weak people without the guidance of a *guru,* these may prove to be dangerous. This is why the science of Yoga was expected to be kept as a secret.

Sense-Control (*Pratyāhāra*)

According to the *Tejobindūpaniṣad*, it is the pleasant experience of the mind after realisation that the Ātman is not different from the object of senses.[133] The *Y.T. Up.* has stated that *pratyāhāra* is the withdrawal of senses from the sensual objects.[134] It is the supression of the organs of senses as mentioned as early as the *Chānd. Up.*[135] Further, the later *Kṣuri. Up.* has explained this concept with illustration, "As a tortoise draws in its limbs, so are all the senses withdrawn into the heart together with the active mind."[136] The senses and the mind are considered to be only the emanations of the Ātman. They are to be checked and controlled.[137] The *Śāṇḍ. Up.* describes the five kinds of *pratyāhāra* as follows:

(*i*) The forcible withdrawal of the senses from their objects of desire.

(*ii*) Seeing everything as one's own Ātman.

(*iii*) Rejection of the fruit, obtained by the *karman*-s.

(*iv*) Turning one's face away from the sensual pleasures.

(*v*) Projecting of the vital air into the eighteen vital regions described in the Upaniṣad in the prescribed order.[138]

Ethical preparation (*yama, niyama*), posture (*āsana*), breath control and abstraction of the senses represent the stage of purgation, while *dhyāna* and *dhāraṇā* are the stages of illumination and *samādhi* is the union.

Dhāraṇā

The restless mind of a man can know the truth by a persistent withdrawal of consciousness from outward acts as well as inward changes. *Dhāraṇā* is the steadfastness of mind. Deussen, P. says that the *Kṣuri. Up.* teaches the concentration of the mind on the limbs and several vessels of the body, whereby they are in turn cut off from it by the knife of the mind itself and thus freedom from desire is attained.[139] Seeing the Brahman everywhere, wherever the mind wanders is *dhāraṇā* according to *Tejobindūpaniṣad.*[140]

Contemplation (*Dhyāna*)

In normal life, concentration is normally sustained at its fullest for a very short time. *Dhyāna* is the resulting state of an even current of thought undisturbed by other thoughts, in which the whole body is brought in harmony with the Supreme Spirit.[141] According to *Tejobindūpaniṣad*, it is the state of the mind when one actually experiences oneself to be the Higher Self.[142] Almost all the later Upaniṣads proclaim *saguṇa* type of meditation, as a means of concentration. They stress the importance of a support (*ālambana*) in the form of one's own favourite deity. Awandering mind can concentrate, easily on this deity and meditate upon it. The Upaniṣads are never weary of offering descriptions of the sacred syllable Oṁ and its *mātrā*-s. It is said that, it is the best support.[143] It is the chariot which carries one to the world of the Brahman.[144] Besides the three *mātrā*-s, the later Upaniṣads describe the half *mātrā* and it is said that it leads one to the Supreme Goal.[145] The point (*bindū*) is the point of strength which bears the deepest meaning.[146] In some Upaniṣads twelve component parts of the syllable Oṁ are described. Though it is said that Oṁ represents higher as well as lower Brahman,[147] the later Upaniṣads advance even beyond the syllable, first to the half *mātrā* and then even beyond this. "Higher than the original syllable, is the point (*bindū*), the *nāda* higher than this; the syllable vanishes with the sound. The highest state is silent."[148] This highest state, is not expressed by any word or combination of words,[149] It cannot be meditated on by means of Oṁ but only in absolute silence.[150] It is the chariot which is to be abandoned where the road ends and the walkway begins.[151] Ascending by this support, man attains to nothingness, where there is no word, no sound. "like the sap of the flowers in liquid honey."[152] Thus, the eighth and the highest stage of Yoga is reached.

Absorption (*Samādhi*)

Meditation becomes absorption when subject and object, the soul and the God are completely blended into one. The consciousness of the separate subject altogether disappears. It is of the nature of the Supreme Bliss.[153] The Upaniṣads look upon this union as an ascent of the soul that meditates from the heart, then it winds upwards through the *suṣumṇā* and breaking through the arch of the skull, it finally gazes the Supreme.[154] The heart is looked upon as a lotus flower – a view already expressed in the *Chānd. Up.* (VIII. 1.1). The *M.N. Up.* says that, a toungue of flame rises from this lotus leaping upwards.[155] According to the *Kṣuri. Up.*, the Prāṇa rises up from the navel to the heart through the *suṣumṇā*, like a spider on its web, and further moves upwards from the heart; and with the knife (*kṣurikā*) of the Yoga cuts through all the veins except *suṣumṇā* and ascends upon it to its destination, *viz.* the Brahman.[156] The *A. Nāda. Up.* also says that Prāṇa is the one which ascends by means of silent Oṁ.[157] According to *Dhyānabindūpaniṣad*, the half *mātrā* of the Oṁ, draws the mind upwards, from the lotus of the heart by the path of veins and between the eyebrows it is lost in the Supreme.[158]

There are two degrees of *samādhi*; *i.e. savikalpa* and *nirvikalpa*. In the former, the mind remains conscious of the object. The latter does not involve any such separate consciousness of either subject or object or even self-consciousness.[159] The *Sarasvatī. R. Up.* speaks of six kinds of *samādhi* and says that *nirvikalpa samādhi* is like a lamp undisturbed by wind.[160] *Samādhi* is nothing, but all void according to *S.L. Up., i.e.* it is marked by the absence of mind, intellect.[161] The later Upaniṣads which have incorporated the principles of Yoga, Vedānta philosophy, Śāktism and other sectarian Upaniṣads, have discussed this Yoga doctrine. Raising the respective deities to the Highest state of the Brahman, they have advised the aspirants to meditate upon them in order to attain the state of *samādhi* and the ultimate union with the Supreme.

In addition to different postures and *prāṇāyāma*; for the progress on this path; the Upaniṣads have described different *bandha*-s. They are complementary to other practices.

Mālabanadha

This *bandha* is helpful in arousing the dormant serpent power. The process consists of arresting the downward movement of the Apāna vāyu, then this Vāyu is forced upwards and is united with the Udāna vāyu. By this process, a great amount of heat is produced by which the dormant serpent power is roused and then it enters the *brahmanāḍī.*[162]

The Uḍḍīyānabandha

This is practised just after inhalation and before exhaltion. The stomach and neck are to be strained in such a way that the Prāṇa goes to the stomach and gradually removing all the disorders, enters the *suṣumṇānāḍī.*[163] The *jālandarabandha* is practised after the exhalation of breath, pressing the chin at the base of the neck. The breath is pressed downward and the Prāṇa passes to the *brahmanāḍī.* This stirs *sarasvatī, nāḍī.* which in turn rouses the serpent power.[164] These are three primary *bandha*-s. Different kinds of *mudrā*-s are also practised by *yogin-s* as accessory to their main Yogic practices. They are meant for cleansing the vessel *i.e.* removing the disorders of the body and making it healthy. Different *mudrā*-s, which constitute another feature of the *haṭhayoga* are explained in detail in the Yoga-Upaniṣads, *viz.* by the practice of *mahāmudrā*, the nerves are purified, diseases are eradicated, one can digest any amount of food, poison also can be digested and it has no evil effect on the body.[165] *Khecarī mudrā* is the most difficult and is to be practised under the guidance of an adept *guru*. In this *mudrā*, the tongue is gradually cut off from its roots; over the period of six months. Then the yogin gradually pulls it out and elongates it. After nine years of practice, the tongue becomes so long, that it reaches the chest, then the *yogin* practises to push the tongue through *brahmarandhra* and rotates it in the cavity of brain. After twelve years, as a fruit of this *vidyā*, the initiate sees the whole universe in this body.[166] The *ṣaṇmukhīmudrā* consists of suspending the Apāna in the head until one feels delighted. By the practice of this *mudrā*, one gains control over mind, reaches the superconscious state and attains oneness with the Brahman.[167] One may hear various sounds (*yoganāda*-s) while practising it. For the mind to be absorbed in spontaneous delight, the *śāmbhavīmudrā* and the *cinmayamudrā* should be practised.

The other processes prescribed by the *haṭhayoga* and described in the Upaniṣads are *vajrolī* and *amrolī*.[168] The aim of all these processes is to acquire the ability of preserving the seed in the body, and direct it upwards (*ūrdhvaretas*). All these processes have more of physiological value and they are practised to gain health and physical immortality.

As the body and mind are used as instruments in Yoga, to reach the desired goal, they must be kept in perfect health. The Yogic practices are the means to the goal.

Physiological Aspect of Yoga

According to Ranade, R.D., "It was the study of Yoga which was the cause of the rise of physiological science which was the precursor of the later fullfledged systems of medicine".[169] It seems that the study of the body; even during the period of the earlier Upaniṣads; was of great importance. In the earlier Upaniṣads, several accounts of veins originating from the heart and surrounding it occur. The number of veins is said to be 72,000 of which 101 are of vital importance. (*Bṛ. Up.* II.1.19). *Ibid.* (IV. 3.20), the *Kau. Up.* (IV. 19), the *Chānd. Up.* (VIII. 6.1) describe the colour of the veins as tawny, green, red etc. or; tawny, white, dark, yellow, red or blue, green, red etc. with little variations. It is evident that the authors of these passages knew the distinction between the blood vessels; a fact of physiological importance. Moreover, the *Mai. Up.* (I. 2) enumerates seven *dhātu*-s, bone, skin, muscles etc. The three *doṣa*-s namely bile, phelgum, wind are also mentioned. It is evident that the physiological details presented in the later Upaniṣads, especially those dealing with the Yoga exhibit an advanced level of knowledge of physiology. The knowledge of the creation of the body, that of different nerve centres, the breaths the veins (*nāḍī*-s), the five great elements and their places in the body, the vital parts of the body, the eight petalled lotus of the heart, the impurities (*doṣa*-s) with reference to the body are some of the important topics dealt with in the later Upaniṣads.

The *Yogaśikhā. Up.* describes sixteen *nāḍī*-s with their names, functions, places and the names of their presiding deities.[170] *Vilambinī, Surā, Sarasvatī, Rākā, Kuhū,* and *Śaṁkhini* etc. are the names of the *nāḍī*-s. Thus, for *e.g. Sarasvatī* reaches the tip of the tongue.[171] *Rākā* enables one to drink water, creates hunger and stores up mucus in the nose.[172] The nerve *Śaṁkhini* carries the essence of food to the head.[173] The *Kuhā* excretes the impurities from the body[174] and so on. The *Yogacāḍāmaṇi. Up.* presents a vivid description of three important nerves. It says that *Suṣumṇā* is well placed at the centre of the body, in the middle of the umbilical knot, resembling a fine fibre of the lotus stalk, proceeding upwards to the *Brahmarandhra. Iḍā* and *Piṅgalā* are at its left and right respectively. *Iḍā* originates from the knot of the navel and terminates in the left nostril and *Piṅgalā*, having the same origin terminates in the right nostril. *Gāndhārī* and *Hastijivā* are at the front and the rear, proceeding to the left and the right eye respectively. *Pūṣā* and *Yaśasvinī*, originate from the navel and reach the left and the right ears respectively. *Kuhū,* originating from the same knot, proceeds to the genitals.[174] Thus, the later Upaniṣads present detailed descriptions of the *nāḍī*-s, describe their course and functions; the places of the Prāṇa-s and their functions. This knowledge is a must for a *yogin*, for the cleanising of the *nāḍī*-s.[175]

The Prāṇa-s

The *A. Nāda. Up.* describes five prominent breaths in the body. Thus, the first and foremost Prāṇa is situated in the heart. The colour of this Prāṇa is red, like that of a ruby. The place of Apāna breath; having the colour of dazzeling Indragopa gem; is at the anus. Vyāna breath is lustrous like the rays of the Sun and pervades all the parts of the body. The Samāna is situated in the navel and is of white colour, like the milk of a cow. The Udāna which is of grey colour is situated in the throat.[176] Nāga, Kūrma, Kṛkara, Devadatta, Dhanañjaya are known as five subordinate breaths.[177] Assimilation of water, food and other liquids in the mouth as well as in the abdomen, is the function of the Prāṇa. Evacuation of the liquids and waste, is the action of the Apāna. Prāṇa and Apāna are assisted by the Vyāna, in their functions. Samāna nourishes the body and Nāga maintains the balance of the body. The Kūrma and Kṛkara perform the function of closing and blinking the eyelids. Devadatta causes yawning and sleep.[178]

The Plexuses and the Serpent Power

The plexuses are known as *cakra*-s or lotuses and play an important part in the Yoga practice. Six *cakra*-s are generally mentioned but the *S. L.. Up.* adds four more and explains them.[179] Again, there are discrepancies as to the number and colour of the petals mentioned with reference to these *cakra*-s. Thus, the *Yoga. K. Up.* speaks of sixteen petals in the *hṛdayacakra* instead of twelve;[180] and the *Dhyānabindūpaniṣad* mentions twelve spokes inestead of ten in the *Nābhicakra.*[181]

1. The Pelvic Plexus (*Mūlādhāra Cakra*) : This is the root support, situated between the anus and the genitals, *i.e.* at the base of spinal column.[182]

It has four petals.[183] Woodroffe, J. opines that the number of petals in any *cakra* is determined by the position and the number of *nāḍī*-s surrounding and passing through the *cakra.* Thus, the four *nāḍī*-s around the pelvic plexus gives it the appearance of a lotus having four petals. The petals are thus, configurations made by the position of the *nāḍī*-s at any particular centre. The *nāḍī*-s are the subtle channels along which the currents of the Prāṇa-s flow.[184]

2. The Aortic Plexus (*Svādhiṣṭhānacakra*) : It has six petals and is situated in the region of the genitals. It is the place of the Apāna-breath.

3. The Solar Plexus or the Abdominal Brain (*Maṇipūra or Nābhicakra*) : It is crooked like a serpent and has fine coverings and consists of ten petals. This plexus is also known as the abdominal brain "because of the abundance of grey and white matter here." opines Vaidya, S.M. Further he says that, these *cakra*-s can be definitely considered as the sympathetic plexuses.[185] Gajendragadkar, K.V. holds that even the modern physiology recognizes the existence of these *cakra*-s.[186] This is the place of the Samāna breath and the subordinate Kṛkara breath. When the three *Vāṇī*-s (*paśyantī, madhyamā*, and *vaikharī*) are dissolved here, one obtains the knowledge of the highest speech (*parā vāṇī*), which is in the form of inspiration.[187]

4. Cardiac Plexus : It is situated in the region of the heart. Hence it is known as the lotus of the heart. It is also named *anāhata cakra*, since the aspirant is able to hear different types of *nāda*-s here while proceeding on the spiritual path. One is advised to dissolute the Prāṇa and the *manas* in this *cakra.* This *cakra* is the abode of the Prāṇa and the Devadattaprāṇa. This also is the place of *paśyantī vāṇī.*[188]

5. Cervical Plexus (*Viśuddhacakra*) : This *cakra* is in the throat, having sixteen petals. The *Kṣuri. Up.* states that after dissipating the *Maṇipūra* and the *Anāhata cakra*-s, the Prāṇa enters into this *cakra*[189] and later proceeds towards the *Ājñā* and the *Sahasrāra cakra.* Of the five prominent breaths, the Udāna and the subordinate breath *Kūrma* reside here. This is the place of *Madhyamā-vāṇī.*[190]

6. Optic Thalamus (*Ājñācakra*) : The *cakra* which consists of two petals is situated between the eye-brows. In this place the Ātman, as well as the Nādabrahman is realized. Commencing from the *Mūlādhāra* and ending in the *Ājñā*, there are fifty petals in all; as are the letters of the alphabets which are in the petals. They are known as *mātṛkā*-s. According to Woodroffe, J., "the *mātṛkā*-s are associated with the *tattva*-s since both are the products of the same Creative Cosmic process manifesting either as physiological or psychological function."[191] It is noteworthy that the number of petals equals that of the letters leaving out either *Kṣa* or *la*; and these fifty multiplied by twenty are in the thousand petals of the *Sahasrāra*. The number is probably indicative of multitude and magnitude.

The Serpent Power (*Kuṇḍalinī Śakti*)

The place of the serpent power is above the *Nābhicakra*, near the navel. There she rests coiled in the dormant form. In the body, in Yoga, this static *śakti* is affected by *prāṇāyāma* and other Yogic process, and becomes dynamic. The *Yogakuṇḍalī Up.* presents details about this process. It is awakened by means of breath, internal fire and mind. The practitioner has to strictly observe celibacy and temperance. When the mind is absorbed by the incessant and regular practice of the *Prāṇāyāma,* the impurities in the body are purged away. The practice of *mālabandha,* forces Apāna breath upwards. Therefore, Apāna passes upwards along with the fire to the seat of the Prāṇa, where these three are blended. This blend proceeds to the serpent power, where it lays dormat. By the push of the Prāṇa, *kuṇḍalinī* is roused by the pressure of the *bandha*-s, the Prāṇa enters the *Suṣumṇānāḍī* and paves her way upwards towards the *Sahasrāracakra*, piercing the *cakra*-s on her way upwards.[192]

Thus, when completely dynamic, *i.e.* when the *kuṇḍalinī śakti* unites with the consciousness of Śiva in the *Sahasrāra,* the polarization of the body gives way. A man's consciousness is merged into that of the Lord's. The body continues to exist and continues it's organic life. The consciousness of one's own body and other objects is withdrawn because the mind is ceased. "When *kuṇḍalī ni* sleeps, man is awake to this world, and when she gets up, he sleeps, *i.e.* loses all consciousness of the world."[193]

The physiological basis of Yoga, which was already discussed in the days of the earlier Upaniṣads, gathered impetus. Deep consideration was given to physiological thought, as is evident in the later Upaniṣads. This was not limited to Yoga but also extended to the advanced study of embryology as is seen in the *Garbhopaniṣ ad*. The Upaniṣad describes that, from the union of the seed and blood, at the periodical time as nodule arises, after a week it forms into a cyst; within fifteen days a lump; after two months the head is formed; after three months the parts of the feet; in the fourth month ankle bones, belly and hips; in the fifth the spine; in the sixth month, mouth, nose and ears. In the seventh month, the body is inhabited by the soul and it is complete in all its parts. In the ninth month, it is complete in knowledge also and recalls the former births. After the completion of the term, when it enters into this world, comes into contact with the Vaiṣṇavavāyu and forgets everything.[194] However, Deussen, P. considers this to be an Indian imagination and compares it to Voltaire's mockery which has reference to similar ideas in the later western philosophy.[195]

The Utility of Yoga

The acquisition of powers through the Yogic practices is subordinated to the chief end of *samādhi* in the Yoga system. But though the highest goal may not be attained, the lower stages are not without their value. Each stage brings its reward. for *e.g.*, control of body through postures results in an indifference towards heat and cold.[196] The *Yogacūdāmaṇi Up.* states that, by the practice of the postures diseases are cured; the *prāṇāyāma* destroys sin, the *Pratyāhāra* ends the mental transformations, the *dhāraṇa* endows one with mental fortitude.[197] Full intuitive knowledge of any object can be obtained through concentration. If one concentrates on muscular powers, one will have a giant's strength.[198] By the hightened powers of the senses through concentration one obtains clairvoyance and clairaudience.[199] Concentration on the threefold modifications which all objects undergo endows one with the power to know the past, present and future. Meditation on the serpent power in the *Nābhicakra* endows the Yogin with all powers[200] (*siddhi*-s).

One acquires larger vision and latent powers get manifested. By following the practice and principles of Yoga; such as hightening the power of concentration, arresting the wanderings of the mind, fixing the attention on the deepest sources of strength, one can master one's own soul. Yoga helps one reach higher levels of consciousness, through a transformation of psychic organism which enables it to get beyond the limits set to ordinary human experience. Thus, Yoga is the means to obtain the desired goal worldly or spiritual. The supernormal powers are considered to be the obstacles in attaining *samādhi*. They are the by-products of the higher life. By disregarding these powers, a true seeker can attain freedom.

Saṁnyāsa

According to Ghosh, A., "There is an established tradition, long favoured by great religious teachings and by men of profound spiritual experience that renunciation must not only be complete as a discipline but a definite means to an end and that it shall fall nothing short of the renunciation of life itself, and of our mundane existence."[201] The history of this tradition can be traced back to the earlier Upaniṣads. According to Ranade, R.D., the foundations of the *āśrama* systems has been already firmly laid down even in the earlier Upaniṣads.[202] Kane, P.V. has also stated that in the times of the earlier Upaniṣads, the three *āśrama*-s were known and all four were known by their specific names at the time of the *Jābālopaniṣad*.[203] Expressing the same views, Deusen, P. stated that in the older Upaniṣads, the separation between the third and fourth orders of life was not marked distinctly. The distinction between *vānaprasthāśrama* and *saṁnyāsāśrama* was gradually established.[204] In the *Chānd. Up.*, the recluses are advised to perform penance.[205] In the *Bṛ. Up.*, persons who fast and practice penance are contrasted with the man who knows the Ātman and becomes a *muni* and a wanderer (*parivrājin*).[206] Again, in the *Bṛ. Up.*, the knowledge of the Ātman as the highest aim is differentiated from sacrifices and practices of penance.[207] An intimation of four *āśrama*-s is provided by the *Muṇḍ. Up.*[208] and the *Jābāla. Up.* names all the four in their correct order.[209] In the post-Vedic age the formal conditions and the rules of ascetic life and other stages of life were set forth by *Dharmasūtra-s* and law givers like Manu.

The later Upaniṣads reveal a clear distinction between the third and the fourth orders of life and lay down strict specific norms for the ascetics to achieve emancipation, the fourth goal of life.

The Rules to be Observed by a *Saṁnyāsin*

The later Upaniṣads, which propound *Saṁnyāsa* as a way to salvation, lay down various rules to be observed by a *saṁnyāsin*. A person who renounces, should abandon relatives, Vedas and objects of desire.[210] After renunciation, he should not mention his caste, nation, name, age, family etc. to anyone.[211] He should not accept gifts from anyone.[212] A *saṁnyāsin* should neither converse with women nor should remember any lady seen by him before.[213] He should always be patient and cool-headed. Honour and dishonour and the dualities such as these should be treated equally by him.[214] He should uproot all desires right from their roots and consider the gold and earth as equal. In short, a *saṁnyāsin* should adhere to the stated rules strictly, in accordance with his own grade.

The Evil Effects of Non-observance of the Rules

If one takes to renunciation with doubtful mind, one will not be released for many lives. An entry into family life of a person who has once renounced the world is as good as death.[215] An ascetic who does not follow the norms of asceticism (*parivrāja*) is called the downfallen (*ārūḍhacyuta*).[216] The *Saṁnyāsopaniṣad* states that those who fail to observe the vow of *Saṁnyāsa* or those that create obstacles on the path of renunciation and those who initiate a down-fallen one are all the fallen ascetics.[217]

Different types of *Saṁnyāsa*

Different types of *Saṁnyāsa* mentioned in the later Upaniṣads are :

(*i*) *Vairāgyasaṁnyāsa* : This *saṁnyāsa* is one which is resorted to by a person who having performed meritorious deeds in his life gets disgusted with worldly pleasures and subdues his passions.[218]

(*ii*) *Jñānasaṁnyāsa* : Is one which is resorted to by a person who has studied various branches of knowledge throughly, has experienced the world in totality, has given up all the desires of the senses.[219]

(*iii*) *Jñānavairāgyasaṁnyāsa* : Renunciation resorted to after studying everything, experiencing everything and renouncing for the sake of contemplation of the Self.[220]

(*iv*) *Karmasaṁnyāsa* : *Karmasaṁnyāsa* is to be resorted to after passing through the first three stages of life, after performing the necessary rite even in the absence of the feeling of detachment.[221] On the contrary, *Āturasaṁnyāsa* can be resorted to with a mere intense desire. For this, there is no need to perform any rite.[222] One can embrace it even while on death-bed.[223]

Classification of Recluses

The later Upaniṣads enlist six types of recluses. A detailed description of all these form a special feature of these, esspecially those propounding Saṁnyāsa.

(*i*) *Kutīcaka* : This is considered as the first order of a *saṁnyāsin*. He is required to retain a tuft of hair on his head and wear a sacred thread. He has to have a water pitcher and a staff as his belongings. He has to wear either a loin-cloth or has to cover his body with tattered rags or grass. As a symbol of his class, he has to wear a white *ūrdhvapuṇḍra*. He is expected to worship gods, and has to wait upon his parents and the preceptor.[224] The *Śāṭyāyanīya. Up.*, has compared five things, *viz* a threefold staff, loin-cloth, *upavīta, śikya* and *pavitra* to five *mātrā*-s of the Praṇava; and the threefold staff according to the Upaniṣad is the *Vaiṣṇavaliṅga* which leads a *saṁnyāsin* to release.[225]

(*ii*) *Bahādaka* : Type of a *saṁnyāsin* stands second in the order of recluses. He has to take his bath twice a day. However, the Kutīcaka is advised to take bath thrice a day. The Kutīcaka is allowed to keep two bath towels with him, but the Bahādaka is allowed to have only one.[226] He can wear matted hair or maintain a tuft. His possessions are a threefold staff and a water-pot. His attire comprises of a loin-cloth or saffron-coloured dress and the sacred thread. He, like Kuṭīcaka wears a *tripuṇḍra* mark. He is allowed to worship gods, practise *mantrajapa,* study and teach the Vedic lores. He is not allowed to initiate others in the order.

(*iii*) *Haṁsa* : This order is the third, in the ascending orders of *saṁnyāsins*. The Haṁsa-s do not worship god and do not utter spells. The *antaḥpraṇava* and meditation on the Veda-s are recommended for him. He is advised to take bath once in a day and should use a rag as his bath-towel. He should wear matted hair. He should wear a *tripuṇḍra* or *ūrdhvapuṇḍra*. He should maintain himself with that much quantity of alms which can be held by him in the palms of his hand. While wandering, he is advised to stay in a village for one night or for five nights in a city, or at a holy place for seven nights. He can stay at the same place for four months only in the rainy season.[227]

(*iv*) *Paramahaṁsa* : Abandonment of all the mental inclinations is looked upon as a real bath for him. He may wear a loin cloth or may stay naked. The *paraṁhamasa* type of *saṁnyāsin* has no belongings like the staff, water-pot etc. He may beg alms in the house of a person belonging to any caste. The palms of his hands serve as the pot and he takes only eight *kavala*-s of food. His outward appearance resembles that of a mad man. However, he has a balanced mind, is well-versed in the knowledge of the Brahman. His characteristics are unmanifest. As the mark of this order, he besmears his body with sacred ashes. He may stay in a vacant house, in a hollow of a tree, or on a pasture, or in a cave or on the mountain in a secluded area. There are no rules or limitations of any sort for the *Paramahaṁsa.* He is one who continually experiences the identity of his Self with the Brahman. He is so called because he has identified himself with the *Paramahaṁsa* (the Supreme Self).[228]

(*v*) *Turīyātīta* : He is always conscious of the feeling 'I am that' (*soham*). He stays naked. He eats food directly by his mouth and is therefore, called '*gomukha*', or he maintains himself with the forest fruits.[229]

(*vi*) *Avadhūta* : The *Avadhūtopaniṣad* deals with the characteristics of this highest order of *saṁnyāsins.* According to this Upaniṣad, the *Avadhūta* has a choice to perform various duties and follow the rules laid down in the *śāstra*-s for the benefit and guidance of the worldly people.[230] But while doing all this, he acts merely as a witness and considers himself to be the non-doer. He treats his body as a corpse. There are no restrictions for him and no special rules of conduct.[231] The Avadhūta roams about all the times.[232] He accepts food from people belonging to all castes. He may eat any amount of food. He is not affected by virtue, merit, vice or sin.[233] He has no belongings and has no sect-mark. There is nothing like religious or non-religious, holy or unholy for the *Avadhūta.*[234] He is unshakable and Supreme. He has to cut off all the ties of worldly existence. He transgresses all distinctions and even the stages of life. He is always in communion with the Highest Self.

The above details indicate that as a *saṁnyāsin* goes on reaching higher levels, there is no need to follow the rules strictly. At the initial stage, it is necessary to control the senses and the wandering mind. In the course of time, a *saṁnyāsin* can easily focus his attention on the Brahman.

The Fruit

The realization of the Brahman forms the main aim of *saṁnyāsa* stage of life. When a person takes to renunciation, it is said that his four hundred generations, a hundred preceding and three hundred succeeding, go to the heaven.[235] According to the *Saṁnyāsopaniṣad,* however, the number of generations is hundred and twenty.[236] The fruit that a *saṁnyāsin* himself obtains is the highest delight of the Brahman; which is fourfold – *priya, moda, pramoda* and *ānanda.*[237] The worlds a *saṁnyāsin* obtains are as follows. The Ātura and Kutīcaka type of *saṁnyāsin*-s obtain *Bhūloka* and *bhuvaḥloka*. Bahūdaka types of *saṁnyāsins* reach the heaven. The Haṁsa goes to *Tapoloka*, the Paramahaṁsa type to *Satyaloka*. Meditating upon his own Self, Turīyātīta and the Avadhāta type obtain release in their own Selves as the *bhrahmarakīṭanyāya.*[238]

Ghosh, Aurobindo says that, many causes have contributed to the growth of this pure, lofty and august tradition of renunciation.

(*i*) The first and the foremost is the radical opposition between the worldly living, which is of imperfect nature and the nature of spiritual living. This results in the entire rejection of world existence as a lie or an unhappy dream.

(*ii*) Soul's thirst for personal salvation; an escape into total and permanent bliss, undisturbed by worldly troubles.

(*iii*) Incidental to spiritual experience can be a strong feeling and practical proof of the difficulties in combining the life of works (action) with spiritual peace, *i.e.* the life of realization.

(*iv*) The lowest cause can be said to be the weakness that arises from the struggle, disgust and disappointment of the soul baffled by things around, which pushes the soul to become free from the evercircling wheel of death and birth.[239]

By discipline or by positive practice of the Yoga, the truth of knowledge, the truth of works etc. are confirmed in oneself. By renunciation, false hoods are uprooted and discarded in such a way that they cannot hamper the harmonious growth of the Divine living by their persistence, resistence and recurrence. According to Ghosh, Aurobindo, "Renunciation is an indispensable instrument of our perfection."[240]

This means can be used only for removing that which stands in the way of positive fulfilment.

This renunciation obviously has to be an inward renunciation of attachment and craving of desires in the senses and the heart; of self will in the thought and action; of egoism in the centre of consciousness. In short, it should be renunciation of all sorts of worldly attachments of body, mind and thought. This will ultimately lead to the renunciation of the subtle desires, and the consciousness of 'I'ness – and only the Divine consciousness will remain.

Tantra

The word '*tantra*' is derived from the root *tan,* which means to stretch, to extend, to spread etc. The word *tantra* connotes various shades of meaning such as, the right way of doing anything (of following a technique); regular order of ceremonies and rites; system; ritual etc. It also means religious treatises teaching magical and mystical doctrine for the worship of the deities or the attainment of superhuman power. The means by which the knowledge of metaphyics or philosophy is advanced is known as a 'Tantraśāstra'. The contemplation of the form, virtue (*guṇa*), deeds of a deity, the worship of *yantra*-s and *cakra*-s, worship by means of *mantra*-s, *japa*, *tarpaṇa-vidhi, nyāsa,* uttering of thousand names (*nāmasahasra*), *stotra*-s and many other worships (*upāsanā*-s) are included in the *tantras.*[241]

The Period

"The Tantras represent a development of the medieval period and the Tāntric literature in its present form belongs mainly to the centuries following 300 A.D." states Zimmer, Heinrich.[242] However, Schomerus, H.W. claims that the beginning of the Āgama literature goes back to a time before the birth of Christ. He states so, considering the following evidences :

(*i*) The Śaiva-Āgama-s are mentioned in the *Sūtasaṁhitā* of the *Skandapurāṇa*. As the Buddhists and Jains are mentioned in the *Sūtasaṁhitā*, that document must have emerged after the 2nd or 3rd Cen. B.C.

(*ii*) The Śaiva-Āgama-s are often mentioned in the Tamil literature. The oldest must be Tirumūlar's 'Tirumanta' which mentions Āgama-s and is considered as more or less reworking of its doctrines. Tamil scholars allot this work to the 2nd or 3rd cen. B.C. on linguistic grounds. Schomerus is of the opinion that the Śaiva-Āgama-s cannot be later than the first Buddhist council. (480 B.C.).[243] But Winternitz opines that, in the latest portion of the *Mahābhārata*, with their frequent allusions to the Purāṇa-s and Itihāsa-s, there is no mention of the Tantra-s.[244] It may be said that the period of the Tantra-s is later that of the *Mahābhārata*. According to Winternitz, M., the *Pañcarātrasaṁhitā* probably originated in the north, the earliest of them perhaps dating from the 5th to the 9th cen. A.D.

Some of the Tantra-s themselves say that there are sixtyfour tantra-s; their original home probably seems to be Bengal from where they spread through Assam, Nepal and even beyond India to Tibet, China through the agency of Buddhism. In reality, they are known throughout the length and breadth of India. The earliest Nepalese manuscripts of Tantra-s date from the 7th to 9th cen. A.D. The worship of Durgā which plays an important part in the Tantra-s goes back to the later Vedic period, does not prove that Tantrism and the Tantra-s are of an equally venerble age. This goddess and her cult do unite traits of different deities-Āryan as well as non-Āryan. It is probable that the system of Tantra-s adopted many characteristics from non-Āryan and non-Brahmanical cult. On the other hand, some essential traits of the tantra-s can be found in the *Av,* as well as in the Brāhmaṇa-s and the earlier Upanișads. Śāktism was prevalent in Bengal from 12th to 16th cen. A.D.[245] The above details indicate that the Tantra can be said to belong to the period ranging from the 3rd to 16th cen. A.D.

As pointed out by Winternitz, M., the Purāṇas, the Tantra-s, and the later Upanișads can be considered to be belonging to the same period.[246]

The Tāntric Literature

(*i*) The Saṁhitā-s are the scared books of the Vaișṇava-s. (*ii*) The Āgama-s are those of the Śaiva-s. (*iii*) The Tantra-s are those of the Śākta-s. However, there is no line of clear demarcation among them. The expression Tantra is frequently used as a general term for this class of works. *viz.* The *Vaișṇava Padmasaṁhitā* is also known as the Padmatantra. According to Eliot, a Tantra also means 'a system of doctrines', a book. An Āgama means a tradition and a Saṁhitā stands for a collection of sacred works.[247] Tantra-s take the form of a dialogue between Śiva and Pārvatī. When the goddess asks questions like a pupil, and Śiva answers them like a teacher, these dialogues are called Āgama-s, whereas when the goddess answers Śiva's questions they are called Nigama-s.

The Tantraśāstra is the presentation of Vedāntic Truth modelled as regards the mode of life and ritual to meet the characteristics of Kaliyuga. It is said that for each *yuga* of a *mahāyuga*, a suitable study (*upāsanā*) is prescribed. For Satyayuga and Tretāyuga, the study of the Veda-s is prescribed. For the *Tretā* and *Kali*, the study of the Purāṇa-s is prescribed. And for the Kaliyuga, the study of Tantraśāstra is advised.[248] The Tāntric writings (*āgama*-s) are divided into five main groups according to the personification celebrated; Sūrya, Gaṇeśa, Śakti, Śiva, and Viṣṇu; the last three being the most important. These are the deities, predominantly worshipped in the later Upaniṣads also. Tāntric principles and practices incorporated into the worship of these deities are evident in the later Upaniṣads. Thus, the deity is worshipped with the help of *mantra, yantra, mudrā*-s etc.

A complete Tantra (Saṁhitā, Āgama) consists of four parts according to the four main themes treated. *viz.*

(*i*) Knowledge (*jñāna*) comprising actual philosophical doctrines, leaning towards monism and sometimes with monotheistic bias, and also occultism including the knowledge of the secret power of the letters, syllables, formulae and figures.

(*ii*) *Yoga* : Meditation and concentration for the attainment of salvation, and also performed for the attainment of various powers.

(*iii*) *Kriyā* : Comprises of instructions for making of idols, construction and consecration of temples.

(*iv*) *Caryā* : Consists of rules regarding rites, festivals, social duties and the code of conduct.[249]

Hence, the Tantra-s are not drawn from popular belief or from popular traditions, either of the non-Āryans or of the Āryan immigrants, but they are "the pseudo-scientific productions of theologians, in which the practice and the theory of Yoga and the doctrines of monist (*advaita*) philosophy are seen mingled with the most extravagant symbolism and occultism."[250]

Philosophy

In Tantra, the theistic attitude practically obliterates the abstract ideal of the formless Brahman in favour of the Brahman endowed with virtues (*guṇa*-s). Tantra-s speak of the Brahman, the highest divine principle in the same expression of the Upaniṣ ads. According to the doctrine of the Śākta philosophers, the Brahman is nothing but the eternal and primitive force (*Śakti*) out of which all things have been created. Typical of a *tāntrika* is the concept of *Śakti*. The power or the active aspect of the immanent God is called *Śakti*. Śiva is the unchanging consciousness and Śakti is his changing power.

Māyāśakti

According to the Tantra, it is that power by which the infinite, formeless consciousness veils itself to itself, so that it may experience itself as a form. Māyāśakti assumes the form of the *tattva*-s which is composed of the three *guṇa*-s, namely *sattva, rajas* and *tamas*. These *guṇa*-s work by mutual supression. *Tamoguṇa* veils consciousness. The *sattva* functions to reveal it. The function of *rajas* is to induce either *tamas* to supress *sattva* or *viceversa*. Evolution takes place when *sattvaguṇa* predominates. *Māyā* or Prakṛti, is the veil of the spirit as *tamoguṇa* The revealer of the spirit is *sattvaguṇa,* and these functions take place due to *rajoguṇa*. The upward and the revealing movement from the predominant *tamas* towards *sattva* present a spiritual progress of the *jīvātman*. The aim of *sādhanā*, therefore, is the cultivation of *sattvaguṇa*.[251]

Creation

The universe has sprung from Mahākuṇḍalinī. In her Supreme form, she is at rest, coiled and static, united with Śiva and with Śivabindū. She uncoils hereself to manifest. The *tattva*-s issue forth. She is, thus, dynamic and continues to move in the *tattva*-s so created. After creating the *pṛthivītattva*, she again rests coiled, *i.e.* assumes a static form.[252]

The Tāntric Worship

The Tāntric worship includes the *mantra* of a deity adored, which is believed to have the essence of the deity. The *mantra*-s of a deity which are the foundations of Tāntric worship, and represent the essential power of a deity, are always disguised and need to be decoded by those who have special knowledge before understanding their exact components. A spiritual master; after determining the capacity of the pupil; imparted the *mantra* and other details of the worship to an initiate. The *dhyānamantra* of a deity describes her physical appearance in some detail. The devotee has to fill his mind with this description, while ritually approaching her. The text of the *mantra* gives her secret (*rahasya*) and lists her armour (*kavaca*), usually in the form of a prayer to protect her devotee from all sides. The worship usually includes *nāmastotra*. Tantra describes the *yantra*-s or *cakra*-s of a deity along with the directions of construction and meditation upon it. A standard sixteen fold worship (*ṣoḍaśopacāra pūjā*) or an abbreviated form of the same are also included in the worship.[253] In the Tāntric religion, the progressive nature of worship (*sādhanā*) is often described as an awakening, arising and an ascent of the serpent power. Through meditative techniques, the aspirant awakens this power and causes it to ascend by the central channel (*suṣumṇā*). *Kuṇḍalinīsādhanā* represents a desire to transcend the normal consciousness. In general, in this worship, the vision of the adored deity and the identity with her is sought.[254] In the logic of the worship, if one is able to acquire the identity, one can obtain that which the deity possesses; be it knowledge or the power to annihilate enemies.[255]

Tāntric Worship Reflected in the Later Upaniṣads

The influence of the Tantra-s on the method of worship is clearly evident in the later Upaniṣads.

Bīja-s

The seers of the Upaniṣads use some mystical Tāntric syllables (*bīja*-s) as the part of the *mantra*-s they recommend for the worship of the deities.[256]

The *bījamantra*-s of the later Tāntrism are similar to the meaningless syllables (such as *hā, bu,* etc.) of the *Sāmaveda*, which are known as *stobha*-s. These syllables are sometimes strung together and are called *bījamāla*; they also may be arranged in *maṇḍala, cakra* or *yantra*.[257] Referring to *Nityaṣoḍaśikhārṇava*, Desai, S.G. states that these syllables carry significant meanings like the syllable *sā* used for the individual Self, *hā* for the Highest Self, *hrīṁ* for *māyā* etc. Each Tāntric word carries *bhāvārtha*, *vacyārtha*, and *saṁpradāyārtha* etc.[258] It is possible that these terms might have been introduced to conceal their real meaning from people other than the initiates.

Nyāsa

The Tāntric ceremony of *nyāsa* resembles the Vedic domestic rites (*gṛhya*) prescribed in connection with the first *saṁskāra, garbhādhāna*; which uses *mantra*-s from the *Rv.* and *Av.*[259] and is referred to in the *Bṛ. Up.* (*Bṛ. Up.* VI.4). This *nyāsa* or 'fixing' is concentrating on the object of meditation in right manner. *Nyāsa* is performed by placing the fingertips and palm of the right hand and touching various limbs of the body accompanied with the recitation of the *mantra*-s. This is done in order, to imbue one's body with the life (Prāṇa) of the deity. For *e.g.* the *Vanadurgopaniṣ ad* describes different *nyāsa*-s with reference to the worship of the deity.[260]

Mudrā-s

Ritual gestures are employed in worship and these, like

words, are the expressions and supports of spiritual resolve. They are used like language to convey the most subtle amplifications of expressions.[261] Different *mudrā*-s and Tantric spells used along with them are mentioned in the *Ātharvaṇadvitīyopaniṣad. e.g. Hrīṁ Śrīṁ yā vai Śivā Bhagavatī hrauṁ trikhaṇḍa mudrā tasyae namo namaḥ*. The *Tripuratāpinyūpaniṣad* explains the *mudrā*-s in detail.[262] One is asked to practise the *mudrā*-s by assuming the lotus-posture.[263] *e.g. Yonimudrā* is performed by placing the middle finger on the *anāmikā*, the little finger uniting the thumb and the first finger held downwards like a stick.[264] It is said that one who practises this *mudrā*, obtains all fruits, knows everything, attracts all and paralyses enemies.[265] In this way, nine other *mudrā*-s and the fruits obtained thereby are explained in this Upaniṣad.[266]

Yantra-s and Cakra-s

A figure drawn on a metal sheet or a paper; in geometrical shapes like triangles, squares, lines; which represents a deity is known as a *yantra*. When this figure is in circular or semicircular shape, it is known as a *cakra*. A yantra is considered to be an abode of the deity. It is used as a complementary to *mantra*. It was believed that when the worship of a *yantra* performed along with the proper *mantra* yielded the desired fruit earlier and easily.[267] Without the worship of *yantra,* a deity was not pleased.[268] It was also believed that the worship of a *yantra* cured diseases, enabled one to secure popularity and prosperity. It seems that the authors of the later Upaniṣads believed that a man could achieve all his desires by means of a *tantra, mantra,* and *yantra* worship. The belief that the *yantra*-s are endowed with an occult power and that they can be used for good and evil purposes led to their misuse in the later period. Some of the later Upaniṣads, especially the *Tripuratāpinyūpaniṣad,* provides information regarding the worship of the *yantra* along with the appropriate *mantra* and the essential technique (*tantra*), which enable a man to entice women and to paralyse or kill enemies.[269]

The later Upanisaḍs describe in detail the construction of a *yantra.* Thus, the *Gaṇeśa. P. Tā. Up.* (II) describes the diagram of *Vināyakayantra*; The *Rāma. P. Tā. Up.* and the *Rāma. U. Tā. Up.* describe two different *Rāmayantra*-s in accordance with different *Rāmamantra*-s. A triangle, a circle around it and a twelve-petalled lotus in the circle is the nature of a *Sūryayantra*. The twelve coverings (*āvaraṇa*-s) are stated; the seventh covering of which comprises of the twelve months of a year; along with their presiding deities.[270] The Upaniṣad glorifies the worship of this *yantra* leading to the attainment of the world of Sūrya.[271] The worship of *Rājyaśyāmalāyantra* is considered as a lower type of Śākta worship, which recommends the worship of either the female genitals or that of the *yantra* of the same; and is to be performed on particular days of the month with particular flowers. Various miraculous fruits obtained by the worship are also described.[272] The *S.L. Up.* presents a beautiful description of the *śrīcakra*, which is still worshipped today in temples and houses. The worshipper obtains plenty of wealth and miraculous powers as a fruit of the worship.[273]

To give an idea of *yantra* worship, the *Vināyakayantra* is described below.

At the centre of a metal-sheet or paper, a triangle with a dot as its centre is drawn. Then twelve spokes (*ārā*-s) with the inscription of the *ṛtu*-s and then sixteen pericarps are drawn. The dot is supposed to be the form of god in the seed syllable. To his left, stands *siddhi* and to his right, *buddhi*. In his front, a cow is drawn, which yields all wishes. Around the triangle, in a hexagon, six Vināyaka-s are to be shown. In an eight petalled lotus, the eight Vināyaka-s are drawn.[274] The dot (*Śūnya*) in the centre of this *yantra* represents the Brahman. The hexagon represents the six worlds and six seasons. The eight petals stand for the *Gāyatrīmantra* having eight syllables in each foot. The twelve petals stand for the twelve Āditya-s and they become the vowels. The sixteen petals represent sixteen digits. The Puruṣa is a *varṇa* and is situated[275] in the world. He is the *Gaṇeśa-anuṣṭubh*.

It is said that if one performs a sacrifice with a lakh of *apūpa*-s and worships Gaṇeśa with this *yantra*, on the fourth day in every fortnight; he will be the giver of wealth from that very moment.[276]

Mantra

One of the continuities between the Vedic and the post-Vedic age, is the class of the Upaniṣads. The Upaniṣads, esspecially the later ones contain numerous discussions, explanations regarding the utility of Oṁ and other *mantra*-s. They provide a mine of information about the evolution of religious practices of the Brāhmanic tradition.

The *mantra*-s are verses, sequences of words in prose which contain prayers and praises in honour of various powers. Through prayers and narration which are fundamentally personalistic in nature, human beings try to encompass the enormity of the cosmos by bringing it into the measure and capacity of human grasp.

In the realm of *mantra*-s, there has been a forward movement. Alper, H. quotes Findley, E. who points out that the *Ṛv.* itself contains the evidence of a fundamental transformation that created the *mantra* as the tradition. Thus, according to him, the journey from poetic inspiration to ritual utilization is noticeable right from the Ṛgvedic age.[277]

Definition of a Mantra

The *mantra*-s are defined differently in different contexts. Gonda, J. suggests that the Vedic seer; in his approach to the Real; is thought of as having been emptied on himself and filled with God. Moreover, he points out that the *mantra*-s are not thought of as the products of discursive thought, human wisdom or poetic fantacy but they are the 'flash-lights' of the eternal truth seen by those eminent men who have come into supersensuous contact with the unseen.[278] Ghosh, Aurobindo puts it more vividly and says, "The language of the Veda itself is a *śṛti*, a rhythm not composed by the intellect but heard; a divine word that came vibrating out of the Infinite to the inner audience of the man who had previously made himself fit for the impersonal knowledge."[279]

Therefore, the word (*mantra*) the seer spoke was not his own but the word of the God. By concentrating on such a *mantra,* the devotee invokes the power inherent in the divine intuition and so purifies his consciousness.

According to Gonda, the Vedic *mantra*-s are "a general name for the 'formulas', verses and sequences of words in prose, which contain praise . . . are believed to have magical, religious and spiritual efficiency which are muttered, sung in the Vedic ritual." Further, he adds that the word applies to comparable formulas of different origin used in the post-Vedic cults.

In the Tāntric context, he defines *mantra* as "a power (*śakti*) in the form of formulated and expressed thought."[280] Agehananda, B., also in the Tāntric context defines *mantra* as "a quasimorpheme or a series of quasimorphemes or a series of genuine and mixed quasimorphemes arranged in conventional patterns based on codified esoteric traditions and passed on from one preceptor to one disciple in the course of prescribed initiation."[281]

The history of the *mantra*-s can be traced back to the Veda-s. With some modifications, they are effectively used in the Tantra-s. In Yoga, *mantra*-s are glorified. Patañjali has stated that as a result of concentrated study (*svādhyāya*) of a *mantra,* the desired deity becomes perceptible. Through the practice of fixed concentraditon (*samādhi*) on the *mantra*, consciousness is purified of the *karmika* obstructions and the deity is 'seen'; The power of such *mantrasamādhi* to induce a perfectly clear identity with the deity is discussed in detailed psychological analysis in the Yogasūtra-s.[282] The authors of the later Upaniṣads appear to have responded to the changes in social, cultural conditions leading to a complicated life with inevitable earthly goals. At that time, it was necessary to adopt simpler and easier means for the common man to achieve spiritual goals. The authors of the later Upaniṣads prescribed *mantra*-s as an effective means; which at times were believed to be bestowing material gains; which ultimately were supposed to be leading to spiritual goal.

The seers of the later Upaniṣads believed that the *mantra*-s had power, to remove all impurities, to overcome the evil, and to transcend death.[283] The *mantra*-s have power to attract all.[284] It was believed that he who utters the royal formula conquers all the worlds.[285]

The seers of the later Upaniṣads glorified *mantra*-s and assured the achievement of goals ranging from purely earthly to totally spiritual. Thus, he who utters the eight syllabled spell in praise of the Sūrya; facing him at noon; is released from the fear of diseases, his poverty is removed, he is purified of certain bodily sins... he is released from five great sins.[286] The *Gaṇeśa. U. Tā. Up.* states that he who utters the *mantra* with reference to Gaṇeśa attains the miraculous power to arrest fire, water, wind etc.[287] Recitation of the *mantra*-s in honour of Nṛsiṁha also yield the miraculous powers.[288] With the *mantra* in praise of Garuḍa, he is asked to remove all kinds of poisons.[289]

The *Sarasvatī. R. Up.* explains ten *mantras* in praise of Sarasvatī along with the *bīja, mātṛka, kīlaka* and the seer of the *mantra* states that when Sarasvatī is worshipped with these *mantra*-s, one understands the books of knowledge,[290] *i.e.* ignorance is removed. Thirtythree different spells equate *Nṛsimaha* with other deities like Sūrya, Rudra, Kāla and Viṣṇu etc., and the Upaniṣad states that God is pleased with him, who adores and worships Him with these *mantra*-s.[291] Again, elsewhere it is said that a *mantra* represents the Brahman, without the recitation of which, God is not pleased.[292] He who always recites the Rāma-*mantras*, 'sees' the God, attains immortality.[293] Through the recitation of Hayagrīvamantra, the meaning of the four *mahāvākya*-s is realized.[294] The worshipper attains everything material and spiritual by the Sūrya *mantra* along with the worship of Sūrya-*yantra*.[295] The *Kalisaṁ. Up.* states that in the *Kali*-age *mantra* alone helps one to cross the ocean of *saṁsāra*. Moreover, he who always recites *mantra*; whether he is pure or impure, attains release.[296]

Dange, S.A. has defined a *mantra* as, the words of praise composed in metres which serve as a means of contemplation.[297]

In the Vedic religion the worship of the supernatural powers began by the recitation of the hymns (*mantra*-s) in praise of such powers while offering oblations in the sacrifice. The accomplishment of the sacrifice depended upon the proper recitation of the hymns. Thus, the *mantra*-s became important means of offering sacrifices.

The *mantra*-s were also the means of meditation and concentration. One knows that human mind is unable to reach the formless, perceive it and concentrate on it. It tries to resort to personified aspect through which he attempts to concentrate on the Abstract.

The Vedic *mantra, Tat Savitur*...etc. (*Rv.* III.62.10) is known either as Gāyatrī after its metre or as Sāvitrī after the deity to whom it is dedicated. Savitṛ is a God identified with the Sun. In the *Gāyatrī. R. Up.* and the *Gāyatrī. Up.*, one can notice the personified aspect of '*Gāyatrī*'.

The Gāyatrī *mantra* is said to be having four feet (*pāda*-s). They are mystically identified with the earth, mid-region and the heaven as also with *ṛc*-s, *sāman*-s, sacrifical formulas and with Prāṇa, Apāna and Vyāna.[298] One meditating on these feet, sees the fourth one (*turīya*). Agni is said to be the mouth of 'Gāyatrī'. The sins of a devotee are burnt by muttering it.[299] The Gāyatrī belongs to Sāṅkhyāyanagotra, and has twenty four syllables in three feet which are compared to twenty four deities sages, metres etc. She has six bellies and five heads.[300] She is said to be threefold in the forms of Gāyatrī, Sāvitrī and Sarasvatī representing the three stages of the Sun as rising, stationary at the mid-day and setting, describing three as belonging to these three periods and as a virgin, youthful lady and an old woman respectively.[301] It is said that the he who knows this secret doctrine of the Gāyatrī *mantra,* obtains the fruit of *mantrajapa,* recited sixty thousand times.[302]

The *Tripuratāpinyūpaniṣad* interprets this Savitṛ Gāyatrī to suit the *Śakti* cult and draws the conclusion that Śiva (the highest God) and *Śakti* (the creator of the beings) are glorified in this *mantra.* The Upaniṣad maintains that the Tāntric words *ka, la, ī* etc. reresent the *pāda*-s of Gāyatrī and explains the comparison in details in a mystic manner.[303] Similarly, the *Nṛsiṁhatāpini Up.*, the *Rāmatāpinī Up.*, the *Gaṇeśa. U. Tā. Up.* and other sectarian Upaniṣads identify this Gāyatrī *mantra* with the *mantra* that they have advocated in honour of their favourite deity.[304]

The authors of the later Upaniṣads composed new Gāyatrī *mantra*-s for glorifying different deities. It is notweworthy that these new Gāyatrī *mantra*-s follow the same Ṛg vedic *mantra*, making only a few changes as are required to make the *mantra* suit the respective deity. They do not give the name of the deity in the first foot, as in the original *mantra*, but in the third, *i.e.* the last foot perhaps to emphasize the greatness of the deity concerned. for *e.g. Tatpuruṣāya vidmahe suparṇapakṣāya dhīmahi tanno Garuḍaḥ pracodayāt.*[305]

The tendency to personify the abstract can be traced back to the *Ṛv*, where the Gods (powers) were conceived as humans in appearance. In the *Ṛv.* even the personification of abstract nouns like *mannyu, śraddhā* is noticed.[306] Though anthropomorphism of its physical appearance is rudimentary in nature, one can observe the personification of 'Gāyatrī' in the Upaniṣads.

Nṛsiṁha Anuṣṭubh

The *Nṛsiṁha. P. Tā. Up.* and the *Nṛsiṁha. U. Tā. Up.* contain the description of *anuṣṭubh*. In the Upaniṣads it is said that the *anuṣṭubh* and the *sāman* are identical and that, because *sāman* is immortal, *anuṣṭubh* also leads to immortality. *Anuṣṭubh* is next identified with Oṁ.[307]

The *Parameṣṭhin* after practising a penance for a thousand years saw this Supreme *Anuṣṭubhvidyā.* He then continued the chanting of the *vidyā* for another thousand years. As a fruit of that penance, he saw lord Nṛsimaha full of radiance, embraced by the goddess Lakṣmī, perched on his vehicle Suparṇa, having the face of a lion and the body of a human being and having three eyes in the form of the Sun, the moon and fire. Thus, inspired, Prajāpati praised him as, "*Ugraṁ Vīraṁ jvalantam...*" etc.[308] The

Nṛsiṁha P. Tā. Up. adores this *Nṛsiṁha aṅuṣṭubh mantra* as the royal spell (*mantrarāja*) in praise of the deity. Thus, the first foot of this *anuṣṭubh* comprises the earth with the seven seas, the mountains, the islands. The second foot is the mid-region inhabited by the *yakṣa*-s, *gandharva*-s etc. The third foot is the celestial region. And the fourth foot is of the form of the Brahman; is of the character of the Bliss, which is equated with the ether of the heart.[309]

All these paths such as *Bhakti, Yoga*, *Saṁnyāsa* etc. are resorted to by the later Upaniṣads, which lead an aspirant towards his goal. Numerous methods of worship such as *pūjā*, muttering of sacred syllables, words or verses (*japa*), worship of *yantra,* etc. have been incorporated in these Upaniṣads. Methods of worship of different paths are also combined, with a view to allow the masses, to choose the *upāsanā* as per one's own wish and temperament and to lead one to the path of spirituality. Meditations on the Abstract were replaced by different forms of worship, which were easier for the masses to follow. It may be observed that changes in society bring about changes in culture and *vice-versa*. When belief system underwent changes, when monism was replaced by polytheism, when community started adoring personified deities, various new modes of worshipping were resorted to, to tread the path of spirituality.

REFERENCES

1. *Bh. G.,* IV. 38[a],

   न हि ज्ञानेन सदृशं पवित्रमिह विद्यते।

2. *Kaṭh. Up.* I.2.7[a].

   श्रवणायापि बहुभिर्यो न लभ्य: शृण्वन्तोऽपि बहवो यं न विद्यु:।

   also *Bh. G.,* II. 29,

   आश्चर्यवत्पश्यति कश्चिदेनमाश्चर्यवद्वदति तथैव चान्य:।
   आश्चर्यवच्चैनमन्य: शृश्रुणोति श्रुत्वाप्येनं वेद न चैव कश्चित्॥

3. *Kaṭh. Up.* I. 3.14[b],
4. *Bh. G.* XII. 5,

क्लेशोऽधिकतरस्तेषामव्यक्तासक्तचेतसाम्।
अव्यक्ता हि गतिर्दुःखं देहवद्भिरवाप्यते॥

5. Tilak, B.G., *op. cit.*, pp. 567-570.
6. Belvalkar, S.K. and Ranade, R.D., *op. cit.,* p. 408.
7. *Bh. G.* X. 9

   मच्चित्ता मद्गतप्राणा बोधयन्तः परस्परम्।
   कथयन्तश्च मां नित्यं तुष्यन्ति च रमन्ति च॥
8. *The Nārada Bhakti Sūtra,* II. 19,

   नारदस्तु तदर्पिताखिलाचारता तद्विस्मरणे परमव्याकुलतेति।
9. Velankar H.D, *Ṛgvedātila Bhaktimārga,* Pune, 1952, pp. 1-10.
10. *Ibid.,* p. 11.
11. Belvalkar, S.K., Ranade, R.D., *op. cit.,* p. 409.
12. *Ṛv.* I. 1.9.

    स नः पितेव सूनवेऽग्ने सूपायनो भव। सचस्वा नः स्वस्तये॥
13. *Ibid,* VIII. 98.11.

    त्वं हि नः पिता वसो त्वं माता शतक्रतो बभूविथ। अधा ते सुम्नमीमहे॥
14. *Ibid.,* X. 7.3,

    अग्निं मन्ये पितरमग्निमापिमग्निं भ्रातरं सदमित्सखायम्।
15. *Ibid.,* II.12.15,

    वयं त इन्द्र विश्वह प्रियासः सुवीरासो विदथमा वदेम।
16. *Ibid.,* IV. 17.9.
17. Belvalkar, S.K., Ranade, R.D., *op. cit.,* p. 79.
18. *Kaṭh Up.* I. 2.22,

    अशरीरँ शरीरेष्वनवस्थेष्ववस्थितम्। महान्तं विभुमात्मानं मत्वा धीरो न शोचति।
19. *Kau. Up,* III.1[f],

    मामेव विजानीह्येतदेवाहं मनुष्याय हिततमं मन्ये। यन्मां विजानीयात्।
20. *Ibid.,* III. 2[a],

    स होवाच प्राणोऽस्मि प्रज्ञात्मा तं मामायुरमृतमित्युपास्स्व।
21. *Muṇḍ. Up.,* III. 2.10[b],

    तेषामेवैतां ब्रह्मविद्यां वदेत शिरोव्रतं विधिवद्यैस्तु चीर्णम्॥

22. *Chānd. Up.,* III. 11.5-6[a],
इदं वाव तज्जेष्ठाय पुत्राय पिता ब्रह्म प्रब्रूयात्प्रणाय्याय वाऽन्तेवासिने॥ नान्यस्मै कस्मैचन...

23. *Śvet. Up.*, VI. 23
यस्य देवे परा भक्तिर्यथा देवे तथा गुरौ।
तस्यैते कथिता ह्यर्थाः प्रकाशन्ते महात्मनः ...।

24. Tiele, C.P., q. by Bakre, A.B., *op. cit.,* pp. 152-153.

25. *Gaṇapatyupaniṣad. Up. S.,* Pt.I.p.571. ll. 7-8,
भक्तानुकंपिनं देवं जगत्कारणमच्युतम्।
अविभूतं च सृष्ट्यादौ प्रकृतेः पुरुषात्परम्॥

26. *Rudrahṛdaya. Up.,* 24[a],
सर्वदेवात्मकं रुद्रं नमस्कुर्यात् पृथक् पृथक्।
also, *Ibid.,* 9,
ब्रह्मविष्णुमयो रुद्र अग्नीषोमात्मकं जगत्।
पुंलिङ्गं सर्वमीशानं स्त्रीलिङ्गं भगवत्युमा॥

27. *Pāramātmika. Up.,* Up. S. pt. II, p. 108,
भक्तिप्रपत्तिप्रमुखैस्तद्वशीकारकारणम्।
also, *Sāmarahasya. Up. Up. S.,* pt. II, p. 220. l. 11,
दास्यभावेनात्मसर्पणम्।

28. *Tvmn. Up., Up. S.pt.I.,* p. 382, ll. 10-16,
तस्मात्सर्वेषामधिकारिणामनधिकारिणां भक्तियोग एव प्रशस्यते। भक्तियोगो निरुपद्रवः। भक्तियोगान्मुक्तिः। ...भक्तवत्सलः स्वयमेव सर्वेभ्यो मोक्षविघ्नेभ्यो भक्तिनिष्ठान्सर्वान्परिपालयति। ... मोक्षं दापयति...। भक्त्या विना ब्रह्मज्ञानं कदापि न जायते।

29. *Sarasvatī. R. Up. Up. S.* pt. I, pp. 646, 647, 7-8[cd]
यः कवित्वं निरातङ्कं भुक्तिमुक्ती च वाञ्छति।
सोऽभ्यर्च्यैनां दशश्लोक्या नित्यं स्तौति सरस्वतीम्॥
भक्तिश्रद्धाभियुक्तस्य षण्मासात्प्रत्ययो भवेत्।

30. *Jābāla. D. Up.* I. 9.2,
ऊर्ध्वरेतं विश्वरूपं विरूपाक्षं महेश्वरम्।
सोऽहमित्यादरेणैव ध्यायेद्योगीश्वरेश्वरम्॥

31. *Vāsudevopaniṣad. Up. S.* Pt. I. p. 406, ll. 13-15,
एकाग्रमनसा यो मां ध्यायते हरिमव्ययम्। हृत्पङ्कजे च स्वात्मानं स मुक्तो नात्र संशयः॥ मद्रूपमद्वयं ब्रह्म आदिमध्यान्तवर्जितम्। स्वप्रभं सच्चिदानन्दं भक्त्या जानाति चाव्ययम्॥
32. *Śivopanisad Up. S.* pt.II, VI.1-25, 43-45, 236, 60, 256, 239, 199.
33. *Ibid., Up. S.* Pt. II, VI. 185,
शिवस्य रथयात्रां तु यः प्रपश्यति भक्तितः।
प्रसङ्गात् कौतुकाद्वापि तेऽपि यान्ति शिवं पुरम्॥
34. *Ibid.,* Pt. II, VI. 284,
शिवयज्ञोपयोगार्थं प्रवक्ष्यामि समासतः।
सर्वेषां शिवभक्तानां दद्याद्यत्किञ्चिदादरात्।
दत्त्वा यज्ञफलं विज्ञात् किमु तद्वस्तुदानतः॥
35. *Ibid.,* Pt. II. VI. 43
तस्मादीश्वरमुद्दिश्य यद्यदात्मनि रोचते।
तत्तदीश्वरभक्तेभ्यः प्रदातव्यं फलार्थिना॥
36. *Gaṇeśa. U. Tā. Up* VI, pp. 639-640.
37. *Kāmarāja. Up, Up. S.* pt. II, p. 401,
...अथ रक्तपुष्पैरर्चयेत्। तदभावे जलैस्तदभावे मानसीं भक्तिमाचरेत्।
38. *Ātmapūjopaniṣad. Up. S.* Pt. II, p. 6
तस्य निश्चिंतनं ध्यानम्। सर्वकर्मनिराकरणमावाहनम्।
निश्चलज्ञानमासनम्। समुन्मनीभावः पाद्यम्। सदामनस्कमर्घ्यम्।
सदादीप्तिराचमनीयम्। वराकृतप्राप्तिः स्नानम्। सर्वात्मकत्वं दृश्यविलयो गन्धः।
...चिदादीप्तिः पुष्पम्। ...सोऽहं भावो नमस्कारः। परमेश्वरस्तुतिर्मौनम्...।
सर्वनिरामयपरिपूर्णोऽहमस्मीति मुमुक्षूणां मोक्षैकसिद्धिर्भवति।
39. *Śivopanisad,* VII. 74[b]
गुरुभक्त्या लभेद्ज्ञानं ज्ञानान्मुक्तिमवाप्नुयात्।
40. *Kalisan. Up.* I.1[bc],
... गोप्यं तत्छृणु येन कलिसंसारं तरिष्यसि...। भगवत् आदिपुरुषस्य नारायणस्य नामोच्चारणमात्रेण निर्धूत कलिर्भवति।
41. *S. Sāra. Up. Up. S.* pt. II. p. 384, l. 1
परमकैवल्यः स एव कैलासः। ईश्वरकृपया परमपरिपक्वचित्ता जानन्ति।

42. *Ibid., Up. S.* pt. II. p. 388, ll. 7-8, 15-18.
43. *Rādhopaniṣad. Up. S.* pt. II, p. 208, ll. 7-18.
44. *Ibid., Up. S.* pt. II. p. 211, ll. 2-6.
45. *Ibid., Up. S.* pt. II. p. 213, ll. 1-2

    मानसपूजया जपेन ध्यानेन कीर्तनेन स्तुत्या मानसेन सर्वेण नित्यस्थलं प्राप्नोति।
46. *Guhyakālī. Up. Up. S.* pt.II, p. 410, ll. 1-20.
47. *Sāma. R. Up. Up. S.* pt. II. p. 235, ll. 1-15.
48. *Bhāgavata. P.*, VII. 5.23.

    श्रवणं कीर्तनं विष्णोः स्मरणं पादसेवनम्।
    अर्चनं वंदनं दास्यं सख्यमात्मनिवेदनम्॥
49. *Sāma. R. Up. Up. S.* pt. II. p. 220, l. 11.
50. *Ibid., Up. S.* pt. II. p. 236, ll. 7-17.
51. *Ibid., Up. S.* pt. II. p. 291.
52. *Ibid., Up. S.* pt. II. p. 290, ll. 3-6.
53. *Ibid., Up. S.* pt. II. p. 290, l. 6
54. *Ibid., Up. S.* pt. II. p. 290, l. 1

    यथा अनादिसंसिद्धोऽयं जीवसंघस्तथा मायाप्यनादिसिद्धा भवति। सा त्रिविधा व्याप्य तिष्ठति।
55. *Ibid., Up. S.* pt. II. p. 291, l. 104.
56. Dasgupta, S.N., *Hindu Mysticism,* Delhi, 1976, pp. 126.f.
57. *Ibid.*, p. 127.
58. Hiriyanna, M., *The Outlines of Indian Philosophy,* pp. 268-297.
59. For more details see Radhakrishnan, S., *Indian Philosophy* (Vol. II), pp. 343 ff.
60. *Bh. G.* XIII. 24

    ध्यानेनात्मनि पश्यन्ति केचिदात्मानमात्मना।
    अन्ये सांख्येन योगेन कर्मयोगेन चापरे॥
61. *Yogayājñavalkya* (I), quoted by Kolhatkar, K.K., *Pātañjala Yogadarśana,* p. 100,

    संयोगो योग इत्युक्तो जीवात्मपरमात्मनोः।

    Mai. Up., VI. 25.

एकत्वं प्राणमनसोरिन्द्रियाणां तथैव च। सर्वभावपरित्यागो योग इत्यभिधीयते।

also *Yogaśikhā. Up.* I. 68[b], 69[a],

सूर्यचन्द्रमसोर्योगो जीवात्मपरमात्मनोः॥
एवं तु द्वन्द्वजालस्य संयोगो योग उच्यते॥

62. Radhakrishnan, S., *Indian Philosophy* (Vol. II), p. 337.
63. Radhakrishnan, S., *Indian Philosophy* (Vol. I), p. 121.
64. Radhakrishnan, S., *The Principal Upaniṣads,* India, 1998, p. 627.
65. Ranade, R.D. *op. cit.,* pp. 135-136.
66. *Praśna. Up.* VI.2[b]

    इहैवान्तःशरीरे सोम्य स पुरुषो यस्मिन्नेताः षोडशकलाः प्रभवन्तीति।

67. *Kaṭh. Up.* I. 3.13

    यच्छेद्वाङ्मनसी प्राज्ञस्तद्यच्छेज्ज्ञान आत्मनि।
    ज्ञानमात्मनि महति नियच्छेत्तद्यच्छेच्छान्त आत्मनि॥

68. *Ibid.,* II. 3.6-7[ab]

    इन्द्रियेभ्यः परं मनो मनसः सत्त्वमुत्तमम्।
    सत्त्वादधि महानात्मा महतोऽव्यक्तमुत्तमम्॥
    अव्यक्तात्तु परः पुरुषो व्यापकोऽलिङ्ग एव च।

69. *Śvet. Up.* VI. 13[b]

    तत्कारणं सांख्ययोगाधिगम्यं ज्ञात्वा देवं मुच्यते सर्वपाशैः।

70. Deussen, P. *The Philosophy of the Upaniṣads,* New York, 1966, p. 387.
71. *Śvet. Up.* II. 10

    समे शुचौ शर्करावह्निवालुकाविवर्जिते शब्दजलाश्रयादिभिः।
    मनोनुकूले न तु चक्षुपीडने गुहानिवाताश्रयणे प्रयोजयेत्॥

72. *Mai. Up.* VI. 30[a]
73. *Śvet. Up.* II. 8[ab]

    त्रिरुन्नतं स्थाप्य समं शरीरं हृदीन्द्रियाणि मनसा संनिवेश्य।

74. *Ibid.*, II. 9[b]

    दुष्टाश्वयुक्तमिववाहमेनं विद्वान्मनो धारयेताप्रमत्तः।

75. *Ibid.*, II. 9[a]

प्राणान्प्रपीड्येह संयुक्तचेष्टः क्षीणे प्राणे नासिकयोच्छ्वसीत।

76. *Ibid.*, II. 11.

नीहारधूमार्कानिलानलानां खद्योतविद्युत्स्फटिकशशीनाम्।
एतानि रूपाणि पुरःसराणि ब्रह्मण्यभिव्यक्तिकराणि योगे॥

77. *Ibid.*, II. 12[b], 13.

न तस्य रोगो न जरा न मृत्युः प्राप्तस्य योगाग्निमयं शरीरम्। लघुत्वमारोग्यमलोलुपत्वं वर्णप्रसादं स्वरसौष्ठवं च। गन्धः शुभो मूत्रपुरीषमल्पं योगप्रवृत्तिं प्रथमां वदन्ति।

78. *Ibid.*, II. 15[ab]

यदात्मतत्त्वेन तु ब्रह्मतत्त्वं दीपोपमेनेह युक्तः प्रपश्येत्।

79. *Patañjali Y.S.*, I. 3,

तदा द्रष्टुः स्वरूपेऽवस्थानम्।

80. *Śvet. Up.* I. 14[cd]

ध्याननिर्मथनाभ्यासाद्देवं पश्येन्निगूढवत्।

81. *Kaṭh. Up.* II. 3.10-11[ab]

यदा पञ्चावतिष्ठन्ते ज्ञानानि मनसा सह। बुद्धिश्च न विचेष्टति तामाहुः परमां गतिम्॥
तां योगमिति मन्यन्ते स्थिरामिन्द्रियधारणाम्।

82. Radhakrishnan, S., *Indian Philosophy,* Vol. II. p. 341.

83. Jacobi, *Dates of Philosophical Sūtra*-s, *JAOS* , 1911, quoted by Hiriyanna, M., *op. cit.,* p.270.

84. *Mantrikopaniṣad.* I.14,

तं षड्विंशक इत्येते सप्तविंशं तथापरे।
पुरुषं निर्गुणं सांख्यमथर्वशिरसो विदुः॥

85. *Y.T. Up.* 19[ab],

योगो हि बहुधा ब्रह्मन्भिद्यते व्यवहारतः।

also *Yogarājopaniṇad.,* 1[b].

मन्त्रयोगो लयश्चैव राजयोगो हठस्तथा।

86. *Kalisan. Up.* 3[c],

सर्वदा शुचिरशुचिर्वा पठन्ब्राह्मणः सलोकतां समीपतां सरूपतां सायुज्यतामेति।

87. *Y.R. Up.* 3[b], 4[a],

ब्रह्मविष्णुशिवादीनां मन्त्रं जाप्यं विशारदैः।

साध्यते मन्त्रयोगस्तु वत्सराजादिभिर्यथा।

88. *Y.T. Up.* 21[b], 22.
89. *Ibid.*, 23,

    लययोगश्चित्तलय: कोटिश: परिकीर्तित:।
    गच्छंस्तिष्ठन्स्वपन्भुंजन्ध्यायेन्निष्कलमीश्वरम्।। स एव लययोग...
90. *Kṣuri. Up.,* 21,

    यथा निर्वाणकाले तु दीपो दग्ध्वा लयं व्रजेत्।
    तथा सर्वाणि कर्माणि योगी दग्ध्वा लयं व्रजेत्।।
91. *Nādabindūpaniṣad,* 38.

    यत्र कुत्रापि वा नादे लगति प्रथमं मन:।
    तत्र तत्र स्थिरीभूत्वा तेन सार्धं विलीयते।।
92. *Ibid.*, 42[cd]

    नादासक्तं सदा चित्तं विषयं न हि कांक्षति।।
93. *Ibid.*, I. 46[cd]

    ब्रह्मप्रणवसंलग्ननादो ज्योतिर्मयात्मक:।।
94. *Ibid.*, 47[ab]

    मनस्तत्र लयं याति तद्विष्णो: परमं पदम्।
95. Woodreff, J. *op. cit.*, p. 643.
96. *Y.R. Up.,* 4[b], 5[a],

    कृष्णद्वैपायनाद्यैस्तु साधितो लयसंज्ञित:।।
    नवस्वेव हि चक्रेषु लयं कृत्वा महात्मभि:।
97. *Ibid.,* 19,

    एतेषां नवचक्राणामेकैकं ध्यायतो मुने:।
    सिद्धयो मुक्तिसहिता: करस्था: स्युर्दिने दिने।।
98. *Tejobindūpaniṣad*, I. 15-16

    यमो हि नियमस्त्यागो मौनं देशश्च कालत:।
    आसनं मूलबन्धश्च देहसाम्यं च दृक्स्थिति:।।
    प्राणसंयमनं चैव प्रत्याहारश्च धारणा।
    आत्मध्यानं समाधिश्च प्रोक्तान्यङ्गानि वै क्रमात्।।
99. *Tejobindūpaniṣad,* I. 23

आदावन्ते च मध्ये च जनो यस्मिन्न विद्यते। येनेदं सततं व्याप्तं स देशो विजनः स्मृतः।

100. *Kṣuri. Up.* 2[a]
निःशब्दं देशमास्थाय तत्रासनमवस्थितः।

101. *A. Nāda. Up.* 18
भूमिभागे समे रम्ये सर्वदोषविवर्जिते।

102. *Y.T. Up.* I. 32[cd], 33[ab]
सुशोभनं मठं कुर्यात् सूक्ष्मद्वारं तु निर्व्रणम्।
सुष्ठु लिप्तं गोमयेन सुधया वा प्रयत्नतः॥
दिने दिने च संमृष्टं संमार्जन्या विशेषतः।
वासितं च सुगन्धेन धूपितं गुग्गुलादिभिः॥

103. *Ibid.,* I. 35[a],
नात्युच्छ्रितं नातिनीचं चैलाजिनकुशोत्तमम्।

104. *Triśikhi. Brā. Up.* 89, 90[a],
योगाङ्गद्रव्यसंपूर्णं तत्र दारुमये शुभे।
आसने कल्पिते दर्भकुशकृष्णाजिनादिभिः॥

105. *Jābāla. D. Up.* V. 4
पर्वताग्रे नदीतीरे बिल्वमूले वनेऽथवा।
मनोरमे शुचौ देशे मठं कृत्वा समाहितः॥

106. *Y.T. Up.,* I. 28[cd], 47.

107. *A. Nāda. Up.* 28.
भयं क्रोधमथालस्यमतिस्वप्नातिजागरम्।
अत्याहारमनाहारं नित्यं योगी विवर्जयेत्॥

108. *Ibid.,* I. 30[b].

109. *Tejobindūpaniṣad,* I. 17,
सर्वं ब्रह्मेति वै ज्ञानादिन्द्रियग्रामसंयमः।
यमोऽयमिति संप्रोक्तोऽभ्यसनीयो मुहुर्मुहुः॥

110. *Maṇḍala. Brā. Up., Up. S.,* pt. I, p. 347,
शीतोष्णाहारनिद्राविजयः सर्वदा शान्तिर्निश्चलत्वं विषयेन्द्रियनिग्रह...।

111. *Patañjali Y.S.,* II. 32,
शौचसन्तोषतपः स्वाध्यायेश्वर प्रणिधानानि नियमाः।

112. *Ibid.*, I. 15
दृष्टानुश्रविकविषयवितृष्णस्य वशीकारसंज्ञा वैराग्यम्।
113. *Bh. G.* VI. 10-15.
114. *Patañjali Y.S.*, III. 46,
रूपलावण्यबलवज्रसंहननत्वानि कायसंपत्।
115. *A. Nāda. Up.* 19,
पद्मकं स्वस्तिकं वापि भद्रासनमथापि वा।
बद्ध्वा योगासनं सम्यगुत्तराभिमुखस्थितः॥
116. *Triśikhi. Brā. Up.*, I. 34-50.
117. *Ibid.*, 52[b]
आसनं विजितं येन जितं तेन जगत्त्रयम्।
118. *Yogaśikhā. Up.*, I. 71[ab],
आसनं पद्मकं बद्ध्वा यच्चान्यदपि रोचते।
नासाग्रे दृष्टिमारोप्य हस्तपादौ च संयतौ।
119. *A. Nāda. Up.*, I. 23,
तिर्यगूर्ध्वमधो दृष्टिं विनिधार्य महामतिः।
स्थिरः स्थायी विनिष्कंपं तदा योगं समभ्यसेत्।
120. *Kṣuri. Up.* 4[a],
उरोमुखकटिग्रीवं किंचिद्धृदयमुन्नतम्।
121. *Y.T. Up.*, I. 124, 125, 126.
122. *Yoga. K. Up.*, I. 4[b],
आसनं द्विविधं प्रोक्तं पद्मं वज्रासनं तथा।
123. *Jābālopa. D. Up.* III. 12
येन केन प्रकारेण सुखं धैर्यं च जायते।
तत्सुखासनमित्युक्तमशक्तस्तत्समाश्रयेत्।
124. *A. Nāda. Up.* 10[b],
प्राणायामास्त्रयः प्रोक्ता रेचकपूरककुम्भकाः।
125. *Kṣuri. Up.* I. 5
also *Y.T. Up.* I. 39[a].
126. *Ibid.*, I. 36[b], 37[a],

ततो दक्षिणहस्तस्य अङ्गुष्ठेनैव पिङ्गलाम्॥ निरुध्य पूरयेद्वायुमिडया तु शनैः शनैः।

127. *A. Nāda. Up.* 13[b], 14[a]

एवं वायुर्ग्रहीतव्यः पूरकस्येति लक्षणम्। वक्त्रेणोत्पलनालेन वायुं कृत्वा निराश्रयम्।

also *Dhyānabindūpaniṣad,* I. 20[a].

128. *Dhyānabindūpaniṣad*, I. 21.

129. *Jābālopa. D. Up.*, VI. 2,

also *Śāṇḍ. Up.*, I. 17[c,d,e]

तस्मात्प्रणव एव प्राणायामः.... रक्ताङ्गी हंसवाहिनी दण्डहस्ता बाला गायत्री भवति। उकारमूर्तिः.... सावित्री भवति। मकारमूर्तिः.... सरस्वती भवति।

130. *Jābālopa. D. Up.* VI. 3[b], 4[a], 6[a],

शनैः षोडशभिमत्रिरकारं तत्र संस्मरेत्। पूरितं धारयेत्पश्चाच्चतुःषष्ट्या तु मात्रया। शनैः पिङ्गलया तत्र द्वात्रिंशन्मात्रया पुनः।

131. *A. Nāda. Up.*7[b], 8[a],

तथेन्द्रियकृता दोषा दह्यन्ते प्राणनिग्रहात् प्राणायामैर्दहेद्दोषान्धारणाभिश्च किल्बिषम्।

also *Jābālopa. D. Up.*, VI. 23,

सर्वरोगविनिर्मुक्तो जीवेद्वर्षशतं नरः।

132. *Yogacūḍāmaṇi. Up.* 109[a],

आसनेन रुजं हन्ति प्राणायामेन पातकम्।

133. *Tejobindūpaniṇad*, I. 34,

विषयेष्वात्मतां दृष्ट्वा मनसश्चित्तरञ्जकम्।
प्रत्याहारः स विज्ञेयोऽभ्यसनीयो मुहुर्मुहुः॥

134. *Y.T. Up.* 68[b],

इन्द्रियाणीन्द्रियार्थेभ्यो यत्प्रत्याहरणं स्फुटम्।

135. *Chānd. Up.,* VIII. 15.1,

...कुटुम्बे शुचौ देशे स्वाध्यायमधीयानो धार्मिकान्विदधदात्मनि सर्वेन्द्रियाणि संप्रतिष्ठाप्याहिंसन्सर्वभूतान्यन्यत्र... ...सखल्वेवं वर्तयन्यावदायुषं ब्रह्मलोकम-भिसंपद्यते...।

136. *Kṣuri. Up.* 2[b],

कूर्मोऽङ्गानीव संहृत्य मनो हृदि निरुध्य च।

also *Bh. G.* II. 58

137. *A. Nāda. Up.* I. 5
शब्दादिविषयाः पञ्च मनश्चैवातिचञ्चलम्।
चिन्तयेदात्मनो रश्मीन्प्रत्याहारः स उच्यते॥

138. *Śāṇḍ. Up.* I. 69

139. *Deussen, P., op. cit.,* p. 390.

140. *Tejobindūpaniṇad,* I. 35,
यत्र यत्र मनो याति ब्रह्मणस्तत्र दर्शनात्।
मनसा धारणं चैव धारणा सा परा मता॥

141. *Manḍalabrā. Up. Up. S.* pt. I, p. 347, l. 22.
सर्वशरीरेषु चैतन्यैकतानता ध्यानम्।

142. *Tejobindūpaniṣad,* I. 36.
ब्रह्मैवास्मीति सद्वृत्त्या निरालम्बतया स्थितिः।
ध्यानशब्देन विख्यातः परमानन्ददायकः॥

143. *Kaṭh. Up.* I. 2.17,
एतदालम्बनं श्रेष्ठमेतदालम्बनं परम्।

144. *A. Nāda. Up.* 2
ओंकारं रथमारुह्य विष्णुं कृत्वाथ सारथिम्।
ब्रह्मलोकपदान्वेषी रुद्राराधनतत्परः॥

145. *Nādabindūpaniṣad,* I. 1[b],
मकारं पुच्छमित्याहुः अर्धमात्रा तु मस्तकम्।
also *Dhyānabindūpaniṣad,* I.17, *Y.T. Up.* I. 139[b]. 140[b]. etc.

146. *Tejobindūpaniṣad*, I. 1,
तेजोबिन्दुः परं ध्यानं विश्वात्महृदि संस्थितम्।

147. *Gauḍapādakārikā*, I. 26[a],
प्रणवो ह्यपरं ब्रह्म प्रणवश्च परः स्मृतः।

148. *Dhyānabindūpaniṣad*. 2
बीजाक्षरं परं बिन्दुं नादं तस्योपरि स्थितम्।
सशब्दं चाक्षरे क्षीणे निःशब्दं परमं पदम्॥

149. *Tejobindūpaniṣad.* I. 7
उपाधिरहितंस्थानं वाङ्मनोऽतीतगोचरम्।
स्वभावं भावसंग्राह्यमसंघातं पदाच्च्युतम्॥

150. *Brahmabindūpaniṣad.* 7[a],

स्वरेण संधयेद्योगमस्वरं भावयेत्परम्।

151. *A. Nāda. Up.*3

तावद्रथेन गन्तव्यं यावद्रथपथि स्थितः।

स्थित्वा रथपथस्थानं रथमुत्सृज्य गच्छति॥

152. Deussen, P., *The Philosophy of the Upaniṣads,* London, 1966, p. 342.

153. *Śāṇḍ. Up.* I. 72

अथ समाधिः। जीवात्मपरमात्मैक्यावस्था त्रिपुटीरहिता परमानन्दस्वरूपा शुद्धचैतन्यात्मिका भवति॥

also, *Y.T. Up.* 107[ab]

समाधिः समतावस्था जीवात्मपरमात्मनोः।

154. *Tait. Up.* I. 6. 1-2

155. *M.N. Up.* 11. 8-12

156. *Kṣuri. Up.* I. 8-18.

157. *A. Nāda. Up.* I. 25[d], 26[ab]

...यदक्षरं न क्षरते कदाचित्॥ येनासौ पश्यते मार्गं प्राणस्तेन हि गच्छति।

158. *Dhyānabindūpaniṣad.* 38.39

यथैवोत्पलनालेन तोयमाकर्षयेन्नरः। तथैवोत्कर्षयेत्वायुं...॥

अर्धमात्रात्मकं कृत्वा कोशीभूतं तु पङ्कजम्। कर्षयेन्नालमात्रेण भ्रुवोर्मध्ये लयं नयेत्॥

159. Radhakrishnan, S., *Indian Philosophy,* Vol. II. p. 358.
also, *Sarasvatī. R. Up.* 25[b],

सविकल्पो निर्विकल्पः समाधिर्द्विविधो हृदि।

160. *Ibid.*, 25-31.

161. *S.L. Up.* I. 15

यदा संक्षीयते प्राणो मानसं च प्रलीयते। तदा समरसत्वं यत्समाधिरभिधीयते॥

162. *Y.T. Up.* 120[b], 121

पार्ष्णिभागेन संपीड्य योनिमाकुञ्चयेद्दृढम्॥ अपानमूर्ध्वमुत्थाप्य योनिबन्धोऽयमुच्यते॥

प्राणापानौ नादबिन्दू मूलबन्धेन चैकताम्॥

Yogaśikhā. Up. I. 83

पायोराकुञ्चनं कुर्यात् कुण्डलीं चालयेत् तदा।
also, *Yoga. K. Up.*, I. 66[a],
तेनाग्निना च संतप्ता पवनेनैव चालिता...।

163. *Dhyānabindūpaniṣad,* I. 76
उड्डियाणं तदेव स्यात् तत्र बन्धो विधीयते॥
उदरे पश्चिमं ताणं नाभेरूर्ध्वं तु कारयेत्।

164. *Yogacūḍāmaṇi. Up.* 50
बध्नाति हि शिरोजातमधोगामि नभोजलम्। ततो जालन्धरोबन्धः कष्टदुखौघनाशनः॥
जालन्धरे कृते बन्धे कण्ठसंकोचलक्षणे। न पीयूषं पतत्यग्नौ न च वायुः प्रधावति॥
Yogaśikhā. Up. I. 111[b], 112[a]
अधस्तात्कुञ्चनेनाशु कण्ठसंकोचने कृते। मध्ये पश्चिमतानेन स्यात्प्राणो ब्रह्मनाडिगः॥
Yoga. K. Up. I. 53
चालनं तु सरस्वत्याः कृत्वा प्राणं निरोधयेत्।

165. *Yogacūḍāmaṇi. Up.* 68[b], 69[b]
अतिभुक्तं विषं घोरं पीयूषमिव जीर्यते।
...तस्य रोगाः क्षयं यान्ति महामुद्रां तु योऽभ्यसेत्॥

166. *Yoga. K. Up.*, II. 1-48.

167 *Maṇḍalabrā . Up.* II. 2[c].

168. *Y.T. Up.*, I. 128.

169. Ranade, R.D., *op. cit.*, p. 139.

170. *Yogaśikhā. Up.*, V. 16-27.

171. *Ibid.*, V. 23[b],
सरस्वती तु या नाडी या जिह्वान्तं प्रसर्पति।

172. *Ibid.*, V. 24
राकाह्वया तु या नाडी पीत्वा च सलिलं क्षणात्।
क्षुतमुत्पादयेद् घ्राणे श्लेष्माणं संचिनोति च॥

173. *Ibid.*, V. 25,
कण्ठकूपोद्भवा नाडी शङ्खिन्याख्या त्वधोमुखी।
अन्नसारं समादाय मूर्ध्नि संचिनुते तदा॥

174. *Ibid.*, V. 26[b]

मलं त्यजेत्कुहूर्नाडी मूत्रं मुञ्चति वारुणी।
Yogacūḍāmaṇi. Up. I. 15-20.

175. *Śāṇḍ. Up.* p. 413, l. 1
एवं नाडीस्थानं वायुस्थानं तत्कर्म च सम्यग्ज्ञात्वा नाडीसंशोधनं कुर्यात्॥

176. *A. Nāda. Up.* 35, 36[a], 37, 38
प्राण आद्यो हृदि स्थाने अपानस्तु पुनर्गुदे।
समानो नाभिदेशे तु उदानः कण्ठमाश्रितः॥
व्यानः सर्वेषु चाङ्गेषु सदा व्यावृत्य तिष्ठति।
रक्तवर्णमणिप्रख्यः प्राणो वायुः प्रकीर्तितः।
अपानस्तस्य मध्ये तु इन्द्रगोपसमप्रभः॥
समानस्तस्य मध्ये तु गोक्षीरधवलप्रभः।
अपाण्डुर उदानश्च व्यानो ह्यर्चिःसमप्रभः॥

177. *Triśikhi. Brā. Up.* I. 76[b].
178. *Ibid.*, I. 77-86.
179. *S.L. Up. Up. S.* pt. I. p. 655, ll. 6-22
180. *Yoga. K. Up.*, I. 69[b],
अनाहताख्यं यच्चक्रं दलैः षोडशभिर्युतम्।

181. *Dhyānabindūpaniṣad.* 49,
तन्नाभिमण्डलं चक्रं प्रोच्यते मणिपूरकम्।
द्वादशारमहाचक्रे पुण्यपापनियन्त्रितः॥

182. *Yogaśikhā. Up.* I. 168[b]
गुदमेढ्रान्तरालस्थं मूलाधारं त्रिकोणम्।

183. *Yogacūḍāmaṇi. Up.* I. 4[b]
चतुर्दलं स्यादाधारं...।

184. Woodroffe, J., *Śakti and Śākta–Essays and addresses on the Śākta Tantraśāstra,* London. 1929. p. 641.
185. Vaidya, S.M., *Ṣaṭ cakra Darśana vā Bhedana* (*Mar.*), Islampur, 1937, pp. 6 ff.
186. Gajendragadkar, K.V., quoted by *Desai, S.G., op. cit.*, p. 317.
187. Vaidya, S.M., *op. cit.,* p. 7.
188. *Ibid.*, p. 7.

189. *Kṣuri. Up.* 9[c]

तद्भित्त्वा कण्ठमायाति तां नाडीं पूरयन्यतः।

190. Vaidya, S.M., *op. cit.,* p. 7.
191. Woodroffe, J., *op. cit.,* pp. 640 f.
192. *Yoga. K. Up.,* I. 63-74.
193. Woodroffe, J., *op. cit.,* p. 656.
194. *Garbhopaniṣad.* 3-4[b].

ऋतुकाले संप्रयोगादेकरात्रोषितं कलिलं भवति सप्तरात्रोषितं बुद्बुदं भवति अर्धमासाभ्यन्तरेण पिण्डो भवति मासाभ्यन्तरेण कठिनो भवति मासद्वयेन शिरः संपद्यते मासत्रयेण पादप्रदेशो भवति ॥ चतुर्थे मासेऽङ्गुल्यजठरकटिप्रदेशो भवति। पञ्चमे मासे पृष्ठवंशो भवति। ...सप्तमे मासे जीवेन संयुक्तो भवति। अष्टमे मासे सर्वसंपूर्णो भवति। ... जातमात्रस्तु वैष्णवेन वायुना संस्पृश्य तदा न स्मरति..।

195. Deussen, P. *op. cit.*, p. 296.
196. *Patañjali. Y.S.,* II. 48,

ततो द्वन्द्वानभिघातः।

197. *Yogacūḍāmaṇi. Up.* I. 109.
198. *Patañjali. Y.S.,* III. 24,

बलेषु हस्तिबलादीनि।

199. *Ibid.*, III. 36.

ततः प्रतिमश्रावणवेदनादर्शास्वादवार्ता जायन्ते।

200. *Ibid.*, III. 29.

नाभिचक्रेकायव्यूहज्ञानम्।

201. Ghosh, Aurobindo., *The Synthesis of Yoga,* Pondicherry, 2002, p. 42.
202. Ranade, R.D., *op. cit.,* p. 326.
203. Kane, P.V., *History of Dharmaśāstra.* Vol. II. pt. II, Pune, 1941, p. 422.
204. Deussen, P., *op. cit.,* p. 367.
205. *Chānd. Up.,* II. 23.1.
206. *Bṛ. Up.,* IV. 3.22.
207. *Ibid.*, III.8.10.

208. *Muṇḍ. Up.* III. 2.6.

वेदान्तविज्ञानसुनिश्चितार्थाः संन्यासयोगाद्यतयः शुद्धसत्त्वाः।
ते ब्रह्मलोकेषु परान्तकाले परामृताः परिमुच्यन्ति सर्वे॥

also, *Ibid.*, I. 2.11

209. *Jābālopaniṣad.* IV. 1[b]

...ब्रह्मचर्यं समाप्य गृही भवेत् गृही भूत्वा वनी भवेत् वनी भूत्वा प्रव्रजेत्।

210. *N.P. Up.* IV. 1[a]

त्यक्त्वा लोकांश्च वेदांश्च विषयानिन्द्रियाणि च।

211. *Ibid.*, IV. 2

नामगोत्रादिवरणं देशं कालं श्रुतं कुलम्।
वयो वृत्तं व्रतं शीलं ख्यापयेन्नेव सद्यतिः॥

212. *Ibid.* IV. 8[b]

प्रतिग्रहं न गृह्णीयान्नैव चान्यं प्रदापयेत्।

213. *Ibid.*, IV. 8[a].3

214. *Śātyāyanīyopaniṣad*, I. 18[c].

द्वन्द्वसहः प्रशान्तः।

215. *Kuṇḍikopaniṣad.* I. 7, 9[b]

लोकवद्भार्ययाऽऽसक्तो वनं गच्छति संयतः। संत्यक्त्वा संसृतिसुखमनुतिष्ठति किं मुधा। ...संन्यस्याग्निमपुनरावर्तनं यन्मृत्यु....।

216. *Śātyāyanīyopaniṣad*, I. 29.

परिव्राज्यं गृहीत्वा तु यः स्वधर्मे न तिष्ठति।
तमारूढच्युतं विद्यादिति वेदानुशासनम्॥

217. *Saṁnyāsopaniṣad*, *Up. S.* pt. I., p. 476. ll. 1-3

संन्यासे निश्चयं कृत्वा पुनर्न च करोति यः।
स कुर्यात्कृच्छ्रमात्रं तु न पुनः संन्यस्तुमर्हति॥

संन्यासं पातयेद्यस्तु पतितं न्यासयेत्तु यः।
संन्यासविघ्नकर्ता च त्रीनेतान् पतितान्विदुः॥

218. *Ibid.*, Up. S. pt. I, p. 476. L. 26

दृष्टानुश्रविकविषयवैतृष्णमेत्यप्राक्पुण्यकर्मविशेषात्संन्यस्तः स वैराग्य संन्यासी।

219. *Ibid.*, Up. S. pt. I, p. 476. ll. 26-30

शास्त्रज्ञानात्पापपुण्यलोकानुभवश्रवणात्प्रपञ्चोपरतो...शास्त्रवासना...त्यक्त्वा...
प्रवृत्तिं सर्व हेयं मत्वा... यः संन्यसति...।

220. *Ibid.*, Up. S. pt. I, p. 477. l. 1,

क्रमेण सर्वमभ्यस्य सर्वमनुभूय...स्वरूपानुसंधानेन देहमात्रावशिष्टः संन्यस्य जातरूपधरो भवति स ज्ञानवैराग्यसंज्ञासी।

221. *Ibid.*, Up. S. pt. I, p. 477.

ब्रह्मचर्यं समाप्य गृहीभूत्वा...वैराग्याभावेऽप्याश्रमक्रमानुसारेण यः संन्यसति स कर्म संन्यासी।

222. *Jābāla. Up.* V. 5.

यद्यातुरः स्यान्मनसा वाचा वा संन्यसेत्।

223. *N.P. Up.*, II. 4,

...प्राणस्योत्क्रामणासन्नकालस्त्वातुरसंज्ञकः।

224. *Ibid.*, pt. I, p. 317. l. 14-16.

...कुटीचकः शिखायज्ञोपवीती दण्डकमण्डलुधरः कौपीकन्थाधरः पितृमातृगुर्वाराधनपरः पिठरखनित्रशिक्या दिमन्त्रसाधनपर एकत्रान्नादनपरः श्वेतोर्ध्वपुण्ड्रधारी त्रिदण्डः।

225. *Śātyāyanīyopaniṣad*. I. 7-9.

त्रिदण्डमुपवीतं च वासःकौपीनवेष्टनम्।
शिक्यं पवित्रमित्येतद्बिभृयाद्यावदायुषम्॥

पञ्चैतास्तु यतेर्मात्रास्ता मात्रा ब्रह्मणे श्रुताः।
...त्रिदण्डं वैष्णवं लिङ्गं विप्राणां मुक्तिसाधनम्॥

226. *N.P. Up. Up. S.* pt. I, p. 317. l. 17.

बहूदकः शिखादिकन्थाधरत्रिपुण्ड्रधारी कुटीचकवत्सर्वसमो मधुकरवृत्त्याष्टकवलाशी
Ibid., Up. S. p. 324.

227. *Ibid., Up. S.* pt. I. pp. 317, 324

...हंसो जटाधारी त्रिपुण्ड्रोर्ध्वपुण्ड्रधारी...
हंसस्येकवारं (स्नानं)... हंसस्य खण्डम्...
...ग्राम एकरात्रं पत्तने पञ्चरात्रं क्षेत्रे पञ्चरात्र तीर्थे...।

228. *Ibid., Up. S.* pt. I. p. 317. l. 19,

परमहंसः शिखायज्ञोपवीतरहितः पञ्चगृहेष्वेकरात्रान्नादनपरः करपात्री एककौपीनधारी शाटीमेकामेकं... भस्मोद्धूलनपरः सर्वत्यागी।

...परमहंसादित्रयाणां न कटिसूत्रं न कौपिनं न वस्त्रं न कमण्डलुर्न दण्डः।

229. *Ibid., Up. S.* pt. I. p. 317.

तुरीयातीतो गोमुखः फलाहारी।

230. *Avadhūtopaniṣad.*12[a], 13[a]

अनुतिष्ठन्तु कर्माणि परलोकयियासवः।
व्याचक्षतां ते शास्त्राणि वेदानध्यापयन्तु वा।

231. *N.P. Up.*, pt. I. p. 317, l. 23

अवधूतस्त्वनियमोऽभिशस्तपतितवर्जनपूर्वकं सर्ववर्णेष्वजगरवृत्त्याहारपरः स्वरूपानुसंधानपरः।

232. *Avadhūtopaniṣad.*6[a].

स्वैरं स्वैरविहरणं तत्संसरणम्।

233. *Ibid.*, 6[i],

यथा रविः सर्वरसान्प्रभुंक्ते हुताशनश्चापि हि सर्वभक्षः।
तथैव योगी विषयान्भुङ्क्ते न लिप्यते पुण्यपापैश्च शुद्धः॥

234. *Ibid.*, 6[c],

न तेषां धर्माधर्मौ न मेध्यामेध्यौ।

235. *Śātyāyanīyopaniṣad.* 30[j].

शतं कुलानां प्रथमं बभूव तथा पराणां त्रिशतं समग्रम।
एते भवन्ति सुकृतस्य लोके येषां कुले संन्यसतीह विद्वान्।

236. *Saṁnyāsopaniṣad.* II. 7

षष्टिं कुलान्यतीतानि षष्टिमागामिकानि च। कुलान्युद्धरते प्राज्ञः संन्यस्तमिति यो वदेत्।

237. *Avadhūtopaniṣad.* 2.

तस्य प्रियं शिरः कृत्वा मोदो दक्षिणपक्षकः। प्रमोदः उत्तरः पक्ष आनन्दो गोष्पदायते।

238. *Saṁnyāsopaniṣad.* I. 59.

...आतुरकुटीचकयोर्भूलोकर्भूवर्लोकौ। बहूदकस्य स्वर्गलोकः। हंसस्य तपोलोकः। परमहंसस्य सत्यलोकः। तुरीयातीतावधूतयोः स्वात्मन्येव कैवल्यं स्वरूपानुसंधानेन भ्रमरकीटन्यायवत्।

239. Ghosh, Arbindo., *The Synthesis of Yoga,* Pondicherry, 2002, pp. 326-329.

240 *Ibid.*, p. 326.

241. Ed. by Joshi, Mahadevashastri and Hodavar, Padmaja *Bhāratīya Saṁskṛti Kośa,* Vol. IV. pp. 795, 796.

242. Zimmer, Henrich, "*The Tantras*", *Philosophies of India,* ed. by Campbell, Joseph, New York, 1951, p. 61.

243. Schomerush, W., *Śaiva Siddhānta,* Delhi, 1979, pp. 8-10.

244. Winternitz, M., *op. cit.,* p. 578.

245. Winternitz, M., *op. cit.,* pp. 564-579.

246. *Ibid.*, p. 222.

247. Eliot, q. by Winternitz, *op. cit.,* p. 559.

248. Woodroffe, J., *op. cit.,* p. 7.

249. Winternitz, M., *op. cit.,* p. 562.

250. *Ibid.*, p. 579.

251. For more details, see Woodroffe, J., *op. cit.,* pp. 7-12.

252. For more details, see Woodroffe, J., *op. cit.,* pp. 652-656.

253. Kinsley David, *op. cit.,* p. 14.

254. *Ibid.,* p. 47.

255. *Ibid.,* p. 3-4.

256. *Devī. Up.,* I. 18.

प्रपद्ये शरणं देवी दुंदुर्गे दुरितं हर।

Tvmn. Up. p. 376. L. 5,

रामाय हुं फट् स्वाहा। ह्रीं ह्रीं श्रीं श्रीं लक्ष्मीवासुदेवाय नमः।

257. Stall Frits, "Vedic Mantra-s"; *Understanding the mantras,* ed. by Alper Harvey, Delhi, 1991, p. 56.

258. Desai, S.G., *op. cit.,* p. 210.

259. Stall Frits, *op. cit.,* p. 83.

260. *Vanadurgopaniṣad, Up. S.* pt. II, p. 426. l. 8.

ओम् हंसिनी ह्रां अङ्गुष्ठाभ्याम् हृदि।
ओम् शिखिनी ह्रीं तर्जनीभ्यां शिरसि।
चक्रिणी ह्रूं मध्यमाभ्यां शिखायां। त्रिशूलधारिणी ह्रैं अनामिकाभ्यां कवचं शींल.

261. Winternitz, M., *op. cit.*, p. 568.

262. *Tripuratāpinyupaniṣad.* pt. I. pp. 537-538.

263. *Ibid., Up. S.* pt. I. p. 537, l. 25
...कृतजानुमण्डलं विस्तीर्य पद्मासनं कृत्वा मुद्राः सृजतेति।

264. *Ibid., Up. S.* pt. I. p. 537, l. 28; p. 538, l. 1
मध्यमे अनामिकोपरि विन्यस्य कनिष्ठिकाङ्गुष्ठतोऽधीते-
मुक्तयोस्तर्जन्योर्दण्डवदधस्तादेवंविधा प्रथमा संपद्यते।

265. *Ibid.*, Up.S. pt. I. p. 537, ll. 26-27
...यो योनिमुद्रामधीते स सर्वं वेत्ति स सर्वफलमश्नुते स सर्वान्भञ्जयति...।

266. *Ibid.*, p. 538.
Mudrā-s namely
योनिमुद्रा, मीलितमध्यमा, अङ्कुशाकृति, तुरीया, मध्यमानखमिलिताङ्गुष्ठौ, अग्रेअङ्कुशाकृतिः, खेचरी, ...त्रिखण्डा।

267. Gajendragadkar, K.V., *op. cit.*, p. 330.

268. *Rama. P.Tā. Up.* I. 13[b]
विना यन्त्रेण चेत्पूजा देवता न प्रसीदति।

269. *Tripuratāpinyupaniṣad*. p. 538. l. 17
नीलीयुक्तं चक्रं शत्रून्मारयति। गतिं स्तम्भयति। लाक्षायुक्तं कृत्वा सकललोकं वशीकरोति...भगाङ्ककुण्डं कृत्वाग्निमाधाय पुरुषो हविषा हुत्वा योषितो वशीकरोति।

270. *Sūryatāpinyupaniṣad, Up. S.* pt. II. V. p. 59.
...वृत्तमादौ विलिख्य साष्टपत्रं ततस्त्रिकोणं वृत्तं षडश्रं वृत्तयुगळं साधुकोणं समालिखेदिति। तत्रैता देवता आवाह्य द्वादशावरणानि कुर्यात्तत्र... माघादिद्वादशमासाधिपतयः सप्तमे...।

271. *Ibid., Up. S.* pt. II. VI. p. 60
देशिकोक्तविधानेन यन्त्रे देवं प्रपूजयेत्...
...सूर्यस्योपासनं कार्यं गच्छेत् सूर्यसँ सदम्।

272. *Rājaśyāmālarahasyopaniṣad, Up. S.* pt. II. p. 423, l. 8[ff].
शुक्रवारे भार्याजगन्मोहनचक्रे त्रिशतं मन्त्रजपेन मन्त्रसिद्धिः।... ...नवाशीतिन्यासानां न्यसनेन देवस्त्री भोगमाप्तोति।... देवताशरीरी भूत्वा विमानवान् भवति।... वर्षर्तौ श्रावणे मासि सर्वरात्रिषु भार्याजगन्मोहनचक्रे चम्पककुसुमैः पूजिता... आरोग्यप्रदा भवति।

273. *S.L. Up. S.* pt. I. p. 655, l. 24.

स सकलधनधान्यसत्पुत्रकलत्रहयभूगजपशुमहिषीदासीदासयोगज्ञानवान् भवति।

274. *Gaṇeśapūrvatāpini. Up.* II. 4-5.

मध्ये बिन्दुं त्रिकोणं तदनु ऋतुगणं वसुदलं द्वादशारं षोडशकर्णिकेति। मध्ये बीजात्मकं देवं यजेत्। वामदक्षिणे सिद्धिर्बुद्धिः। अग्रे कामदुधा। षट्कोणे सुमुखादयः षड्विनायकाः। वसुदले वक्रतुण्डाद्यष्टविनायकाः।...

275. *Ibid.*, III. 1.

...मूले शून्यं विजानीयात्। शून्यं वै परं ब्रह्म। ... षट्कोणं भवति षड् हीमे लोकाः षड्वा ऋतवो भवन्ति। .. अष्टपत्रं भवत्यष्टाक्षरा गायत्री... द्वादशपत्रं भवति द्वादशादित्या भवन्ति ते स्वरा भवन्ति। ... षोडशपत्रं भवति षोडशकलो वै... पुरुषः स लोकाधितिष्ठितो भवत्यनुष्टुब् वै पुरुषः।

276. *Ibid.*, II. 5.

य एतेन चतुर्थीषु पक्षयोरुभयोरपि। लक्षं जुहूयादपूपानां तत्क्षणाद्धनदो भवेत्।

277. Alper, Harvey, "*Introduction*" *Understanding the Mantras*, p. 3.

278. Gonda, J. q. by Crawford, Harold "*The meaning and power of Mantras in Bhartṛhari's Vākyapadīya*", *op. cit.*, ed. Alper, Harvey, p. 165.

279. Ghosh, A., *On the Vedas*, Pondicherry, 1956, p. 6.

280. Gonda q. by Alper H. *op. cit.*, p. 3.

281. Bharati, Agehananda. *The Tantrika Tradition*, p. 111.

282. *Patañjali Y.S.* I. 42.

तत्र शब्दार्थज्ञानविकल्पैः संकीर्णा सवितर्का समापत्तिः।

283. *Nṛsiṁha. P.Tā. Up.*, V. 2.1.

य एतं मन्त्रराजं नारसिंहानुष्टुभं नित्यमधीते स मृत्युं तरति स पाप्मानं तरति स ब्रह्महत्यां तरति स भ्रूणहत्यां तरति... स सर्वं तरति। ...यो नारसिंहानुष्टुभं नित्यमधीते सोऽग्निपूतो भवति स वायुपूतो भवति ... सर्वपूतो भवति।

284. *Ibid.*, V. 5.1.

... स मनुष्यानाकर्षयति स देवानाकर्षयति ... स ग्रहानाकर्षयति स सर्वानाकर्षयति।

285. *Ibid.*, V. 4.1.

य एतं ... नित्यमधीते स भूर्लोकं जयति स भुवर्लोकं जयति... स सत्यलोकं जयति स सर्वलोकं जयति।

286. *Sūryopaniṣad*, *Up. S.*, pt. I. p. 510. ll. 12-14.

...सूर्याभिमुखो जप्त्वा महाव्याधिभयात्प्रमुच्यते। अलक्ष्मीर्नश्यति। अभक्ष्यभक्षणात्पूतो भवति ...असत्संभाषणात्पूतो भवति।... मध्याह्ने सूर्याभिमुख: पठेत्। सद्योत्पन्नपञ्चमहापापान्प्रमुच्यते।

287. *Gaṇeśa. U. Ta. Up. S.*, pt. I, p. 638. l. 4.

य एनं मन्त्रराजं गणपते: सर्वदं नित्यं जपति सोऽग्निं स्तम्भयति स उदकं स्तम्भयति स वायुं स्तम्भयति... ...स सर्वोपद्रवान्स्तम्भयति।

288. *Nṛsiṁha. P. Tā. Up. S.* pt. I. p. 226, ll. 10-13.

289. *Gāruḍopaniṣad Up. S.* pt. I. p. 624, ll. 17-18.

also, *Vanadurgopaniṣad Up. S.*, pt. II. p. 465, L. 5

ह्रीं दुंसर्पोलूककाककपोतवृश्चिकदंष्ट्राग्निविषं नो भयं भूतप्रेतपिशाच्च-ब्रह्मराक्षस-सकलकिल्बिषादिमहारोगविषं निर्विषं कुरु कुरु।

290. *Sarasvatī. R. Up.* I.9-10[a]

तत: प्रवर्तते वाणी स्वेच्छया ललिताक्षरा। गद्यपद्यात्मकै: शब्दैरप्रमेयैर्विवक्षितै:। अश्रुतो बुध्यते ग्रन्थ: प्राय: सारस्वत: कवि:।

291. *Nṛsiṁha. P.Tā. Up.*, IV. 3.

एतैर्द्वात्रिंशत्मन्त्रैर्नित्यं देवं स्तुवते ततो देव: प्रीतो भवति ...।

292. *Rāma. P.Tā. Up.*, I. 11.

ब्रह्मादीनां वाचकोऽयं मन्त्रोऽन्वर्थादिसंज्ञक:। जप्तव्यो मन्त्रिणा नैवं विना देव: प्रसीदति।

293. *Rāma. U.Tā. Up. Up. S.*, pt. I. p. 405. l. 8.

तस्माद्य एतैर्मन्त्रैर्नित्यं देवं स्तौति स देवं पश्यति सोऽमृतत्वं गच्छति।

294. *Hayagrīvopaniṣad Up. S.* pt. I. p. 620, l. 28.

प्रज्ञानमानन्दं ब्रह्म तत्त्वमसि अयमात्मा ब्रह्म अहं ब्रह्मास्मीति महावाक्यै: प्रतिपादितमर्थं, त एते मन्त्रा: प्रतिपादयन्ति।

295. *Sūryatāpinī. Up.*, pt. II, p. 60.

296. *Kalisan. Up.* 1[c].

Ibid., 2[c]

सर्वदा शुचिरशुचिर्वा पठन्ब्राह्मण: सलोकता समीपतां सरूपतां सायुज्यमेति।

297. Dange, S.A., *Hindu Dharmāṇi Tattvajñāna,* Pune. 1973. p. 342.

298. *Gāyatrī. Up. Up. S.* pt. II. p. 409, ll. 1-10.

299. *Ibid., Up. S.*, pt. II. p. 410, ll. 6-8.

तस्या अग्निरेव मुखं यदिह वापि वह्निमानग्नावभ्यादधाति सर्वमेतत्सन्दहत्येवं-विद्यद्यपवह्नीव पापं करोति सर्वमेवैतत्सम्यग्विशुद्धो यतोऽजरोऽमृत स भवतीति।

300. *Gāyatrī. R. Up. Up. S.*, pt. II, p. 406, ll. 2-3.
सांख्यायनगोत्रा सा चतुर्विंशत्यक्षरा गायत्री त्रिपादा चतुष्पादा।
पुनस्तस्याश्चत्वार: पादा: षट् कुक्षिका: पञ्च शीर्षाणि भवति।

301. *Ibid., Up. S.*, pt. II. p. 406, ll. 16-23.
पूर्वाह्नकालिका संध्या गायत्री कुमारी रक्ता रक्ताङ्गी रक्तवासिनी रक्तगन्ध-माल्यानुलेपनी...। मध्याह्नकालिका सन्ध्या सावित्री युवती श्वेताङ्गी श्वेतवासिनी श्वेतगन्धमाल्यानुलेपनी त्रिशूलडमरुहस्ता वृषभारूढा रुद्रदैवत्या यजुर्वेदसहिता आदित्यपथगामिनी भुवोलोके व्यवस्थिता। सायं संध्या सरस्वती वृद्धा कृष्णाङ्गी... स्वर्गलोकव्यवस्थिता।

302. *Gāyatrī. R. Up. Up. S.*, pt. II, p. 408, l. 16.
य इदं गायत्रीरहस्यं ब्राह्मण: पठेत् तेन गायत्र्या: षष्टिसहस्रलक्षाणि जप्त्वा भवन्ति।

303. *Tripuratāpinupaniṣad*, (I), pt. I. pp. 532-533.

304. *Nṛsiṁha. P.Tā. Up. Up. S.*, pt. I. p. 223, l. 23
नृसिंहाय विद्महे वज्रनखाय धीमहि। तन्न: सिंह: प्रचोदयादित्येषा वै नृसिंहगायत्री वेदानां देवानां... भवति।

305. *M.N. Up.*, III. 15.

306. Macdonell, A.A. *The Vedic Mythology*, Varanasi, 1963. p. 119.

307. *Nṛsiṁha. P.Tā. Up.*, I. 3.
...तस्मादिदं साङ्गं साम जानीयाद्यो जानीते सोऽमृतत्वं च गच्छति।
...सर्वे वेदा: प्रणवादिकास्तं प्रणवं तत्साम्नोङ्गं वेद।

308. *Avyaktopaniṣad*, pt. I, p. 489. ll. 8-18.
ततोऽपश्यज्ज्योतिर्मयं श्रियालिङ्गितं सुपर्णरथं शेषफणाच्छादितमौलिं मृगमुखं नरवपुषं शशिसूर्यहव्यवाहनात्मक-नयनत्रयम्। ...तथैवचार्थ तमस्तौत्। उग्रमित्याह... महाविष्णुमित्याह...

309. *Nṛsiṁha. P. Tā. Up.*, I. 2.
ससागरां सपर्वतां सप्तद्वीपां वसुंधरां तत्साम्न: प्रथमं पादं..
जानीयाद्यक्षगन्धर्वाप्सरोगणसेवितमन्तरिक्षं तत्साम्नो द्वितीयं पादं..
जानीयाद्वसुरुद्रादित्यै: सर्वैर्देवै: सेवितं दिवं तत्साम्नस्तृतीयं पादं...
जानीयाद्यो जानीते सोऽमृतत्वं गच्छति।

CHAPTER VI

MISCELLANEOUS

Besides the topics dealt with, so far, some Upaniṣads reflect a few more points such as the doctrine of *karman*, the concept of release etc. which are examined in the following chapter.

Social Conditions Reflected in the Upaniṣads

"Social structure can be defined as the totality of patterns of collected human phenomena that cannot be explained solely on the basis of human heridity and/or the non-human environment".[1] It is a composite of several components such as norms, religion, values, belief systems etc. These are parts of a larger whole and always relate with each other. Religion, philosophy and society always interact with each other. So, also literary works and society. It would be interesting to examine social conditions existing in the days of the Upaniṣads which are reflected in them.

Relation of Brāhmins and Kṣatriya-s

Some Upaniṣads refer to Brāhmins who had approached Kṣ atriyas in order to attain the highest knowledge of philosophy. Obviously, they indicate an earnest urge on the part of Kṣatriyas to indulge in philosophic enquiries. Thus, the *Bṛ. Up.* refers to a Brāhmin who accepted a seat lower than that of a Kṣatriya, at *Rājasūya* sacrifice to give him his due honour. On the other hand, ạ Kṣatriya was expected to remember that his Kṣatrahood was born of Brāhminhood and even though he attained the highest state, he will have to depend upon the Brāhmins, *i.e.* to live under the control and guidance of the Brāhmins.[2] The Upaniṣad further states that a Brāhmin Āruṇi desirous of having spiritual knowledge went to Jaivali as a pupil. He regarded Jaivali to be superior to himself.[3] "Since this (sacred) lore (or knowledge) did not approach Brāhmins, in the past, only Kṣatriya-s were the administrators (wielded the supreme authority)," states the *Chānd.Up.*[4] In the *Kau.Up.* the king Citra Gārgyāyaṇi is seen to have praised Āruṇi, who approached him in a humble manner, with sacrificial fuel in hands. Āruṇi who was really worthy of receiving the highest knowledge was instructed by the king.[5] All these Upaniṣadic passages are indicative of the earthly and spiritual supremacy of the Kṣatriya-s.

On the contrary, there are other passages from the Upani- ṣads which hint at the superiority of Brāhmins over Kṣatriya-s. They mention that the Kṣatriya-s gained spiritual knowledge from their Brāhmin preceptors. Thus, revering Yājñavalkya's spiritual wisdom, the king Janaka was inclined to bow down before him.[6] The *Mai.Up.* stated that the king Bṛhadratha filled with remorse went to Śākyāyana and begged him to help him out from the world of existence as one would help a frog out from a well without water.[7] These passages show Brāhmins to be superior to Kṣatriya-s in respect of spiritual wisdom.

Thus, it may be said that the intellectual and spiritual wisdom was solely dependent on the ability of a person, and was not the monopoly of any caste.

Āśrama System

Āśrama system constituted an important integral part of ancient Indian social structure. Deussen, P. has derived the term *āśrama* from the root *śram*, which means to exert oneself. The term according to him means, a place where austerities are performed, and the action of performing austerities.[8] Again, Deussen, P. has explained the meaning of the word *āśrama* as "the places of mortification." He did so, on the basis of the use of the word *atyāśramin* in the *Śvet. Up.* (VI.21) followed by the *Mai. Up.* (IV. 3) etc. Accordingly, he has stated "The whole life should be passed in a series of gradually intensifying ascetic stages, through which a man, more and more purified from all earthly attachment should become fit for his home (*astam*)."[9] Although the original meaning of the term is doubtful, in the course of time, the word came to mean 'an order of life', and over a passage of time it became a custom and a law for the life of the Āryans.[10]

As regards the number of *āśrama*-s existing during the period of the earlier Upaniṣads, the relevant details from the Upaniṣads are given below.

Brahmacaryāśrama

It was the period of instructions to be received by a student from the teacher. The duration of the period of instruction generally was that of twelve years,[11] or a series of years,[12] Śvetaketu began to get instruction at the age of twelve and continued his study for twelve years. During this period, he studied all the Vedā-s.[13]

The student was supposed to approach the preceptor with a request saying, '*upaimi ahaṁ bhavantam*.'[14] Formally, the student had to carry sacrificial fuel in his hands as a token of his assent to serve the teacher and tend to the sacred fires.[15] Sometimes, the duration of this period is stretched longer. Accordingly, Upakosala in the *Chānd.Up.* stayed with his preceptor for twelve years and tended the sacred fires. The teacher, Satyakāma Jābāla allowed other pupils to return to their homes but did not allow Upakosala to depart.[16] Further, it is told that, after the teacher went away, the sacrificial fires imparted him the knowledge. Then the fires said, "Upakosala, you have the knowledge of (the form of) ourselves and the knowledge of the Self. But the teacher will show you the way."[17] And after the teacher returned, he showed Upakosala the way. Similarly, in another story, Satyakāma was sent at first with the teacher's herds of cattle into a distant country, where he remained for a number of years. A part of knowledge was imparted to him by a bull, a swan etc.[18] From the story of Śvetaketu, it seems that it was possible for an aspirant to receive instruction from a worthy father.[19] The act of service to the teacher also included begging alms for one's own teacher, to await for his commands and obey them. As a rule, the students lived in the house of a teacher (*antevāsins*) for a series of years and some continued to do so and settled permanently in the teachers house.[20]

Gṛhasthāśrama

In a passage of the *Tait.Up.*, when the students have completed their Vedic study, a pupil is advised by the teacher; to speak truth, to perform his own duty, to revise whatever he had learnt, and to continue the line of progeny.[21] The *Chānd. Up.* has mentioned that one who returns from his teacher's house after the completion of his studies, pursues the study of the Veda in his household, trains and teaches students, subdues all his organs in the Ātman, and does not cause harm to anybody, one who maintains this mode of life enters the world of the Brahman, from where there is no return.[22] The duty of the householder was to establish a family and have progeny to continue his lineage. Other duties of a householder included the performance of sacrifices, the Vedic study and alms giving.

From these passages one may conclude that the orders of students (*brahmacarya*) and householders (*gṛhasthāśrama*) did definitely exist during the period of the Upaniṣads.

In the *Chānd. Up.*, three branches of *dharma* are enumerated. The householders are advised to perform sacrifices, study and value charity, the recluses are advised to perform penance; and the students are advised to observe celibacy and serve the teacher. Then, it is said, all these reach the holy worlds after death.[23] In the later Upaniṣads, a clear distinction between the *vānaprasthāśrama* and the *saṁnyāsāśrama* is observed, and further, a finer classification of these orders is also noticed. Thus, the *Āśramopaniṣad* has recorded sixteen classifications of the four *āśrama*-s.[24] The four types of *brahmacārins* as enumerated in the Upaniṣad are as follows :

(*i*) ***The Gāyatra :*** One who recites *Gāyatrī* spell following his thread ceremony for three nights without eating salt is called as *Gāyatra brahmacārin.*[25]

(*ii*) ***The Brāhmaṇa :*** One who pursues the study of the Veda-s for forty eight years, *i.e.* twelve years for each of the Veda-s or till the realization of the knowledge of the Veda-s is known as a *Brāhmaṇa*.[26]

(*iii*) ***The Prājāpatya :*** One who is devoted to his own wife, avoids relations with the wives of others, enjoys sexual pleasures with one's own wife at proper times is known as a *Prājāpatya brahmacārin*. Or one who resides in the *gurukula* for twenty four years or forty eight years (studyig the Veda-s) is also known as a *Prājāpatya*.[27]

(*iv*) ***Bṛhat :*** One who stays with his own teacher, till death and observes celibacy is called a *Naiṣṭhika* or *Bṛhat*.[28]

Similarly, the householders (*gṛhastha*-s) are also of four types.

(*i*) ***Vārtākavṛtti :*** He indulges in various activities as his occupation such as agriculture, cattle breeding, trade etc., without blemish. He engages himself in various religious activities, performs sacrifices and leads a life searching for the Self.[29]

(*ii*) ***Śālīnavṛtti :*** This type of householder performs sacrifices for himself and not for others. He studies the lores but does not teach. He donates or bestows gifts upon others but does not accept any. In this way, he leads a life of hundred years in search of the Ātman.[30]

(*iii*) ***Yāyāvara :*** This type of a householder performs sacrifices for himself and even for others. He studies and even teaches others, gives away and accepts gifts from others. Leading a life of hundred years in this way, he is engaged in search of the Ātman.[31]

(*iv*) ***Ghorasaṁnyāsin :*** This type of a person lives by pure water drawn fresh (from well) and by gleaning grains (*Uñchavṛtti*).[32] The four types of *Vānaprasthāś-rama* recorded in the Upaniṣad are as follows :

(*i*) ***Vaikhānasa-s :*** The *vaikhānasa*-s perform five great sacrifices (*pañcamahāyajña*-s) stay outside the city, maintain themselves on the herbs and roots of the trees, and try to have the knowledge of the Self.[33]

(*ii*) ***Udumbara-s :*** *Udumbara*-s get up early in the morning and whichever direction they happen to see first, they perform sacrifices there with the berries (*badara*), grains (*nīvāra*-s) *udumbara*-s etc. Performing these activities, they search for the Self.[34]

(*iii*) ***The Bālakhilya-s :*** Wear matted hair, a hide or a bark (*Valakala*), earn their livehood by growing fruit and flowers for eight months, they worship fire, perform sacrifices and contemplate on the Self.[35]

(*iv*) ***The Phenapā*-s :** Maintain themselves on dried leaves and fruits. Wherever they stay, they worship fire, perform *pañcamahāyajña*-s and meditate on the Self.[36]

The above details indicate that the stage of a *Vānaprasthāśrama* was a preparatory stage leading to that of an ascetic (*Saṁnyāsāśrama*). However, it must be noted that the Upaniṣadic authors were liberal in allowing people who were capable of renouncing the world and worldly pleasures at an early stage to do so.[37] The details regarding this stage of life have been already dealt with (*Ibid.*, pp. 264-272).

The Position of Women in Society

In the earlier Upaniṣads, three different types of women are seen. The *Bṛ. Up.* (IV. 5.1) narrates a story of Yājñavalkya and his two wives. Of these two, Maitreyī was eager to have knowledge of the Highest Reality. She considered wealth to be emphemeral and was eager to follow the path leading to immortality. Kātyāyanī was interested in worldly matters and material pleasures. Gārgī is depicted as an intelligent woman, taking part in philosophical discussion in the court of king Janaka. She was bold and sturdy and dared to defy Yājñavalkya.[38] Hence, in the earlier Upaniṣads,

Kātyāyanī represented common women, Maitreyī represented spiritual minded women and Gārgī represented intelligent women with a philosophical bend of mind.

During the period of the later Upaniṣads, the position of women went on deteriorating and women were no longer praised. Some Upaniṣads are seen to be particularly warning persons desirous of being *Saṁnyāsin*-s or *yogin*-s to be more watchful about women. Thus, the *Y.T. Up.* advised ascetics to avoid the company of women.[39] The *N. P. Up.* stated that a *yati* should not converse with women, nor should he remember a woman seen earlier and should avoid listening to stories about them. He should not see the picture of a woman.[40] A wise person should never trust a woman.[41] The *N.P. Up.* says that as one is intoxicated after drinking wine, similarly one is intoxicated after having seen a beautiful woman. Hence, one should avoid being in the company of a woman having poison in her eyes.[42] The *Mahopaniṣad* stated that as the fire burns the grass, women destroy men.[43] Even though she is far off, a woman torments a man. Although, outwardly she appears to be full of affection, at heart she is quite dry.[44] She is the trap for catching the birds in the form of men.[45] A woman is comparable to a casket full of gems with blemishes (*doṣa*-s) and she is said to be a chain of sorrow. The same thoughts are echoed in the *Yājñ. Up.*[46]

The System of Education

The earlier Upaniṣads present a glorious picture of the educational system that prevailed in ancient India. The system is known as *gurukula* system which is still considered to be a special characteristic of Indian civilization. The two noteworthy features of this system are (*i*) the type of instruction imparted and (*ii*) the method of instruction adopted. The combination of these two made the system sound and memorable. The seers of the Upaniṣ ads made no distinction between the philosophy of life and philosophy of education. They considered them both to be co-ordinated and co-related. The *Gurukula* was an institution of intellectual speculation and research.

"The recognition of the importance of association and imitation was one of the main reasons for the great emphasis laid on *gurukula* system."[47] Direct, personal and continuous contact with the teacher of noble character naturally produced favourable impact on the mind of students during their formative period of childhood and adolescence. Due to close association with the preceptors and fellow students they could make progress in education. A healthy dialogue between a teacher and a student and between the fellow students was established.

Liberal Outlook of the System

It is evident from the story of Satyakāma that simplicity of mind and respect for truth were considered to be the sufficient qualities for one's admission to the *gurukula*.[48] Thus, it may be said that the birth or caste could not create a barrier in the pursuit of knowledge of the earnest enquirer. In the Upaniṣadic age, education was never a monopoly of Brāhmins.

The Physical Mobility

The students went far and wide in order to learn from the renowned scholars. Celebrated teachers, sages, students travelled from place to place to indulge in philosophical discussions. Thus, the *Bṛ. Up.* has stated that Śvetaketu Āruṇeya went to Pravāhaṇa Jaivali of Pañcāla.[49] The *Chānd. Up.* mentions that Uddālaka Āruṇi along with other sages; Prācīnaśāla etc. went to the king Aśvapati Kaikeya to have the knowledge of the Universal Self.[50] Persons proficient in holding philosophical discussions from different parts of the country used to interact with each other. There is a frequent mention of such gathering, in the court of king Janaka, in the earlier Upaniṣads.[51] Even the teachers wished that students of good calibre should come to them for learning.[52]

Moral and Spiritual Values in the System

The cultivation of a sense of spiritual values and adherence to delegation of duty made the educational system efficient in fulfilling its desired end, namely the realization of the Self. The values of truth, loyalty, reverence and courtesy, discipline and self-sacrifice were impressed on the minds of young disciples.[53] These values were looked upon as the most vital and dynamic instruments capable of transforming the outlooks and behaviour of students.

The system of education considered knowledge as a means and not an end in itself. It is clear from the story of Śvetaketu. When Śvetaketu returned home, having completed his studies, he was taught the Supreme Truth by his father Āruṇi.[54] Even Nārada who had studied all the Veda-s and other branches of learning, approached Sanatkumāra for spiritual knowledge.[55] Thus, learning was a life long process, to obtain the knowledge of the Highest Reality that leads to the Eternal Bliss which was believed to be making oneself free from the cycle of births and deaths.

The Upaniṣadic teachers made a distinction between the knowledge and wisdom. In the *Muṇḍ.Up.*, the study of the Veda-s and its branches is considered to be an inferior type of knowledge (*aparā vidyā*). Higher knowledge is said to be that of the immortal Self (*parā vidyā*).[56] The *Kaṭh.Up.* has stated that the real end of education which is the eternal truth cannot be achieved by mere learning, reciting or listening.[57] As Sarma, J. has opined, the thinking man so acts in the world as to make his body a fit receptacle for immortality, uses his knowledge for attaining immortality and the system of education was meant for securing Bliss, the final beatitude.[58]

Education of Women

As Besant, Annie has put it, the position of women in any civilization shows a stage of evolution. The high standard of women's education in ancient India and the position of wives in ancient Indian families hint at the remarkable progress of ancient Indian civilization which is evident from a large number of educated women mentioned in the Vedic literature.[59] In the Upaniṣ adic age, the pattern of education seems to be mainly philosophical in nature. Though there is no mention of a female student undertaking formal education in a *gurukula*, women adept in philosophy are mentioned. Thus, in the *Bṛ. Up.*, an erudite scholar Gārgī Vācaknavī is seen to be engaged in philosophical debate with the philosopher Yājñavalkya, at the court of Janaka.[60] A dialogue between Yājñavalkya and his wife Maitreyī indicates the earnest quest of Maitreyī to seek immortality.[61] It can be presumed that women were given a status of honour and liberty to mix with people freely and also to engage in debates and philosophical symposiums, and that, the knowledge enhanced their status. The *Bṛ. Up.* records "the parents who wished to have scholarly daughters", should perform some rituals.[62]

However, the later Upaniṣads contain no reference either to education of women or to educated women.

The Doctrine of Karman

The word *Karman* is derived from the root *kṛ.* which means 'to do'. It stands for all actions. *Karman* thus, etymologically means an action, work, deed, activity etc. Accordingly, any action performed is a *karman.* Logically, it means an effect or a consequence arising out of action.

According to Garg, R.K., the doctrine of *karman* is a natural and normal outcome of the inarticulate views of the pre-Upaniṣ adic sages which assume a definite and articulate shape in the Upaniṣads.[63] The sacrificial texts regarded sacrifices to be bestowing various fruits, whereas according to the Upaniṣads, the knowledge of the Brahman or the Ātman is the sole means of release. Both these texts place the doctrine of *karman* on solid foundation by providing the necessary details regarding the destiny of the embodied soul and the means of liberation from the cycle of births and deaths. Thus, the *karman* doctrine and the doctrine of rebirth were intertwined.

According to *karman* doctrine, actions produce twofold effects; tangible and intangible. The latter are carried from one body to another along with the soul by means of the subtle body.

The new body assumed after death is what the individual soul has become eligible for, at the moment of decay of the previous body. The doctrine, thus, means that every action in will, thought, speech and act produces a necessary effect, good or bad. In the words of Eliot Charles, "At the end of a man's life, his character or personality is practically the sum of his acts, and when extraneous circumstances such as worldly position etc. disappear, the soul is left with nothing but these acts and character they have formed, called in Indian language the fruit of life. It is these acts which determine its next dwelling."[64]

In the Upaniṣads, the law of action is fairly and precisely formulated. The *Bṛ. Up.* says that a man becomes good by good actions and bad by bad actions;[65] which means, as we sow, so do we reap. The *Praśna. Up.* says, "Good actions lead to the good world and the bad actions lead to the bad world."[66] The *Śevt. Up.* asserts that, whoever has qualities and is the doer of actions that bring recompense, he is the enjoyer, surely, of the consequences of whatever he had done. Assuming all forms, characterised by the three qualities, treading the three paths, he, the ruler of the breath (*viz.* individual soul) roams about in accordance with his actions.[67] The *Bṛ. Up.* says that when the soul departs, it is followed by knowledge, actions and past experiences. When the body is destroyed and ignorance is removed, the soul fashions a newer and fairer form as of the manes, that of the celestial beings... or of the Gods; to enjoy what he has earned. According to actions performed in this life, one acquires a newer body of a higher or lower being."[68] The *Chānd.Up.* says, "Those whose conduct here is good, will quickly attain good womb (birth) the birth of a Brāhmin, or a Kṣatriya or that of a Vaiśya. But those whose conduct here has been evil, will quickly attain an evil birth; the birth of a dog, that of a hog or of a Cāṇḍala.[69] The character which is, thus, decisive of one's condition in the next life is determined not only by action but also by knowledge. Again, the *Śvet.Up.* asserts that according to the deeds, the embodied Self assumes successively various forms in various conditions.[70] Nothing goes unrewarded. The evil doers also have to accept the fruit of evil. There are many passages in the Upaniṣads which disclose the fate of the evil doers.[71] The Upaniṣads speak of the path of Gods and that of the fathers, that the departed souls follow. The former is the path of light and suggests spiritual elevation and *vice versa*.[72] Both the action and the fruit form an endless chain of cause and effect, the chain of *saṁsāra*. Liberation from the bondage of desire and *karman* can be effected by the right knowledge of the Individual Self which is the same as the Brahman. This is why the Upaniṣads stress the need for the knowledge of the Brahman. The *Bṛ. Up.* says that he who knows Brahman passes beyond all sorrows. He transcends both the thoughts, "Hence, I did wrong." "Hence, I did right."[73] The *Chānd.Up.* states, "As water does not cling to the leaf of lotus, so action does not cling to him who knows Brahman",[74] Moreover, it says that he who knows the Brahman burns all his evil to ashes.[75] The *Śvet.Up.* asserts that knowledge is the only way to break the fetters of *saṁsāra*.[76]

By the cultivation of penance, faith, chastity, knowledge, detachment and equanimity, one can elevate oneself to the region where the law of action stops functioning and from where there is no return to the cycle of births and deaths.[77]

The above observations show that the law of *karman* was a logical scientific principle which governs the cosmos. It involves the law of causation, the law of conservation of energy, the law of action and reaction.

The Karman-s Enjoined in the Later Upaniṣads

The Later Upaniṣads enjoined various *Karman*-s as a part of *upāsanā*. The symbols like sacred ashes *tripuṇḍra,* and *rudrākṣa, gopicandana* are the marks of different sects which were worn by a devotee in honour of a particular deity and a specific sect.

Glorification of Sacred Ashes (*Bhasma*)

The method of preparation of *bhasma* and its importance

constitute a significant topic of discussion in some of the later Upaniṣads. Here, four types of sacred ashes are described, *i.e.* (*i*) *Anukalpa* – the sacred ashes resulting from an Agnihotra sacrifice. (*ii*) *Upakalpa* – the *bhasma* collected in dry form in the forest and then consecrated according to the scriptures. (*iii*) *Upopakalpa* – the *bhasma* prepared from dry cowdung found in the forest. (*iv*) *Akalpa* or *Śatakalpa* – is the *bhasma* obtained from the temple of Śiva.[78] The *Bṛ. Jābāla. Up.* has laid down several injunctions for preparing the sacred ashes. It stated that the cow should be healthy with strong limbs.[79] One desirous of preparing *bhasma* should fast on the fourteenth day of either in the white or the dark half of the month. Next day, getting up early in the morning, he should have a bath, wear holy clothes, awaken the cow and collect her urine in a silver, copper or earthen pot.[80] One should collect the dung without letting it fall on the ground.[81] All these acts are accompanied with different spells mentioned in the Upaniṣad. One should prepare fourteen balls out of this dung and let them dry in the rays of the Sun. Later, placing the dried balls in a pot, one should follow domestic religious rites and enkindle the fire.[82] This ceremony should begin with an utterance of the syllable Oṁ, oblations of sesame, rice, ghee etc. are to be offered while worshipping fire. During this period of three days, one should feed Brāhmins and offer gifts (*dakṣiṇā*). The sacred ashes, thus prepared are then to be mixed with powdered *agaru* or with *Candrakumkuma* or Kaśmirian *uśīra*.[83]

After doing so, they are ready for the application.The *Bṛ. Jābāla.Up.* stated that wearing of sacred ashes and *tripuṇḍra* is allowed for the persons belonging to three classes (*traivarṇika*-s) and the Śūdra-s can use the ashes of the fire enkindled for cooking the food of learned Brāhmins.[84] These details clearly indicate the Varṇa distinctions in general and the wide gap between the *triavarṇika*-s and Śūdra-s in particular. Different *mantra*-s to be uttered while applying the sacred ashes are also prescribed by the Upaniṣad *e.g.* It should be applied to the head while reciting the spell Īśāna, to the mouth with the receitation of the spell *tatpuruṣ a,* to the thighs, with that of the spell *aghora* and so on, to be accompanied by the utterance of the syllable Oṁ.[85] This Upaniṣ ad exalts *bhasma* as the primary existence, the inner Self of all beings which assumes various forms as does the fire when it enters the world.[86] According to this Upaniṣad, *bhasma* has a power even to revive a dead man to life, heavenly gods can regain their lost lustre. *Bhasma* was believed to be destroying evils and bestow wealth. It was considered to be a means with which the knowledge of Hari and Śaṅkara could be secured. It is stated that one who besmears sacred ashes is released and attains oneness with the Brahman.[87]

Tripuṇḍra

Bhasma was the material used for wearing a *tripuṇḍra*. The symbolical significance of the three horizontal lines drawn on the forehead has been variously explained. Thus these three lines were believed to be representing the syllables *A, U, M* of Oṁkāra, or the three fires *viz.*, Gārhapatya, Dakṣiṇāgni and Āhavanīya. Maheśvara, Sadāśiva, and Mahādeva were considered to be the presiding deities of these lines. The *Vāsudevopaniṣad* has identified this symbol of the three vertical lines with trinity of Gods, the three *vyāhṛti*-s, the three metres, the three durations of time, conditions of the soul etc.[88]

Rudrākṣa Beads

Like the sacred ashes, the Śaiva sect considered *rudrākṣa*-s to be equally important. The Upaniṣads described beads of four colours, white, red, yellow and black to be used by Brāhmins, Kṣatriya-s, Vaiśyas and Śūdras respectively.[89] The *R. Jābāla. Up.* reflects *Varṇu* distinctions as it recommends the different coloured *rudrākṣa*-s for persons belonging to different *varṇa*-s. According to this Upaniṣad, the different facets of *rudrākṣa*-s represent different gods and the act of wearing them naturally leads to different results. Thus, the *rudrākṣa*-s with one facet verily represent the Absolute and one who wears it gains control over his senses and is merged into the Absolute. Those with two facets represent the god Ardhanārīnaṭeśvara etc.[90]

One who wears them pleases the gods and secures wealth, health, happiness, knowledge and intellect. A person wearing them with devotion is instantly freed from all sins. The *rudrākṣa*-s are to be worn by a devotee on all the parts of the body.

According to a mythological account presented in the Upaniṣad, the *rudrākṣa*-s are the tears that trickled down from the eyes of Kālāgnirudra as he opened his eyes after performing penance for several years, in order to kill the demon Tripura.[91]

The Upaniṣads expected people to perform *karman*-s such as preparing the sacred ashes, besmearing the sacred ashes, preparing and cleaning a rosary of *rudrākṣa*-s etc. These acts were enjoined with the accompaniment of appropriate *mantra*-s.

(*i*) ***Bhasma Mantra-s :*** The *mantra*-s to be uttered while applying *bhasma* to the various limbs of the body are given in detail in the *Bṛ. Jābāla. Up.* The dative form of the adjectives of Śiva or Rudra are to be uttered with the word *namaḥ*. Thus, *e.g.* while applying *bhasma* on the forehead, obesiance should be paid to Tryambaka.[92] Similarly, the Upaniṣad has stated *mantra*-s to be uttered while wearing a *tripuṇḍra,* which when worn according to the rites and along with the *mantra*-s give desired fruit to a devotee.[93]

(*ii*) ***Rudrākṣa Mantra-s :*** The *Akṣamālikā.Up.* has enjoined the utterance of *mantra*-s, based on the syllables '*a*' to '*kṣa*' while preparing and cleansing the rosary of *rudrākṣa* beads.[94] Śiva is glorified through these *mantra*-s. A great importance was attached to the utterance of *mantra*-s when the Vedic sacrifices were performed. The authors of the later Upaniṣads followed the same practice and enjoined *mantra*-s for every activity probably for the purpose of remembering God, to control the wandering mind, to curb evil thoughts and to strengthen belief and faith.

The later Upaniṣads enjoined the *karman*-s like sixteenfold ritual (*ṣoḍaśopacāra pūjā*) and the act of muttering (*japa*). They have been discussed earlier to be performed as different parts of *upāsanā*.

The Act of Sipping Water (*Ācamanavidhi*)

The method of sipping water at the time of religious performances is illustrated in the *Ācamanopaniṣad*. According to the Upaniṣad, should begin the act of sipping water after having washed hands and feet and the tuft tied up in a knot. While performing this act, one is expected to face the eastern or northern direction. Further, it is said that five holy waters (*pañcatīrthāni*) exist in the right hand of a Brāhmin. At the tip of the little finger exists, Devatīrtha, at its root the Ārṣikātīrtha etc.[95] The *Śivopaniṣ ad* mentions the places of these *tīrtha*-s differently.[96] One is asked to sip the water thrice, for it pleases the Veda-s. The act of sipping water is, thus, expected to please all the Gods. Sacred importance is attached to this simple act of *ācamana*. Similarly, the *Śivopaniṣ ad* has glorified the eightfold bath (*aṣṭavidhāsnāna*) and the merit obtained thereby. Thus, the Āgneya bath destroys poverty and evil, this divine bath brings about growth in wealth, success and penance.[97] The Vāruṇa bath can be performed by everyone. It makes one hale and hearty.[98] Other types of bath mentioned in the Upaniṣad are Manatra, Vāyavya, Aindra, Mānasa, Śānta and Jñāna.[99] The Jñānasnāna is said to be performed by an ascetic in the clean water of knowledge. The *Śivopaniṣad* says that one who has bathed in pure water in the form of knowledge, is always pure.[100] Water, *manatra*, compassion, charity, truth, control over the senses, knowledge and purity of soul are the eightfold means of purity according to the Upaniṣad.[101]

Śrāddhakarma : *Śrāddha*-s as acts of homage and as means of satisfying the departed ancestors had formed a significant part of the *Smārta* religion.[102] The authors of the Purāṇa-s have continued the same tradition.[103] It has been already stated that the later Upaniṣads and the Purāṇa-s belong to the same time. For the same reason, it was but natural if some of the later Upaniṣads reflect the same belief system.

The references to *Śrāddhakarma-s* are conspicuous by their absence in the earlier Upaniṣads. However, the later *Itihāsa. Up.* and the *Piṇḍ. Up.* stressed their significance. *The Itihāsa. Up.* expected people to perform *śrāddha* in honour of ancestors stating that the ancestors are immensly satisfied thereby.[104] According to this Upaniṣad, a person who does not perform a *śrāddha* correctly, cannot tread *devayāna* path, which is regarded as an ideal one. On the contrary, he falls down from the heaven.[105] The Upaniṣad has laid down various injunctions and prohibitions regarding the performance of this ceremony. According to the Upaniṣad, sixteen *śrāddha*-s are not accepted by the *pitṛ*-s from one who feeds the Brāhmins that are not learned.[106] If the husband of a *vṛṣalī* performs a *śrāddha*, the manes do not accept it and the performer does not reach the heaven.[107] The later Upaniṣads have also emphasized the importance of giving away lumps of rice to the manes. Emphasizing the importance of *piṇḍadāna*, the *Piṇḍ. Up.* stated that every *piṇḍa* would lead to the association of an individual with a (new) body.[108] Ten *piṇḍa*-s offered successively one after the other would lead to the formation of new bodies of the departed ones.[109] Following the tradition of the works on *Dharmaśāstra*, the *Purāṇa-s* have laid down three varieties of *śrāddha viz. nitya, naimittika* and *kāmya.*[110] However, the later Upaniṣads did not deal with such details.

The Literary Aspect of the Upaniṣads

Language is a medium with which feelings, thoughts etc. are expressed. Some Upaniṣads such as the *Bṛ. Up.* the *Chānd. Up.*, the *Sūryopaniṣad* are composed in prose, while others like the *Īśa.Up.*, the *Śivopaniṣad* etc. are in versical form. Some are also composed in mixed form. At times, to break the monotony of prose and to infuse them with vivacity and beauty, verses are inserted, *e.g.* the *Sūrya. Tā. Up.*, and some metrical Upaniṣads contain prose commentary *viz.* the *Vanadurgopaniṣad.*

Language is usually considered to be one of the criteria, with which the period of the Upaniṣads can be examined. Many scholars hold that the language of the earlier Upaniṣads seems to be similar to that of the sacrificial texts (*Brāhmaṇa*-s). Thus, about the nature of the prose of the earlier Upaniṣads, Oldenberg stated, "It is not a lively prose of a real spoken language with its alterations of light and shadow, with its spontaneity and arbitrariness, moved by the impulse of the moment. It is rather a solemnly measured prose of the Brāhmaṇa texts from which the Upaniṣads grew."[111] Gajendragadkar, K.V. has stated that, "the language of the later Upaniṣads is mostly simple but sometimes ornate. Further, he states that the Upaniṣadic authors are seen to be using simple language, as their principal aim was to preach the doctrines of Vedānta."[112]

However, it is observed that it is difficult to draw a line of demarcation between the earlier and the later Upaniṣads on the basis of the criteria of simplicity and complexity or ornateness as also spontaenity and arbitrariness. Thus, for *e.g.* the earlier Upaniṣ ads contain quite a few verses while reading which one feels that to read is to understand.[113] At the same time, these Upaniṣads contain verses or sentences characterised by complexity.[114]

Similar examples are found even in the later Upaniṣads.[115] This shows that the Upaniṣadic authors could mould the language in accordance with the contents. Moreover, it is well-known that even though the language of some portions of the earlier Upaniṣads appears to be simple, it expresses profound philosophical thoughts which can only be comprehended with effort.[116] Sometimes, though the sentence is complex especially because of long compounds, the thought that it expresses is very simple. One can immediately know that the Upaniṣad is laying down a specific rite of worship.[117]

Dialogue Form

"The dialogue emerges particularly strongly from among the elements which constitutes the Upaniṣads.[118] This method of dialogue is used effectively in the earlier Upaniṣads to impart knowledge. Brief conversations between those experienced in sacrifice and those having ritualistic problems occur in the Brāhmaṇa texts. Dialogue form in the Upaniṣads seems to have ensued from it."

The dialogues here appear more often and are employed to convey the Upaniṣadic philosophy. There are dialogues between the exalted knowers and the ardent aspirants. These dialogues reflect a great revolution in the intellectual life of ancient India and show how speculations regarding the doctrine of Brahman developed.

There is a dialogue between husband Yājñavalkya, who decided to renounce the world and Maitreyī, his wife who is shown to be scorning material possessions and was eager to know about the immortality. "You are truly dear to me... I shall explain it to you now" says Yājñavalkya and there begin those profound discourses of Yājñavalkya.[119]

In another instance, the son having completed his studies returned home, was boasting of his knowledge. Unfortunately, however, he did not have that precious knowledge by which the unheard becomes heard, the unknown which was '*Tat*' becomes known and his father talks to him about '*Sat*' which represented the Highest Reality, that was identical with the individual Self.[120]

There are conversations between the generous and pious king of Videha, *i.e.* Janaka and Yājñavalkya who is the wisest of the wise.[121] Sometimes, the preacher is a Kṣatriya king and the aspirant a Brāhmin exemplified by a dialogue between Ajātaśatru and Gārgya.[122] Elsewhere, it is seen that several intelligent men come together. They approach a reputed expert to have the Highest knowledge. However, the teacher himself was not sure about his own knowledge. Hence, they all approached a king. Ultimately, through a dialogue with him they could reach their goal.[123] Again, in another section of the *Chānd. Up.* (IV. 4-8), animals are seen to be revealing the secret. A bull talks to a pupil who was faithfully protecting the herds of his teacher. He imparts to him knowledge which constituted only a quarter of the Brahman (*pāda*). Thereafter, the fire, the swan, the bird Madgu impart knowledge of the Brahman to the pupil. It seems to be an interesting adaptation of a fable.

Occasionally, a dialogue is converted into a dispute as *e.g.* at the symposium in the court of the king Janaka. (*Bṛ. Up.*, III 9.1.26). The superiority of the philosopher Yājñavalkya was not implicitly acknowledged by Śākalya, and he was defeated tragically.

The authors of the later Upaniṣads generally present their doctrines in the following manner. Sometimes, in the beginning, a question is asked by some sage or a God about the topic to be discussed. The entire remaining part of the Upaniṣad is the reply given to that question *e.g.* the *Annapūrṇopaniṣad.* At times, the principles are taught directly in the form of a narration on certain topic. *e.g.* the *Turīyātīta Up.* Sometimes again, an account, *viz.* creation is presented in the beginning and then it is explained *e.g.* the *Bṛ. Jābāla. Up.*, the *Caturvedopaniṣad.*

Similies and Illustrations

The Upaniṣadic authors knew very well how the appropriate similies and illustrations selected from the things and beings of wordly life could simplify the most profound incomprehensible philosophical thought. Thus, it is stated, "As a mass of salt is salt through and through, even so, verily this Self is knowledge through and through – it rises from these elements and vanishes again in them."[124] This simile is used to show the real nature of the Self which is just knowledge. "As a large fish moves along both banks of river, both the nearer and the farther, so also Person moves along both these states, the dreaming one and the waking one."[125] This simile denotes the states of consciousness of the Self. A beautiful simile describes the emergence of all existence and knowledge from the Supreme Being. "As when a lute is played, one is not able to grasp the external sound but by grasping the lute, or the player of the lute, the sound is grasped."[126] This simile is used to show that when one knows Him, everything becomes known.

Illustration

The author of the *Chānd.Up.* has cited the example of rivers flowing from eastern to western direction and again from the western to the eastern one, which ultimately merge into an ocean and losing their individual identity become an ocean, and has very appropriately and ably indicated that from the highest point of view, none has his or her own separate identity. (*Chānd. Up.* VI. 10.1).

The later Upaniṣads also abound in similies, *e.g.* to describe the state of a *Yogin* a simile of fire is used. The ascetic whose mind is free from desires realizes the Truth and obtains peace of mind, "like the fire without fuel, on its own accord gets extinguished."[127]

Along with the similies, the later Upaniṣads make use of figures of speech such as alliteration (*anuprāsa*),[128] illustra-tion (*nidarśana*),[129] metaphor (*rūpaka*),[130] exemplification (*dṛṣṭānta*)[131] etc.

While propounding their doctrine, the authors of the earlier Upaniṣads occasionally furnish etymological meanings of cetain words. Thus, '*svapiti*' means *svamāpito bhavati, i.e.* becomes one with himself, *pipāsati* means, "that is how heat dries up what is drunk."[132] The *Bṛ. Up.* explained the meaning of the word 'Puruṣ a' as the one inhabiting the citadel of the body.[133] In the *Māṇḍ. Up.*, the significance of the syllables *A.U.M.* is mentioned.[134] Even the authors of the later Upaniṣads have attempted some interesting explanations and etymologies of words. Thus, the meaning of the words like Ātman, Viṣṇu, Durgā, *Vāraṇā,* and *Vṛṣ aḷī*, etc. is explained in the Upaniṣads.[135]

Most of the later Upaniṣads end with a verse or a sentence which serves as an *arthavāda* or mention the fruit which may be obtained through the study or recitation of the Upaniṣad.

As Raman, N.S.S. has put it "No one but a foolish can subject the poetry of the Upaniṣads to fruitless analytical scrutiny."[136] One may further say that, it may not be appropriate to scrutinize the literary attributes of the Upaniṣadic language or to contemplate upon their contribution to Sanskrit literature, for the analytical approach cannot simply appreciate the power of various types of philosophical expressions in the ancient Indian thought. One may simply say that, it was the language of the heart meant to be understood by the heart.

Mystical Experiences

Through the long process of purification, contemplation, that is the spiritual journey, the aspirant of the Brahman may encounter some mysterious experiences. One may experience colour, sound, light, form etc. These may be called as the harbingers of the Self-realization. The *Śvet. Up.* tells us that, as a mirror, cleansed of its impurities becomes lustrous and is capable of reflecting lustrous images, so does the embodied one see Himself and reach the goal of his endeavour. And as with the help of a lamp one is able to see an object, similarly by the help of the Individual Self, he sees the lustrous Universal Self – the Unborn, the Highest Reality, the One beyond all existences.[137] "The meaning implied with the above quotation of the *Śvet. Up.* is brought out clearly in the teaching of Maitrī who imparted to his disciple, the highest secret of the Upaniṣads. He said, that at the peak of spiritual experience, the seeker sees his own form in a flood of Supreme light arising from within, which indeed constitutes the realization of the immortal and fearless Ātman."[138]

Mystics speak of vision and audition. On the path of spirituality, one may obtain clairvoyance and clairaudience. Wakeful and alert, with the eyes of the spirit and with the inward ears one may perceive the visions according to the will of God. Though God transcends all forms, He may still use them and convey His presence through them. The images are sent to comfort and instruct us. Many of these visions have a symbolic character. As pointed out by Radhakrishnan, S., they represent truths of the spiritual life.[139]

Out of the above said types of experiences recorded in the earlier Upaniṣads, most of them refer to the vision of light, form and colour. There are only a few references to the experience of audition, and the seers do not give their reasons, and also their exact nature is not explained.

Experiences of Light, Form, Colour

The *Muṇḍ.Up*, tells us that, "on a golden sheath, (vessel disc.) is the spotless and immaculate Brahman, which is the light of all lights which the seeker of the Brahman experiences."[140] The *Chānd. Up.* records that, "after having crossed the bridge of phenomenal existence, even though a man may be blind, he ceases to be blind, the very night becomes like a day because before the vision of the seeker the world is suddenly and once for all illumined."[141] Another passage from the same Upaniṣad says that, "when there is neither any Sun-rise nor Sun-set, there is an eternal day before the aspiring soul."[142] This idea is reflected in the *Śvet. Up.* where it is said that, "when there is neither day nor night, when there is neither Being nor non-Being, before the seeker, God alone is."[143] This statement explains the transcendence of God beyond both night and day, beyond both Being and non-Being. It also implies the inclusion of these in the divine omnipresence. In the second chapter of the Upaniṣad, there is a reference to different forms and lights that are experienced by an aspirant (*yogin*) while treading the path of spirituality. He experiences forms such as those of mist and smoke, the sun, the fire and the wind, the fire-fly and the lightning, the crystal and the moon.[144] The *Bṛ. Up.* points out the glory of the seeeker as, – "before the vision of the aspirant appear forms such as a red coloured beetle, a flame of fire, a lotus flower and a sudden flash of lightning."[145]

Experiences of Sound

The *Bṛ. Up.* and the *Mai.Up.* have mentioned that, one experiences certain sounds within himself; which are attributed by the authors of those Upaniṣads to the process of digestion and assimilation. They have stated that, by shutting the ears, a man is able to hear the sounds which are due to the process of digestion and at the time of death, he is not able to hear those sounds.[146] The *Chānd. Up.* says, "merely by shutting the ears, and by being able to hear the sounds such as roaring of an ox, or a peal of thunder or the crackling of fire, the indication of presence of Reality within us can be obtained."[147] But these experiences of primitive mind sound absurd today for one cannot say that the sound of digestion is a 'mystic' sound. A mystic sound (*anāhatanāda*) can be heard with the ears open and even a deaf man is able to hear the sound. The later Upaniṣads go a step further and explain the types of *anāhatanāda*, which are the landmarks on the way to the Brahman.

The later Upaniṣads profusely describe the experience of the mystical light and sound on one's way of spiritual journey. The purpose behind this may be to indicate the landmarks on the way and to develop the indulgence of the aspirant in his own study.

Experiences of Vision in the Later Upaniṣads

An experience of a very high order is exhibited in the *Maṇḍala. Brā. Up.* It describes in detail, the mystical lights. While meditating, a Yogin concentrates his mind on God, in the centre of the eye-brows, a mountain of light is seen; which is called as Tāraka Brahman.[148] When the ears are closed with the tips of fingers, a hissing noise is heard, and when the mind gets engrossed in that one sees blue light in the middle of the eyes and also in the heart.[149] In the first stage of spiritual experience, a man sees various lustrous things, crystal, stars, smoke, fire-flies, lamps, luminous gold, lights of various colours which the precious jewels emit. One who practises Yoga, a star appears, before him, he sees a mirror made of diamonds, then a disc of the full moon, then a disc of jewels, then the orb of the mid-day Sun and finally a sphere of fire-flames,[150] above it an orb of the Sun and in its centre, the disc of the moon full of nectar. The full orb of the light of the Brahman is seen in the middle of the lunar disc which is dazzling, like a flash of lightning.[151] When a Yogin concentrates his gaze on the tip of his nose, and meditates on the Tāraka-Brahman, he sees a sky filled with blue light at a distance of four fingers, a sky with dark green colour at a distance of six fingers, of a blood red colour at a distance of eight, and the sky of brilliant yellow, and ordinary yellow are seen at a distance of ten and twelve fingers respectively.[152] The Yogin sees the rays of variegated light when he lifts up his gaze from the tip of his nose, to look at the sky and his eyes become steady. When he sees a flame of light above his head covering a distance of twelve *aṅgula*-s,[153] he becomes immortal. The Upaniṣad says that the practitioner sees various colours of radiant morning sky, the light of the sun, the mellow light of the moon and curling flames of fire and he enjoys beholding the sky without all these lights.[154] Further study reveals the sky as changeless and qualityless. This is preceded by the light of shining stars and the sky assumes the form of infinite expanse, blazing with the world destroying fire. Then it assumes the form of *sūryākāśa,* bright as billions of Suns put together. The Yogin's mind is absorbed (*laya*) in these lights during his spiritual practices.[155]

Experiences of Audition in the Later Upaniṣads

Various types of mystical sounds are described in the Yogopaniṣads. It is known as *anāhatanāda*. *Anāhata* means 'unbeaten', *i.e.* the sound which exists without beating anything, also, it does not proceed from speech. This sound is described as supreme and imperishable.[156] *Anāhatanāda* is the Chief means of atonement. The *Haṁsopaniṣad* mentions ten kinds of sounds that a Yogin hears. These are initially *ciṇi* sound, then *ciñciṇi* sound, the sound of a bell, that of conch, that of stringed musical instruments, that of a pair of tabors, sweet notes of flute and drums, the sound of *mṛdaṅga* and of the rumbling of clouds thereafter.[157] According to this Upaniṣad, these sounds bring about various physiological effects. When the sound *ciṇi* is heard, a thrilling sensation passes through the body of the hearer. When the second is heard, one feels as if one's own limbs are being torn away from the body. Engrossed in hearing the third sound, one perspires. When the fourth sound is heard, one experiences tremor in one's own head. There is a feeling of dropping down of the palate at hearing the fifth. On hearing the fifth sound one feels that liquid is flowing from the palate of the mouth. On hearing the sixth one, one gets the pleasure of drinking ambrosia. He acquires the knowledge of secret things by hearing the seventh, the Supreme Speech by the eighth. One is endowed with pure divine vision and invisible subtle body when the ninth sound is heard. Finally, one becomes the Brahman incarnate by hearing the tenth sound.[158] One transcends the normal consciousness by hearing the mystic sounds. *Yoganāda* leads the aspirant to the realization of the Ātman. The *Dhyānabindū. Up.* tells us that the *Yoganāda* resembles the notes of a peacock and when it is heard, one sees the Ātman in the ventricle of his brain, shining like the Sun and his mind is united with the Self.[159] The *Nādabindū. Up.* describes the sounds that are heard by a Yogin; sitting in the *siddhāsana* posture, maintaining *vaiṣṇavīmudrā*, with the eyes wide open and all the while contemplating. The different types of sounds that are heard are the sound of the ocean, that of the thundering of clouds, that of the spring (stream), that of *kiṅkiṇī*, that of *vīṇā* then that of buzzing of bees etc.[160] The Upaniṣad, however, states that the Brahman is beyond the mystical sound and is of the nature of Supreme Silence. The mind exists as long as the sound is heard, but when it merges into the sound, the sound is not heard. The function of the mind, thus is at rest and finally the mind merges into the supreme state of Silence.[161]

The Concept of Deliverance

Various means of knowledge are valid so long as the final illumination does not occur. They are not an end, but lead to immortality (*amṛtatva*). This attainment is generally known by the term *mokṣa* which is the last and the highest of the fourfold aims of life (*dharma, artha, kāma*, and *mokṣa*). The *Ṛv.* speaks of the abode of Yama which is called the abode of the Gods (*Ṛv.* X. 135.7). The Ṛgvedic people aspired to reach this abode. The sacrificial texts (*Brāhmaṇa*-s) stressed the importance of various rituals with an assurance that those who perform them would reach the heavenly world and get an opportunity of being in the company of gods. (*Śat. Brā.* II. 6.4.8, VI. 1.2.3). The concept of deliverance is unique in itself. The stay in the heaven is temporary. When the merits get exhausted, one is forced to come back to the mortal world. Deliverance is permanent union with the Highest Reality. The fact that the individual consciousness has for its essential reality the Universal Self, implies the possibility that every human being can lift the veil of separateness from other things and begin to know his true nature.

The Upaniṣads conceive of *mokṣa* as the knowledge of the Ātman or the Brahman which leads to the highest Bliss. According to the earlier Upaniṣads, everything in this world is the manifestation of the Brahman, is same as the Brahman.[162] It is beginningless (*aja, anādi*) (*Kaṭh. Up.* I. 3.15) and endless (*ananta*) (*Śvet. Up.* I. 1.9). It creates and maintains the world, which gets dissolved in it, which merges into it. (*Ibid.*, I. 1.7). It is omniscient, omnipresent and omnipotent. (*Ibid.*, VI. 8, 11). Like the Brahman, Individual Self (Ātman) also is without a beginning, endless and indestructible. It is the same as the Brahman. There is complete identity between the Ātman and the Brahman.[163] The Brahman is unmanifest (*avyākṛta*), imperceptible.[164] The knowledge of the Brahman frees one from the cycle of births and deaths. It enables one to merge into Brahman and achieve salvation.[165] One should know the basic difference between the limited world and the unlimited Brahman. "In an unlimited state, one does not see any other thing, hear any other thing (besides Oneself). If however, one sees, hears any other thing other than Oneself that state is a limited state."[166] One has to know that beings are within us and one is within beings.[167] Thus, the knowledge of unity in diversity (*sarvātmaikyajñāna*) leads to immortality.

Mokṣa literally means release, which necessarily presupposes a state of bondage. There are certain general characteristics of the state of liberation. (*i*) It is conceived as freedom from the subjection of time. As birth and death are the marks of time, *mokṣa* is liberation from births and death. It is the fourth state of consciousness (*turīya*) which is the same as Parama Brahma (*Bh. G.* VIII. 3.21) (*ii*) *Mokṣa* is freedom from the subjection to the law of *karman*. The deeds good or evil, of the liberated cease to have any effect on him says the *Bṛ. Up.*[169] "As a horse shakes its mane, the liberated soul shakes off his sins; as the moon comes out fully after an eclipse from Rāhu, so does the liberated individual frees him from mortal bondage."[170] His works burn themselves like a reed stalk in the fire.[171] As water does not cling to a lotus leaf, works do not cling to him.[172] Thus, the sentences like these prove that liberation transcends all *karman*-s. (*iii*) *Mokṣa* is the destruction of ignorance, *i.e.* this bondage constitutes the absence of awareness of true nature of the Self; and release is gaining back that awareness. Śaṅkara pointed out that *mokṣa* is neither a thing to be generated (*utpādya*), nor something to be changed (*vikārya*), nor a thing which is acquired (*āpya*) and modified (*saṁskārya*).[173] The *Bṛ. Up.* stated that this Ātman is dearer than one's own son, dearer than everything else and it is supremely dear because it is so close to the heart.[174] Hence, according to the Upaniṣads, emancipation is not to be regarded as becoming something which previously had no existence. But it is the perception of that which existed from eternity, though concealed from us due to ignorance.

When the knowledge of the Ātman dawns upon, attainment comes all at once, total and complete and not by stages and degrees. There is no intermediate state between knowing and not knowing.

Gradual Release (*Kramamukti*)

When the release is only partial or temporary, the individual soul descends again into earthly life. It is not possible for everyone to remove the ignorance all at once and hence a long period of preparation and contemplation is found necessary to make one gradually fit to lift the barrier of ignorance. It is not possible for some people to complete the whole process within the span of one life. Some may stop with the preparation, others may with a part of contemplation and so on. Hence, after death, one attains the status equal to one's own spiritual moral achievements in life. (*Bṛ. Up.* IV. 4.2-4). The Upaniṣads speak of two paths by which the soul proceeds after death; which have been discussed earlier. (*ibid.,* pp. 83ff). As against the way of light, smoky way is not the way of release but a subsequent return.

The Conception of Brahmaloka in the Earlier Upaniṣads

In the *Kaṭh. Up.*, the treasure house (*śevadhi*) referred to by Yama, is impermanent.[175] Yama called this *śevadhi* as impermanent as he spoke about it after teaching the science of sacrifice to Naciketas. It is evident that it is won through the worship of fire and hence its impermenance becomes inevitable. This *śevadhi* referred to by Yama indicates Brahmaloka.[176] The *Muṇḍ. Up.* states that the radiant offerings of the sacrificer in the form of the rays of the Sun invite him with sweet words and lead him to that world saying "this is your holy world of Brahmā won through good deeds."[177] Finally, the Upaniṣad speaks of the way of the enlightened and there it does not speak of Brahmaloka but simply states that they depart by the door of the Sun where exists the immortal Puruṣa.[178] Thus, the *Muṇḍ. Up.* does not consider it as the sphere of gradual liberation. But the Brahmaloka which is referred to in connection of *Daharavidyā* in the *Chānd. Up.* appears to be almost identical with the Brahman itself.[179] Śaṅkara explained the term as 'Brahman itself is the sphere'.[180]

However, the conception of Brahmaloka reflected in the Upaniṣads is vague. In the *Kaṭh. Up.* (I.2.10[a]), Brahmaloka denotes the world of Brahmā, while in the *Chānd.Up.* (VIII. 5.4), it stands for the Brahman.

Concept of Release in the Later Upaniṣads

There are four aspects of release distinguished by the later Upaniṣads. (*i*) Intimacy with the Divine (*sāmīpya*) (*ii*) Similarity of the nature with the Divine, reflecting his glory (*sārūpya*). (*iii*) Co-existence with the Divine, in the same world (*sālokya*). (*iv*) Communion with the Divine (*sāyujya*).

In the *Muktikopaniṣad*, Rāma himself said, "He who worships me is entitled to obtain the fourfold release."[181] Thus, one who mutters his name attains *sālokyamukti*, even a man who has obtained instruction if dies in a holy place like Kāśī attains *sālokya*.[182] One who worships Me and perceives Me as the Ātman of all, attains *sāmīpya* type of release.[183]

He, who has obtained instruction, shaking off his sins, attains to *sārūpya* type of release.[184] When one, who is always associated with Me, that itself is *sāyujya* type of release, pure and of the form of the Bliss of the Brahman.[185]

The *Akṣupaniṣad* described seven stages serving as a ladder enabling a man to rise up from the material life through moral virtues to a mystical union with God-head.[186] The idea of seven stages leading to release is echoed in the *Annapūrṇā. Up.*[187] The *Varāha. Up.* describes these stages in brief as follows : entertaining good desires is the first stage, invest-igating the second one, functioning with refined mind is the third, attainment of the *sattva* is the fourth one, detachment is the fifth, that of right conception is the sixth and the seventh one is the attainment of *turīya* state.[188]

The later sectarian Upaniṣads describe different worlds such as the world of Viṣṇu (*vaikuṇṭha*), the world of *Kṛṣṇa* (*Goloka*), that of Śiva etc. These worlds and their character-istics are described in detail by these Upaniṣads which have been referred to earlier (*Ibid.,* pp. 230 ff) Thus, the later sectarian Upaniṣads have mentioned the attainment of respective worlds as the rewards to be secured by the aspirants, and to induce the masses to follow the easier path thereby.

The *Nirālamba.Up.* defines *mukti* as breaking off the ties of affection by discriminating between eternal and non-eternal things.[189] According to *Bṛ. Jābāla. Up.* one should heat one's own body in the fire of Śiva and then may cool it down by resorting to the path of Yoga.[190] Release is attained thereby. The *Tejobindū. Up.* has described two types of *mukta*-s *viz. jīvanmukta* and *videhamukta*.[191] *Jivanmukti* is deliverance during life. *Videha-mukti* is deliverance after death, when out of bodily form.[192]

Life Eternal (*Jīvanmukti*)

The end of all endeavour is the realization of the Self. At many places, the Upaniṣads discuss the effects produced by Self realization. Thus, "He becomes fearless" says the *Tait. Up.* because he has obtained a support in that invisible, indefinable, fearless, supportless support of all. To the free spirits, life has no terrors, for he has attained Oneness.[193] The *Īśa.Up.* stated that for a man to whom all these beings have become Ātman, what grief what infatuation can there be when he has seen the unity in all things.[194] "All his desires are satisfied when he has fulfilled the highest desire, the realization of the Self." says the *Muṇḍ. Up.*[195] There is no feeling of repentance for him because he never tortures himself thinking, why he did not do any good actions or he did only evil ones. He has known the nature of Reality and has thus gone beyond dualities.[195] The *Tait. Up.* presents a classic description of the limitless Bliss experienced by one after his communion with the Highest.[197] Having realized the Ātman, they find eternal happiness everywhere, stated the *Śvet. Up.*[198]

Thus, *jīvanmukta* is one who has achieved the Final Beautitude but is still an embodied one. He is fearless, desireless, without any grief and is endowed with bliss and happiness.

Contemplation of the Enlightened Soul

The Upaniṣads have presented a few mystic monologues that contain the essence of the ecstasy of spiritual experience. They really are the contemplations of the enlightened soul. Vāmadeva of the *Bṛ. Up.* has said, "The Brahman is the first and the foremost. I am the Brahman, from That everything proceeded. The one among the Gods or the mortals or the sages whoever comes to Self consciousness becomes verily the All. It was me, who was Manu and the Sun too."[199] Similarly. Triśaṅku who knew the Brahman said, "I am the mover of the tree, my fame is like a peak of mountain. The exalted one making me pure, as the Sun, I am the Immortal one. I am a shining treasure, wise, immortal, indestructible.[200] Again, in the same Upaniṣad the enlightened one sings the song of joy. When for him the manifold diveristy of life is attuned to a single harmony. He said, "I am food..... I am the food eater..... I am the first born of the world order, earlier than gods, in the centre of immortality .... I am brilliant (like the Sun)."[201]

The later Upaniṣads are replete with such words of rapture. The contemplation of the enlightened soul is as follows : "I am neither this body, nor the Prāṇa-s, I am not affected by hunger and thirst. I am beyound the states of waking, dream and deep sleep. Neither have I birth, nor death. I am not the *citta*, hence not affected by grief and infatuation, I neither have bondage, nor release. I am without decay, qualityless, taintless and beyond the time. I have no beginning and no end. I am omniscient, omnipotent and omnipresent. I am the creator, sustainer and dissipator of all. I am the Brahman, the Consciousness, the Highest. I take enjoyment in my own Ātman, seeing him alone; having seated on the throne of the Ātman, I think of the Ātaman and nothing else."[202]

Having discussed some of the miscellaneous topics in the Upaniṣads, this comparative study may now be concluded in the next chapter.

REFERENCES

1. Parson Tolcott q. by Bakre, A.B.

   Glimpses of Social Religious Structure in the Mahābhārata, Purāṇa, Vol. XIII no. 2, July 2000, p. 107.

2. *Bṛ. Up.* I. 4.11[cd]

   तस्मात् क्षत्रात्परं नास्ति तस्माद् ब्राह्मण: क्षत्रियमधस्तादुपास्ते राजसूये क्षत्र एव तद्यशो दधाति सैषा क्षत्रस्य योनिर्यद्ब्रह्म। तस्माद्यद्यपि राजा परमतां गच्छति ब्रह्मैवान्तत उपनिश्रयति... ।

3. *Ibid.*, VI. 2.5-7

4. *Chānd. Up.* V. 3.7

   ...यथेयं न प्राक् त्वत्त: पुरा विद्या ब्राह्मणान्गच्छति तस्मादु सर्वेषु लोकेषु क्षत्रस्यैव प्रशासनमभूदिति ...।

5. *Kau. Up.*, I. 1[cd].

स ह समित्पाणिश्चित्रं गार्ग्यायणिं प्रतिचक्रम उपायानीति।
तं होवाच ब्रह्मार्घोऽसि गौतम यो न मानमुपागा एहि व्येव त्वा ज्ञपयिष्यामीति।

6. *Br. Up.*, IV. 2.4[b].

...याज्ञवल्क्य यो नो भगवन्नभयं वेदयसे नमस्तेऽस्त्विमे विदेहा अयमहमस्मि॥

7. *Mai. Up.*, I. 1.1-7.
8. Deussen, P., *Encyclopaedia of Religion and Ethics.* Vol. II. ed. by Hastings, James, New York, 1958., pp. 128, 129.
9. Deussen, P., *The Philosophy of the Upaniṣads,* New York, 1966., p. 367.
10. For more details see : Bakre, A.B., *op. cit.*, p. 111.
11. *Chānd. Up.*, IV. 10.1.

उपकोसलो ह वै कामलायन: सत्यकामे जाबाले ब्रह्मचर्यमुवास। तस्य ह द्वादशवर्षाण्यग्नीन्परिचचार स ह स्माऽन्यानन्तेवासिन: समावर्तयँ स्तँ ह स्मैव न समावर्तयति।

12. *Ibid.* IV. 4.5

...स ह वर्षगणं प्रोवास...।

13. *Ibid.* VI. 1.2[a]

...स ह द्वादशवर्षं उपेत्य चतुर्विंशतिवर्ष: सर्वान्वेदानधीत्य...।

14. *Br. Up.* VI. 2.7
15. *Chānd. Up.* IV. 4.5[a]

...समिधँ सोम्य आहर...।

Ibid., V. 11.7.

... ते ह समित्पाणय: पूर्वाह्णे प्रतिचक्रमिरे तान्हानुपनीयैवैतदुवाच।

also, *Muṇḍ. Up.* I. 1.12.

also, *Praśna. Up.* I. 1. etc.

16. *Chānd. Up.* IV. 10.1.
17. *Ibid.*, IV, 13.1-2
18. *Ibid.*, IV, 5, 6, 7.
19. *Ibid.*, V, 3.1

श्वेतकेतुर्हारुणेय: पञ्चालानाँ समितिमेयाय तँ ह प्रवाहणो जैवलिरुवाच कुमारानु त्वाऽशिषत्पितेत्यनु हि भगव इति॥

also, *Bṛ. Up.* VI. 2.1., *Kau. Up.* I.1

20. *Chānd. Up.* II. 23.1[b].

प्रथमस्तप एव द्वितीयो ब्रह्मचार्याचार्यकुलवासी तृतीयोऽत्यन्तमात्मानमाचार्य-कुलेऽवसादयन्सर्व एते पुण्यलोका: भवन्ति ब्रह्मसँस्थोऽमृतत्वमेति।

21. *Tait. Up.* I. 11.1

वेदमनूच्याचार्योऽन्तेवासिनमनुशास्ति। सत्यं वद। धर्मं चर। स्वाध्यायान्मा प्रमद:। आचार्याय प्रियं धनमाहृत्य प्रजातन्तुं मा व्यवच्छेत्सी:।

22. *Chānd. Up.* VIII. 15.1

23. *Ibid.*, II. 23.1

त्रयो धर्मस्कन्धा यज्ञोऽध्ययनं दानमिति।...

24. *Āśramopaniṣad.* 1[a].

अथातश्चत्वार आश्रमा: षोडशभेदा भवन्ति।

25. *Ibid.*, 1[c]

य उपनयनादूर्ध्वं त्रिरात्रमक्षारलवणाशी गायत्रीमन्त्रे स गायत्र:।

26. *Ibid.*, 1[d]

योऽष्टाचत्वारिंशद्वर्षाणिवेदब्रह्मचर्यं चरेत्प्रतिवेदं द्वादश वा यावद् ग्रहणान्तं वा वेदस्य स ब्राह्मण:।

27. *Ibid.*, 1[e].

स्वदारनिरत ऋतुकालाभिगामी सदा परदारवर्जी स प्राजापत्य:।
अथवा चतुर्विंशतिवर्षाणि गुरुकुलवासी ब्राह्मणोऽष्टाचत्वारिंशद्वर्षवासी च प्राजापत्य:।

28. *Ibid.*, 1[f].

आ प्रायणाद्गुरोरपरित्यागी नैष्ठिको बृहन्निति।

29. *Ibid.*, 2[b].

तत्र वार्ताकवृत्तय: कृषिगोरक्षवणिज्यमगर्हितमुपयुञ्जाना: शतसंवत्सराभि: क्रियाभिर्यजन्त आत्मानं प्रार्थयन्ते।

30. *Ibid.*, 2[c]

शालीनवृत्तयो यजन्तो न याजयन्तोऽधीयाना नाध्यापयन्तो ददतो न प्रतिगृह्णन्त: शतसंवत्सराभि: क्रियाभिर्यजन्त आत्मानं प्रार्थयन्ते।

31. *Ibid.*, 2[d]

यायावरा यजन्तो याजयन्तोऽधीयाना अध्यापयन्तो ददत: प्रतिगृह्णन्त: शतसंवत्सराभि: क्रियाभिर्यजन्त आत्मानं प्रार्थयन्ते।

32. *Ibid.*, 2[e]

घोरसंन्यासिका उध्दृतपरिपूताभिरद्भिः कार्यं कुर्वन्तः प्रतिदिवस-माहृतोञ्छवृत्ति-मुपयुञ्जानाः... ।

33. *Ibid.*, 3[b]

तत्र वैखानसा अकृष्टपच्यौषधिवनस्पतिभिर्ग्रामबहिष्कृताभिरग्निपरिचरणं कृत्वा पञ्चमहायज्ञक्रियां निर्वर्तयन्त आत्मानं प्रार्थयन्ते।

34. *Ibid.*, 3[c]

उदुम्बराः प्रातरुत्थाय यां दिशमभिप्रेक्षन्ते तदाहृतोदुम्बरबदरनीवारश्यामा-कैराग्निपरिचरणं कृत्वा पञ्चमहायज्ञक्रियां निर्वर्तयन्त आत्मानं प्रार्थयन्ते।

35. *Ibid.*, 3[d]

बालखिल्या जटाधराश्चीरचर्मवल्कलपरिवृत्ताः कार्तिक्यां पौर्णमास्यां पुष्पफलमुत्सृजन्तः शेषानष्टौ मासान् वृत्त्युपार्जनं कृत्वाऽग्निपरिचरणं कृत्वा पञ्चमहायज्ञक्रियां निर्वर्तयन्त आत्मानं प्रार्थयन्ते।

36. *Ibid.*, 3[e]

फेनपा उन्मत्तकाः शीर्णपर्णफलभोजिनो यत्र यत्र वसन्तोऽग्निपरिचरणं कृत्वा पञ्चमहायज्ञक्रियां निर्वर्तयन्त आत्मानं प्रार्थयन्ते।

37. *Jābāla. Up.,* IV. 4[e]

...यदहरेव विरजेत् तदहरेव प्रव्रजेत्।

38. *Bṛ. Up.,* III. 8.2.

39. *Y.T. Up.*62[a].

वर्जयित्वा स्त्रियाः सङ्गं कुर्यादभ्यासमादरात्।

40. *N.P. Up.,* IV. 3[abc].

न संभाषेत्स्त्रियं कांचित्पूर्वदृष्टां च न स्मरेत्। कथां च वर्जयेत्तासां ...।

41. *Saṁnyāsopaniṣad.* II. 90[a]

सुजीर्णोऽपि सुजीर्णासु विद्वान्स्त्रीषु न विश्वसेत्।

42. *N.P. Up.* VI. 31.

माद्यति प्रमदां दृष्ट्वा सुरां पीत्वा च माद्यति।
तस्माद् दृष्टिविषां नारीं दूरतः परिवर्जयेत्।

43. *M. Up.* III. 43

केशकज्जलधारिण्यो दुःस्पर्शा लोचनप्रियाः।
दृष्कृताग्निशिखा नार्यो दहन्ति तृणवन्नरम्॥

44. *Ibid.*, III. 44[a].

    ज्वलतामतिदूरेऽपि सरसा अपि नीरसाः।

45. *Ibid.*, III. 45[b]

    नार्यो नरविहङ्गानामङ्गबन्धनवागुराः।

46. *Ibid.*, III. 47

    सर्वेषां दोषरत्नानां सुसमुद्रिक्यानया।
    दुःखशृङ्खलया नित्यमलमस्तु मम स्त्रिया॥

    also, *Yājña. Up.*, I. 9-13.

47. Altekar, A.S., *Education in Ancient India,* Benaras, 1948, p. 32.
48. *Chānd. Up.*, IV. 4.1-4.
49. *Bṛ. Up.* VI. 2.1.

    श्वेतकेतुर्ह वा आरुणेयः पञ्चालानां परिषदमाजगाम स आजगाम जैवलिं प्रवाहणं परिचारयमाणं...

    also, *Chānd. Up.* V. 3.1.

50. *Ibid.*, V. 11.1-4.
51. *Bṛ. Up.*, III. 1.1.
52. *Tait. Up., I. 4.2.*

    आ मा यन्तु ब्रह्मचारिणः.... वि मायन्तु ब्रह्मचारिणः.. दमायन्तु ब्रह्मचारिणः ...। शमायन्तु ब्रह्मचारिणः।

53. *Ibid.*, I. 11.1-4.
54. *Chānd. Up.*, VI. 8-16.
55. *Ibid.*, VII. 1.
56. *Muṇḍ. Up.*, I. 1.4.

    द्वे विद्ये वेदितव्ये इति ह स्न यद् ब्रह्मविदो वदन्ति परा चैवापरा च।
    तत्रापरा ऋग्वेदो यजुर्वेदः सामवेदोऽथर्ववेदः शिक्षा कल्पो व्याकरणं निरुक्तं छन्दो ज्योतिषमिति।

    अथ परा यया तदक्षरमधिगम्यते।

57. *Kaṭh. Up.* I. 2.22[a]

    नायमात्मा प्रवचनेन लभ्यो न मेधया न बहुना श्रुतेन।

58. Sarma, J., *The Philosophy of Education in the Upaniṣads.,* New Delhi, 1978, p. 58.

59. Besant, Annie, *Ancient Ideals in Modern Life*, London, 1901, p. 106.
60. *Bṛ.Up.* III 8.1.
61. *Ibid.,* II. 4.1-15.
62. *Ibid.*, VI. 4.17

    अथ य इच्छेद्दुहिता मे पण्डिता जायेत..।
63. Garg, R.K., *Upaniṣadic Challenge to Science,* Delhi, 1978, p. 45.
64. Eliot Charls q. by Garg, R.K., *op. cit.,* p. 45.
65. *Bṛ. Up.* III. 2.13[b]

    ...पुण्यो वै पुण्येन कर्मणा भवति पाप: पापेनेति।

    also, *Chānd. Up.,* III. 14.1[b]

    अथ खलु क्रतुमय: पुरुषो: ...।
66. *Praśna. Up.* III. 7

    अथैकयोर्ध्व उदान: पुण्येन पुण्यं लोकं नयति पापेन पापमुभाभ्यामेव मनुष्यलोकम्।

    also, *Muṇḍ. Up.* III. 1.10[B]

    तं तं लोकं जयते तांश्च कामांस्तस्मादात्मज्ञं ह्यर्चयेद्भूतिकाम:।
67. *Śvet. Up.* V. 7

    गुणान्वयो य: फलकर्मकर्ता कृतस्य तस्यैव स चोपभोक्ता।
    स विश्वरूपस्त्रिगुणस्त्रिवर्त्मा प्राणाधिप: संचरति स्वकर्मभि:॥
68. *Bṛ. Up.* IV. 4.2[b]. 4[b]

    तं विद्याकर्मणी समन्वारभेते पूर्वप्रज्ञा च।

    ...एवमेवायमात्मेदँ शरीरं निहत्याऽविद्यां गमयित्वाऽन्यन्नवतरं कल्याणतरं रूपं कुरुते पित्र्यं वा गान्धर्वं वा...।
69. *Chānd. Up.,* V. 10.7.
70. *Śvet. Up.* V. 11[b]

    कर्मानुगान्यनुक्रमेण देही स्थानेषु रूपाण्यभिसंप्रपद्यते।
71. *Kaṭh. Up.,* I. 1.3[b].

    अनन्दा नाम ते लोकास्तान्स गच्छति ता ददत्।

    also, *Īśa. Up.*3[a]

असूर्या नाम ते लोका अन्धेन तमसावृता:।

also, *Bṛ. Up.*, IV. 4.9-11.

72. For more details, *Ibid.*, pp. 83ff.

73. *Bṛ. Up.*, IV. 4.22[b].

न व्यथते रिषत्येतमु हेवैते न तरत इत्यत: पापमकरवमित्यत: कल्याणमकरवमित्युभे उ हैवैष एते तरति नैनं कृताकृते तपत:।

74. *Chānd. Up.*, IV. 14.3[b].

...यथा पुष्करपलाश आपो न श्लिष्यन्त एवमेवंविदि पापं कर्म न श्लिष्यत इति...।

75. *Ibid.*, V. 24.3.

तद्यैथेषीकातूलमग्नौ प्रोतं प्रदूयेतैवँ-हास्य सर्वे पाप्मान: प्रदूयन्ते य एतदेवं विद्वानग्निहोत्रं जुहोति।

76. *Śvet. Up.*, I. 11[a].

ज्ञात्वा देवं सर्वपाशापहानि: क्षीणै: क्लेशैर्जन्ममृत्युप्रहाणि:।

also, *Ibid.*, V. 13[b]

विश्वस्यैकं परिवेष्टितारं ज्ञात्वा देवं मुच्यते सर्वपाशै:।

77. *Chānd. Up*, V. 10.1.

ये चेमेऽरण्ये श्रद्धा तप इत्युपासते तेऽर्चिषमभिसंभवन्त्यर्चिषोऽहरह्न आपूर्यमाण-पक्षमापूर्यमाणपक्षाद्यान्षडुदङ्गेति मासाँ-स्तान्।

78. *Bṛhajjābālopaniṣad,* III. 34.

अथ चतुर्विधं भस्मकल्पम्। प्रथममनुकल्पम्। द्वितीयमुपकल्पम्। उपोपकल्पं तृतीयम्। अकल्पं चतुर्थम्। अग्निहोत्रसमुद्भूतं विरजानलजमनुकल्पम्। वने शुष्कं शकृत्संगृह्य कल्पोक्तविधिना कल्पितमुपकल्पं स्यात्। अरण्ये शुष्कं गोमयं चूर्णीकृत्यानुसंगृह्य गोमूत्रै: पिण्डीकृत्य यथाकल्पं संस्कृतमुपोपकल्पम्। शिवालयस्थमकल्पं शतकल्पं च।

79. *Ibid.*, III. 1,

कृशाङ्गां वत्सहीनामशान्ताम्... जग्धतृणां ... रोगार्तां गां विहाय प्रशस्तगोमयमाहरेद्गोमयं स्वस्थं...।

80. *Ibid.*, III. 5, 6,

परेद्यु: प्रातरुत्थाय शुचिर्भूत्वा समाहित:।
कृतस्नानो धौतवस्त्र: पयोर्धं च सृजेच्च गाम्॥

उत्थाप्य गां प्रयत्नेन गायत्र्या मूत्रमाहरेत्।
सौवर्णे राजते ताम्रे धारयेन्मृन्मये घटे॥

81. *Ibid.*, III. 8[a].
अभूमिपातं गृह्णीयात्पात्रे पूर्वोदिते गृही।

82. *Ibid.*, III. 10.11[b].
पञ्चानां त्विति मन्त्रेण पिण्डानां तु चतुर्दश।
कुर्यात्संशोध्य किरणैः सौरकैराहरेत्ततः॥
...स्वगृह्योक्तविधानेन प्रतिष्ठाप्याग्निमीजयेत्।

83. *Ibid.*, III. 12, 13, 23, 26[b], 27[a].

84. *Ibid.*, V. 3[a], 5[b].
त्रैवर्णिकानां सर्वेषामग्निहोत्रसमुद्भवम्।
...शूद्राणां श्रोत्रियागारपचनाग्निसमुद्भवम्।

85. *Ibid.*, III. 31.
ईशानेति शिरोदेशं मुखं तत्पुरुषेण तु।
ऊरुदेशमघोरेण गुह्यं वामेन मन्त्रयेत्।

86. *Ibid.*, II. 1[b-c].
अग्निर्यथैको भुवनं प्रविष्टो रूपं रूपं प्रतिरूपो बभूव।
एवं भस्म सर्वभूतान्तरात्मा रूपं रूपं प्रतिरूपो बहिश्च॥

87. *Ibid.*, VI. 1-7.

88. *Vāsudevopaniṣad,* pt. I. p. 406, ll. 3-5.
ब्रह्मादयस्त्रयो मूर्तयस्तिस्रो व्याहृतयस्त्रीणि छन्दांसि त्रयोऽग्नय ज्योतिष्मन्तस्त्रयः कालास्तिस्त्रोऽवस्थास्त्रय आत्मानः पुण्ड्रास्त्रय ऊर्ध्वा अकार उकारो मकार एते प्रणवमयोर्ध्वपुण्ड्रः..।

89. *R. Jābāla. Up.* 9
श्वेतास्तु ब्राह्मणा ज्ञेयाः क्षत्रिया रक्तवर्णकाः।
पीतास्तु वैश्या विज्ञेयाः कृष्णाः शूद्रा उदाहृताः।।

90. *Ibid., Up. S.* I. p. 568.
एकवक्त्रं तु रुद्राक्षं परतत्त्वस्वरूपकम्।
तद्धारणात्परे तत्त्वे लीयते विजितेन्द्रियः॥
द्विवक्त्रं तु मुनिश्रेष्ठ चार्धनारीश्वरात्मकम्।
धारणादर्धनारीशः प्रीयते तस्य नित्यशः॥

91. *Ibid., Up. S.*I. p. 567.

त्रिपुरवधार्थमहं निमीलिताक्षोऽभवम्। तेभ्यो जलबिन्दवो भूमौ पतितास्ते रुद्राक्षा जाता:।

92. *Br. Jābāla. Up.*, IV. 29-32.
93. *Ibid.*, IV. 11-16.
94. *Akṣamālikā. Up* pt. I, pp. 486-488.
95. *Ācamanopaniṣad, Up. S.*, pt. II. pp. 5-6.

    आचमनविधिं व्याख्यास्याम:। जङ्घे पाणिपादौ प्रक्षाल्य प्राङ्मुख उदङ्मुखो वा बद्धशिखो यज्ञोपवीती। ब्राह्मणस्य दक्षिणे हस्ते पञ्च तीर्थानि भवन्ति। अङ्गुल्यग्रे देवतीर्थं कनिष्ठामूले आर्षिकं...।

96. *Śivopaniṣad,* V. 45-48.
97. *Ibid.*, V. 1[a]

    यथाग्नेयं महास्नानमलक्ष्मीमलनाशनम्।

98. *Ibid.*, V. 16

    त्रिकालं वारुणस्नानादनारोग्यं प्रजायते।
    आग्नेयं रोगशमनमेतस्मात् सार्वकामिकम्।।

99. *Ibid.*, V. 31.

    आग्नेयं वारुणं मान्त्रं वायव्यं त्वैन्द्रपञ्चमम्।
    मानसं शान्तितोयं च ज्ञानस्नानम् तथाष्टमम्।

100. *Ibid.*, V. 41.

    ज्ञानामलाम्भसा स्नात: सर्वदैव मुनि: शुचि:।
    निर्मलस्सुविशुद्धश्च विज्ञेय: सूर्यरश्मिवत्।।

101. *Ibid.*, V. 44.

    जलं मन्त्रं दया दानं सत्यमिन्द्रियसंयम:।
    ज्ञानं भावात्मशुद्धिश्च शौचमष्टविधं स्मृतम्।।

102. *Yāj. S.*, I.217[ff].

    Uśana. S., III. 113, 115.

    Atri. S., 357, 360.

103. *Agn. P.*, 163.37-39, also, *Mārk. P.*, 390.1-7.

    also, *Brahmāṇḍ. P.*, II. 3.17.10[cd]-20.

104. *Itihāsa. Up. Up. S.* pt. II. p. 10. l. 11

    एवमस्य पितृणामनन्ता तृप्तिर्भवति।

105. *Ibid.*, *Up. S.* pt. II. p. 12
य: च्छ्राद्धानि कुरुतेऽसंगतानि न देवयानेन पथा स याति।
परिमुक्तं पिप्पलं बन्धनादिव स्वर्गाल्लोकाच्च्यवतेऽश्राद्धमित्र: ॥

106. *Ibid. Up. S.* pt. II. p. 13
अश्रोत्रियं ब्राह्मणं भोजयानस्य षोडश श्राद्धानि पितरो न भुञ्जते।

107. *Ibid. Up. S.* pt. II. p. 16
वृषळीपतिभुक्तानि श्राद्धानि च हवींषि च।
पितरो न प्रतिगृह्णन्ति दाता स्वर्गं न गच्छति॥

108. *Piṇḍ. Up. Up. S.* pt. II. p. 30.

109. *Ibid.*, *Up. S.,* pt. II. pp. 1-8.

110. *Mat. P.* 16.5-6[ab].

111. Oldenberg, H., *op. cit.,* p. 101.

112. Gajendragadkar, K.V. *op. cit.,* p. 325.

113. *Tait. Up.,* I. 11.1
सत्यं वद। धर्मं चर...।
also, *Praśna. Up.* I. 8.
विश्वरूपं हरिणं जातवेदसं परायणं ज्योतिरेकं तपन्तम्। सहस्त्ररश्मि: शतधा वर्तमान: प्राण: प्रजानामुदयत्येष सूर्य:।

114. *Chānd. Up.* VI. 8.3.
अशनापिपासे मे सोम्य विजानीहीति यत्रैतत्पुरुषोऽशिशिषति...।
also, *Bṛ. Up.* I. 2.

115. *Yogaśikhā. Up.* VI. 57
त्रय: कालास्त्रयो देवास्त्रयो लोकास्त्रय: स्वरा:।
त्रयो वेदा: स्थिता यत्र तत्परं ज्योतिरोमिति॥
also, *Śivopaniṣad.* V. 87.
P. Haṁsa. P. Up. Up. S. pt. I. p. 484. ll. 14-19
भैक्षमाचरन्...परमहंसपरिव्राजको भवति।
also, *N.P. Up. Up. S.* pt. I. pp. 316-317.
तथेत्यंङ्गीकृत्य... ज्ञानवैराग्यसंन्यासी।

116. *Īśa. Up.* 1[a]
ईशा वास्यमिदँ सर्वं यत्किंच जगत्यां जगत्।

also, *Ken. Up.*, I.4, I.5.

117. *Gaṇeśa. U. Ta. Up. Up. S.* pt. I. p. 639.

... तेन पञ्चवारं सकृद्वाऽभिषिच्य नित्येन संतर्प्य... दर्शयेत्।

118. Oldenberg, H., *op. cit.*, p. 94.

119. *Bṛ. Up.* II. 4. 1-4.

120. *Chānd. Up.* VI. 1-16.

121. *Bṛ. Up.* IV. 2.1-4. IV. 3.1-38.

122. *Ibid.*, II. 1.15

123. *Chānd. Up.*, V. 11-1-7.

124. *Bṛ. Up.*, IV. 5.13,

स यथा सैन्धवघनोऽनन्तरोऽबाह्यः कृत्स्नो रसघन एवैवं वा अरेऽयमात्माऽनन्तरोऽबाह्यः कृत्स्नः प्रज्ञानघनः एवैतेभ्यो भूतेभ्यः समुत्थाय तान्येवानुविनश्यति ...।

125. *Ibid.*, IV. 3.18

तद्यथा महामत्स्य उभे कूलेऽनुसंचरति पूर्वं चापरं चैवमेवायं पुरुष एतावुभावन्तावनु-संचरति स्वप्नान्तं च बुद्धान्तं च।

126. *Ibid.*, II. 4.9.

स यथा वीणायै वाद्यमानायै न बाह्याञ्छब्दाञ्छक्नुयाद्ग्रहणाय वीणायै तु ग्रहणेन वीणावादस्य वा शब्दो गृहीतः॥

127. *Triśikhi. brā. Up.* 162

एवं विशोध्य तत्त्वानि योगी निःस्पृहचेतसा।
यथा निरिन्धनो वह्निः स्वयमेव प्रशाम्यति ॥

128. *Annapūrṇā. Up.* V. 24[b],

न नन्दन्ति न निन्दन्ति जीवितं मरणं तथा।

129. *Tejobindūpaniṣad.* VI. 74.

शशशृङ्गेण नागेन्द्रो मृतश्चेज्जगदस्ति तत्।
मृगतृष्णाजलं पीत्वा तृप्तश्चेदस्त्विदं जगत्॥

130. *Pāramātmika. Up. Up. S.* pt. II. p. 88.

सोमसूर्यौ नयनोर्मरुतं पक्षयोर्द्वयो।

also, *Yājñavalkya. Up.* I. 10[b],

स्त्रियो हि नरकाग्नीनामिन्धनं चारु दारुणम्।

131. *Mahopaniṣad*, IV. 133.
अहो नु चित्रं पद्मोत्थैर्बद्धास्तन्तुभिरद्रय:।

132. *Chānd. Up.* VI. 8.1-3.

133. *Bṛ. Up.* II. 5.18.

134. *Māṇḍ. Up.* I.9-11.

135. *Śāṇḍilya. Up. Up. S.* pt. I. p. 419.
Ātman – यस्मात्सर्वमाप्नोति सर्वमादत्ते सर्वमत्ति च तस्मादुच्यते आत्मेति।
Pāramātmika. Up. Up. S. II. p. 86.
Viṣṇu – व्याप्नोतीति विष्णु: सर्वव्यापक इत्यर्थ:।
Devī. Up. I.18
Durgā – दुर्गात्संत्रायते यस्मात् देवी दुर्गेति कथ्यते।
Itihāsa. Up. Up. S. pt. II., p. 16. ll. 18-19.
Vṛṣali – पितृगेहेषु या कन्या रज: पश्यति असंस्कृता सा कन्या वृषळी नाम।

136. Raman, N.S.S., "*Is Comparative Philosohy Possible*", *Indian Philosophy Today.* Delhi, 1975, p. 210.

137. *Śvet. Up.* II. 14-15.

138. *Mai. Up.* II. 1.2[b]
अथ य एष संप्रसादोऽस्माच्छरीरात्समुत्थाय परं ज्योतिरुपसंपद्य स्वेन रूपेणाभिनिष्पद्यत इत्येष आत्मेति होवाचैतदमृतमभयमेतद्ब्रह्मेति। अथ खल्वियं ब्रह्मविद्या सर्वोपनिषद्विद्या वा राजन्नस्माकं भगवता मैत्रिणाऽख्याता ...॥

139. Radhakishnan, S., *The Principal Upaniṣads,* p. 722.

140. *Muṇḍ. Up.* II. 2.9
हिरण्मये परे कोशे विरजं ब्रह्म निष्कलम्।
तत्छुभ्रं ज्योतिषां ज्योतिस्तद्यदात्मविदो विदु:॥

141. *Chānd. Up.* VIII. 4.2
...एतं सेतुं तीर्त्वाऽन्ध: सन्ननंधो भवति विद्ध: सन्नविद्धो भवति... तस्माद्वा एतं सेतुं तीर्त्वापि नक्तमहरेवाभिनिष्पद्यते ...।

142. *Ibid.*, III. 11.2-3
न दै तत्र न निम्लोच नोदियाय कदाचन। देवास्तेनाहं सत्येन मा विराधिषि ब्रह्मणेति॥
न ह वा अस्मा उदेति न निम्लोचति सकृद्दिवा हैवास्मै भवति य एतां एतामेवं ब्रह्मोपनिषदं वेद॥

143. *Śvet. Up.* IV. 18

यदाऽतमः तन्न दिवा न रात्रिर्न न सन्न चासन् शिव एव केवलः॥

144. *Ibid,* II. 11,

नीहारधूमार्कानलानिलानां खद्योतविद्युत्स्फटिकशशिनाम्।
एतानि रूपाणि पुरःसराणि ब्रह्मण्यभिव्यक्तिकराणि योगे॥

145. *Bṛ. Up.*, II. 3.6,

146. *Ibid.*, V. 9.1, *Mai. Up.*, II. 6,

अयमग्निर्वैश्वानरो योऽयमंतः पुरुषे येनेदमन्नं पच्यते यदिदमद्यते तस्यैष घोषो भवति यमेतत्कर्णावपिधाय शृणोति स यदोत्क्रमिष्यन् भवति नैनं घोषं शृणोति॥

147. *Chānd. Up.*, III. 13, 7[b]

यत्रैत्कर्णावपिगृह्य निनदमिव नदथुरिवाग्नेरिव ज्वलत उपशृणोति ...।

148. *Maṇḍala. Brā. Up. Up. S.* pt. I. p. 348. l. 5,

भ्रूमध्ये सच्चिदानंदतेजःकूटरूपं तारकं ब्रह्म।

149. *Ibid.*, p. 348. ll. 8-10,

...तर्जन्यग्रोन्मीलितकर्णरन्ध्रद्वये फूत्कारशब्दो जायते। तत्र स्थिते मनसि चक्षुर्मध्यनील-ज्योतिः पश्यति। एवं हृदयेऽपि।

150. *Ibid.*, p. 349. ll. 19-33.

151. *Ibid.*, p. 349. ll. 11-13.

आदावग्निमण्डलम्। तदुपरिसूर्यमण्डलं। तन्मध्ये सुधाचन्द्रमण्डलम्।
तन्मध्येऽखण्डब्रह्मतेजोमण्डलम्। तद्विद्युल्लेखावच्छुक्लभास्वरम्॥

152. *Ibid.*, p. 348. l. 9

बहिर्लक्ष्यं तु नासाग्रे चतुःषडष्टदशद्वादशाङ्गुलीभिः क्रमान्नीलद्युतिश्यामत्व-सदृग्रक्तभङ्गीस्फुरत्पीतवर्णद्वयोपेतं व्योमत्वं पश्यति।

153. *Ibid.*, p. 348. ll. 12-14,

पुरुषस्य दृष्ट्यग्रे ज्योतिर्मयूखा वर्तन्ते। तद्दृष्टिः स्थिरा भवति। शीर्षोपरि द्वादशाङ्गुलिमानं ज्योतिः पश्यति तदाऽमृतत्वमेति।

154. *Ibid.*, p. 348. l. 15,

मध्यलक्ष्यं तु प्रातःश्चित्रादिवर्णसूर्यचन्द्रवह्निज्वालावलीवत्तद्विहीनान्तरिक्षवत्पश्यति ...।

155. *Ibid.*, p. 348. ll. 16-19.

156. *Yogaśikhā. Up.*, III. 2[a],

अक्षरं परमो नादः।

157. *Haṁsopaniṣad. Up. S.* pt. I. p. 147. ll. 19-22.

नादो दशविधो जायते। चिणिति प्रथमः। चिञ्चिणीति द्वितीयः। घण्टानादस्तृतीयः। शङ्खनादश्चतुर्थम्। पञ्चपस्तन्त्रीनादः। षष्ठस्तालनादः। सप्तमो वेणुनादः। अष्टमो मृदङ्गनादः। नवमो भेरीनादः। दशमो मेघनादः।

158. *Ibid., Up. S.,* pt. I. 147. ll. 22-25,

प्रथमे चिञ्चिणीगात्रं द्वितीये गात्रभज्जनम्। तृतीये स्वेदनं याति चतुर्थे कम्पते शिरः। पञ्चमे स्त्रवते तालु षष्ठेऽमृतनिवेषणम् सप्तमे गूढविज्ञानं परा वाचा तथाऽष्टमे। अदृश्यं नवमे देहं दिव्यचक्षुस्तथाऽमलम्। दशमं परमं ब्रह्म भवेत्ब्रह्मात्मसंन्निधौ।

159. *Dhyānabindūpaniṣad,* I. 102-105,

अमूर्तो वर्तते नादो वीणादण्डसमुत्थितः। शङ्खनादादिभिश्चैव मध्यमेव ध्वनिर्यथा॥ व्योमरन्ध्रगतो नादो मायूरं नादमेव च। कपालकुहरे मध्ये चतुर्द्वारस्य मध्यमे॥ तदात्मा राजते तत्र यथा व्योम्नि दिवाकरः।... स्वात्मानं पुरुषं पश्येन्मनस्तत्र लयं गतम्।

160. *Nādbindūpaniṣad,* I. 34-35,

आदौ जलधिजीमूतभेरीनिर्झरसंभवः। मध्ये मर्दलशब्दाभो घण्टाकाहलजस्तथा॥ अन्ते तु किंकिणीवंशवीणाभ्रमरनिःस्वनः। इति नानाविध नादाः श्रूयन्ते सूक्ष्मसूक्ष्मतः।

161. *Ibid.,* 47-49[a],

मनस्तत्र लयं याति तद्विष्णोः परमं पदम्।
तावदाकाशसंकल्पो यावच्छब्दः प्रवर्तते॥
निःशब्दं तत्परं ब्रह्म परमात्मा समीयते।
नादो यावन्मनस्तावन्नादान्तेऽपि मनोन्मनी॥
सशब्दक्षरे क्षीणे निःशब्दं परमं पदम्॥

162. *Chānd. Up.,* III. 14.1[a].

163. *Bṛ. Up.,* IV. 4.5[a].

164. *Ibid.,* I. 4.7[a],

तद्धेदं तर्ह्यव्याकृतमासीत्...।

165. *Ibid.,* IV. 4.25.

166. *Chānd. Up.,* VII. 24.1.

यत्र नान्यत्पश्यति नान्यच्छृणोति नान्यद्विजानाति स भूमाऽथ यत्रान्यत्पश्यति... तदल्पं...।

167. *Īśa. Up.*, 6.

यस्तु सर्वाणि भूतान्यात्मन्येवानुपश्यति।
सर्वभूतेषु चात्मानं ततो न विजुगुप्सते॥

168. *Ibid.*, 7,

यस्मिन्सर्वाणिभूतान्यात्मैवाभूद्विजानतः।
तत्र को मोहः कः शोकः एकत्वमनुपश्यतः।

169. *Bṛ. Up.*, IV. 4.22[b].

170. *Chānd. Up.*, VIII. 13.1.

श्यामाच्छबलं प्रपद्ये शबलाच्छ्यामं प्रपद्येऽश्व इव रोमाणि विधूय पापं चन्द्र इव राहोर्मुखात्प्रमुच्य धूत्वा शरीरमकृतं कृतात्मा...।

171. *Ibid.*, V. 24.3.

172. *Ibid.*, Iv. 14.3.

173. *Bṛ. Sū. Sā. Bh.*, I. 1.4.

174. *Bṛ. Up.*, I. 4.8[a]

तदेतत्प्रेयः पुत्रात्प्रेयो वित्तात्प्रेयोऽन्यस्मात्सर्वस्मादन्तरतरं यदयमात्मा।

175. *Kaṭh. Up.*, I. 2.10[a].

जानाम्यहं शेवधिरित्यनित्यं न ह्यध्रुवैः प्राप्यते हि ध्रुवं तत्।

176. Swami, Paramananda, *Encyclopaedic Dictionary of Upanisadic Words* (Vol. II), Delhi, 2000, p. 336.

177. *Muṇḍ. Up.*, I. 2.6.

एह्येहीति तमाहुतयः सुवर्चसः सूर्यस्य रश्मिभिर्यजमानं वहन्ति।
प्रियां वाचमभिवदन्त्योऽर्चयन्त्य एष वः पुण्यः सुकृतो ब्रह्मलोकः॥

178. *Ibid.*, I. 2.11[b],

सूर्यद्वारेण ते विरजाः प्रयान्ति यत्रामृतः स पुरुषो ह्यव्ययात्मा।

179. *Chānd. Up.*, VIII. 5.4.

180. Śaṅkara's commentry on *Chānd. Up.* VIII. 5.4.

181. *Muktikopaniṣad,* I. 25[b],

चतुर्विधा तु या मुक्तिर्मदुपासनया भवेत्।

182. *Ibid.*, I.18[b], 19.

दूराचाररतो वापि मन्नामभजनात्कपे।

सालोक्य मुक्तिमाप्नोति न तु लोकान्तरादिकम्।
काश्यां तु ब्रह्मनालेऽस्मिन्मृतो मत्तारमाप्नुयात्॥

183. *Ibid.*, I. 23,

मयि सर्वात्मके भावो मत्सामीप्यं भजत्ययम्।
सैव सालोक्यसारूप्यसामीप्या मुक्तिरिष्यते॥

184. *Ibid.*, I. 21,

जन्तोर्दक्षिणकर्णे तु मत्तारं समुपादिशेत्।
निर्धूताशेषपापौघो मत्सारूप्यं भजत्ययम्।

185. *Ibid.*, I. 24[b], 25[a],

मत्सायुज्यं द्विजः सम्यग्भजेद्भ्रमरकीटवत्।
सैव सायुज्यमुक्तिः स्याद्ब्रह्मानन्दकरी शिवा॥

186. *Akṣyupaniṣad*, I. 27-41.

187. *Annapūrṇā. Up.* V. 81-85.

188. *Varāha. Up.*, IV. 1.

...शुभेच्छा प्रथमा भूमिका भवति। विचारणा द्वितीया। तनुमानसी तृतीया। सत्त्वापत्तिस्तुरीया। असंसक्तिः पञ्चमी। पदार्थभावना षष्ठी। तुरीयगा सप्तमी।...

189. *Nirālamba. Up. Up. S.*, pt. I. p. 256. ll. 8-10.

मोक्ष इति च नित्यानित्यवस्तुविचारादनित्यसंसारसुखदुःखविषयसमस्त-क्षेत्रममताबन्धक्षयो मोक्षः।

190. *Br. Jābāla. Up.*, II. 4-9.

191. *Tejobindū. Up.*, IV. 3[bc], 53[a].

यस्य देहादिकं नास्ति यस्य ब्रह्मेति निश्चयः।
परमानन्दपूर्णो यः जीवनमुक्त उच्यते॥

अतीतातीतभावो यो वैदेही मुक्त एव सः।

192. Radhakrishnan, S., *The Principal Upaniṣads.*, p. 121.

193. *Tait. Up.*, II. 7[1.]

यदा हयेवैष एतस्मिन्नदृश्येऽनात्म्येऽनिरुक्तेऽनिलयनेऽभयं प्रतिष्ठां विन्दते। अथ सोऽभयं गतो भवति।

194. *Īśa. Up.*, I. 7.

195. *Muṇḍ. Up.*, III. 2.2[b].

पर्याप्तकामस्य कृतात्मनस्तु इहैव सर्वे प्रविलीयन्ति कामाः ॥

196. *Tait. Up.*, II. 9. (*Up. S.*, I. pp. 27-28)

एतं ह वाव न तपति किमहं साधु नाकरवम्। किमहं पापमकरवमिति।

197. *Tait. Up.*, II.8.

ते ये शतं मानुषा आनन्दाः। स एको मनुष्यगन्धर्वाणामानन्दः
... ते ये शतं प्रजापतेरानन्दाः। स एको ब्रह्मण आनन्दः।

198. *Śvet. Up.*, VI. 12[b].

तमात्मस्थं येऽनुपश्यन्ति धीरास्तेषां सुखं शाश्वतं नेतरेषाम्।

199. *Bṛ. Up.*, I. 4.10

ब्रह्म वा इदमग्र आसीत्तदात्मानमेवावेदहं ब्रह्मास्मीति। तस्मात्तत्सर्वमभवत् तद्यो यो देवानां प्रत्यबुध्यत स एव तदभवत्तथर्षीणां तथा मनुष्याणां तद्धैतत्पश्यन्नृषिर्वामदेवः प्रतिपेदेऽहं मनुरभवं सूर्यश्चेति ॥

200. *Tait. Up. Up. S.*, pt. I. p. 24.

अहं वृक्षस्य रेरिवा। कीर्तिः पृष्ठं गिरेरिव। ऊर्ध्वपवित्रो वाजिनीव स्वमृतमस्मि। द्रविणं सर्ववर्चसम्। सुमेधा अमृतोऽक्षितः।

201. *Ibid.*, III. 10.5-6.

202. *Tejobindū. Up.*, IV. 8-31. also, *Ātmaprabodha. Up.* 2-30, also *Avadhūta*. Up. 20-30 etc.

CHAPTER VII

CONCLUSION

Unceasing motion is the natural course of the universe. With the changing time, changes in the society are inevitable. With the developments in the fields of science and technology, the world has been set to a course of modernization, which in its turn has brought about cultural and social changes. The progress made by man on the basis of scientific and technological knowledge has been enabling him to have increasing material benefits. However, mere comforts and pleasures that he can have in the modern world may not enable him to have lasting happiness and peace of mind. Cultural and social upheaval has now brought man at the cross roads, where he will have to rethink, know the importance of philosophy and metaphysics and choose the path which will tend him to commune with the Infinite and attain its knowledge. The Upaniṣads direct towards such a path which makes one turn inwards towards the power and the sanctity of one's own Self wherein abide happiness, peace and bliss. In this connection, one can take note of the fact that Schopenhaur found 'the solace of his life and solace of his death' after comprehending the Upaniṣadic philosophy.[1]

Man has always been anxious to know his origin as also that of the world. The attempts to know the same led to the origin and development of philosophy. In India, the roots of philosophical concepts can be traced back to the Ṛgvedic age. The Ṛgvedic seers contemplated upon the concept of the origin of the world and presented different accounts of creation. The composer of the *Puruṣasūkta* glorified the greatness of the highest cause. It indicated the origin of the world through a sacrifice at which Puruṣa born from the great Puruṣa was sacrificed by the gods.

Sāndhya-s and Ṛṣi-s were their offerings. (*Ṛv*. X. 10.16.). Another seer imagined the world to be the outcome of Unborn (*Ṛv*. X. 81) and yet another stated that Prajāpati who created the primeval waters as the golden germ (*Hiraṇyagarbha*) and created the world thereafter (*Ṛv*. X. 121). The Nāsadīyasūkta reflects the in-ability to state the nature of the cause of the world (*Ṛv*. X. 129). The composers of the Atharvanic hymns termed the first cause of the world variously as the red one (Rohita) (*A*v. XIII. 3), an ox (*anadvān*) (*Av*. X. 10), the cow (*vaśā*) (*Av*. XI. 5), time (*kāla*) (*Av*. XIV. 53). Even the sacrificial texts presented creation accounts wherein at times Prajāpati is said to have entertained a desire to become many, performed austerities thereafter and created the world (*Tait*. S., V. 6.4.2, VII. 1.5.1). Elsewhere, waters are imagined to have desired to reproduce, performed penance, produced golden egg and created the world (*Śat. Brā*. XI. 1.6.1 ff). However, the full-fledged development of philosophical thought is reflected only in the Upaniṣads which can broadly be categorized as :

(*i*) the earlier thirteen principal Upaniṣads composed between 1200 B.C. and 600 B.C. and

(*ii*) the later ones ranging between a long span of time of nearly 1200 years, *i.e.* between 200 A.D. and 1400 A.D.

As there is a wide time lapse between the period of the earlier and the later Upaniṣads, there are bound to be some changes.

Although it is difficult to tackle the issue of the priority and posteriority of philosophy and religion, it is certain that these two are always closely associated with each other. In fact, philosophical concepts have always formed an integral part of religion.

It is observed that religious and social changes mutually influence each other. At times, changes in society lead to changes in religion. At the same time, changes in religion can lead to changes in society.[2]

Since religion and philosophy are closely related with each other, changes in the field of philosophical concepts can be the outcome of changing social circumstances. At the same time, changing religio-philosophical thoughts can lead to changes in society. Literature is the mirror to the society of its time. It reflects social and religious phenomena of that time and even philosophical thoughts of people existing in those days. The composition of the Upaniṣads are not an exception to this observation. Thus, the Ṛgvedic Āryans who had to depend upon the natural forces were inclined to adore, revere and deify them. They named them variously such as Indra, Varuṇa, Agni, Uṣas etc. and showered praises on them. The Ṛgvedic religion thus, was the religion of the multiplicity of gods with an awareness of the fact that all these divinities are the manifestations of the same Reality.[3]

The sacrificial texts subordinated the importance of gods to the institution of sacrifice. They narrated cosmogonic, cosmological accounts and also indulged in philosophical speculations. They stressed the importance of rituals as bestowing different fruits upon the sacrificer. However, different benefits derived through the performance of sacrifices were only for a shorter duration and hence just temporary in nature. The earlier Upaniṣads replaced the ritualistic (*karmakāṇḍātmaka*) portion of the sacrificial texts with the philosophical (*jñānakāṇḍātmaka*) portion. They are the philosophical reflections of the seers, which are scattered in the Veda-s and sacrificial texts. They propounded the doctrine of complete identity between the individual Self (Ātman) and the Supreme Self (Brahman) through statements such as "the universe is Brahman and Brahman is Ātman." (*Sarvaṁ khalu idaṁ Brahma. Ayam Ātmā Brahma.*).

According to the earlier Upaniṣads, the knowledge of the Highest Reality enabled the aspirant to free himself from the cycle of births and deaths forever and achieve salvation. Thus, as contrasted with the fruits laid down by the sacrificial texts, the fruit laid down by the earlier Upaniṣads was permanent in nature. To comprehend the Highest Reality which is abstract in nature, the Upaniṣads propounded *upāsanā*-s that are known as *vidyā*-s which expected the aspirants to meditate on the perceptible form of the abstract Brahman (*pratīka*-s) and which lead to the knowledge of the imperceptible Brahman. The path of knowledge (*jñāna*) was difficult to tread upon, and could be pursued only by a limited few who could concentrate their attention on the abstract, transcendental Supreme Reality. Knowing very well that the attempt to focus on the formless Reality is not only difficult but even painful;[4] and man is inclined to seek shelter of the personified aspect. This personified aspect is an intermediary stage through which he can ultimately reach the final goal. The authors of the later Upaniṣads knew the importance of personified aspect and accordingly described five prominent deities *viz.* Viṣṇu, Śiva, Sūrya, Devī, Gaṇapati and their different forms. On the one hand, they tried to replace the attempt to pursue the Highest Reality in the form of Brahman which was imagined to be without any attribute, shape or concrete form with that of worshipping different gods and goddesses with different forms and on the other hand, they replaced the difficult attempt to meditate upon the formless Supreme Reality with easy means. The later Upaniṣads propounded different paths such as *bhakti*, Yoga Saṁnyāsa etc. and tried to amalgamate the modes of worships propounded by these paths as means to attain the knowledge of the Supreme Reality.

The chronological overview of the Sanskrit texts of the Vedic period indicates a polytheistic tendency culminating into a monistic one and again a monistic tendency leading to a polytheistic one. It must however, be remembered that the worship of gods and goddesses, *japa* and the like laid down in the later Upaniṣads were different means through which finally the same goal *viz.* the knowledge of the Supreme Reality was to be attained. Thus, it is evident in the ultimate analysis that the earlier and later Upaniṣads expected the aspirants to have the knowledge of the Highest Reality and achieve salvation.

As concluding remarks it can again be stated that the earlier Upaniṣads stressed the importance of the knowledge of the attributeless (*nirguṇa, nirviśeṣa*) Brahman which was believed to be the only cause of the world and the knowledge of which led to salvation. Being the knowledge of the transcendental Reality, it was difficult to comprehend. The later Upaniṣads replaced Brahman with a number of divinities, monism with pluralism, the abstract (*amūrta*) principle with the concerete (*mūrta*). At the same time, they identified these divinities with the Brahman. Simplifying the act of 'focussing attention', they left ample choice for the aspirants to choose the divinity as per their own appeal, liking, convenience, suitability. They widened the scope of the aspirants towards the pursuit of *dharma,* the first goal of human life. They transformed philosophy for a few into a religion for the masses and at the same time retained the importance of philosophy. One may hope that even in the modern period and the time to come this vision of the authors of the Upaniṣads will enhance the progress of the aspirant on his spiritual path and will fulfill the purpose of life.

REFERENCES

1. Schopenhaur q. by Hume, R.E., *Op. Cit.*, p. 4.
2. For more details, Nottingham, Elizabeth, q. by Bakre, A.B. *Op. Cit.* pp. 16-17.
3. *Ṛv.* X. 164.46.

   एकं सद्विप्रा बहुधा वदन्ति अग्निं यमं मातरिश्वानमाहुः।
4. *Bh. G.* XII. 5^{ab}.

   क्लेशोऽधिकतरस्तेषामव्यक्तासक्त चेतसाम्।

APPENDIX

CHRONOLOGICAL REVIEW : *(Of Important Works)*

It is very difficult to fix an exact date for each of the earlier Upaniṣads for all the Upaniṣads are seen to be having earlier and later parts.[1] But when the Upaniṣads as a whole are taken into consideration, the period can roughly be estimated. Ranade, R.D. has scrutinized the period of the earlier Upaniṣads by applying various tests such as (*i*) The language, the style, the vocabulary, grammatical peculiarties etc. (*ii*) Successive eleaboration of details. (iii) Ideological development. (*iv*) Inter quotation. etc.

Accordingly, he arranged them in chronological order as follows :

(*i*) *Bṛ. Up., Chānd. Up.*

(*ii*) *Īśa. Up, Ken. Up.*

(*iii*) *Ait. Up., Tait. Up., Kau. Up.*

(*iv*) *Kaṭh. Up., Mūṇḍ. Up., Śvet. Up.,*

(*v*) *Praśna. Up., Mai. Up., Maṇḍ. Up.*

and stated that the Upaniṣadic period may be fixed between 1000 and 600 B.C., prior to the rise of Buddhism.[2]

Taking into consideration the vast literature of the later Upaniṣads, it is even more difficult to fix an exact date for each of the composition. Desai, S.G. has fixed the tentative period of some of the later Upaniṣads. Thus, in consonance with Deussen, he treats the *Cūlikā. Up.* as contemporaneous to the *Bh. G.* (200 B.C. - 200 A.D.), taking into account its theistic Yoga and Sāṁkhya conception. According to him, the Saṁnyāsa Upaniṣads, *Āruṇeya. Up. Jābāla. Up. Kaṇṭhaśṛti. Up. Paramahaṁsa. Up.* are not later than 200 A.D. In the Yoga group of the Upaniṣads *Cūlikā. Up.* and *Brahmabindū. Ups.* are the earliest belonging to 200 B.C. The *Kṣurikā. Up.*, the *Tejobindū. Up.*, the *Brahmavidyā. Up.*, the *Nādabindū. Up.*, the *Yogaśikhā. Up.*, the *Dhyānabindū* and *Amṛtabindū. Up.* may be placed in about 200 A.D.

As the worship of Rāma is implied in the *Rāma. P. Tā. Up.* it may be placed around 200 A.D. The *Rāma. U. Tā. Up.* contains passages from the earlier Upaniṣads. Hence, it is of the late origin. The *Nṛsiṁha. Tā. Up.* have been commented uon by Gauḍapāda, hence, they cannot be later than 700 A.D. The *Gopālatāpinī Upaniṣ ads*, containing an element of Rādhā are of later period, propably around 900 A.D. Further, he says that though this chronology is provisional the major creative activity of the Atharvanic authors of the Upaniṣads must have been between 500 B.C. and 500 A.D. and the *Allopaniṣad* can be placed between A.D. 1300 and A.D. 1400. Thus, he inferred that the Upaniṣads cover a very long period of 1200 years. (A.D. 200-1400).[3] The period of *Rāmarahasya Up.* seems to be later than that of eighteen *Purāṇa*-s (later than 900 A.D.)[4], since it makes the mention of the eighteen *Purāṇa*-s.

According to Kinsley, D., a group of *mahāvidyā*-s (*devī*-s) existed since the tenth cen. A.D. Though, the worship of Durgā and Kālī hark back to the 4th - 5th cen. A.D. this group flourished around 10th cen. A.D.[5] Mahākāla Saṁhitā (10th cen. A.D.) mentions nine *mahāvidyā*-s except Dhūmāvatī.[6] It may be inferred that the period of the Śākta Upaniṣads is parallel to this period and that of the *Tantra*-s. According to Zimmer, H, the *Tantra*-s represent a development of the medieval period and the Tāntric literture belongs mainly to the centuries following 300 A.D.[7] According to Winternitz, the *Pañcarātra Saṁhitā*, which probably might have originated in the north belongs to the 5th to 9th cen. A.D. Thus, according to him the Viṣṇuite Upaniṣads of these sects which worship Viṣṇu as Nṛsiṁha and Rāma in the *mantra*-s and the *yantra*-s possibly belong to the same period.[8]

The *Y.S.* of Patañjali is assigned to the second century B.C. Patañjali systematised the conceptions of the Yoga and set them forth on the background of the metaphysics of the Sāṁkhya.[9]

According to Kane, P.V., the probable dates of the Purāṇa-s are from 300 A.D. to 900 A.D.[10]

About the later Upaniṣads Macdonell has said that "all but three are contemporaneous with the Purāṇa-s."[11] Even Winternitz, M., stated that the later Upaniṣads are on same chronological level as the Purāṇa-s and the Tantra-s.[12]

All the work has been carried out keeping in view these guidelines.

REFERENCES

1. Deussen, P., *The Philosophy of the Upaniṣads,* pp. 8-9.
2. For more details see Ranade R.D. *op. cit.,* pp. 9-12.

   also, Belvalkar S.K. and Ranade, R.D. *History of Indian Philosophy* Vol. II pp. 87 ff.
3. Desai S.G., *op. cit.* pp. xxxiii, xxxiv.
4. *Rāmarahasya. Up. Up. S.* pp. 386

   ...पुराणेषु अष्टादशसु... ।
5. Kinsley, David, *op. cit.*, p. 1.
6. *Mahākāla Saṁhitā, Kāmakalākhaṇḍa,* pp. 65-66.
7. Zimmer, H. *op. cit.*, p. 61.
8. Winternitz, M. *op. cit.*, p. 563.
9. Radhakrishnan, S. *Indian Philosophy*, Vol. II, p. 341.
10. Kane, P.V. *History of Dharmaśāstra* Vol. IV. Pune, 1953, p. ix.
11. Macdonell, A., *op. cit.*, p. 238 (*A History of Sanskrit Literature*).
12. Winternitz, M., *op. cit.*, p. 222.

BIBLIOGRAPHY

(A) SANSKRIT TEXTS AND COMMENTARIES

Agni Purāṇa : Nag Publishers, Delhi, 1985.

Atri-Saṁhitā : Ed. Dutta, M.N., T.D.S. Vol. II. pp. 181-214, Cosmo Publications, New Delhi, 1979.

Bhāgavata Purāṇa : Geeta Press, Gorakhpur, Śaka 2010.

Bhāratīya Mānasaśāstra Athavā Sārth Āṇi Savivaraṇa Pātañjala Yoga Darśana (Marathi) : D.B. Dhavale, K.B. Dhavale, Mumbai, 1951.

Brahmasūtrabhāṣya of Śaṅkarācārya : Translated by Gambhirananda Advaita Ashrama Publication Trust, Calcutta, 1993.

Brahmasūtra-s with Śāṅkara Bhāṣya. Vol. III. (works of Śānakarācārya in original Sanskrit) : Motilal Banarasidass, Delhi, 1998.

Brahmāṇḍa Purāṇa : Motilal Banarasidass, Delhi, 1985.

Gauḍapādakārikā : Ed. Karmarkar, R.D., with notes and translation into English, B.O.R.I., Poona, 1973 (first published in 1953).

Īśa Upaniṣad : With original text and exposition by Ghosh, Aurobindo, Aurobindo Ashram Pub., Pondicherry, 2002.

Īśādi Daśopaniṣadaḥ with Śāṅkara Bhāṣya : Brijbhushan Das, Vanivilas Sanskrit Pustakalaya, Benaras.

Mahābhārata : Bhandarkar Oriental Research Institute (B.O. R.I.) Vol. III. Pune, 1974.

Manusmṛti : Ed. Ravishastri, with Sanskrit text and commentary by Surendrakumar (Hindi) Arsha Sahitya Prachara Trust, Delhi, 1985.

Matsya Purāṇa (Vol. I-II) : Nag Publishers, Delhi, 1983.

The Nārada-Bhakti-Sātra : With Text and commentary by Swami PrabhupadaThe Bhaktivedanta Trust, Mumbai, London, 1991.

Ṛgveda : Vaidika Samshodhan Mandal, Pune, 1933-51.

Śatapatha Brāhmaṇa : Ed. by Several Learned Persons, Parts III and IV, Nag Publishers, Delhi, 1990.

Śrībhāṣya of Rāmānuja (Part I) : Ed. Karmarkar, R.D., University of Poona, Poona, 1959.

Taittirīya Saṁhitā : Ed. Weber Albrecht, F.A. Brockhaus, Leipzip, 1871.

The Bhagvadgītā (The Song Divine) : With Sanskrit text and translation, Gita Press, Gorakhpur, 1991. (first pub. in 1943).

The Mīmaṁsā Sātras of 'Jaimini : Mohanlal Sandal, Motilal Banarasidass, New Delhi, 1997 (first pub. in 1993).

Uśanaḥ-Samahitā : Ed. Dutta M.N., T.D.S. Vol. I. pp. 111-164, Cosmo Publications, New Delhi, 1978.

Vaiṣṇava Upaniṣads : Ed. Mahadevashastri, with Commentary of Sri Upanishad Brahmayogin, Theosophical Society for Adyar Library, Madras, 1923.

Upaniṣads in Sankar's Wwn Words (Khanda-3) : Vidya-vachaspati Panoli,Matrubhumi Printing and Publishing, Calicut, 1993.

Upaniṣadsamagrahaḥ : Ed. Jagadishashastri, Motilal Banarasidass, Delhi, 1998.

Yājñavalkya-smṛti : Ed. Vasudev Laxman Sastri Panshikar, with Mitākṣarā of Vijñāneśvara, Nirnayasagar Press, Bombay, 1909.

(B) ENGLISH AND MARATHI BOOKS

Alper, Harvey (Ed.) : *Understanding the Mantras.* Motilal Banarasidass, Delhi, 1991. (First pub. in N.Y. 1988).

Altekar, A.S. : *Education in Ancient India,* Benaras Indian Book Shop. Rev. enlarged edition. no. 3. Benaras, 1948 (first pub. in 1934).

Antarkar, W.R. (Śaṅkara-Vijayas) : *A Comparative and Critical Study.* Veda Shastra Pandita Raksha Sabha, Mumbai, 2003.

Bagchi, Prabhodhanchandra : *Studies in the Tantras,* University of Calcutta, Calcutta, 1975.

Bakre, A.B. : *Religion in Social Flux (as seen in the main Purāṇa-s)* Eastern Book Linkers, Delhi, 1998.

Banerji, Sureshchandra : *A Companion to Indian Philosophy,* B.R. Publishing Corporation, Delhi, 1996.

Banerji, Sureshchandra : *Tantra in Bengal : A Study of its Origin, Development and Influence,*Nyaya Prakash, Calcutta, 1977.

Basu, B.D. (Ed.) : *The Sacred Book of the Hindus. "Philosophical Teachings of the Upaniṣads"-* extra Vol. V by Sandal Mohanlal, Basu B.D., Panini Office, Allahabad, 1945.

Besant, Annie : *Ancient Ideals in Modern Life,* Theosophical Publishing Society, London, Benaras, 1901.

Belvalkar, S.K. and Ranade, R.D. : *History of Indian Philosophy* (*the Creative Period*) Vol. II. Oriental Books Reprint Corporation Book Publishers, Delhi, 1974 (first pub. in 1927).

Bhandarkar, R.G. : *Vaiṣṇavism, Śaivism and Minor Religious Systems,* Oxford University Press, Bombay, 1913.

Bharati Agehananda : *The Tantric Tradition* Rider and Company, London, 1965.

Campbell, Joseph : Bollingen Series XXVI, Zimmer, Henrich, *Philosophies of India* Pantheon Books, New York, 1951.

Chakravarti Sureshchandra : *The Philosophy of the Upaniṣads.* University of Calcutta, Calcutta, 1935.

C.V. Narayana Iyer : *Origin and Early History of Śaivism in South India,* University of Madras, Madras, 1974.

Dange, S.A. : *Hindu Dharma āṇi Tattvajñāna* (Mar.) Srilekhan vāchan Bhāndar, Poona, 1973.

Dange, S.A. : *Towards Understanding Hindu Myths,* Aryan Books International, New Delhi, 1996.

Dange, S.S. (Ed.) : *Sacrifices in India Concept and Evolution,* Viveka Publications, Aligarh, 1987.

Dasgupta, S.N. : *Hindu Mysticism,* Motilal Banarasidass, Delhi, 1976 (first pub. in 1927).

Dasgupta, S.N. : *The History of Indian Philosophy* (Vol. I) Cambridge University Press, London, 1922.

Desai, S.G. : *A Critical Study of the Later Upaniṣads,* Bharatiya Vidya Bhavan, Mumbai, 1996.

Deussen, Paul, (translation into English by Geden, A.S.) : *The Philosophy of the Upaniṣads.* Dover Publications, INC, New York, 1966, (first pub. in 1906).

Deussen, Paul, (translated by Bedekar V.M. and Palsule G.B.): *Sixty Upaniṣads of the Veda* (Vol. II) Motilal Banarasidass, Delhi, 1995.

Devaraja, N.K. : *Indian Philosophy Today* Macmillan Cor-poration of India Ltd., Delhi, 1975.

Dixit, S.H. : *Bhāratīya Tattvajñāna* (Marathi) Suvichar Prakashan Mandal, Pune, 1963.

Durant, Will : *Pleasures of Philosophy – A Survey of Human Life and Destiny.* Simon and Schuster, New York, 1953.

Frauwllner, Erich (translation by Bedekar, V.M.) : *History of Indian Philosophy* (Vol. I) Motilal Banarasidass, Delhi, 1993 (first pub. in 1973).

Gajendragadkar, K.V. : *Upaniṣadrahasya* (Marathi.) A.V. Lokasamgraha Karkhana, Poona, 1938.

Garg, R.K. : *Upaniṣadic Challenge to Science,* Sundeep Prakashan, Delhi, 1978.

Ghosh, Aurobindo : *The Synthesis of Yoga* Sri Aurobindo Ashram Publications dept. Pondicherry, 2002. (first pub. in 1948).

Ghosh, Aurobindo : *The Upaniṣads,* Sri Aurobindo Ashram Publications, Pondicherry, 1972.

Hiriyanna, M. : *Outlines of Indian Philosophy,* Motilal Banarasidass, Delhi, 2000 (first pub. in 1943).

Hume, R.E. : *The Thirteen Principal Upaniṣads,* Oxford University Press, London, 1949.

Kane, P.V. : *History of Dharmaśāstra,* B.O.R.I., Pune, Vol. II. pt. II. 1941.

Kinsley, David : *Tāntric Visions of the Divine Feminine (The Ten Mahāvidyās),* Motilal Banarasidass, Delhi, 1998.

Macdonell, Arthur : *A History of Sanskrit Literature,* Munshiram Manoharlal Oriental and Foregin Book Sellers, Delhi, 1958.

Macdonell, Arthur : *A Vedic Mythology,* Indological Book House, Varanasi, 1963.

Max Müller (Ed. And translated by Max Müller) : *The Sacred Books of the East* (Vol. I.) Motilal Banarasidass, Delhi, 1993.

Mishra, Umesh : *History of Indian Philosophy,* Vol. I, Tirabhukri Publications, Allahabad, 1957.

Monier Williams, Monier : *Brahmanism and Hinduism,* John Murray, London, 1887.

Mukhopadhyaya, G.G. : *Studies in the Upaniṣads,* The Principal Sanskrit College, Calcutta, 1960.

Oldenberg, Herman : *The Doctrine of the Upaniṣads and Early Buddhism* (translated by Shrotri, S.B.) Motilal Banarasidass, Delhi, 1991.

Radhakrishnan, S. and Moore, C.A. : *A Sourcebook in Indian Philosophy,* Princeton University Press, New Jersey, 1957.

Radhakrishnan S. : *The Principal Upaniṣads,* Harper Collins India, Delhi, 1998, (first pub. in 1953).

Radhakrishnan S. : *Indian Philosophy,* George Allen and Unwin Ltd., London, Vol. I. (1923), Vol. II (1927).

Ranade, R.D. : *A Constructive Survey of Upanishadic Philosophy,* Bharatiya Vidya Bhavan, Bombay, 1986, (first pub. in 1926).

Sarma, Jogeshwar : *The Philosophy of Education in the Upaniṣads,* Oriental Publishers and Distributors, Delhi, 1978.

Schomerus, H.W. (translated by Law, Mary) : *Śaiva Siddhānta* Motilal Banarasidass, Delhi, 1979 (first pub. in 1912).

Shende, N.J. : *The Religion and Philosophy of the Atharva-veda,* B.O.R.I., Poona, 1952.

Tilak, B.G. (translated by Sukhtankar, B.S.) : *Gitarahasya* Vol. I Lokmanya Tilak Mandir, Poona, 1935.

Vaidya, Sripad M. : *Śat Cakra Darśana Vā Bhedana* (Marathi) Islampur, 1937.

Velankar, H.D. : *Ṛgvedātīla Bhaktimārga* (Marathi) Shikshana Prasarak Mandali, Poona, 1952.

Vidya, C.V. : *History of Sanskrit Literature,* Vol. II, Parimal Publications, Delhi, 1986.

Winternitz, Maurice : *A History of Sanskrit Literature,* Vol. 1, (translated by Shreenivas Sharma) Motilal Banarasidass, Delhi, 1981.

Woodroffe, John : *Śakti and Śākta – Essays and Addresses on Śākta Tantraśāstra* 3rd ed., Luzac and Co., London, 1929.

(C) ENCYCLOPAEDIA

Encyclopaedia of Religion and Ethics, Vol. VIII : Ed. Hastings James, T. & T. Clark, Edinburgh, 1953 (first pub. in 1915).

Encyclopaedia of Religion and Ethics, Vol. II : T. & T Clark, New York 1958.

Encyclopaedia of Philosophy, Vol. III, V : Ed. Edwards Paul, Macmillan Publishing Co. Inc. New York, 1972.

(D) JOURNALS AND RESEARCH PAPERS

Bakre, A.B. : *Purāṇa*, Vol. XLII No. 2, Kashi Publication Trust, Varanasi, July 2000.

Balasubramanyam, R. and Raghvan, V.K.S.N. : *Indian Philosophical Annual* Vol. 14, University of Madras, Madras, 1982.

(E) DICTIONARIES AND KOŚA-S

Bhāratīya Saṁskṛti Kośa Vol. IV. (Marathi) : Joshi Mahadevashastri and Hodavar Padmaja, Maharashtra Samskriti Mandal, Pune, 1967.

Encyclopaedic Dictionary of Upaniṣads Vol. I, II, III : Ed. Swami Paramananda Sarupa and Sons, New Delhi, 2000.

Oxford English Dictionary, Reissue of a New English Dictionary on Historical Principles Vol. VI : Clarendon Press, Oxford, 1993.

The Concise Oxford Dictionary : Ed. Thompsun Della, Oxford University Press, Oxford, 1995 (First pub. in 1911).

INDEX

P